# *The Expectation of the Poor*

*The American Society of Missiology Series,* in collaboration with Orbis Books, seeks to publish scholarly works of high merit and wide interest on numerous aspects of missiology—the study of mission. Able presentations on new and creative approaches to the practice of mission will receive close attention.

*American Society of Missiology Series, No. 9*

# The Expectation of the Poor

## *LATIN AMERICAN BASE ECCLESIAL COMMUNITIES*
## *IN PROTESTANT PERSPECTIVE*

## GUILLERMO COOK

ORBIS BOOKS

Maryknoll, New York 10545

The Catholic Foreign Mission Society of America (Maryknoll) recruits and trains people for overseas missionary service. Through Orbis Books Maryknoll aims to foster the international dialogue that is essential to mission. The books published, however, reflect the opinions of their authors and are not meant to represent the official position of the society.

Copyright © 1985 by Guillermo Cook
Published by Orbis Books, Maryknoll, NY 10545
All rights reserved
Manufactured in the United States of America

Manuscript editor: William E. Jerman

**Library of Congress Cataloging in Publication Data**

Cook, Guillermo
  The expectation of the poor.

  Bibliography: p.
  Includes index.
  1. Christian communities—Catholic Church.
2. Christian communities—Brazil.   3. Catholic Church—
Brazil—History.   4. Protestant churches—Brazil—
History.   5. Brazil—Church history.   I. Title.
BX2347.72.B6C66   1985      250        85-5131
ISBN 0-88344-209-4 (pbk.)

*To the growing number of evangelical base ecclesial communities
in Latin America that remain faithful
to their Christian vocation
in contexts of violence and oppression*

# Contents

# Preface to the Series

The purpose of the ASM Series is to publish, without regard for disciplinary, national, or denominational boundaries, scholarly works of high quality and wide interest on missiological themes from the entire spectrum of scholarly pursuits, e.g., theology, history, anthropology, sociology, linguistics, health, education, art, political science, economics, and development, to articulate but a partial list. Always the focus will be on Christian mission.

By "mission" in this context is meant a cross-cultural passage over the boundary between faith in Jesus Christ and its absence. In this understanding of mission, the basic functions of Christian proclamation, dialogue, witness, service, fellowship, worship, and nurture are of special concern. How does the transition from one cultural context to another influence the shape and interaction of these dynamic functions?

Missiologists know that they need the other disciplines. And other disciplines, we dare to suggest, need missiology, perhaps more than they sometimes realize. Neither the insider's nor the outsider's view is complete in itself. The world Christian mission has through two millennia amassed a rich and well-documented body of experience to share with other disciplines.

Interaction will be the hallmark of this Series. It desires to be a channel for talking to one another instead of about one another. Secular scholars and church-related missiologists have too long engaged in a sterile venting of feelings about one another, often lacking in full evidence. Ignorance of and indifference to one another's work has been no less harmful to good scholarship.

The promotion of scholarly dialogue among missiologists may, at times, involve the publication of views and positions that other missiologists cannot accept, and with which members of the Editorial Committee do not agree. The manuscripts published reflect the opinions of their authors and are not meant to represent the position of the American Society of Missiology or the Editorial Committee of the ASM Series.

We express our warm thanks to various mission agencies whose financial contributions enabled leaders of vision in the ASM to launch this new venture. The future of the ASM series will, we feel sure, fully justify their confidence and support.

*William J. Danker, Chairperson,*
*ASM Series Editorial Committee*

# Foreword

The future of the Roman Catholic Church in Latin America in general, and in Brazil in particular, depends to a large extent on what happens to the *comunidades eclesiais de base* (CEBs) within the next few years. These small groups made up of poor and oppressed Christians who seek to understand and to respond to their concrete problems in light of Scripture have, therefore, become a very important reference point in the study of contemporary Christianity. Herein lies in the first place the significance of this work.

Written from a radical evangelical perspective, *The Expectation of the Poor* is the most complete treatment of the CEB movement in Brazil available at present. One outstanding feature of this scholarly work is its missiological thrust. It is obvious that Guillermo Cook has carried out his research with an eye on the implications that the CEBs have for the evangelization of Latin America. His study makes it clear that in this area the CEBs pose a powerful challenge not only to their own church but also to the Protestant churches.

In fact, Cook shows that in a real sense the CEBs are more "Protestant" than the Protestant churches, most of which started in Brazil as "base ecclesial communities" but have become institutionalized and accommodated to the status quo. Of particular importance here is the emphasis of the CEBs on the Gospel as good news to the poor, on "the priesthood of all believers," and on creative protest (the so-called "Protestant principle"). Cook is quite correct in understanding the CEBs as a call to Protestants of all colors to return to their roots in order to overcome the inherent contradiction of their present predicament.

On the other hand, the challenge that the CEBs represent for the Roman Catholic Church can hardly be exaggerated. Would it sound too bold to say that since the Protestant Reformation in the sixteenth century there has been no crisis in this church comparable to the one produced by the CEBs in Latin America? Perhaps. The fact remains, however, that there is plenty of evidence to show the very deep concern that these Catholic communities have been causing to the hierarchy since the Latin American Conference of Bishops (CELAM) in 1968. As Cook demonstrates, since then the Vatican itself has been evincing signs of a growing anxiety over the CEBs. Certainly, at the level of sociology, ecclesiology, theology, and mission, they are the greatest challenge to the Roman See!

An important occurrence that has taken place within the Roman Catholic Church after Cook had finished his research points in the same direction. I am here referring to the silencing of Leonardo Boff by the Sacred Congregation for the Doctrine of the Faith. As the most distinguished theologian in Brazil, Boff had eloquently articulated in *The Church: Charism and Power* and other writings the challenge of the CEBs to his church. Now he has been punished as a result. The logical inference is that the Vatican is prepared to use its power to keep the charisma of the CEBs within institutional bounds. Cook's carefully researched work provides important clues on the effects that such policy may have on the future of the Roman Catholic Church in Latin America.

C. RENÉ PADILLA
General Secretary
Latin American Theological Fraternity

# Acknowledgments

As impossible as it is to name everyone who has made a contribution to this book, I gratefully acknowledge my debt to the following:

To my Lord Jesus Christ, for confronting me with the reality of the poor, transforming my evangelical ministry.

To the "church of the poor," for teaching me the real meaning of *comunidad*, and for trusting in me, a foreigner and a Protestant.

To the Catholic CEB leaders and guides, from laity to prelates, who have given the expression "pastoral ministry" a new depth of meaning.

To my dear wife Beverly who, in spite of the frequent absences that my research required, was always supportive. To my daughter Beth, for her efficient typing, and for her commitment to the integral liberation of the poor in Latin America.

To my colleagues in the Latin American Evangelical Center for Pastoral Studies (CELEP), who channeled the funds, provided a typist, and allowed me time to complete this book. CELEP's ever deeper commitment to the poor in Latin America is, in a way, both the cause and the result of this venture.

To Faith Annette Sand, a friend and colleague of many years, who was the processor of the final drafts of the manuscript. Along with her computer expertise, she contributed her knowledge of subject and context, and her editorial savvy.

To my colleague and onetime mentor, Orlando E. Costas, who first suggested the topic to me, and counseled and encouraged me in my research.

To Profs. Paul E. Pierson and Arthur F. Glasser, for their continual encouragement and guidance as the original version of this work was taking shape.

To the tiny Gethsemani Church in a marginalized barrio of San José, Costa Rica, for allowing me to worship, witness, serve—and reflect—in a Protestant *comunidad*.

To the handful of evangelical pastors in our region who, in spite of hostility, and in some cases martyrdom, are not afraid to express their commitment to the poor and oppressed in Latin America—in obedience to Jesus Christ and his word. To them I dedicate this book.

# Acronyms and Abbreviations

| | |
|---|---|
| AC | *Ação Católica,* Catholic Action |
| AG | *Ad Gentes* (Vatican II) |
| AP | *Ação Popular,* Popular Action |
| ASTE | *Associação de Seminários Teológicos Evangélicos,* São Paulo |
| AV | Authorized (King James) Version |
| CBB | *Convenção Batista Brasileira,* Brazilian Baptist Convention |
| CCB | *Congregação Cristã do Brasil,* Christian Congregation of Brazil |
| CEB | *Comunidades Eclesiais* (Spanish: *Eclesiales*) *de Base,* Basic (Grassroots) Ecclesial Communities |
| CEDI | *Centro Ecuménico de Documentação e Informação,* Rio de Janeiro/São Paulo |
| CELAM | *Consejo Episcopal Latinoamericano,* Latin American Episcopal Council |
| CEP | *Centro de Estudios y Publicaciones,* Lima, Peru |
| CERIS | *Centro de Estudos Religiosos e Sociedade* |
| CIET | *Congresso Internacional Ecuménico de Teologia* (São Paulo, 1980) |
| CNBB | *Conferência Nacional dos Bispos do Brasil,* National Conference of the Bishops of Brazil |
| CNS | *Conselho Nacional de Segurança,* National Security Council, Brazil |
| CRIE | *Centro Regional de Informaciones Ecuménicas,* Mexico City |
| DEI | *Departamento Ecuménico de Investigación,* San José, Costa Rica |
| DIAL | *Diffusion de l'Information sur l'Amérique Latine,* Paris |
| EAME | "Ecumenical Affirmation on Mission and Evangelism" (WCC) |
| EMW | "Evangelization of the Modern World" (1974 Synod of Bishops, Rome) |
| EN | *Evangelii Nuntiandi* (Pope Paul VI) |
| FASE | *Federação de Orgãos para a Assistência Social e Educacional,* Rio de Janeiro |
| FENIP | *Federação Evangélica Nacional de Igrejas Presbiterianas,* National Evangelical Federation of Presbyterian Churches |

| | |
|---|---|
| GS | *Gaudium et Spes* (Vatican II) |
| IBGE | *Instituto Brasileiro de Geografia e Estatística* |
| IBRADES | *Instituto Brasileiro de Estudos Sociais,* São Paulo |
| IDOC | Information-Documentation, New York/Rome |
| IECL | *Igreja Evangélica de Confissão Luterana,* Evangelical Church, Lutheran Confession |
| IECT | International Ecumenical Congress of Theology; *see* CIET |
| IPB | *Igreja Presbiteriana do Brasil,* Presbyterian Church of Brazil |
| IPI | *Igreja Presbiteriana Independente,* Independent Presbyterian Church |
| IRM | *International Review of Mission,* Geneva, Switzerland |
| JB | *Jerusalem Bible* |
| JUC | *Juventude Universitária Cristã,* University Christian Youth |
| LADOC | Latin American Documentation, Washington, D.C. |
| MEB | *Movimento de Educação de Base,* Basic (Grassroots) Education Movement |
| MM | *Mater et Magistra* (Pope John XXIII) |
| NEB | *New English Bible* |
| NIDCC | *New International Dictionary of the Christian Church* |
| NIV | *New International Version* |
| PP | *Populorum Progressio* (Pope Paul VI) |
| PPC | *Plano Pastoral de Conjunto,* Combined Pastoral Plan (of the CNBB—for CEB, rural, urban, and family ministry) |
| PT | *Partido dos Trabalhadores,* Workers' Party |
| QA | *Quadragesimo Anno* (Pope Pius XI) |
| REB | *Revista Eclesiástica Brasileira,* Petrópolis, Brazil |
| RN | *Rerum Novarum* (Pope Leo XIII) |
| SEDOC | *Serviço de Documentação,* Petrópolis, Brazil |
| SNI | *Serviço Nacional de Infromação,* National Information ("intelligence") Service, Brazil |
| WCC | World Council of Churches |

# List of Tables

# Introduction

*For the needy shall not always be forgotten; the expectation of the poor shall not perish forever [Ps. 9:18].*

The small, yellowish object was carefully and even reverently passed around the tight circle of persons who had crowded into the clapboard shack of a Brazilian *favelado*.[1] Several months earlier it had been smuggled out of a South American jail by members of the Catholic basic community, *comunidade de base*, movement. A young priest had painstakingly carved his meager soup bone into the crude form of a dove and sent it from his prison as a "greeting" to the thousands of Catholic grassroots communities in Latin America. His crime? He had dared to live out the consequences of his Christian faith as a coordinator of several small CEBs (*comunidades eclesiais de base*)[2] in one of the miserable shantytowns that encircle the major cities of Latin America.

Scores of *comunidade* leaders have been murdered in Latin America by the death squads of some of the most repressive governments on earth. Countless others have been harassed, imprisoned, tortured, or have simply disappeared. The crudely carved bone symbol was a vivid reminder to members of one of the most influential movements in contemporary Latin American Catholicism of the possible consequences of fully obeying the Holy Spirit in the Latin America of today.

The early church attempted to relate in much the same way to fellow Christians who had been martyred for their faith; it gave rise to some of the relics that for centuries have been sacred to Catholics. At first, they helped to remind members of Christian communities of the price that some of their number had paid for proclaiming the authority of Christ over that of the Caesars. When Christianity became "respectable" and powerful, the relics of long-ago martyrs ceased to communicate their original meanings and became objects of superstitious veneration and worship.

Persecution and martyrdom have always been part of the life of the church when it remained faithful to the Lord in the midst of a hostile world order. Victims of the Roman circus and the Spanish Inquisition, members of the German "Confessing Church," Christians in the salt mines and slave camps of Siberia, and Protestant martyrs in Spain and Colombia are only a few of the

1

better known examples. Latin American Protestants had grown accustomed to persecution at the hands of Catholics, but they have found it extremely difficult to relate to a Latin American martyr church bearing the Catholic label. Traditional Protestants have found it even more difficult to comprehend the new social, political, and religious dimensions of the contextual reality in which this incredible phenomenon is taking place.

Reality is *the* operative word in many *comunidades de base*, as well as in Catholic liberation theologies.[3] The components of this reality are the poverty, alienation, marginalization, and oppression in which *comunidade* members find themselves. Reality, in the reflection of these grassroots communities, also has spiritual and ecclesial dimensions.

One salient aspect of Brazilian social and religious reality is that of the *comunidades eclesiais de base* (CEBs). They are small groups of about ten to thirty persons "from the same area and same class who come together to discuss concrete problems in light of the Bible," and to discuss lines of action in response to their situation. "The overwhelming majority of the *comunidades* are poor" and come from "the margins" of society (Bruneau 1979: 227, 229).

The immediate purpose of this work is to investigate, analyze, and interpret this movement in terms of its significance, if any, to Christian mission and to the integral growth of the Latin American church, both Protestant and Catholic. I am approaching the subject scientifically, making use of analytical tools— social and historical, political and economic, cultural and theological—all of them placed at the service of missiology. I have gathered data from an abundance of published and unpublished sources in Brazil, Spanish-speaking Latin America, and elsewhere.[4] This information has been correlated with personal interviews and with my own participant observation in Protestant and Catholic movements.

## SIGNIFICANCE OF THE *COMUNIDADES DE BASE*

As a result of over twenty years of active involvement in Protestant mission in Latin America, and of my more recent interaction with the Catholic *comunidades de base* movement, I have developed the following theses:

1. The *comunidades* are *historically* significant because they challenge the monolithic self-understanding of the Catholic Church—a self-understanding that is now in crisis. They are genuine expressions of both the inherent unity and rich diversity in the church of Jesus Christ. The *comunidades* challenge Latin American and world Catholicism to the degree that their ecclesial style is a quiet revolt against ecclesiastical institutionalism and lack of community, as well as against centuries-old church-state alliances. These grassroots communities are calling the Catholic Church back to its historical and sociological roots, forcing it to become an active participant in the struggles of the impoverished in Latin America.

But the *comunidades de base* are also significant in that they challenge the well established and often prosperous Protestant churches in Latin America, whose roots can be found among base communities of the dispossessed and oppressed of Europe from the sixteenth through the eighteenth century.

2. The *comunidades* are *sociologically* significant because they are both a critique and a creative consequence of Catholic institutionalism. They are yet another example of a grassroots "revolt" against institutional fossilization— the systemic rigidity and theological sterility that gripped the Catholic Church for more than a millennium and a half of its history. But, unlike a number of earlier grassroots protest movements, the *comunidades* have not spun off into a new church. Nor has the Vatican, to date, been able to mold the movement into an instrument of its ecclesiastical policies, as happened, for example, with the Franciscan movement (see Bruneau 1979: 225-26).

In this sense, the Catholic *comunidades* are a "Protestant" phenomenon (IDOC 1978:50). But they also challenge Protestantism, at the level of its own institutionalization, while pointing out an alternative, so far at least, to the fissiparous tendencies of the protest movements in historical Protestantism.

3. These Catholic grassroots communities are *ecclesiologically significant* because they are challenging the traditional Catholic pyramidal church structure. The monopoly of word and sacrament by the clergy and the concentration of ministries and privileges in the hierarchy are being questioned by the ecclesial praxis of the *comunidades*. This challenge has been thrown at the Catholic Church in part by Protestant Scripture dissemination and by the emphasis upon the universal priesthood of believers that is most evident in grassroots Pentecostalism.

The priesthood of the all believers has largely become a theoretical doctrine in traditional Protestantism. The *comunidades de base*, therefore, are significant because they are now challenging the creeping clericalization of the very Protestant churches that originated as grassroots protests against the institutionalism of state churches.

4. Finally, the grassroots communities *challenge traditional Catholicism in its missionary theory and practice*. The *comunidades* are a creative response to the challenge that has been posed to the Catholic Church by Protestant numerical growth in Latin America. The *comunidades*, in turn, pose a counter-challenge to Protestant mission. They first challenge Protestant churches to rethink their long-standing polemical attitude toward Catholicism, however justified it may have seemed in the past. And they challenge them to rethink their present and future mission in the light of the return of a significant segment of church membership to the grassroots of society—from which several Protestant churches originated—with the liberating message of Jesus Christ.

The Catholic *comunidades* are also significant for Protestant mission because they call into question our vaunted growth, forcing us to evaluate it in the context of the socio-economic marginalization and oppression of the Latin American masses. The *comunidades de base*, together with other Catholic revitalization movements, call into question the Evangelical-Protestant understanding of church growth in Latin America. Until recently, Protestant growth had taken place almost exclusively as conversion *out of* nominal Catholicism. This criterion can no longer serve as the sole basis for evaluating church growth. Because of renewal movements such as the *comunidades*, students of church growth must ask questions such as the following:

1. What is the nature and depth of Protestant growth in Brazil and Latin America? Is there a necessary cause-and-effect relationship between its quantitative increase and growth in the knowledgeable application of biblical truth to the total life and witness of the church? Or are the causes of the numerical growth more superficial?

2. How does the Protestant message as a whole relate to the kingdom message? Does acceptance or rejection of this message have any bearing upon Protestant growth and nongrowth? Why do more Latin Americans turn to spiritism, secular materialism, and Catholic renewal movements than to Protestant alternatives?

3. In the light of the above considerations, what should the Evangelical-Protestant attitude be toward reevangelization and revitalization movements within the Catholic Church? What does the Catholic Church mean today by "evangelization" and "conversion"? Does the Catholic understanding have anything to contribute to the traditional Protestant definition and practice of doing evangelism?

4. How can the Catholic doctrine of the church be squared with an Evangelical-Protestant interpretation of church growth? Is membership head-counting adequate for assessing numerical growth that is the fruit of reevangelization within sacramental churches with large nominal memberships? Indeed, how adequate are such criteria for measuring revitalization movements in third- and fourth-generation Protestant churches where membership has grown increasingly nominal?

5. Finally, and more importantly, how much does membership quantification really tell us about the style and witness of a church in response to the challenges of its environment?

## THE THEOLOGICAL CONTEXT: A PERSONAL STATEMENT

Whether out of ignorance or design, Evangelical Protestantism in Latin America has heretofore largely overlooked recent missiological developments within the Catholic Church—except to call them into question or react violently against them. Perhaps we have been too preoccupied with our own ecclesiastical endeavors, or we have been too jealous of our religious patrimony. More to the point, our ideological and theological presuppositions seem to have subtly influenced our choice of missiological studies. Perhaps we have deliberately chosen to remain ignorant—ostrichlike—in order to avoid the suspicion of commitment to political and religious options that seem dangerous to many Evangelicals. If this is the case, we are deluding ourselves. The radical "people movements"—that is, the ground swell of grassroots protest movements in the church—will not go away, however much we might wish them to do so. The comments of social anthropologist Marvin Harris are to the point:

> Contributions to the political expression of particular value positions consist of both action and interaction. Merely to refrain from opinion is not therefore to avoid the expression of opinion. Thus. . .the selection of subjects about which one will *not* carry on research, teach, or publish represents as much of a commitment as the reverse.[5]

As an Evangelical, I am not entirely unaware of the biases of my coreligionists, particularly those who seem to be the least informed about Latin American reality. Because of these biases and misinformation, I found it vitally important for an Evangelical of very conservative stock, such as I, to break out of one's shell and begin to study Catholic phenomena objectively. I have observed, participated in, and studied at close range a movement that is having a profound impact upon the life of a church that I had been taught to consider dead. My own commitment to Jesus Christ, to his one church, and to the world that he gave his life to redeem and to set free, forced me to accept the challenge of this research project.

Being human, I, too, must admit to certain biases. I approach this study, as would anyone else, with my own set of ideologically conditioned theological presuppositions. They are convictions that have developed slowly over the years as the result of my own often unwilling confrontation with human reality in the light of God's word.

My theological convictions are Evangelical, with all that this implies: belief in the authority of Scripture; in the creation of humankind in the divine image and its subsequent fall; in the incarnation of the Son of God in a virgin's womb; in his death, resurrection, and exaltation for our redemption; and in the imperative of reconciliation with God by personal acts of repentance and faith.

But over the years, the worldview that informs this study of the Catholic *comunidades* in Brazil became *Radical* Evangelical. The "radical" (from *radix*, "root") nature of the evangel demands a return to its christological roots in Scripture and human history, as well as to the historical sources of the church. The doctrines that I have just affirmed have become for the Radical Evangelical more than a creed that must be frequently repeated in order to maintain institutional credibility. They are a ringing call to action—to total involvement in the present history of humankind. In essence, they announce the kingdom of God wherein the church, the firstfruits, begins to demonstrate and proclaim the rule of God over every facet of human history.[6]

Ultimately, the radicalness of the gospel is a call for us to move out of the "safety" of our ecclesiastical structures and theological formulations into a world where human beings suffer because God's laws are flaunted. It is a world where risks must be taken for the cause of Christ and his brothers and sisters who suffer because of human rapacity and the oppressiveness of the structures to which they belong.

The reader of this work should take my theological assumptions for granted throughout and not expect periodical expressions of my personal views ("security blankets"!) regarding phenomena or positions with which some might disagree. My personal interaction with the subject will begin in chapter 9.

## THE SOCIOLOGICAL CONTEXT: THE MEANING OF "BASE"

The strength of most anthropological studies lies in their long-term involvement in the research object—which contrasts with North Atlantic sociology, which often focuses upon the analysis of impersonal and "objective" statistical studies. In contrast, the critico-analytical sciences and theology of the Latin American dialectical school, from which I will draw heavily in my research, insists that aseptic objectivity is a myth. Researchers always approach their subject from the perspective of their set of values that have been formed in concrete historical situations. These values make up one's ideological frame of reference.[7] Students of Latin American social phenomena will understand the reality under investigation to the degree in which they involve themselves in its processes and come to understand their inherently political nature.

J. B. Libânio defines the Iberian word *base* at three interrelated levels. The *psychological* (cultural) meaning has the sense of "cellular," "nuclear," or "fundamental." *Sociologically* it refers to the "popular classes"—that is, to the poor. *Theologically* it has to do with the "elemental Christian fabric," the *koinonia* of lay persons (1979b: 5).

The sociological meaning of *base*, which will frequently engage our attention, admits of several nuances.[8] In functionalist sociology, the concept refers simply to the base in the pyramid model of society where the "lower classes" are to be found.[9]

Marcel Garaudy, a Marxist convert to Catholicism, gives us a dialectical definition of *base* at four interrelated levels. (1) At the level of *society* "the base is that sector of the population that finds itself at the same time deprived of ownership, power, and knowledge." (2) At the *economic* level the "base is the sector that, through its labor, creates wealth, but does not have within its power the possibility of determining the orientation of this labor, or the distribution of its fruits." (3) Nor can the base "participate in *political* decisions, except, perhaps, by delegation in nondespotic societies." (4) Finally, the *culture* of the base is determined by the ideology of the dominant class "that has as its object the legitimization of the established order." But, Garaudy warns:

> The essential fact is not that. . .the base is poor, lacks effective political power, and has no culture of its own, but that its masters have deprived it of ownership, power, and knowledge by means of an interplay of forms of exploitation, oppression, and domination. . . . What characterizes the base is that *it has been denied its own future* [Concilium 1975: Sp. 104:62–64; emphasis added].

But, as we shall see, *base* culture is not totally determined by the dominant class. The poor are refusing to give up their own future. This is why I call the *comunidades de base* "the expectation of the poor."

## THE GEOGRAPHICAL CONTEXT: BRAZIL

Catholic CEBs are to be found in a number of Latin American countries, most notably Brazil, Chile, Peru, Ecuador, Bolivia, Colombia, Panama, Honduras, Nicaragua, El Salvador, Guatemala, and Mexico. I have chosen Brazil as a special case study for a number of reasons. In the course of several years of work in that country I came into contact for the first time with the *comunidades*. More than half of the estimated 150,000 Latin American CEBs (as of 1979) were in Brazil (*Time*, 1979c:88).[10]

I am impressed by the fact that the largest and, until recently, the fastest growing Protestant churches in Latin America are to be found in Brazil—and that several of these institutions can trace their beginnings to grassroots movements in Europe, with some similarities to the CEBs. Meanwhile, a momentous change in traditional church-state relationships has been taking place in Brazil. To a certain degree, it has placed Catholicism in the adversary role that was once occupied, also to a certain degree, by Protestantism. Conversely, Protestantism has displayed a disquieting tendency to seek to replace Catholicism as the privileged beneficiary of state support, not only in Brazil, but elsewhere in Latin America. The Brazilian paradigm is, therefore, pertinent to the entire region, with allowances made for different histories and socio-cultural environments.

The Brazilian Catholic Church has considerable clout in the Latin American Episcopal Conference (CELAM), despite recent setbacks for the progressive wing. This and the sheer size and energy of Brazilian Protestantism that serves as a model for Latin American evangelicalism—not to mention the socio-economic influence of Brazil in the region—should make a study of Brazilian *comunidades* significant for all of Latin America, as well as for the universal church.

## BACK TO OUR ROOTS

The reader should be advised that, ultimately, this study of the CEBs is a call to the universal church to return to the simplicity of its New Testament origins, and to its early commitment to the poor, persecuted, and oppressed. The rich and powerful ecclesiastical institutions, of whatever theological color and shade, are an affront to the suffering servant of Yahweh—our Lord Jesus Christ—who on a certain occasion chided his ambitious disciples:

You know those who are regarded as rulers of the Gentiles lord it over them, and their high officials exercise authority over them. Not so with you. Instead, whoever wants to become great among you must be your servant, and whoever wants to be first must be a slave of all. For even the Son of Man did not come to be served, but to serve, and to give his life a ransom for many [Mark 10:42–45, NIV].

My interest transcends the Catholic CEBs, as grateful as I am for their prophetic call. As a child of the Reformation, I am concerned about the institutional drift of Protestantism. We seem to be passing the Catholic Church—or a certain segment of it—but in the wrong direction! I am concerned about the mission of the church to the poor and from the poor. This concern stems not so much from "strategic" considerations—because of the decisive role of the masses as agents of change in history, or because they are often more open to the gospel. My preoccupation is founded upon the Word of a God who, in the incarnation, became poor—a God who in the Old and New Testaments spoke the harshest words against those who, although professing to obey God, oppressed the poor, even as they idolized their institutions. It is at this point, more than any other, that the *comunidades de base* challenge us today.

# PART I

# THE *COMUNIDADES* IN HISTORICAL PERSPECTIVE

# Chapter 1

# The Socio-Cultural Environment
# of the *Comunidades*

*Doomed is the man who builds his house by injustice . . . who makes his countrymen work for nothing and does not pay their wages [Jer. 22:13].*

The Catholic *comunidades de base* were not born in a historical vacuum. In order to understand their development it is important to comprehend the social and cultural environment in which they germinated—as well as the historical processes that brought them into being. Culture cannot be understood apart from social structure. Neither can the processes of history. This will become clear as we begin to look at some key aspects of Latin American culture—with particular reference to Brazil, our case study—before moving on to the more specifically sociological and historical milieu in which the CEBs have appeared.

## THE CULTURAL ENVIRONMENT

There is no such thing as *a* Latin American culture—that is, verifiable throughout the Latin American peoples and nations. There is not even *a* Brazilian culture, for that matter. What we have is a complex of subcultures—European, Amerindian, African, Asian, Middle Eastern, and their mixes. The dominant culture, Iberian—Spanish and Portuguese—developed over several millennia as the Iberian peninsula was overrun by a succession of peoples.[11] Apart from the Latin heritage, it was the Arabic culture that, over a period of five centuries, left the deepest imprint upon the Iberian ethos. Iberian culture, itself varied, was modified in countless ways in the New World.

Latin American culture and society have been studied in considerable depth, and from a number of perspectives, by a distinguished list of autochthonous

11

social scientists. Two pioneers in this field are the Brazilian anthropologists Gilberto Freyre and Darcy Ribeiro.[12] I am indebted to them for some valuable insights into Latin American and Brazilian cultural reality, within a global historical context. They can throw some light upon factors that have contributed to the emergence of the CEBs.[13]

## A Structural Analysis of Civilization and Culture

Ribeiro singles out eight great "cultural-historical configurations," four of which have had a direct bearing upon Latin American culture.[14] Of interest to us are the two configurations that encompass the autochthonous peoples of Middle America—Mexico and Central America—and the Andean region and, in particular, the "new peoples" configuration that is developing in the unique Brazilian melting pot.

Each of the racial elements in this configuration has contributed to the whole in a different measure and in accordance with its own particular strengths and weaknesses. The indigenous Amerindians offered their capacity for adaptability to a hostile environment. Blacks provided their hardiness and strength for manual labor that made possible the production of goods and services. Whites contributed their single-minded drive toward colonization, their enormous productive capacity, their social order and, above all, their dominant European worldview—as well as their Iberian ethos. Black peoples shared with Amerindian peoples nonincorporation into the European-dominated mainstream. The new society was structured in such a way as to maintain social order and cohesion in favor of colonial metropolises. The cultural distinctives of the Amerindian and black components of Brazil's "new peoples" culture were encouraged only to the degree in which they contributed to the enterprise of the colonizers.

The numerous grassroots protests during colonial times were, initially, attempts to return to ancient communal tribal ways. But the process of acculturation was so efficient that today their children struggle to attain a lifestyle akin to that of their European peers in the work force. For a long time, they were incapable of finding socio-cultural structures more in harmony with their needs. Their only hope lay in either finding a place in the sun within the capitalist system or in surmounting capitalism with new socio-economic patterns (Ribeiro 1980: 74–79). This, of course, is one of the fundamental reasons for the significance of the *comunidades*.

Ribeiro's analysis is helpful because it shows how the various subcultures of Latin America and, in particular, Brazil have interacted with sociological and technological factors to produce the social structures and related class struggle of today. At the same time, he warns that these processes are complex and never—as in doctrinaire Marxism—"rigidly deterministic nor linearly evolutionary." Ultimate control of the process is in the hands of the prevailing power structure (ibid., 38–86). The contrasting dyads figuring in the next three paragraphs are useful for an understanding of the tensions at work in Latin

American society, which have also contributed to the rise of the CEBs, particularly among the aboriginal peoples of Central and Andean America and the new cultural mix that is evolving in Brazil.

## Cultural Alienation and Creativity

The ethnic African and Amerindian cultures were distorted by the ideology of the colonialist system. The resultant "spurious culture" of these marginalized peoples that have grown up under the shadow of a dominant culture is ideologically rationalized not only by the dominators, but by the subordinate peoples who have lost their own cultural identity (Ribeiro 127–32). But it is the capacity for creativity of an alienated culture that opens up the possibility of "eradicating the spurious elements in it, through self-constructive processes that amount to cultural revolutions." Latin American popular religiosity and the *comunidades* are manifestations of the dealienating creativity of marginalized peoples (ibid., 137).

## Cultural Homogeneity and Heterogeneity

Although cultural homogeneity is an important factor in many of the Amerindian subcultures, complex cultures such as that of Brazil contain within them a variety of differentiations, conditions of relative dependence, and variations in social and regional development (Ribeiro 1980: 138). The heterogeneity of Brazilian culture—even at its base—calls into question a Christian mission that is predicated upon mere cultural homogeneity. The only homogeneity there, Ribeiro insists, is that which has resulted from the all-pervasive social institutions that came from Europe (ibid., 140–41).[15] The homogeneous element in grassroots Latin American society is the all-pervasive "culture of poverty." The significance of this for Protestantism in Brazil cannot be overemphasized.

## Cultural Spuriousness and Authenticity

The spurious character of Latin American culture is evidenced in the crisis of identity that its people have expressed in various ways throughout history. If the colonial *mameluco* (or mestizo) of Brazil identified with the culture of his white father, ipso facto he identified with those who oppressed the family of his Indian mother. Blacks aped the ways of whites, and after the Amerindians had been pushed out of their ancestral lands, mulattoes adopted Amerindian names and ways in order to identify with an idealized vanished culture.[16] As we shall see, the authentic elements in Hispanic and Brazilian culture are those that have developed among the subordinate classes as creative adaptations for survival and resistance, despite the inroads of alien cultures (Ribeiro 140–54).

It is the purpose of this study to consider one aspect of grassroots creativity, the *comunidades,* and to verify its uniqueness in the context of the total history of Brazil.

## THE SOCIO-ECONOMIC REALITY OF BRAZIL

The sociological milieu in which the CEBs have made their appearance partakes of the same overwhelming character throughout Latin America. Although microstructures may vary between Hispanic and Lusitanian cultures, and from country to country, the macrostructure of the region is one and the same: poverty and marginalization, as well as socio-economic and political dependence. In Brazil, as the largest nation in every respect, despite its grandiose pretentions, the social contradictions may be more acute than in any other nation in Latin America.

This gigantic nation has an estimated 125 million inhabitants who live within an area that encompasses more than 8.5 million square kilometers (3.3 million square miles). It is larger than the forty-eight contiguous United States. Its population, though only about two-thirds of that of the "lower 48," is twice that of Mexico and its land mass more than four times that of Mexico.

Because of the vast geographical surface of Brazil—roughly half of the South American continent—and despite its rapid population growth, its population density is still less than fifteen persons per square kilometer or thirty-six per square mile (World Almanac 1983: 504). But the Brazilian population is heavily concentrated in a roughly 900-kilometer (500-mile) strip along the Atlantic seaboard. Since the founding of Brasilia in 1960, a government-planned colonization of the vast and underpopulated interior is being put into effect to reduce the pressure on the overpopulated seaboard and to exploit the untapped natural resources of the Amazon.

Nonetheless, the coastal cities of Brazil have continued to grow as the masses of impoverished peasants swell their already bloated populations. Whereas in 1945 approximately 70 percent of all Brazilians dwelt in rural areas and 30 percent in the cities, by 1976 the percentages had been exactly reversed. The overall population is growing at the rate of 2.8 percent a year, whereas the urban population grows at 4.8 percent. In the industrial southeast, three-quarters of the population are urban dwellers.[17] Greater São Paulo, with over 15 million inhabitants, is the second largest metropolis in the Western Hemisphere and one of the fastest-growing urban centers in the world. If its present 5.5 percent yearly growth rate continues, greater São Paulo will reach 25 million inhabitants by the year 2000 (São Paulo 1978: 35, 86; *Realidade* 1972: 57).

Perhaps more than any other nation on earth, Brazil is a cultural melting pot. To the early Amerindian inhabitants, the Portuguese colonizers, and the forcibly imported black African slaves have been added over the years successive waves of Italian, Germanic, Slavic, Baltic, Far Eastern (Japanese, Chinese, and Korean), and Spanish-American immigrants (Poppino 1968: 157, 169; L. T. Smith 1972: 118, 143). It is even possible to find a colony of the descendants of a party of Confederate immigrants from South Carolina in the state of São Paulo! One-tenth of the population is classified by the census bureau—the IBGE— as black, 18 percent as "mixed" (including mulattoes and a very small minority of ethnic Amerindians), and the rest as white. The majority of blacks and a large segment of mulattoes are to be found at the bottom of the social pyramid (Read and Ineson: 6; São Paulo 1978: 74, 84).

The most relevant statistics for the purposes of this study are for the period of 1960 to 1975 when the CEBs were beginning to emerge. In 1970, 42 percent of the population was under 15 years of age (Read and Ineson: 5–9). By 1976, 74 percent of the 15–30 age-group was classified as literate, though about one-third of the total population was illiterate. Although the average life expectancy increased to 57.6 years, the infant mortality rate continued to climb.

### The Two Sides of the "Economic Miracle"

The per capita income in 1968, four years after the military regime came to power with promises of reform, was $350. Yet even a figure as low as this one is deceptive. It hides the misery of the marginalized masses who somehow manage to subsist on much less. The real extent of their plight is covered up and offset by the exorbitance of the handful of those who enjoy the benefits of the Brazilian "economic miracle" (see Table 1). Although the per capita income had risen to $1,523 by 1978 (World Almanac 1983: 504), this reflected only the increasing wealth of the very few rich; the overwhelming mass of the poor continued to grow poorer. It also fails to take into account a staggering rate of inflation that, in 1981, had reached 120 percent.

### Table 1

### Distribution of Total Income in Brazil

| % of population | % of total income in Brazil | |
|---|---|---|
| | 1960 | 1970 |
| A. Top 1% of income scale | 11.7 | 17.8 |
| B. Upper 4% | 15.6 | 18.5 |
| C. Middle 15% | 27.2 | 26.9 |
| D. Lower 30% | 27.8 | 23.1 |
| E. Bottom 50% | 17.7 | 13.1 |

Source: J. C. Duarte, "Aspectos da distribuição de renda no Brazil em 1970," Piracicaba, ESALQ-USP, 1971 (*São Paulo* 1978: 60).

In the late 1960s and early 70s much was made of the Brazilian "economic miracle." And, indeed, when one does not dig too deeply into the social effects of the growth of the Brazilian economy since 1964, the statistics are impressive.

The gross national product (GNP) rose steadily at 9 percent or more per year between 1967 and 1973, after which it began to slow down and then went into a tailspin as a consequence of the rise in petroleum prices, gross overspending, and graft. Only nine years after a recent military regime initiated its new economic policies, Brazilian manufactured goods had jumped from a mere 3 percent to almost one-third of its total exports. During the same period, exports spurted from $1.4 billion to $4 billion. By 1973 its foreign reserves were four billion dollars—twice what they had been the year before.

---

### Table 2

### Distribution of Income in Brazil Based on Units of the Minimum Wage

| Income in terms of units of the minimum wages | % of population with monetary income | |
|---|---|---|
| | 1970 | 1972 |
| Less than 1 (minimum wage) | 50.2 | 52.5 |
| From 1 to 2 (minimum wages) | 28.6 | 22.8 |
| From 2 to 3 | 10.2 | 9.8 |
| From 3 to 7 | 7.1 | 9.4 |
| From 7 to 10 | 1.7 | 2.3 |
| More than 10 | 2.2 | 3.2 |

Source: P. Singer, *"Mais pobres e mais ricos,"* *Opinião,* no. 116, Jan. 24, 1975 (quoted in *São Paulo* 1978: 61).

---

Nonetheless, this amazing growth represented only one side of the economic reality in Brazil, for it reaped "benefits for the rich sweated out the poor." For a time, Brazil had as its model Japan, and its economic planners were proud of the fact that by 1973 both the Brazilian GNP and its exports had attained the levels reached by their Asian model barely twelve to fifteen years earlier. At that time, before the sudden rise in petroleum prices, they confidently predicted that they would catch up with Japan by 1985.

Meanwhile, other economists, taking into account the totality of the national socio-economic and cultural reality, were predicting that within a dozen years Brazil would be "a small Japan within a giant India." Both predictions had substance, before the current national economic crisis, because Brazil has enormous untapped resources: mineral wealth, hydroelectric capacity, vast agricultural production (it leads the world in coffee and sugar exports and is second only to the United States in soybean production)—and a large undernourished and uneducated work force that, until recently, was "willing to put in long hours at low pay, because the alternative is no work and no pay" (*Washington Post,* May 27, 1973, quoted in LADOC Keyhole 8: 17–18).

In theory, the "economic miracle" was to have benefited the impoverished masses, which make up 80 percent of the population of Brazil. According to a study in which the University of São Paulo participated, fully half of all Brazilians are living at a bare subsistence level (Table 2).

As in all Latin America, there were glaring inequities in the distribution of income in Brazil in 1960—a fact at the root of the social unrest that, as we shall see in the following chapter, led to the military coup of 1964. (Such disparities are also the root cause of most of the social tensions in Central and South America.) Yet, six years after the present regime came to power with the avowed intention of giving all Brazilians a just portion of the national wealth, the top 5 percent of the population had increased its cut of the total income from 27.3 to 36.3 percent. This percentage parallels that of the bottom 80 percent of the population, which during the same period dropped from 45 to 36.6 percent in total income (Table 3).

The middle 15 percent of Brazilians, who in the early days of the new regime rejoiced in their new affluence, had by 1970 begun to feel the economic pinch. As their share of the benefits of the economic boom continued to erode, their mounting disenchantment was one of the factors behind more recent changes in Brazilian economic and political policies.

The distribution of income can also be measured in terms of the number of minimum wages that each sector of the population receives. A minimum wage is, in theory, the amount of money that a family needs to support its basic needs, including rent, transportation, recreation, and a minimum essential diet. Yet the minimum wage has always been unrealistically low, and many workers receive less than a minimum wage (contrary to the law).

Table 2 highlights two opposite tendencies: whereas 3.9 percent of wage earners (those making more than three minimum wages) rose on the income scale, 2.3 percent (those making less than one minimum wage) declined. These figures for the period between 1970 and 1972 revealed a trend that, in the words of a Brazilian newspaper, was one of "a growing wretched majority." If this trend continued, "by 1980 we should have over 60 percent of the population earning less than one minimum wage, and around 30 percent earning over three minimum wages" (*Opinião,* no. 119, Feb. 14, 1975, pp. 11–12; quoted in São Paulo 1978: 61). The overall picture is one of massive imbalance in the distribution of the economic resources of the nation.

### São Paulo: Cheap Stockings under a Silk Dress

Oh, São Paulo! A queen that vainly shows her skyscrapers that are her crown of gold. All dressed up in velvet and silk but with cheap stockings underneath—the *favela* [de Jesus 1962: 42].

The limitations of this study do not allow a region-by-region analysis of the socio-economic condition of Brazilians. Because over 30 percent of those who

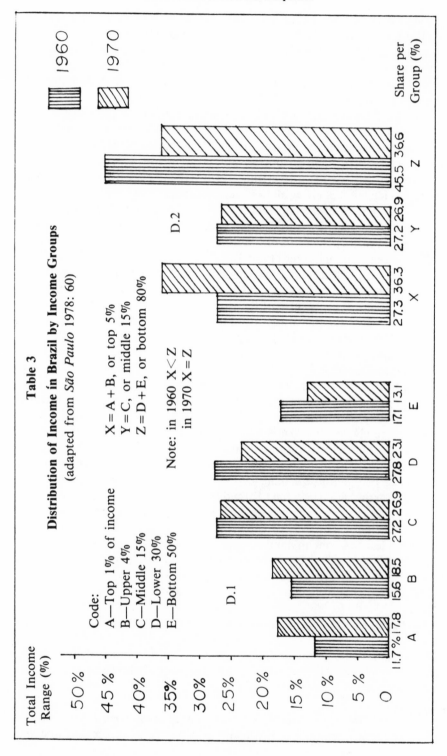

**Table 3**

**Distribution of Income in Brazil by Income Groups**

(adapted from *São Paulo* 1978: 60)

Code:
A—Top 1% of income
B—Upper 4%
C—Middle 15%
D—Lower 30%
E—Bottom 50%

X = A + B, or top 5%
Y = C, or middle 15%
Z = D + E, or bottom 80%

Note: in 1960 X < Z
      in 1970 X = Z

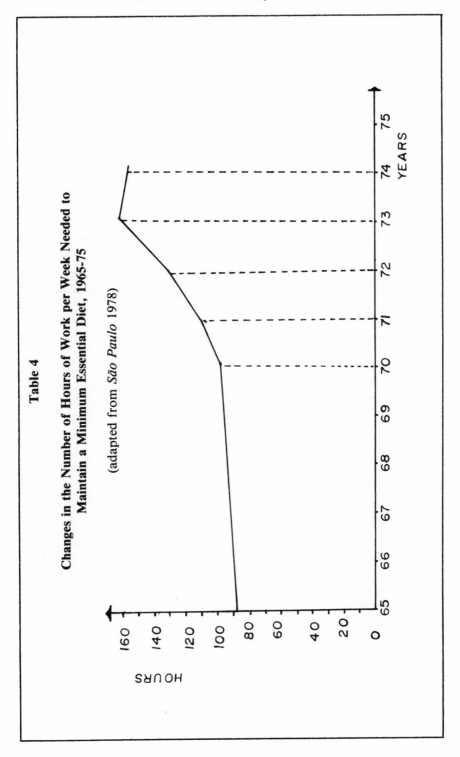

Table 4

Changes in the Number of Hours of Work per Week Needed to
Maintain a Minimum Essential Diet, 1965-75

(adapted from *São Paulo* 1978)

receive a monthly income of over five minimum wages live in greater São Paulo, it should be illustrative to analyze the economic reality of the inhabitants of this, the most prosperous city in Brazil and Latin America and the capital of its most wealthy state. More than one-third of all domestic productivity, 44 percent of all capital issues, and 44 percent of all accumulations in Brazil are concentrated in greater São Paulo (São Paulo 1978: 19).

But there is another, dismal, reality in São Paulo. Although only 19 percent of all *paulistanos* receive less than one minimum wage—as compared with 48.2 percent in the nation as a whole—over twice as many persons per hundred receive over five minimum wages as in the entire nation, according to official IBGE figures. Table 4 shows the increase in the number of working hours needed to acquire the minimum essential diet, based on the São Paulo minimum wage. (Minimum wages in the industrial heartland in the southeast are proportionately higher than in the rest of Brazil.)

Over the 11-year period between 1958 and 1969, there was a 36.5 percent decrease in the purchasing power of the wages of the average wage earner in São Paulo. The trend has accelerated since 1973. This caused a corresponding increase in the number of working hours per person in order to keep up with the cost of living. In 1972, one-fifth of those earning up to one minimum wage and one-fourth of those earning between one and two minimum wages were forced to work more than fifty hours a week:

> Even so, labor productivity grows considerably faster than the average real wage in greater São Paulo. In this way, productivity gains do not lead to wage increases for the workers as a whole, but constitute, instead, an additional source of capital accumulation for the firm [São Paulo 1978: 62–65].

As a result, São Paulo and all the large cities of Brazil are surrounded by festering *favelas* to feed the insatiable labor market (see *Folha* 1981 a, b: 26).

The results of this economic imbalance, even in so prosperous an industrial center as greater São Paulo, can be seen at both ends of the age scale. "A cycle of productive life has been created that allows employers to abuse their employees by excluding older workers from the labor market." Although the proportion of unemployed men aged 40–49 is only 4.7 percent in greater São Paulo, for the 50–59 age-group the percentage of unemployed escalates to 19.4 percent. And even if we take into account the retirement age of 65, the 47.9 percent unemployment for men in the 60–69 age-group and 80 percent for men above 70 are still very high (São Paulo 1978: 76).

Sadder still is the condition of children. From 1940 to 1960 the general mortality rate in the city descended steeply, as did the infant mortality rate, probably as a result of the efforts of several activist mayors. Although these rates decreased much less dramatically in the surrounding metropolitan area, from 1950 the infant mortality rate for the entire megalopolis, including the core city, fell by 30 percent and in the following decade 32 percent. Beginning in

1960 the overall mortality rates and the infant mortality rates increased steadily. From 1961 to 1975 the infant mortality rate in greater São Paulo increased by 45 percent.

The reduction in the real value of the wages of the laborers in São Paulo has had a marked impact on their eating habits. Malnutrition can be both the direct and indirect cause of death because it is "the most important aggravating factor on infectious diseases" (São Paulo: 46–48), as well as in mental retardation.

If this is the situation in a region so economically favored as São Paulo, what can be the economic reality of the poorer sections of Brazil?

The daily *O Estado de São Paulo,* in its May 24, 1970 edition, published a summary of a recently completed study underwritten by the Bank of the Northeast. In the fourth largest city in Brazil, Recife (population 1 million-plus at that time), a bustling metropolis on the "hump" of Brazil, the 40 percent of the population with the lowest income received only 1.55 percent of the total revenues in 1967, as against 16.5 percent in 1960. In Salvador da Bahia, the fifth city (just under one million at the time) and the colonial capital of Brazil, the 20 percent at the bottom of the income scale received only 3.8 percent of city revenue in 1966, compared with 5.6 percent in 1962. The same trend could be observed in all the state capitals of the depressed northeast during these seminal years of the CEBs (LADOC Keyhole 8: 13).

### The Rural Poor of Brazil—the "Culture of Silence"

Shephard Foreman points out that very early in Brazilian history there developed alongside the plantation system a diversified peasant sector composed of small owners *(lavradores),* tenant farmers *(foreiros),* and sharecroppers *(moradores)* "who served as both commodity producers and a labor force within the system, as well as suppliers of food-crops on it." Each had different socio-economic ties to the plantation masters. Subsequently, squatters from coastal regions swarmed into uncultivated private and public lands. They hastened the end of the land-grant system (Foreman 1975: 20–27).

Caio Prado, Jr., observes in this regard that during the colonial period there was a large mass of persons between the minority of landholders and the multitude of slaves. The latter were economically taken care of. But for the ones in the middle—the "unclassed"—there was nothing but a hand-to-mouth existence. This large group consisted of runaway slaves, semiacculturated Amerindians, mestizos of all color gradations, whites, and down-in-the-mouth younger sons of "illustrious Portuguese family trees" (C. Prado 1963: 279–81; Foreman: 29–30).

Foreman points out that the present land-tenure system in rural Brazil is not just a throwback to an earlier socio-economic order. It is, in fact, a functional response to present socio-economic realities. Even in colonial times, he reminds us, the system was adapted to "agricultural exploitation for an international market."

Foreman estimates that in 1950 "62 percent of the people who depended upon agriculture for their livelihood were landless agricultural workers." If we include "those whose land is not economically viable," the number of de facto landless agricultural laborers climbs to 81 percent. The overall pattern remained the same in the 1970s.

There are today, says Foreman, at least three major types of wage-labor arrangements in rural Brazil: (1) a worker is allotted a plot for subsistence crops, or (2) he is loaned a house on plantation lands, but with no land to farm, or (3) he becomes a *trabalhador braçal,* "day-laborer." The last-named are the ones who most closely resemble a rural proletariat (1975: 40–62). This is much the case in all Latin America.

Foreman points out that "a two-class system was not an adequate description of the social system in colonial Brazil when social differentiation was already taking place." He adds that it certainly does not adequately describe the Brazil of today where "we find considerable intermediate ranking between the upper and lower echelons of rural society." He goes on to show that power is not the exclusive monopoly of the landed class, but that it is wielded, perhaps even more brutally, "by various intermediaries in the system who do not have the status of the rural gentry but who have access to them and, thus, to a relative share of strategic resources." This group of "intermediaries" is distinct from the upper and lower echelons of society, but is not yet, properly speaking, a middle class. Nevertheless:

> The social differentiation that is now taking place in rural Brazil increasingly reflects the changes that are occurring in the nation at large . . . .
> The social, economic, and political components of the rural "subsystem" articulate in rather precise and identifiable ways with the ongoing social, economic, and political processes of the nation-state [Foreman: 66–68].

Foreman shows how, after the 1964 *revolução,* "the landowning elite and some rural industrialists have become, more than ever before, the critical underpinnings of a national political system" that is looking for support among the rural poor in order to centralize and legitimize its authority. He shows how the system works. The large landholders' control of available land, whether public or private, forces the landless to align themselves with those who are in a position to help them. Lacking any kind of legal infrastructure to support them, those of the "silent generation" are obligated to "subject themselves to patrons who can facilitate access to strategic resources, and who offer them some measure of security and protection."

Patrons make few demands upon their dependents as long as they remain loyal, obedient, and dependable. The landlord's word is law. If dependents become restless, and "reason" fails, the patron has recourse to the "law," and, as a last recourse, to violence (Foreman: 68:77).

For their part, they can either submit in silence, escape into some folk religious group, migrate to the overpopulated cities in search of an elusive "better life," or join some form of protest movement, such as, in the 1960s, the activist Peasant Leagues of political leader Francisco Julião (Foreman: 185–240). In the 1970s and 80s, it has been the *comunidades* that have provided the ideological "space" where the rural poor can begin to be free.

## The "Wasted Generation"

The unequal distribution of the benefits of the Brazilian "economic miracle" has exacted its toll in what *Time Magazine* (Sept. 11, 1978) has called "Brazil's wasted generation"—the 16 million hopelessly deprived children, one-third of the youth of Brazil:

> Amid all the delights of Brazil live more than 2 million children who have been abandoned by their destitute parents and another 14 million who live in such poverty that abandonment almost seems preferable . . . .
> The outcasts among them have been called "nobody's children," and they range from infants to teenagers. They have been turned into the streets of every major city in the land . . . . They rove in gypsy bands, sleep in construction pipes, in rat-infested cellars of abandoned buildings, or on street corners in miserable heaps. Their beds are torn newspapers, their clothing, mere scraps of cloth. Their days are spent in hustling, prostitution, and petty crime. The children who remain with their parents are similarly corrupted [32–33].

The article goes on to state that the "children who fall into the hands of the authorities are not necessarily better off." One 13-year-old boy told of his mistreatment in a detention center at the hands of the police: "They beat me on the back and throat with boards and pieces of rubber with nails in it. Sometimes at night, four or five guards would come and rape us."

*Time* points out that this "scandal" is the result of the Brazilian economic "advance." Millions of rural poor have fled the countryside in search of city jobs. Lacking basic skills and education they have had to settle for low-paying jobs—while continuing to contribute to a "stunningly high birth rate (37.1 per thousand)." As a result, many impoverished parents are forced to treat their children like rubbish in order to survive. The miserable plight of these *favelados* is told by Carolina Maria de Jesus, who, in the midst of the "human garbage dump" of her São Paulo *favela,* fought for herself and her three illegitimate children, and kept a graphic account of her experiences on scraps of paper picked up from the gutters.

Her words—harshly realistic—are poignantly poetic. "Hard is the bread that we eat. Hard is the bed on which we sleep. Hard is the life of a *favelado*" (de Jesus 1962: 42).

## Violence as a Way of Life

Illicit and institutionalized violence has increasingly become part of the way of life in the large cities of Brazil. According to a study published in 1972, one of every five *paulistanos* and *cariocas* has experienced some kind of criminal violence. Another survey found that one of every two of the inhabitants of São Paulo could tell some personal story of violence. Seventy percent of armed attacks and of violent crimes are perpetrated by persons younger than 21; most of them are between 14 and 17 years of age.

Violence breeds violence. During the late 1960s, the *escuadrãos da morte* (death squads of off-duty policemen) took matters into their own hands, summarily executing anyone caught in or suspected of any crime, including political subversion. In the opinion of informed observers, the panic that this produced among the marginalized masses only bred more violence as the desperate fought back in self-defense. Two-thirds of the respondents to a survey taken in nine cities of various sizes answered that they did not feel safe on the streets at night. A slightly smaller percentage said that they felt safe in their own homes. Over two-thirds of those questioned, including 41 percent of the poor persons interviewed, answered that they had installed special protective devices in their homes. Over half of the respondents stated that the level of police protection was "very bad" *(Realidade:* 181–89*)*. During the 1970s and 80s, the climate of fear and violence continued to increase.

In the rural areas of Brazil, the impoverished masses are kept in bondage to the vast *fazenda* or landholding system as indentured labor. Most attempts to remedy their situation have been met by the violence of *fazendeiros* and of their allies in the local government and police. We shall look more closely at the historical roots of this aspect of Brazilian reality in the following chapter.

These, then, are some of the socio-economic facts of Brazil today. Eighty percent of its population—as in a number of Spanish American countries— belong to the impoverished bases of society. They dwell primarily in the feudal and drought-ridden northeast and in the *mucambos* (shantytowns) that fester around its enormous cities. It is for these people that Afro-Brazilian spiritism and Pentecostalism have had their greatest appeal. It is also where the *comunidades* seem to be growing more rapidly.

A very small and extremely wealthy military, industrial, and landholding elite forcibly controls the reins of power at the top of the social pyramid. Its members profess traditional Catholicism and are attracted to more "sophisticated" forms of spiritism. Between these two extremes is a small and relatively affluent middle class. Many traditional Protestants and most Catholic charismatics belong to it.

From 1964 through 1984, the reins of government have been in the hands of the *Revolução,* the military and secret service complex that rules with a heavy hand, despite a superficial appearance of democracy. The social and economic policies of the present regime are the social context—the *realidade*—in which the grassroots communities of Brazil have taken root. A better understanding of the implications of these *comunidades* for Christian mission demands that they be studied within the context of this reality and as a part of a complex social and historical process. To this task we turn our attention in the following chapter.

## Chapter 2

# The Historical and Political Dimensions of Brazil: The View from Below

*Again I looked and saw all the oppression that was taking place under the sun: I saw the tears of the oppressed—and they have no comforter; power was on the side of the oppressors [Eccles. 4:1].*

The socio-economic and cultural context in which the CEBs have appeared is the result of particular historical processes that we must understand in order to appreciate the significance of this grassroots movement. History does not just happen. It is conditioned by particular interacting forces—economic, political, social, cultural, and religious—and by their corresponding ideological representations.

Eduardo Hoornaert, a Catholic missioner working in Brazil, makes this clear:

It is impossible to study colonial Christendom without situating it within the complex that can be called "the reality," i.e., the complex of structures, social organizations, mental representations that are interrelated and which reveal the complexity of a human existence that has economic, political, social, and cultural dimensions . . . . Christianity is a characterizing element of the society in which we live and we will only be able to understand clearly the Christian culture which we inherited from the past, if we study how it functioned in the complex of Portuguese-Brazilian life, and what were its connections with elements of the economic, political, and social order [Hoornaert 1979: 251].

25

Hoornaert and like-minded historians write a complete history of Latin American Christianity—both Catholic and Protestant—from the perspective of the subordinate classes. Hoornaert's work will provide us with the substance of a historical overview of the social reality that is the seedbed of the CEBs. Brazil can serve as a model and point of reference for an understanding of all Latin American socio-political history.

## COLONIZATION AND CHRISTIANIZATION: TWO SIDES OF THE SAME HISTORICAL UNDERTAKING (1500–1759)

The first stage in the history of Brazil merits more attention than all other periods except for the most recent. It was during the first sixty years of its history that the directions were set for the next two centuries. In fact, this is where the roots of the *comunidades* may be found. Although the political and ecclesiastical structures of Latin America experienced many changes, neither the colonies and later independent nations nor the church were able to evade the path set for them at the beginning of their history.

This history began, as a matter of fact, long before the European discovery of this bountiful region. Iberian-American history is rooted in the medieval concept of Christendom, which gradually became the policy of the church from the time of Constantine the Great in the fourth century (Hoornaert: 160–61).[18] It was only in the middle of our present century that the Brazilian Catholic Church began to take hesitant steps toward freeing itself from the stranglehold of its past. In the process, it initiated small but significant changes in the social and political institutions of the nation.

### Missionary-Colonialist Expansion in Brazil: A Case in Point

Brazil was accidentally discovered by Europe in 1500 when the Portuguese navigator Pedro Alvarez Cabral was blown too far west as he attempted to sail around Africa to the Indies. There are strong hints, however, that these Western lands were already known to far-ranging Phoenician navigators many centuries earlier. Spanish and French explorers may have chanced upon the eastward-jutting "hump" of South America without realizing what they had found, a few years before Columbus "discovered" America.

Those who claimed this new territory in the name of the Holy Cross and of the king of Portugal, and who began to settle it a quarter of a century later, did not bother to inquire of its inhabitants by what name *they* called it. They first baptized the land *Santa Cruz* or *Ilha da Vera Cruz* (Island of the True Cross). It later came to be known as Brazil—from the word *brasa* (live coal)—because of its thickly forested brazil-wood coasts, the source of a much-prized red dye (Poppino 1968: 44–47). Those who made their fortunes cutting and transporting the wood back to the metropolis were called *brasileiros,* a term much later applied to all those born in the new land. The numerous and varied native tribes were arbitrarily lumped under the name of *brasiles.*

*Brasilico*—a trade language based on Portuguese and the dominant Tupi-

Guarani dialect—was the language of the masses, until Portuguese was imposed upon them in the eighteenth century by the Marquis of Pombal (Hoornaert 1979: 32,280–81).

In the naming of the Brazilian people its destiny can be viewed as decided by alien imperium, because, as Enrique Dussel has observed, "in the biblical understanding of this process, to give someone or something a name is to gain dominion over what is named" (1976: 78). In the religious and mercantilist names that were imposed upon Brazil can be found significant foreshadowings of the history of religious and economic exploitation of this vast colony.

Three historical facts interacted in the colonization of Latin America:

1. The "spirit of the Crusades," which had as its constant goal the forcible conversion of infidel gentiles to the Christian faith, was based upon the Christendom worldview. Long after the ardor to free the Holy Sepulcher had cooled in Europe, the fires of the Crusades burned bright in an Iberian peninsula that had been ruled for half a millennium by the Muslim infidel.[19]

Only a handful of years after the total liberation of their lands from the infidel, the same crusading fanaticism served as a justification for Iberian colonizers as they fought, enslaved, and exterminated the hapless Amerindians, and later expelled the Protestant French and Dutch from their territories (dos Santos: 24–25, 45–46; Hoornaert 1979: 157).

2. The second historical determinant in the colonization of Latin America was the royal patronage system.[20] By papal decree, it granted to the monarchs of Portugal and Spain both temporal and spiritual authority over all the lands that they would conquer.[21]

In theory, according to official state documents, the crown was guided primarily by spiritual motives such as preaching the gospel and converting the infidel. In practice, temporal objectives—commercial expansion; exploitation of land and human beings—predominated. This was a consequence of the medieval identification of church and society as a unified whole. There was no operative conception of the church as church (Hoornaert: 162, 170, 172; dos Santos: 25, 42; Bruneau 1974: 18–19).

3. The third factor was the imperative of defending doctrinal orthodoxy. Its instrument was the Inquisition, put into effect to defend the religious, political, and economic hegemony of the crown. This was not as important a factor in the Portuguese colonies as it was in Spanish America.[22] Nevertheless, Amerindians in Portuguese lands also were baptized and enslaved, Jews forced to become Catholics, and Protestants traders harassed and expelled—all in the name of the preservation of the Christian faith. The political and economic imperatives of the colonizing enterprise were justified in missionary writings (dos Santos: 47–48; Galilea 1978: 41–42).

### Dimensions of Iberian Colonialism

The history of the colonization of Brazil must be appreciated from intersecting economic, political, cultural, and ecclesial perspectives.

*Economics.* In a perceptive model to which he returns at various times throughout his work, Hoornaert suggests that the Portuguese-Brazilian relationship during the colonial period—and this would apply, as well, to Spanish colonization—consisted in three distinct "moments":

1. The moment of the *outward journey,* from the European metropolis to the colony, was characterized by a "commercial exclusiveness" designed to protect Portuguese mercantile interests from competition with other European powers.

2. The moment of *contact with the new colonies* was highlighted by controversy over the ownership of the new lands. The indigenous inhabitants were immediately perceived as a hindrance to colonial territorial monopoly for the benefit of the European metropolis.[23] Those missionaries who upheld the rights of the natives against landlords could not avoid entering into conflict with robber priests and barons.[24]

3. The third moment of the colonial venture was the *return to the metropolis* with the fruit of the slave labor of the native population. During the first colonial period, slavery was open and legalized. In subsequent periods of Brazilian history, the enslavement of the original inhabitants of Brazil, though modified and camouflaged, continued to be real.

These three "moments" had their counterparts in the trajectory of the Spanish-Portuguese Catholic Church in its relationship to the colonies. Revenues from colonial churches were sent to the monarchs who were entitled to collect tithes from all their domains. Much smaller sums returned to the colonies in the form of benefices and ecclesiastical emoluments designed to uphold the religious-colonial status quo (Hoornaert 1979: 31–32, 252–55).

*Politics.* The political dimension of colonial Latin America was characterized by plantation feudalism. Real political power was in the hands of local landholders (Port., *fazendeiros*; Sp., *hacendados*) who exercized absolute and uncontested authority over the lives—and deaths—of all their subjects. Although Brazil did not have a colonial army, land-barons were protected by their own private armies, which, when necessary, protected the colony from foreign invasion.[25] Yet there were differences. In marked contrast with the better-trained civil and ecclesiastical representatives of the Spanish crown, who followed on the heels of the conquistadores, Portuguese governors were professional soldiers who relied upon the feudal *fazenda* owners to administer their vast provinces (Hoornaert: 255–57). Sixty years of unified Spanish-Portuguese rule under Philip II (1580–1640) were not sufficient to influence Portuguese colonial structures along the lines of the more efficient Spanish imperial administration. This same patron-client relationship obtains today in many places and is at the root of much of the marginalization and social unrest in Latin America (de Kadt 1970: 14).

*Sociology.* Colonial Brazil was dominated by the institution of slavery much more than in the Spanish colonies—which relied on the subjected Amerindian nations for forced labor. In this, Brazil was closer to the British colonial and southern U. S. slave systems. After the native population had been virtually exterminated by war, disease, overwork, and cultural alienation, African slaves took its place. In colonial Brazil slavery was never open to question. It was deeply imbedded in the social fabric of the colony without which it would never have existed.

One of the saddest chapters in the history of the Brazilian Catholic Church is its involvement in this bleak practice. The Jesuits, who had generally championed the cause of Amerindians while they remained free, not only owned African slaves and used them as legal tender, but sought to justify the practice in theological terms.[26]

*Culture.* In a vast and complex colonial milieu such as Portuguese and Spanish America, it is not possible to study culture as a unitary whole. From an anthropological perspective, three overlapping elements should be considered in order to gain an understanding of the impact of colonialist culture upon contemporary Latin America: cultural areas, cultural environments, and cultural discrimination (Hoornaert 1979: 264–72).

1. The *cultural areas* of this period were superimposed willy-nilly upon earlier Amerindian cultural areas without any awareness on the part of the conquistadores of the existence of complex indigenous subcultures (Leers 1977: 15ff.). Though goodwill toward the natives was not absent in certain ecclesiastical quarters, the internal logic of the colonial enterprise demanded the imposition of an alien culture upon the aboriginal inhabitants of the land. In the case of Brazil, the principal cultural areas were: the *sugar plantation "frontier"* along the northeastern seaboard, the *cattle ranches in the north-central plains,* and the *gold and diamond fields of central Brazil.* In each region new cultural areas developed, based upon the exploitation of the wealth of the land and of the labor of its rightful owners for the benefit of a greedy colonial power.

2. There were fundamentally three *cultural environments* in colonial Brazil. They all developed the conditions in which the CEBs of today have grown: the sugar mills *(engenhos),* the closely related plantations *(fazendas),* and *the built-up population centers.*[27] Much of what can be said about the *engenho* system of the northeastern seaboard of Brazil can also be said about the cotton, cocoa, and coffee *fazendas* of the interior, and about similar cultural areas in Spanish America. The principal difference was that in Brazil absentee landlords were often represented by harsh plantation managers and that, for a time at least, the slaves were Amerindian. Their protected villages (Sp., *aldeamientos*; Port., *aldeamentos*) were the counterparts of the African *senzalas* in the Brazilian and Spanish Caribbean sugar mills.

The cultural environment of the population centers was, in many ways, very different from rural plantation life. Slaves lived and worked on the ground floors of the mansions; the masters and their families lived on the second story. Gilberto Freyre points out that, in one respect—their natural, high-protein food—slaves had fared better on the plantations than their masters, for whom custom dictated a vitamin-poor diet. In the cities, however, the slaves began to imitate their masters' diets and widespread malnutrition followed (Freyre 1968: 120–21, 186–87).

The coastal cities divided their living space into two clearly defined areas.

The upper city, cooler and healthier, where the colonizers dwelt, was comprised of neighborhoods graced by cathedrals and baroque churches with gold-leaf altars, large convents, and numerous parochial schools. In the swampy and malaria-infested lower city, the simple churches were frequented by slaves and poor "freemen" who practiced their popular religions. Later, as the rich began to move down into the lower city, the crowding of the *favelas* began, as shanties appeared on the rugged hillsides.

In stark contrast to white-dominated urban centers was the Palmares community, a black parasocialist dictatorship in the arid northeastern Brazilian hinterland, the *sertão*. A well-governed city of straw huts built by runaway slaves was able to defend itself for seventy years in opposition to the forces of the white slave masters. It had a community granary, used crop diversification instead of monoculture, and pooled the products of its fields, ranches, and mills for distribution among all the inhabitants. Perhaps in search of legitimization, the Palmares blacks and their native wives took the white man's religion. They worshiped the saints of the white religion but had their own priestly hierarchy (Freyre 1968: 134, 170–71) after the Jesuit provincial turned down their request for a father confessor (Azzi 1984: 8–9).

The urban phenomenon in Brazil differed markedly from its colonial Spanish American counterpart. This was due to geographical as well as sociocultural factors. The Spanish conquerors found advanced civilizations in the high plateaus and lush valleys of the central western South American hinterland. They built their major administrative and trade centers on the highland ruins of conquered Amerindian cities. The mountain ranges of Brazil are relatively low and rise abruptly from the Atlantic seaboard, creating well-protected deep-sea harbors. The Portuguese colonizers, finding no cities, and being by long tradition a nation of seafarers and merchants, established their trade centers along the coast.

The cities that sprang up haphazardly on the long stretch of Brazilian seacoast were in marked contrast with Palmares or even with the medieval European model of a relatively harmonious interaction between city and surrounding areas, which also somewhat characterized Spanish colonial cities. Brazilian cities were open in their attitude toward their European metropolis but hostile toward their own vast interior. They were merely clearinghouses through which the riches of the interior passed in order to feed the coffers of the distant metropolitan capital.[28] The colonial cities of Brazil were, in fact, black cities that functioned for the benefit of a white world.

3. Another integral aspect of colonial life was that of *racial-cultural discrimination*. Exploding the myth that extols Brazil as a model of racial harmony, Hoornaert underlines the socio-economic reasons behind the Portuguese colonists' leaning toward miscegenation. He insists that "the masters of the *engenhos* soon discovered that it was more productive to produce slaves *in loco* than to import them at exhorbitant prices" (1979: 270).[29]

The "romantic" facade of miscegenation must not be allowed to obscure the harsh reality of racial discrimination in colonial Brazil. Racial discrimination was also very much a part of the life of the church, much more so than in most of Spanish America. The religious orders accepted only native Portuguese into their ranks, and the sons of Portuguese and Amerindian halfbreeds *(mamelucos)*, to the fourth degree. Mulattoes (offspring of Portuguese and blacks) were very rarely accepted into a religious order, and then only on their death-beds as a special favor. Blacks were totally excluded from the religious orders. In consequence, it became impossible for the majority black and mulatto population to express their religious values and worldviews through their own leadership and worship styles. This contributed to the shortage of local priests that has always plagued the Brazilian church (P. Pierson 1974: 306), and it was to have a profound effect upon the popular religiosity of Brazil. This is a fact that we must not forget when we analyze the socio-economic composition of the *comunidades* in Brazil today (Hoornaert 1979: 264–73).[30]

## The Role of the Colonial Church as an Instrument of Domination

The ecclesial dimension of colonialism is inseparable from the other components of the total reality of colonialism. In order to understand the significance of the ecclesial life of the CEBs, it is important to understand the impact of the colonial church upon society up to the twentieth century.

1. The *self-understanding of the colonial church* derived from the Council of Trent (1545). The Christendom model that for over a thousand years had gradually taken over the Catholic Church became official dogma. The true church was the society of Christian faithful spread across the globe—the *orbis Christianus*—who lived under the authority of the pope. As a logical extension of this belief, evangelization and mission were viewed exclusively as a function of the creation of a Christian society through participation in the sacraments.[31]

Although the colonizers saw their church in this light, it probably appeared very different to their slaves. Though it is not easy to determine how those illiterate subjects understood Christianity, we may conjecture from indirect allusions that they perceived the church in exactly the terms that their conquerors intended it to be for them—the religious expression of an overwhelming political and economic power. For some of the indigenous inhabitants, the church may have been perceived as the means to social advancement. Yet for the majority it was a religion that barely disguised their true animistic beliefs; a religiosity to be shucked just as quickly as they were able, if they were fortunate enough to escape their *aldeamentos* into the safety of the jungle or the *sertão* (Hoornaert 1979: 155–59; 245–349; Montenegro 1972: 7–41).

2. Because of its dependence upon the Portuguese crown, the *structure of the colonial church* was extremely feeble.[32] The authority of the Holy See was purely symbolic, and that of the episcopacy limited, for the most part, to jurisdictional matters. Bishops often filled important positions in the colonial government, to which they owed their first allegiance.

There were, in fact, two Catholic churches in colonial Latin America: the "official" church of the cities with its cathedrals, parish priests, vicars, and bishops, which had very little to do with the grassroots church of the lay brotherhoods or with the baronial church of the plantation chaplains. Priests lived from royal benefices, chaplains from the offerings of the faithful.[33]

3. The *doctrine of the colonial church* was decisively influenced by the fact of slavery and by the entire socio-economic structure of the colonial enterprise. In the face of this reality, says Hoornaert, the church responded with two contradictory "doctrines": a minority *prophetic* doctrine, which dimly saw Christ's presence even in the despised Amerindians and blacks, and a *legitimizing* doctrine that sacralized the demonic institution of slavery with religious symbols (cf. Galila 1978: 42). Unfortunately, the proponents of the former doctrine (unlike CEB members today) lacked the analytical tools to comprehend fully the context in which they ministered. Because of this they were perplexed, hesitant, and often ambiguous in their reactions, as can be perceived from a close study of the theology, preaching, and catechesis of the colonial church (Hoornaert 1979: 320–22).[34]

It is therefore not surprising that Christianity came to mean one thing to the Portuguese overlords and something else to the poor of Brazil. The austere and wrathful God whom the all-powerful masters worshiped as the legitimizer of their world was perceived by their slaves as a source of spiritual strength to support them in the midst of injustice. The Christ of the colonizers was a kind of Greek hero—a blond warrior who died heroically on a cross in defense of the kind of Christianity they identified with.[35]

The colonial church was equally unable to communicate the biblical truth about the Holy Spirit. The reason is well put by Hoornaert:

> The institution could hardly "preach" the Holy Spirit, because he inspires, thrills, moves, and can only be communicated through a living experience, and not so much through words. The theme of the Holy Spirit escaped manipulation by the dominant powers and surfaced, instead, as manifestations closer to the popular religion of more recent times. The rapid popular acceptance of the ecstatic experience which is cultivated particularly in Pentecostal cults demonstrates that there always was an affinity between the theme of the Holy Spirit and popular religion [1979: 346].[36]

4. The *pedagogy of the colonial church* was at the service of this alienating and domesticating catechesis. There were two general ways of carrying out mission—sedentary and itinerant. The former—done by chaplains, plantations masters, and religious—failed to take into account the tribal reality of the subjugated peoples and destroyed it in the massification and paternalism of the native *reducciones* and African slaves sheds. Because of the vastness of the territory and the small number of clergymen, itinerant catechesis gradually replaced sedentary missions.

The concentration of the sacraments into the hands of the specialized clergy inevitably reduced the laity to the role of passive recipients of divine grace. The infrequent priestly visits were the principal events of every population center and were attended by large and enthusiastic crowds. The emphasis was on numbers. The needs of individual persons and of local communities continued to be swallowed up in the anonymity of the masses (Hoornaert 1979: 125–35; dos Santos: 28), until the emergence of the CEBs in our time.

5. The colonial Catholic Church perceived itself as a church in mission. But its *concept of mission* was, of course, thoroughly conditioned by its Christendom worldview. The CEBs today present what is doubtless the most significant challenge to this traditional approach to mission, because of its starting point—the long-forgotten and oppressed poor.

The *evangelizing discourse* of colonial Catholic missions in Brazil was, as Hoornaert puts it, *universalist,* encompassing every free and conquered subject in its pale. It legitimized the universal right of colonizers to impose their absolute understanding of total reality upon conquered peoples in the name of Christianity. It was a *doctrinaire* discourse, because evangelization was conceived almost entirely in terms of a mechanical transmission of church dogma without reference to the existential situation of the receiver. It was also a *martial* discourse, justifying war, massacre, and slavery in the name of the Prince of Peace who died to make men and women whole and free. Finally, it was a *reductionist* discourse in that it reduced its subjects from individual persons in their own right to indistinguishable members of a mass. The oppressed of colonial Brazil, says Hoornaert, were reduced from heterogeneity to homogeneity, from adult personhood to a state of minority dependence, from language complexity and diversity to the sameness of a single trade language (1979: 23–28, 142–51; dos Santos: 28–29).

## THE MORE THINGS CHANGE, THE MORE THEY ARE THE SAME: THE NONHISTORY OF THE POOR

The profoundly alienating evangelization that characterized the colonial period—in itself merely a reflection of vaster socio-economic, political, and ecclesial realities—determined the course that Christianity would take in Latin America for the next two centuries, until the emergence of the grassroots church. And in Brazil, despite superficial changes in the components of the reality of church and society, the Christendom model continued to guide church and society throughout the subsequent periods of its history until the middle of this century, as the following summary will show.

The foregoing descriptive analysis of the colonial history of Latin America, with particular reference to the case of Brazil—the nation with the largest number of *comunidades de base*—has been necessary in order to establish the pattern that would obtain from the middle of the eighteenth century until today, despite momentous political changes in the emerging Latin American republics.

Three major "realities" are apparent in what has gone before—and they will continue to be operative for years to come, as far as the masses of Latin

American poor are concerned: *cultural alienation, socio-economic marginalization,* yet *religious vitality* against all odds. Herein we find the roots of the CEBs. Out of their perduring struggle to create and maintain free "spaces"of communal solidarity as a defense against alienation, the poor have discovered the meaning of *comunidade.* In the solidarity of *base* communities they are discovering their own human worth and have begun to act politically, demanding their place in the sun. But none of this would probably have any ultimate value were it not for the religious dimension of their struggles. The popular religiosity—perhaps the only element of hope in their centuries of otherwise hopeless existence (see chap. 3)—is now acquiring an *ecclesial* dimension, thanks to the "option for the poor" taken by the Catholic Church.

But two centuries were to pass before any of this would begin to emerge. Meanwhile, the poor of Latin America continued to be nonpersons, despite the political changes that were taking place at the top. They were ignored, then used, by both state and church, even while the magic words of the French Revolution—freedom, liberty, equality—were being proclaimed throughout Latin America. As a case in point, Brazil passed through four distinct political periods between 1759 and 1954, during which the lot of poor masses remained unaltered.

### The Challenge of Regalism and Jansenism (1759–1822)

In a desperate attempt to shore up the tottering Portuguese empire, Sebastião Carvalho e Mello—the Marquis of Pombal and chief minister from 1750 to 1777—brought the nobility and the church under his absolute control. For the Portuguese church, it was a time of stagnation and decadence that would continue until 1884.

Pastoral inattention in sees and parishes bereft of bishops and pastors further strengthened the syncretistic and baroque popular religion of the colonial era, which was now dependent upon ill-trained Brazilian monks and the penitential lay brotherhoods (Galilea 1978: 45–46). This was also a time of unsettling changes in the agrarian base of the colony—including the replacement of colonial monocultures by African coffee; it would set in motion an accelerating migration to the cities (Poppino: 147ff.; Freyre 1968: 45–47).

Regalism was reinforced as a conscious state policy aimed at revitalizing the colonial-mercantile enterprise. In the process, the Jesuits and other non-Portuguese religious orders were expelled from the colonies. Attracted to the independent ideas of Jansenism and Gallicanism, Pombal severed the Portuguese church from Rome for a decade (1760–1770). The cumulative effect of these policies dealt a blow to Portuguese Catholicism in Brazil from which it would take years to recover.[37] From the onetime Jesuit University of Coimbra, committed ecclesiastical agents of "Pombalism" were sent throughout the empire. Many of these priests were to become prominent in the Brazilian independence movement.

After the Napoleonic wars—which had sent the Portuguese court into temporary Brazilian exile—the colony was elevated to the status of coequal partner with Portugal. But this only glossed over deep-seated tensions and failed to arouse a mortally wounded church. In 1822, the Portuguese prince regent of Brazil was installed as emperor of an independent nation (Bruneau 1974: 19–22; dos Santos: 32–37). Yet, for the masses of the poor, this was but a cosmetic change.

### The Empire, Regalism, and the Revitalization of the Church (1822–1889)

The new emperor soon abdicated in favor of his 14-year-old son, Dom Pedro II, who ruled for fifty years as a constitutional monarch. He was a nominal Catholic, a Voltairian rationalist, a dabbler in science and esoterics (Montenegro 1972: 43–77), and a close friend and neighbor in Rio de Janeiro of the first resident Protestant missionary, of whom we shall hear more in a later chapter (Léonard 1963: 40ff.).

The emperor maintained a tight rein on the church, which he treated as just another department of state—an extension of the regalist ideology of the colonial period (Montenegro 1972: 109–25). All this might have led to the demise of Catholicism in Brazil, when a Catholic revitalization movement in Europe, Ultramontanism, turned events around in Brazil from about 1900 (Léonard: 28; dos Santos: 37–38).[38] A revitalized Roman church clashed with the emperor's policies. Two countermovements worked against him. His best bishops, the austere and disciplined men whom Ultramontanism had produced, began to demand greater autonomy for the church. Meanwhile, anticlericalism and political liberalism of a French-trained elite also brought pressure to bear. Together they forced the emperor's abdication, which led to the proclamation of the First Republic in 1889 (Bruneau 1974: 23–30; Montenegro 1972: 79–108; 126–33).

Toward the end of the empire there was a growing class consciousness and popular discontent of which both church and state were oblivious. Official Catholicism, for example, played no part in the successful abolitionist movement during this period. Having lost touch with the masses, the church was also losing the intelligentsia, increasingly attracted to scientific positivism and a pseudo-scientific spiritism (Kardecism). Republicanism and a laicized state eventually won the day (dos Santos: 37–41; de Kadt: 15ff.).

### The First Republic and Church Autonomy (1889–1930)

A new constitution was proclaimed; it virtually ignored the church and excluded it from the public realm. The reaction of the church was ambivalent. Although rejoicing in a new autonomy, it felt very insecure, lamenting its loss of influence over the state. In order to understand subsequent developments in the Brazilian Catholic Church lasting even until today, it is important to bear in mind, as Bruneau points out, that henceforth the church would always be seeking to regain its lost influence over the state and the social order, while all the time insisting upon its own autonomy (1974: 30–31).

Under the direct authority of the Holy See, for the first time in five hundred years the Brazilian church would begin to experience a series of administrative measures to strengthen it. Despite this, it never became more than a pale copy of the post-Tridentine model.[39] And more significantly for our study, even with an increase in dioceses, seminaries, and priests, it remained almost totally out of touch with the people. It was a middle-class, urban, and elitist church—centralized, dogmatic, and reactionary; a "moralist" ideology molded its character (Montenegro 1972: 93–98). After Vatican I it was continually on the defensive against all the fashionable "isms"—modernism, socialism, secularism, and Protestantism (Bruneau 1974: 30–36; Galilea 1978: 47–48; de Kadt: 16–19).

Although the church had preserved its institutional integrity, it seemed to be completely unaware of the existence of the poor—the majority of the faithful—and of the folk religiosity that flourished at the grassroots unrelated to official dogma and structure. Nor did it understand the implications of the half dozen or so grassroots messianic movements that took place in various parts of Brazil from 1817 through the Second Republic (Foreman 1975: 221–36). Significantly, it was at midpoint in this period (1910) that Pentecostalism began its steady growth among the masses in Brazil (Read and Ineson: 31).

## The Second Republic: State Populism and Church Authoritarianism—an Alliance of Convenience (1930–1954)

The strong personalities of Getulio Vargas and Cardinal Leme dominated this quarter century of Brazilian history. Leme was the key ecclesiastical figure during the first half of the twentieth century. Vargas was probably the ablest and one of the most colorful political figures in Brazilian—and perhaps even in all Latin American—history. He ruled provisionally from 1930 to 1934, constitutionally until 1937, dictatorially until 1945, and again as an elected president from 1950 until his suicide in 1954.[40]

The Vargas period saw the beginning of profound changes in the political structure of Brazil as new forces appeared on the political horizon—a rising urban middle class and radical movements of both left and right. Traditional regionalization was giving way to an increasing concentration of power into the hands of the federal government. But the plantation system was left untouched. At the same time Vargas encouraged industrial production for the domestic market and sought to lessen Brazilian dependence upon its principal agricultural exports.

Dom Leme, archbishop of the northeast see of Olinda-Recife and later cardinal-archbishop of Rio, was a convinced upholder of the Christendom social order. He set about to return the church to a position of influence with the state—a first in postindependence Latin America. In exchange for church support, Vargas allowed Dom Leme to shape the church ideologically according to his own moralistic and activist ideas (Montenegro: 154ff.).

Catholicism continued to be a superficial and traditional religion, allied with the rich and powerful in maintaining the status quo. Meanwhile, it continued to lose its influence over the subordinate masses—the bulk of the population of Brazil.

The post–World War II period was marked by accelerated economic growth that masked a creeping crisis in the socio-economic system in Latin America. This was to become more obvious in the decade of the 60s. Capitalism and the so-called free-enterprise system was benefiting only the very few at the top of the social pyramid. The postwar era set in motion a drive toward industrialization, as the U.S.A., and later a revitalized Europe, searched for new markets for their products—products that only a very few could afford.

Masses of rural poor headed for the cities in search of a better life, which most would never attain. Enormous slums sprang up seemingly overnight on the periphery of the principal cities of Latin America. Later, lands that peasants had cultivated for centuries were absorbed, often ruthlessly, by new agribusinesses, adding to the growing stream of urban-bound dispossessed. Conditions were particularly acute in Brazil.

## Bankruptcy of the System and Inertia of the Church (1954–1964)

In Brazil this was a time of extraordinary European immigration and of vast internal migrations related to the coffee boom and to the beginning of the urbanization movement. Brazil was moving rapidly from a predominantly rural (60 percent in 1945) to a predominantly urban (60 percent in 1976) society. During the brief period when Brazil enjoyed a semblance of democracy, fiscal mismanagement and increasing independence upon international capitalism contributed to galloping inflation.

The Vargas period was followed briefly by caretaker governments and political intrigues. During a full presidential term, Juscelino Kubitscheck, the founder of Brasilia, managed to mask the growing social unrest by his astute balancing of opposing political forces. But his grandiose spending set in motion a galloping inflation that would reach 96 percent by 1964. The remaining years of this period were chaotic as social contradictions intensified.

A conservative reformist, Jânio Quadros, was quickly succeeded by vice-president João Goulart, a politically radical rancher who was much feared by the military-landholding-industrial alliance that controlled Brazil.[41] In the wake of growing chaos and polarization, Goulart was deposed by the military on March 31, 1964, thus ending the brief Brazilian experiment with democratic rule (Skidmore: 143–302; Antoine: 11–31).

Meanwhile, the masses of the oppressed were beginning to awaken from centuries of enforced apathy, as Marxist cadres, Catholic radicals, Pentecostals, and Afro-spiritist cults vied for their allegiance. During the early part of this period, a reactionary hierarchy could not respond creatively to the rapidly changing situation. The traditional link of the church with the poor had always been through the extended family, but these nuclei were breaking up during the mass urban migrations. The church offered no alternative to this breakdown of community life. Its only link with the poor was through folk religiosity. The various spiritist cults experienced a growth rate of 224 percent during this decade. Pentecostal growth also accelerated.

Although a few perceptive prelates were beginning to read the handwriting on the wall and to advocate changes, the church did not begin its process of change until political events disrupted its comfortable relationship with the state and set it on an unprecedented course toward radicalization (Bruneau 1974: 69–77).[42]

## Military Rule and the Doctrine of National Security (1964)

The plot that would lead to more than two decades of military rule had begun at least two years before 1964. By December of 1963, the commanders of key garrisons were involved in the conspiracy, supported by a political coalition of liberals, social and Christian democrats, and conservatives. The coup, which began on March 30, 1964, spread quickly, forcing President Goulart to flee the country the following day. Despite avowals of constitutionality by the conspirators, the military high command imposed one of its most distinguished World War II veterans, Marshal Humberto Castello Branco, as president. This so-called bloodless revolution was, in fact, not without bloodshed (Mourão Filho 1978: 47–48, 171–72, 231; Skidmore 1967: 311; Antoine 1973: 19–25, 61–64).

Castello Branco was followed by Marshall Arthur Costa e Silva, whose halting steps toward limited democracy were interpreted by both political extremes as signs of weakness. The *Revolução* had clearly failed. Subversion was more widespread than before. Corruption was rampant at every level of a paralyzed government, and a sense of malaise had infected the armed forces. During a brief experiment in "constitutional" liberalization (between March 1967 and December 1968), student uprisings and a defiant congress drove the military hard-liners to stage a "coup within a coup." They closed congress and forced the president to renege on his promises of liberalization. Institutional Act no. 5 (AI-5),[43] which the ultrarightist army faction proclaimed in the ailing president's name, announced the beginning of an overt policy of repression against any social or political sector that opposed the goals of the *Revolução* (Antoine 1973: 95, 205–53).[44]

In 1969, an ailing Costa e Silva was shunted aside in favor of another general, the hard-line director of the SNI. President Emilio Garastaçu Medici's answer to the violence of the left was the repression, torture, and elimination of any group or person even suspected of Marxist leanings. The broad definitions that the police gave to these labels encompassed communist cadres, social democrats, and Catholic activists (Antoine 1973: 254–359; Moureira Alvez 1968).

The ideology that guided the dictatorship of the *Revolução* and legitimized its crass violation of fundamental human rights is the so-called doctrine of national security. This doctrine was born in the pre–World War II "Munich School" of political science and revived in recent decades in the National War College and in the Industrial College of the Armed Forces in Washington. The Latin American graduates of these institutions have made the doctrine of national security the cornerstone of their political and military science curricula in their respective military academies, and the cornerstone of the national policies of the countries they control. National security was also central in the geopolitical thinking and planning of the Nixon administration under Henry Kissinger (Comblin 1978: 21ff.), and an obsession with the Reagan administration.

According to one of its Brazilian theorists, "National Security is the guarantee given by the state for the conquest or defense of the national objectives, in the face of opposition and pressure" (Comblin: 54). The two key concepts in this ideology are *bipolarity* and *total war*, both of them seen within a geopolitical context.

The principal tenet of this view of global politics is that the world is divided into two mutually antagonistic power blocs or poles and that Latin America must inevitably fall into one of these two camps. For moral and strategic reasons, Latin America—and in particular Brazil because of its strategic importance as "the anchor of Western defense in the South Atlantic"—are identified with the anticommunist and "democratic" nations of the West. This conviction is fortified by the fear of communist subversion, a fear kept alive by the memory of the attempted Marxist coups in 1935 and 1955 (Comblin 1978: 19–32, 154; Couto e Silva 1981: 217–50).

The fundamental geopolitical fact of life today, writes scholarly General Golbery do Couto e Silva, the principal Brazilian ideologue of national security, is that the Western and freedom-loving democracies are engaged, like it or not, in a total war for their survival. In fact, the very existence of Christianity and of its cherished institutions are at stake. The common enemy is Marxism, under any guise. Total war demands of the nations involved in it wartime measures and exceptional sacrifices for as long as necessary.

While the war lasts, he warns, heavy burdens will of necessity be imposed upon the citizens of Brazil—burdens that will cause increasing tensions between the common good and national security. The only way out is to sacrifice the common good on behalf of national security for as long as it continues to be threatened. In the past, nations that did not perceive this paid for it by the decadence that followed. For the foreseeable future, national security will require the limitation of a number of basic freedoms. But the more that Brazilians are willing to sacrifice today, the more they will appreciate their liberty when it is finally attained (Pro Mundi Vita: Dossiers 1975: 15; Couto e Silva 1981: 139–216). [45]

The nation-state, according to the national security doctrine, is a homogeneous whole guided by a unified will toward certain specific goals. These goals have to do with the preservation of three fundamental patrimonies of the Brazilian people (the same would apply to other national security states): (1)

the *moral and spiritual heritage* of Western civilization;[46] (2) *national character and values* of Brazilians; and (3) *national sovereignty.* These goals are intimately related to the economic development of the nation (Couto e Silva: 259–66).

Curiously, the doctrine of national security, despite its roots in the anticommunist geopolitics of the United States, and its avowedly anti-Marxist rationale, sounds very similar—in its utopic, pragmatic, and ultranationalistic language—to the very ideology it claims to oppose. Its professed concern for Christian values notwithstanding, it has its roots in the same atheistic, materialistic, and dehumanizing philosophy as Leninist communism, and may ultimately be much more damaging.[47] It is for this reason that the Catholic Church in Brazil has dared to confront the government of the *Revolução.*

### The Collapse of the "Brazilian Miracle"

During the administration of General Ernesto Geisel (1974–1979), the son of a German Lutheran pastor, the world economic crisis became more acute. The Brazilian "economic miracle" was reeling under the impact of the dramatic increase in Arab oil prices, and of the slow erosion of the dollar and bureaucratic corruption. Discontent, always present among the long-suffering masses, was now becoming increasingly vocal in the hard-pressed middle class. It was also manifest among students, long passive because, by military law, they had no political voice. Opposition to government policies came from an unexpected quarter when spokesmen for the industrial elite began to ask for a return to constitutionality. Popular unrest manifested itself in unexpectedly large votes in congressional and municipal elections for what had once been a tame "opposition party." On the international front, Brazil was under pressure for human rights from the newly installed Carter administration, as part of a short-lived "trilateral" global strategy.

The Catholic Church played a key role in bringing pressure to bear upon political structures by its almost unified stance in behalf of the oppressed and marginalized masses of Brazil. The rapid multiplication of the *comunidades* during this period helped to awaken the consciousness of the grass roots of Brazil to their rights and duties as Christians and as citizens.

Tactically, it was time for *distenção*—a cautious, limited, political liberalization.[48] Ten years after it has been promulgated, AI-5 was revoked, but only after several of its national security safeguards had been permanently incorporated into the constitution. At the same time, Geisel picked a fellow "moderate" to succeed him, bypassing the high command that had always chosen the official candidates for the presidency before they were "elected" by the senate.

General João Batista Figuereido, the head of the INS, seemed an unlikely person to lead an opening toward greater democracy. Yet, guided by General Golbery, this hard-eyed, no-nonsense career officer permitted a degree of freedom in his first months in office that the Brazilian people had not enjoyed for almost fifteen years. The most obvious forms of press and film censorship were abolished, labor strikes were tolerated "within limits," the rights of disenfranchised political leaders were reinstated, a large number of political prisoners released, and a few prominent exiles—including the aging secretary of the Communist Party—began to return. A more equitable distribution of the GNP was announced, although it did little to ameliorate the plight of the poor, and the more flagrant violations of human rights were toned down. Yet the fundamental structural problem of Brazil remains: the concentration of land and industrial profits in the hands of a minute percentage of the population.

The policies of the Figuereido administration and more recent events have some disquieting similarities to what was attempted by President Costa e Silva. For a while, pragmatists and those in the military who favor a return to civilian rule outnumbered the hard-liners. But the balance may be tipping again in the opposite direction as conservatives have become increasingly alarmed at the extent of popular manifestations of discontent.

The year 1981 evoked pessimism tempered by cautious optimism. The growing strength of the hard-liners may have been dramatized by the fall of General Golbery and his replacement by a close adviser to ex-president Medici. Yet, this same adviser has a more recent record of support for political *distenção*. Aureliano Chavez, the first civilian vice-president in the *Revolução* was twice allowed to become, briefly, the first civilian president of Brazil since 1964, when Figuereido was physically incapacitated.

The collapse of the Brazilian economy in 1982, highlighted by its mind-boggling debt, brought new stresses—while demonstrating to the world the bankruptcy of international capitalism, particularly in Latin America. The harsh belt-tightening required by the International Monetary Fund (IMF) in order to shore up a tottering system added an intolerable burden to the already unbearable plight of the traditionally poor. More recently, persons at the lower fringe of the shrinking middle class are being forced to join the impoverished *favelados*. The periodic readjustment of the minimum wage—already inadequate—to allow for inflation has been virtually frozen. Little wonder that the masses began to riot and, perhaps manipulated by political interests of whatever kind, to express their desperation through violence.[49] Nevertheless, at the close of 1984, a series of unforeseen events and some very astute political maneuvering allowed Tancredo Neves to be elected—by indirect ballot—the first civilian president since 1964, on an opposition ticket.

The rulers of Brazil, as well as in nations such as Chile, Guatemala, and El Salvador, know that they are sitting on a powder keg. It remains to be seen whether these countries indeed will ever become the social democracies that most of their citizens wish them to be. If they do, the Catholic *comunidades* may play a determining role in forging the type of democracy that these nations will enjoy. These communities are not only an expression of the church, they are also "schools for life" where the disenfranchised are learning to tackle their problems through democratic community action (LADOC 1978: 48). The only hope for Brazil—for radical social change and an effective evangelization of the masses—may, in fact, be these grassroots expressions of the Christian gospel. As such, they offer a model to other countries with similarly acute social contradictions, where CEBs can be a potential force in an integral liberation of oppressed peoples.

The religious expressions of Latin American peoples today are as inseparable from ideological forces and political events as they were in the colonial era. This will concern us in the following chapter, particularly as it relates to the emergence of the CEBs.

# Chapter 3

# Religion, Ideology, and Grassroots Revolt

*Those who worship other gods will vanish from this land. You will listen, O Lord, to the prayers of the lowly; you will give them courage. You will hear the cries of the oppressed and the orphans; you will judge in their favor [Ps. 10:16–18].*

Religion is the expression of the constant quest of humanity for meaningful links between immanent and transcendent reality.[50] As a cultural and ideological phenomenon, religion can also be understood as a complex (or complexes) of symbols that bind persons to spiritually oppressive worldviews. Religion, as well, can be used by those who control or manipulate ideological symbols to enslave millions of hapless human beings to dehumanizing social systems. But "the kind of religion," says St. James, "which is without stain or fault in the sight of God our Father is this: to go to the help of orphans and widows in their distress and keep oneself untarnished by the world" (James 1:27, NIV). The "world" of which James speaks is the systemic *kosmos* that must be taken into account in any study of religion.

Bernardino Leers, a student of popular religiosity in rural Brazil, points out:

No religion is independent of the culture, of the historical period nor of the cosmic conditioning of the human society of which it has become a part. . . . Whatever its origin, the more that a religion tries to penetrate the life of mankind, and to reform the human world, the more that society, culture, language as a life expression, and, in short, the world itself, will infiltrate it and mix with it—with its doctrine and praxis. This mutual interpenetration can be severally appraised as mutual enrichment or danger, expansion or limitation, growth or degeneration. But religion will always act this way—if it is truly alive and wishes to communicate itself [Leers 1977: 15].

43

It is my purpose in this chapter to study the complex religious phenomena of Brazil in historical context and from the perspective of both the cultural worldview and the socio-political ideology of those who adhere to the various forms of religiosity. Although the mix of religious variables is different in every country and region, there is enough basic similarity between them—because of their common heritage and socio-cultural reality—to make this study of Brazilian religiosity paradigmatic for all of Latin America.

Brazil is the largest Catholic nation in the world. Its most populous city, São Paulo, has the distinction of being the second largest urban area in Latin America (after Mexico City) and the largest Catholic diocese in the world. Nevertheless, Brazil is not, strictly speaking, a Catholic country, as even Catholic representatives are quick to point out (LADOC 1973: III/36a: 1–3). Although 85 percent of the population calls itself Catholic, an estimated 30 million Brazilians (or 25 percent of the total population and almost one-third of all professing Catholics) practice some form of spiritism. In 1973, only 20 percent of the total population could be considered practicing Catholics, according to a leading Brazilian newspaper (*O Estado* 1973).

Brazil also has the largest Protestant population—more than 4.5 million communicants and 22.5 million adherents—and the third largest Protestant membership-to-population ratio (after Guatemala and Chile) in Latin America.[51] More than two-thirds of the Latin American Protestant membership is to be found in Brazil (Read, Monterroso, and Johnson 1970: 28, 36).

The *comunidades* movement in Brazil cannot be fully understood apart from an understanding of the major dimensions of Brazilian religious reality in general. In this chapter we shall attempt to understand this reality from several different perspectives. The religious modalities that we shall seek to understand are: (1) so-called traditional Catholicism, (2) popular or "folk" Catholic religiosity, and (3), briefly, the spiritism of Amerindian, African, and European origins. Pentecostal popular religiosity will be studied in chapter 11.

## TRADITIONAL CATHOLICISM

Fr. José Comblin makes the point that there is no such thing as a living traditional Catholic religion. What there is, he insists, is an official Catholicism that is taught in seminaries, and can be found in papal encyclicals and pastoral letters, and in the decisions of church councils. The practice of the Catholic faithful departs, to one degree or another, from official dogma (quoted in dos Santos 1978: 118).

Yet from another perspective, it is possible to speak of a traditional Catholicism—if by it we mean the priest-and-parish-centered church that was institutionalized by the Council of Trent and strengthened by the Ultramontane movement. It is the religion of vestured priests, pompous Sunday masses, baroque images, numerous saints' days, and solemn processions in which participation is regimented according to a well-defined social pecking order.

In contrast with the voluntary lay fellowships that arose during colonial times, the participation of the laity in the traditional post-Tridentine and Ultramontane church was highly structured and clergy-dominated. Reacting against this traditional religiosity, and against the ideology that undergirds it, the masses of Brazil—and of Latin America—turned to popular Catholicism, spiritism, Pentecostalism, and more recently to the *comunidades*, in search of a more relevant expression of their faith (dos Santos 1978: 72-80).

Segundo Galilea points out that the well-off classes of society do not really practice traditional or official Catholicism any more or less than do the marginalized masses. The difference between the religion of the masses and of the elite, he insists, lies not so much in the content of their religiosities as in the fact that the religion of the rich is more individualistic and "furtive"—that is, less culturally integrated and more privatized than the religion of the poor. Because of this privatization, says Galilea, the popular element in the religiosity of the elite may be less evident, but it exists nonetheless (1978: 13). Many of the cultic elements that we find in folk religion are, in varying degrees, present in the devotions of the Brazilian elite.

Despite the overlap of traditional and popular religiosity, there is one aspect of traditional Catholicism that we must study because it is in radical discontinuity with the religiosity of the masses. Liberation theology sees the religion of the people as ultimately related to the "historical praxis" of the oppressed poor who make up the majority of the Latin American population. It sees traditional Catholicism as allied with the socio-economic elites who are the oppressors of the poor. As we shall see in chapter 4, the dividing lines are both cultic and ideological. It is the ideological dimension of traditional Catholicism—and not the cultic elements, which in many cases are shared with popular religiosity—that we must now attempt to understand.

## Ideology

Ivan Vallier points out, correctly, that the hierarchy of the Catholic Church in postindependence Latin America realized that its privileged position could be maintained only by political alliances with the state. A highly politicized clergy lost its spiritual authority. The conservative hierarchy failed to initiate new relationships with the state and thus forfeited the opportunity to achieve a greater degree of autonomy and new forms of political leverage. "The church became a major political factor on behalf of the forces that promsied to protect it as an institution, *rather than a differentiated religious system with roots in the spiritual life of autonomous membership groups*" (Vallier 1970: 7-8, 28, emphasis added).

Contrary to Protestant perceptions, the Latin American (and Brazilian) Catholic Church is not an integrated and monolithic whole (de Kadt: 51). Ideologically it is divided. Structurally it is segmented both vertically and horizontally at both national and diocesan levels. Its administrative and pastoral efforts are, for the most part, uncoordinated. Lacking both organizational autonomy and institutional cohesiveness, the traditional church has been forced to extemporize as problems arose in order to maintain its privileged position and simultaneously achieve its objectives. Its survival strategy, says Vallier, has consisted of the "maximization of short-run gains when conditions are favorable, an exercising of restraint in periods of uncertainty, and an ever-ready willingness to be inconsistent if the situation demands it" (1970: 23–26).

The church, adds Vallier in a very perceptive analysis, was structured horizontally—both as a problem-solving unit at each hierarchical level and in its relationship to civil authority—instead of vertically, as a united and central-ized system in ultimate contact with the grass roots. The structure of the church at the parish level is also anachronistic, says Vallier, because the primary religious units in Latin America are not the parish but smaller units such as the village, the family, and lay devotional associations (Vallier 1970: 25–27).

### Radicalization

In recent years, however, a new element has been introduced in traditional Catholicism. Bruneau (1974: 30–36), Vallier (1970: 56–57), and Della Cava (IDOC 1978: 43–47) analyze changes in Brazilian and Latin American Catholi-cism as expressions of the continuing search pursued by the church to find ways to maintain its social influence and control. And Brandão (1980a: 96) refers to differentiated "modes of ecclesiastical control" in his ground-breaking study of Brazilian popular religion, to which I shall have occasion to refer.

In a helpful typology, Vallier outlines five stages in the history of the Latin American Catholic Church, and shows how a succession of "influence strate-gies" interacted with various dimensions of Catholic reality. He also shows how the church at each stage responded to outside pressures.

In chapter 2 we covered Vallier's stage I, the *monopolistic strategy* of the colonial church, as well as stage II, the *political strategy* that was implemented under the strong leadership of Dom Leme in the early twentieth century through the newly organized Catholic Action. We can now turn to an analysis of stage IV, the *social development strategy*, and stage V, the *cultural-pastoral strategy* in Vallier's model, with particular application to traditional Catholi-cism.

Following World War II, and in particular during the late 1950s, there was a shift in the Catholic strategy as the "progressive" elements in the church were brought increasingly into contact with the socio-economic reality of the poor who make up more than two-thirds of the population of Brazil. The theological underpinning of this concern was the revival of interest in the social philosophy of Thomas Aquinas through the writings of Jacques Maritain. The two institu-tional evidences of the Brazilian church's response to newly perceived social challenges was the creation of the National Conference of the Bishops of Brazil (*Conferência Nacional dos Bispos do Brasil*, CNBB) and *Ação Católica*, or Catholic Action. There was no precedent either in canon law or in Catholic history for a national conference of bishops. Heretofore, each bishop has related vertically to Rome through the papal nuncio and not horizontally to his colleagues in the same nation (IDOC 1978: 43–44). The action arm of the CNBB was *Açâo Católica* (AC).

AC became the organizational core for a wide variety of development projects carried out by youth, labor, and peasant organizations. The most prominent of these, the JUC, became the seedbed for future pastoral agents in the *comunidade* movement. Rural vocational centers, literacy programs, a variety of cooperatives, health clinics, and agrarian reform programs became the concern of an idealistic, young Catholic laity and clergy (de Kadt: 58–65). But their growing involvement in the socio-economic reality of the poor brought about their gradual radicalization, which in turn led to the present pastoral strategy of the Brazilian Catholic Church.[52]

### "Cultural-Pastoral" Strategy

The Brazilian Catholic Church has led the way in this more recent strategy of the Latin American church. The evidences of it can be found in its increased sensitivity to cultural and social values, together with an attempt at reordering the internal life of the church. Although this has resulted in a withdrawal from the traditional political arena, it does not by any means signify a withdrawal from society. On the contrary, because of this new pastoral approach to Brazilian reality—and as a result of the political pressures that it brought about—the Brazilian hierarchy got into trouble with the new military regime.

Concerted action along these lines was accomplished, though not without sharp dissension within the hierarchy. Nevertheless, by 1962, the CNBB was able to announce a *Plano de Emergência*. It was followed in 1963 by the Combined Pastoral Plan, which was in large measure a tribute to the determination and skill of Dom Hélder Câmara, the auxiliary archbishop of Rio and secretary general of the CNBB. He was encouraged in his efforts by his close friend and advisor, the Vatican secretary of state, soon to become Pope Paul VI (Antoine: 52–59; de Kadt: 80–101).

Catholic lobbying was partially instrumental in bringing before congress in 1964 the first agrarian reform bill in the history of Brazil—which, as it turned out, would never be implemented. Operating at the grassroots level, between 1961 and 1965, the Catholic-sponsored and government-supported *Movimento de Educação de Base* (MEB) attempted a somewhat paternalistic program of grassroots education. Despite its shortcomings, it was to become—as we shall see in the next chapter—both a laboratory and a seedbed for the CEB movement.

But the military-industrial-landholding alliance that controlled Brazil was incapable of distinguishing between the goals of the socialist-oriented peasant leagues and the Catholic MEB.[53] Both movements, in fact, represented a threat to their absolute control, and were important factors in the decision of the military to topple the Goulart regime. Though the MEB continued to exist, it was gradually emasculated until it became a mere shadow of its former self.

Under pressure, the radical leader of AC, Dom Hélder Câmara, was "exiled" to Recife, in the remote northeast.

But meanwhile, moderate bishops had gained control of the CNBB, serving as a buffer between the reactionary and radical elements at both poles of the Brazilian hierarchy. Then the individual and courageous actions of a handful of more progressive bishops, in defense of the civil rights of their activist clergy and AC-related laity, gradually created a situation that increasingly forced direct confrontation with the state (Vallier 1970: 68; de Kadt: 65–68).

Backed by the moral authority of the encyclicals *Mater et Magistra* (1961) and *Pacem in Terris* (1963), the progressive leadership of the newly created CNBB set in motion a program of conscientization (*conscientização*) among the hierarchy and clergy. A total of eighteen hundred workshops, conducted over a 5-year period, laid the foundations for the eventual commitment of the church to the defense of the rights of its own poor and oppressed. By 1967 the CNBB had moved ideologically beyond Pope Paul's *Populorum Progressio* into action programs that would eventually amount to a challenge to the state. Paradoxically, the moderates eventually became the leaders of the progressive wing of the Catholic Church, after the radicals had been pushed aside. This moderate hierarchy probably acted at first more out of the need to preserve institutional solidarity than out of ideological commitment (Bruneau 1974: 80–137; de Kadt: 80–81, 113–14, 125–210; Libânio 1979: 2–4; see also LADOC 1970: I/13: 1–3; I/47b: 1–5; IDOC: 43–45).

Gradually winning back the leadership of their church, the progressive bishops began to confront head-on, with public statements, specific situations of injustice. The key turning point came in 1973, the twenty-fifth anniversary of the Universal Declaration of Human Rights, when the CNBB "circulated throughout the land an exegetical document demonstrating the biblical origins of each of the declarations" (IDOC: 45; see also LADOC 1973: IV/5:1–7).

Incidents of imprisonment and torture of Catholic activists who were accused of subverting national security mounted until they reached a crescendo in the 1967 "coup within a coup" (LADOC 1970: II/13:1–3; I/26:1–10; Moureira Alvez 1968: 88–89, 124–27, 140–41). Quoting the French Catholic news agency DIAL, the Associated Press stated that a total of 347 religious leaders including 2 bishops and 185 priests had been either imprisoned or called in for questioning between 1964 and 1978. In addition, 29 were tortured, 3 assassinated, and 27 expelled from the country. Eighty-eight, including 23 bishops, had either been defamed or threatened with death.[54]

The reaction of the Vatican was not long in coming. Following immediately upon the heels of a strongly worded statement condemning torture and violence in the world, Paul VI pointedly removed the ultraconservative cardinal of São Paulo by promoting him to a prestigious Vatican position. He then appointed as his successor the moderate auxiliary archbishop of São Paulo, the respected Franciscan scholar, Paulo Evaristo Arns (Bruneau 1974: 209–13).

Quite unexpectedly, Cardinal Arns became the outspoken leader of the only effective opposition to the absolutism of the Brazilian government. Under his inspiration the "church has either pioneered or endorsed most of the basic planks in the civilian opposition's platform": the end of torture, abolition of censorship, the abrogation of AI-5, the reinstatement of habeas corpus, and full amnesty for thousands of exiles (IDOC: 46). Most of these demands were met by 1980. For the first time in Catholic history, the power base of the progressive wing of the church was, fundamentally, a grassroots community movement, the *comunidades*.

A new generation of activist bishops came to the fore. Several of them, like Cardinal Arns, are the product of the strong lay community tradition among German immigrants (IDOC: 48). Cardinals Aloísio Lorscheider and Ivo Lorscheiter became, respectively, the CNBB executive secretary and CELAM chairman, and the chairman of the CNBB.

The social credo of the Brazilian church, as it began to develop in the late 1960s, is the expression of Vatican concern for justice in the encyclicals from this period, backed by Vatican II and Medellín. In 1975, Paul VI's *Evangelii Nuntiandi* further emphasized the prophetic dimension as an integral part of evangelization and related it to the CEBs (1975: 25–40, 58).

As early as 1970, the Brazilian bishops had published a document entitled "Total Rejection of Torture." Then the CNBB, at its twenty-fifth annual conference in 1977, prepared a landmark document entitled "The Christian Requirements of a Political Order."

This statement by more than 250 bishops who met at Itaici, São Paulo, begins by grounding the Catholic understanding of salvation upon the incarnation and resurrection of Jesus Christ. Because of this, the church "in the performance of its mission, according to the example of Jesus, . . . has to commit itself to the poor (Matt. 11:5; Luke 4:18), whose condition of misery is eloquent witness of the sin that is imbedded in the human heart and contaminates all personal, family, and social life." This commitment to the poor places the church squarely within the political realm, though not in the traditional sense of the word "political." Faith, not power, is the driving force behind the new-found social commitment of the church. "For the church, faith must order all of human life and activities, including those that pertain to the political order [which]. . . is subject to the moral order."

The document proceeds to relate the social nature of humanity and the political order to the order of creation. It then clearly defines the rights and duties of the state within the divinely appointed order. "It is not the state that grants . . . rights to persons . . . [for] the state exists for persons." Because of this, "it is the duty of the state to respect, defend, and promote the rights of persons, families, and institutions." All the rights the state enjoys derive "from its responsibility for the common good." The common welfare is also the foundation of the power and authority of the state.

Having clearly set forth its theological and sociological premises, the CNBB document flatly declares that socio-economic marginalization denies the common good. The document takes a hard look at marginalization through the lenses of dialectical sociology and unembarrassedly defines it in terms of class struggle and ideological manipulation (LADOC 1978: VIII/3: 7–8).

In closing, the Brazilian hierarchy insists that "the church does not contest the right of the modern state to elaborate a policy of national security [but] . . . security should not be the privilege of systems, classes, and parties; it is a responsibility of the state, which should be at the service of all the people." The same logic that justifies "regimes of exception" in times of crisis in favor of the common good "requires that the exception not become permanent and unending rule." The challenge of development cannot be divorced from the common good. This requires a holistic development that includes the social, cultural, and religious, as well as the economic, dimensions of human development. Such development is incommensurable because "it is primarily measured by incalculable values" (LADOC 1978:VIII/3: 1–14).

This document represents the position of a church whose organizational principle has moved, in the words of Bruneau, "from territorial coverage to the legitimization of social change through religious justification." In the process, the church is discarding old mechanisms and is searching for new ones. The church as an apparatus may, in some respects, be on the wane, but the church as a living organism is growing because it is gaining back the allegiance of the laity and, in the process, creating the conditions for a higher level of religious influence (1974: 327–40).

The transformation of traditional Catholicism into a "living organism" is taking place through the instrumentality of a number of movements—such as the CEBs—which are a part of the broader post-Vatican II aggiornamento. But before we study the CEBs as such, we must turn from traditional or official Catholicism to the religion of the grass roots of Brazil. This will help us to understand two important dimensions of Brazilian Catholicism: popular or "folk" religiosity, and African and Amerindian spiritism. It will also prepare us for a subsequent analysis of traditional Protestantism and Pentecostalism.

## POPULAR CATHOLIC RELIGIOSITY

Comblin points out that "in discerning popular religiosity, it is not enough to avail oneself of moral criteria," such as were used by the Council of Trent—or, we might add, by early Protestant leaders. As we study this phenomenon, we must ask about the survival potential of this religiosity as an expression of the numerous Latin American subcultures. And, above all, we want to discover if it has any potential for human promotion. In order to do this, we need to differentiate between the several types of popular religiosity.

Comblin suggests a five-point typology: (1) a religiosity that is simply the participation of the people in official and soteriologically necessary religious acts; (2) a religiosity that is the true and living expression of the Christian faith and values that are transmitted in the family; (3) a popular religiosity that manifests itself in the faith and committed life of Christian workers who have been able to create a different lifestyle—for example, the *comunidades*; (4) the popular religion that consists primarily of fulfilling secondary religious acts such as devotion to saints and is mainly concerned with the material benefits of religion; (5) syncretistic popular piety that often is nothing more than a veneer that thinly covers ancient pagan rites and implies a degraded and dominated human condition (Comblin 1978: 214).

The first kind of religiosity in Comblin's typology could probably be classed with what I have preferred to call "traditional" Catholicism. Types 2 and 3 are what Catholic liberation theologians prefer to call "religion of the people," as distinct from "popular religiosity," in order to accentuate the positive elements that they believe are the seeds of the liberation of the poor. The last two categories in the Comblin typology will now concern us as we seek to understand Brazilian popular religiosity.

Throughout the first section of this chapter I have made several references to "popular Catholic religiosity." We need now to become more precise in our use of the term. As Segundo Galilea points out, this term is imprecise because it encompasses syncretistic spiritism, popular (i.e., Pentecostal) Protestantism, as well as popular Catholicism. Galilea recognizes that popular belief is "the religious expression of our large majorities who have not been instructed in the faith." It is characterized in general by (1) the predominance of a *devotional spirituality* that meets the cultural and social needs of the people and (2) an "*ecclesial marginalization*" that takes place by mutual consent because the spirituality of the people does not coincide with official religion" (Galilea 1978: 14-16).

There is a disturbing tendency in progressive Catholic circles to idealize popular religion—disturbing because, as a WCC study warns, "There is no . . . mechanical link," no "elective affinity," between popular movements and the subordinated classes. Rather, folk religion "is popular only in appearance, or, at least, only in the first stage of this history. It never exists in the pure state." Personal values (codes, worship, festivities, sufferings) are quickly manipulated by various ideologies and, in capitalist systems, become the object of commercial exploitation (Santa Ana 1981: 50-53). The tendency to manipulate popular beliefs is, of course, not a capitalist monopoly. It happens, as well, in socialist states!

### The Context of Popular Catholicism

A study of popular religiosity in Latin America, prepared for the Third General Conference of the Latin American Bishops (CELAM III), analyzes popular Catholicism at four structural levels: (1) large groups in religious precincts; (2) collectivities (societal groupings) at the parish level; (3) families and grassroots Christian communities; and (4) the individual or personal level, ranging from the veneration of an image to the fetishistic use of an amulet.

It is at these levels, the CELAM study goes on to state, that the following most frequent manifestations of popular Catholic religion can be found: cults of the images of Christ (either suffering or dead), of Mary, and of certain miracle-working saints, the cult of the dead, the use of medals and scapulars, celebration of novenas, paying mass stipends, and consulting diviners and horoscopes.

The CELAM study observes that several expressions of popular religion (the rosary, the month of Mary, Friday abstinence, etc.) are disappearing. They are being replaced by such alternatives as the liturgy of the Word and by Bible novenas, on the one hand, and by spiritism and astrology on the other (LADOC 1976: VII/13a: 35–39; dos Santos 1978: 126–34). As in other current Catholic renewal movements, there is also an attempt to refocus Mary and the saints within the new prophetic hermeneutic of the *comunidades* (Leon 1978).[55]

Galilea adds that the seven church sacraments are either little used in popular religion or reinterpreted by the people. He points out that the folk devotion to Mary, the saints, and Christ (who is often seen as just another saint) has in it more of the element of respectful appreciation of their power over nature than imitation of their lives as in classic Catholicism (1978: 17–18).

Folk Catholicism has its roots in the religious worldview of colonial and early postcolonial Brazil. Because rural Brazil remains in many places profoundly feudal, what we saw in the previous chapter concerning the interaction of religion, culture, and socio-economic structures in the *fazenda-engenho* system holds true in large measure today (Brandão 1980a: 21–27). Industrialization and mass migrations to the cities have, however, produced an urban variant of popular Catholicism that has made important contributions to the worldview of grassroots communities.

## Rural Catholic Religion

Leers makes the point that there is not just one rural Brazil but many worlds different each from the other. Each has its own social structure, despite the unifying factors of religion and language. Some of these worlds have been affected more than others by the inroads of urbanization and secularization. Leers cautions that the study of Catholic folk religion is complicated by the fact that at several points it shades into African and Amerindian spiritism. Nonetheless, even at the risk of overgeneralization, it is possible to study rural religiosity as a whole, in part because:

> Rural Catholicism is first of all life before it is systematic knowledge, environment and not organization, mystique and not dogma. It is more of a sentimental consciousness than rational science; more *cultus* than theology; more action than doctrine; more praxis than theory; more intuition than logical rationale [Leers 1977: 109].

*Religious ideals and practices in peasant religiosity.* The women in grassroots cultures participate much more intensely in religious practices than do their menfolk. As Carlos Brandão observes, the attitude among men is that "as long as they don't injure others, personal morals are a person's own business and are irrelevant if he compensates for them with social virtues that are founded upon the honor of one's social class and upon group solidarity." He points out that "religion is a stock of rules and of sacred resources which are at the service of daily demands which are essentially earthly," but that the poor "lay hold of the *sacred* in order to resolve the *mundane* needs of their daily struggles for existence." In the presence of priests, they are humble and submissive learners, but away from them they are "re-inventors" and autonomous practitioners of the faith. Their religiosity serves as a seedbed for popular dissidence and resistance to oppression (1980a: 125, 170–75, 203, 287; see also T. Azevedo 1963).

## Urban Catholic Religion

Urbanization is one of the most important contributors toward social change in contemporary Latin America. This is particularly so in Brazil. As Segundo Galilea points out,

Urbanization is not merely an urban majority in a continent that until recently was agrarian. It is, above all, the inauguration of a new mentality, of a new culture, and of another religious lifestyle which is also of the people [1978:26–27].

The mass urban migrations in Brazil in recent decades suggest that the religiosity of the cities is, in great measure, an extension of rural popular religiosity. Yet it is a religiosity that is being conditioned and in the process transformed by the challenges and threats of the alien secular environment in which the uprooted find themselves (Leers 1977: 180–99; dos Santos 1978:13). Urban popular religion is so new that it remains to be studied in depth.

Galilea proposes some guidelines for recognizing and studying this phenomenon found throughout Latin America. Urban Catholicism is characterized by: (1) a devaluation of traditional religious symbols; (2) increasing heterogeneity; (3) depersonalized human relationships; and (4) more specialized areas of work and dwelling. The interaction of these four factors is producing a crisis in urban religiosity. The *comunidades*, although fewer in number in large cities than in rural areas, are an attempt to provide the necessary ideological "space" for a revitalized and more relevant Catholic religiosity (Galilea 1978: 26–40).

It is also in the larger cities that the many forms of spiritism are multiplying in geometric proportion, after being practiced for centuries in the hinterlands. This phenomenon, far too complex to be treated in depth here, merits at least a brief comment because it is part of the reality in which the CEBs are growing in Brazil. (Although by no means the same, its counterpart in Mexico, Central America, and the Andean nations is Amerindian animism.)

### Spiritism in Brazil

Spiritism is a vital component of Afro-Iberian religiosity in Brazil as well as in a number of Caribbean nations. A staggering 25 percent of the population of

Brazil (including almost one-third of all professing Catholics) practices some form of spiritism.

The term "spiritism" alone does not adequately describe the Brazilian phenomenon. It is, in fact, a mix, in varying proportions—and with many local variations—of Portuguese-Catholic popular religiosity (which, like most Iberian Catholicism, was at one time significantly influenced by Moorish and Sephardic esotericism),[56] Amerindian animism,[57] well-developed West African tribal religions (the preponderant element), and animistic Bantu beliefs and practices.[58] More recently it has taken on accretions of French Kardecism (with its quasi-Hindu belief in reincarnation), which was fashionable among the Brazilian elite in the nineteenth century.[59] Each of these streams is contributing to a loosely-structured "new religion"—Umbanda—which claims millions of adherents from the middle and upper levels of Brazilian society, reaching even into the presidential palace. Umbanda aspires to be the "national religion" of Brazil.[60]

Several of the most respected students of Afro-Brazilian spiritism point out that the spiritist cults are, fundamentally, a revolt against socio-cultural alienation. For centuries the religions of their ancestors have been the only "cultural spaces" that the subjugated and exploited descendants of blacks and Amerindians have controlled to any degree (Bastide 1971: 23, 25). In the twentieth century even this escape mechanism is being denied them: it is rapidly being domesticated by the state and by the mass media at the service of the ideology of national security. Afro-Brazilian spiritism is being transmogrified into a kind of "new religion"—partly for tourist consumption. Its cultural symbols are ideologically manipulated for financial gain and, one suspects, in order to maintain social control over the masses.

It is not without significance that appreciable minorities from these same dominated classes are searching in the Catholic *comunidades* and in grassroots Pentecostalism for socio-cultural as well as spiritual liberation (Johnson 1969: 96–128; Willems 1967: 258–60). The role of the Pentecostal movement in this process will engage our interest in the second half of chapter 11.

Meanwhile, it is important to bring together the different strands we have treated separately in pursuing the subject of this chapter. We must weave them into the tapestry of Brazilian social and religious life into which the grassroots ecclesial communities have threaded themselves since the early 1970s. The pattern I shall use is one that is appropriate for the analysis of a phenomenon that is, after all, not only religious but social, economic, and political.

## "POOR PERSONS—RICH GODS"

This is the heading with which Carlos Rodrigues Brandão begins one of the chapters in a recent pioneering anthropological study of folk religiosity—Catholic, spiritist, and Pentecostal. Brandão, a Catholic associate of Rubem Alves, uses dialectical structuralism as his analytical tool (1980: 296–97). Evangelical Protestant studies of folk religiosity have usually been based upon functionalist ethnographic presuppositions, which are useful but tell only the upper half of the story. Aided by Brandão's insights, we shall approach our subject from a very different perspective—what has been called the "underside of history."

From the foregoing description of the religious variants in Brazil—excluding Protestantism[61]—one might conclude that each religious subculture is a discrete and fairly self-contained phenomenon, largely static, and having only a peripheral—and preponderantly functional—relationship to the other religious subcultures within the macrostructure. Nothing could be further from the truth. The religious subcultures all interact dynamically with each other, and all with the political sphere. To quote Brandão's epigrammatic statement, "The process of the genesis and transformation of religious instruments and ideologies . . . is not functionally social but socially political" (1980a: 87). Although socio-cultural functions cannot be totally ignored as factors in popular religions, the study of popular religiosity must not be limited to a description of models of religious phenomena.[62] It should also seek to understand the complex socio-economic as well as cultural interrelationships in grassroots religious practice and belief. This will help us to avoid the pitfalls of purely historiographic and ethnographic analysis on the one hand, and of premature conclusions concerning the functions of "folk religion" on the other hand (1980a: 296).[63]

Sprinkled throughout Brandão's writings are a number of conclusions, based on his observations of grassroots religiosity in a representative segment of rural Brazil. They are germane to our analysis of the CEBs, not only in Brazil but, probably, in any Latin American nation where social contradictions are clearly evident. I have singled out seven that appear to me particularly relevant.

1. *"Religion serves the ideology of the social structures of class dominance* because it produces both the sacred symbols and . . . the knowledge that covers the evidence and contradictions of domination." This is, of course, a Marxist dictum, but what follows contradicts Marxism, because, as Brandão points out, religion is also capable, at a later stage, of planting the seeds of social transformation and of hope "through acts of dissidence and rebellion." Erstwhile symbols of domination can become the basis of hope and belief in the existence of other social alternatives, while helping to create new religious forms that are more in harmony with this new dream (1980: 297).[64]

2. *Latin American religiosity must be analyzed along intersecting social (vertical) and confessional (horizontal) lines before we can truly understand the interaction of its complex variables.*[65] Brandão locates true popular religiosity at the very base of the social pyramid (1980a: 121). As a case in point, he demonstrates that the major Afro-Brazilian spiritist cults and larger Pentecostal denominations in Brazil, as well as the practitioners of certain kinds of Catholic folk religion, are not truly "popular religions," but rather what he calls "intermediate religions." He shows that these supposedly "popular religions" are, in fact, at the service of an upwardly mobile social sector of society

with innately middle-class aspirations.[66] The very base of the socio-religious pyramid is occupied by nonliterate popular religious "agents" whose services are restricted totally to the socio-economically deprived, of which they are a part (1980a: 74, 114, 121–22).

3. *Confessional distinctions tend to blur the closer one gets to the grass roots.* Brandão's "discoveries" in this direction are fascinating to a student of the phenomenology of religion, though perhaps disquieting to a religious purist.

On certain sacred days a Brazilian *camponês,* "peasant," will take candles to the padre for his blessing—one of the few times he steps into the parish church, because this is a function that only a priest is deemed powerful enough to perform. The remainder of the *camponês's* day will be taken up with religious observances where unauthorized lay practitioners play a prominent role. This same *camponês* may attend the tent meeting of a grassroots Pentecostal healer in order to resolve a physical problem that the *santos* were either unwilling or unable to address. Or he may seek the services of a local *macumbeiro* whose magic has been found to be powerful in specific instances (Brandão 1980a: 125–27).[67]

4. *Popular religion is not an apolitical phenomenon; in its own way, it is a grassroots struggle to retain a degree of freedom from the domination of more structured religious forms.* Brandão astutely observes that the elements that constitute the very essence of popular religiosity, and set it apart as a distinct form of religion, are precisely what priests, pastors, and "necktied mediums" find objectionable in it (1980b: 120–21). When these distinctives are removed, or gradually mitigated, the devotees of the several forms of popular religion are, in fact, yielding to subtle upward pulls from the established religions.[68] This same principle is at work when the popular domain of the miraculous is gradually preempted by the traditional religions and placed at the service of their ideologies. As Brandão wryly observes, "If [miracles] are any measure of the vigor of community belief in God and in the verities of the faith, nothing is stronger than the religions of the weak" (1980b: 131).[69]

The essential moments in the religion of grassroots Catholics are not the rites administered by priests. Brandão points out that in the worldview of the people the padre is accepted as a legitimate specialist, though a "dominator." He is accepted by them as a necessary factor in official Catholic rites, but he is not looked upon as an agent of the miraculous. That realm is the exclusive purview of the religion of the poor. Basically, rural and urban proletarian workers, says Brandão, view their faith as an available resource at their disposal, not as an institution to be served. Consequently, their religiosity is, among other things, a form of resistance to attempts at drawing them into the service of a form of domination that they detest, or at least distrust, as they do all official authority. Grassroots resistance to outside domination extends to efforts by Catholic parishes to transform their diffuse religiosity into a more structured kind of basic community. This, in fact, he concludes, is in itself a very political act.[70]

5. *The upward mobility of the natural leaders of the people will gradually*

*separate them, and those who follow them, from their own base communities.*[71] Popular agents and practitioners are intimately related to the group they serve. The closer natural leaders are to the grass roots, the more numerous are the opportunities for them to become the leaders of a popular religious movement. In the *bairros* "down below," any well-known adults who are involved in a legitimate "mystery" can present themselves as grassroots practitioners. But, Brandão points out, the success of religious leaders will depend, in the end, not upon their upward mobility but upon the community that they serve and from which they draw their following. It is their own followers who will evaluate them in terms of their felt needs and who will help determine the nature of the religious practice that leaders exercise (1980b: 47–48).[72]

The watershed where base community begins to flow toward religious institutionalization is at the point where the popular Pentecostal or spiritual "healer" and the Catholic grassroots "pray-er" have begun to renounce their community and class representativeness in exchange for the legitimization and status that an outside agency can provide.

Grassroots Pentecostal and spiritist leaders have one of two avenues open to them: they can either raise up a following and await the day when their movements may become respectable, or they can subordinate their activities to an outside agency, preferably one that has its roots in the same geographical region and socio-cultural area (1980b: 54–56). A process is then initiated whereby their diffuse and highly creative popular religiosity is gradually systematized into a concise and manipulable body of ideas and doctrines. These ideas are then pressed upon future initiates in the sect as it gradually becomes transformed into a church (ibid., 154).

6. *The breakdown of the religious monopoly of Roman Catholicism has brought with it a change in the relationships between religious confessions.* These relationships, Brandão insists, can no longer be traced along purely horizontal, confessional lines. The pull is increasingly toward vertical realignments based on class interests. Vestiges of the old confessional antagonisms still exist in Latin America between different religious groups that compete for converts within the same social class. But with increasing frequency one begins to see representatives of the same "established" confessions standing together on the same political platform—both literally and figuratively—in defense of their own class interests.

However, antagonisms that pit one social class against another within the same religious confession are sufficiently frequent in Latin America to cause one to reflect seriously upon the validity of Brandão's thesis. Ideological kinship, more often than not, is thicker than the blood of credal fellowship.

7. *CEBs can be instances of grassroots resistance to manipulation.*[73] In certain cases, the *comunidades* can be just another evidence of popular resistance to the institutional church—more specifically, its "strategy of conquest of subordinated peoples." The mere fact of the CEBs, though they represent only a small minority within popular Catholicism, is another sign of the ultimate

failure of all attempts to dominate disadvantaged peoples—either politically or symbolically—or to adequately provide the services and symbols that they require (Brandão 1980b: 145).[74]

This is the challenge that faces the Catholic Church in Latin America, a challenge that is even greater for Evangelical Protestantism. It calls for an understanding of the socio-economic and cultural variables at work at the grass roots of Latin American society from the perspective of the poor and oppressed (Santa Ana 1981: 48, 498). This is the only way we can profitably begin to comprehend the CEB phenomenon.

# PART II

# GRASSROOTS COMMUNITIES
# IN THE PERSPECTIVE
# OF RENEWAL

# Chapter 4

# Genesis of the CEBs:
# Renewal from the Underside of History

*I have seen how cruelly my people are being treated. . . . I have heard them cry out to be rescued from their slave drivers. I know all about their sufferings, and so I have come down to rescue them [Exod. 3:7–8].*

The *comunidades* would probably have never been allowed to arise as *Catholic* ecclesial communities had it not been for the general climate of renewal in worldwide Catholicism. The various dimensions of this renewal— biblical, liturgical, socio-pastoral—have all had something to contribute to the CEB movement. But the greatest single factor has been the emergence of the poor and underprivileged as a force to be reckoned with in Latin America.

The cold war between communism and capitalism has indisputably provided ideological frames of reference within which one could interpret the genesis of the grassroots ecclesial communities in Latin America. It has probably exacerbated the issues, but it is not the cause of the CEBs. Socio-politically, the Catholic *comunidades* are the most notable evidence in Christendom today of the poor demanding their place in the sun. (As I shall seek to demonstrate in chapter 10, the CEBs are the most recent, and one of the most significant, manifestations of insurgence in a very long history of grassroots dissidence in the Christian church.)

## THE *COMUNIDADES* IN THE CONTEXT OF CATHOLIC RENEWAL

Beginning with Leo XIII's watershed encyclical *Rerum Novarum* in 1888, and Pius XI's *Quadragesimo Anno* forty years later, the Vatican began to demonstrate a small degree of awareness of the social reality of the subordinated peoples of the world.[75] *Quadragesimo Anno* would remain normative until the second half of the twentieth century.

Then, in the short span of ten years, five epochal social documents burst upon the Catholic world.[76] A little more than a year after *Populorum Progressio*, Pope Paul VI inaugurated the sessions of the Second General Conference of Latin American Bishops (CELAM II) in Medellín, Colombia. CELAM II was the contextualization of official Catholic social doctrine in Latin America. At its very beginning the Medellín document describes the Latin American reality as one of "misery," which collectively "expresses itself as injustice that cries to the heavens" (CELAM II:1/1).

But Medellín did more than describe the situation. It also analyzed. Its analytical instrument was the three-step methodology of Catholic Action—"observe, judge, act"—which had been recommended by John XXIII (MM: 236). Doctrinal reflection follows social analysis and is followed in turn by pastoral recommendations and mediations. The *comunidades* occupied a key position in the pastoral strategy of Medellín (CELAM II: 6/3, 13–14; 10/3, 12, etc.). In all probability, the CEBs could not have arisen without this newfound Roman Catholic openness to renewal—even though the institutional approach was often cautious and at times manipulative.

### Grassroots Movements in the History of Brazil

*The Seeds of Lay Renewal.* More than in perhaps any other Latin American country, Brazilian Catholicism has been uniquely molded throughout its long history by the vitality of its lay movements, as well as by a strong grassroots and unofficial lay leadership. In all Latin America the official church catered to the needs of the dominant classes. Neglected by the official church, the subordinated masses created their own self-sufficient religiosity.

Lay Catholicism, in Brazil and in all Latin America, has been characterized by two interrelated streams: (1) *the family dimension of lay religiosity*, where the cultic elements of the faith "assume a greater degree of warmth through the devotions that are practiced in family oratories";[77] and (2) *the social dimension* of lay Catholicism, characterized by festivity and manifested in two distinct forms: the joyous dances of the blacks and the solemn processions of the whites (dos Santos: 50–51). In both forms of festivity, believers were able to externalize values that they were not free to express in the clergy-dominated Catholicism that followed the Ultramontane reforms in Rome.

*The Role of the Clergy vis-à-vis the Laity.* Particularly in the rural areas of Brazil, this role is an ambiguous one. Power—that is, control of the official symbols of religion—was fairly well concentrated in the clergy within a vertical and dependent relationship under which the laity was expected to remain in passive submission. Consequently, a curious mixture of respect, fear, and anticlericalism has traditionally informed the attitude of the subordinate Catholics toward their spiritual leaders (Leers: 95–97). Leers candidly admits:

> In the Catholic universe the people and the clergy function as social roles in mutual interdependence. As the slave master conditions the role of the slave who, for his own part, finds in the acceptance of his role a way to

survive, in the same way the clergy, conscious of its power by means of the traditional theological rationalizing of the celibate priesthood, had created on the secular plane the general role of submission, obedience, and silent respect on the part of the people, as mute cattle in a time of rain, who celebrate their freedom somewhere else [1977:97].

In stark contrast, an important dimension of the present Catholic church renewal in Brazil, and in a number of other Latin American countries, is the growing identification of the clergy with the subordinated classes. Concretely, this identification is evidenced by the number of priestly functions, as we shall subsequently note, that are being surrendered (Marins 1977a: 16, 33–37). Nevertheless, the traditionally privileged position of the clergy contributed, from colonial times onward, to the development of a number of *autonomous lay institutions—cofrarias* and *irmandades*—and, somewhat closer to the official church, third orders.

At the same time, the absence of effective religious leaders at the grass roots left a vacuum within which a number of lay roles appeared in order to satisfy the religious needs of the people. These are the "blessers," "pray-ers," "pious ones" (*beatos*), and fetishists who were once despised and ignored. But there is now a new appreciation of the value of these lay leaders, to the extent that more progressive bishops are permitting them to assume certain priestly functions.

*Messianic Movements.* This is another significant aspect of the long tradition of grassroots leadership in Brazilian Catholicism (Foreman 1975: 221–36) of significance for today.[78] The messianic potential in present-day Catholic lay religious movements is a fact that probably has not been lost on the Catholic hierarchy or on the political authorities of Brazil.

### The *Comunidades* in the Context of Lay Renewal

In the light of the strong current of lay grassroots movements in Brazil, what is the place of the *comunidades* today? In one very significant sense, the CEBs do not represent a break with the mainstream of grassroots Brazilian Catholicism, which from colonial times has been lay-centered and fundamentally at odds with official Catholicism. Yet in another sense, the *comunidades* are a radically new development within the Catholic Church. In order to understand the significance of this development for the Christian churches in Brazil, we must pick up a few strings that were left loose in the woof of the complex tapestry of contemporary Brazilian Catholicism.

### EMERGENCE OF THE *COMUNIDADES*

### Early History of the Grassroots Communities

Historians of the movement single out a handful of experiments in popular catechesis that began in the 1950s as being particularly significant milestones in the process that produced the *comunidades* in Brazil.

1. The popular catechesis experiment of Barra do Pirai (Northeastern Brazil), in 1956, provides us with the first known link between popular Protestantism and what was later to become the CEB movement:

It began when an old woman said to the bishop during a pastoral visitation of her area, "In Natal the three Protestant churches are lit up and crowded. We hear their hymn-singing. . . and our Catholic church, closed, is in darkness. . .because we don't get a priest." This challenge prompted some fundamental questions such as: If there aren't any priests, does everything have to stop? Cannot anyone else do anything for the life of the church community? [Marins in IRM 271:237, or in Concilium 104:30–31; see also Guimarães 1977:18; LADOC Keyhole 14:2].

A conservative bishop, Dom Agnelo Rossi, was stung into initiating a lay missionary movement.[79] He mobilized 372 community coordinators (lay catechists) who gathered groups of Catholics to pray and listen to the reading of scripture, to hold "Mass without a priest," and in other ways to maintain a sense of community. Instead of the traditional chapels, they built community meeting halls to be used for catechetical instruction, public schooling, and trade schooling (IRM 271:237–38, Concilium 104:130–31; Guimarães: 18–19; Libânio 1979b; LADOC Keyhole 14: 2–4).

2. The *Movimento de Natal* was inspired by an earlier experiment in mass education by Radio Sutatienza in Colombia. In the early 1950s the Catholic Church in the Brazilian Northeastern state capital of Natal became conscious of the abysmal poverty—the malnutrition, illiteracy, endemic diseases, and exploitation—of the majority of its members. The first response to these needs came under the leadership of Archbishop Eugenio Sales. It took the form of treatment centers and of schools for the semiliterate, demonstrating how to mobilize them to attend to their own more urgent basic needs. Literacy training, basic sanitation, and agricultural information were used as vehicles for awakening the political consciousness of the people.

The principal goals of the Natal movement were (1) grassroots literacy programs (*educação de base*) and (2) conscientization with a view to effecting changes in political, social, and economic structures (*conscientização*),[80] (3) so as "to take God to neglected communities" (*evangelização*). By 1963 there were 1,410 radio schools in the archdiocese of Natal alone, and the movement had begun to multiply throughout the impoverished northeast in the form of a network of "evangelical and evangelizing" small CEBs. The Natal experiment is considered the beginning of the grassroots education movement or *Movimento de Educação de Base* (MEB), which laid the groundwork nationwide for the future of CEBs (IRM 271:238–39; Concilium 104: 31; Libânio 1979: 3; de Kadt: 122, 134; LADOC Keyhole 14:4).

3. There were other isolated experiments in lay catechesis, such as that which was undertaken by the nuns of the small town in Nizia Floresta near Natal.

Each such experiment fed into the swelling stream of grassroots Christian education that would eventually empty into the Amazon of the *comunidades* movement. On a vaster scale, a team of fifteen religious workers appointed by the CNBB traveled the entire country over a 5-year period, teaching a total of 1,800 courses on grassroots methodology for members of religious congregations. The CNBB later brought all these experiments together under the Emergency Plan, which five years later became the first of a series (1965–70) of Combined National Pastoral Plans (Libânio 1979b: 3; Alicino 1977: 9, 14–17, 21–23; CNBB 1977).

The stated objectives of these plans were the revitalization of parish structures and the evangelization of "natural communities" existing in the form of spontaneous social units of the grass roots, in order to transform them into "authentic ecclesial communities."[81] Marins explains:

> The beginning of the basic ecclesial communities in Latin America was marked by the concern to evangelize in a continent of baptized persons who lacked contact with the life of the sacraments, with the Word of God, and with one another. They did not have the possibility of devoting their time to the evangelization of others and to announcing the message of salvation to the world. Together with this concern for evangelization, and deriving from it, there was a consciousness of responsibility for facing the reality of the world and for embarking on the work of liberating the world by devoting themselves to the poorest and most unjustly treated. For this reason, too, the communities sprang up most intensely in the most challenging areas, where persons were crushed by adverse conditions [IRM 271: 240; Concilium 104:33].

### The Grassroots Education Movement (MEB)

The earliest experiments in popular catechesis in Brazil were still very much under the thumb of the hierarchy and the local clergy. Libânio characterizes these experiments as "vertical" and "paternalistic" (1979b: 2–3). So, initially, was the MEB. The first four years of the decade of the 1960s were characterized by an intensive competition between Marxist cadres and the Catholic Church for the allegiance of the masses. Catholicism in Brazil pioneered in the creation of labor unions and launched a quasi-political movement known as Popular Action (AP). The lay leaders of these movements had been trained in Catholic Action youth movements. This intellectual, idealistic, and radical elite gradually led the MEB from a mere literacy program to a movement that had a growing stake in changing the basic socio-economic structures of Brazil (de Kadt: 102–21). The MEB, a uniquely Brazilian movement, can be credited with laying the foundations for the CEBs. This is probably one reason why the *comunidades* have proliferated more in Brazil than anywhere else in Latin America.

*Organizational Structure.* The organizational structure of the MEB was bureaucratically top-heavy. Its strategy and directive were sent down through a chain of command from a national directorate of bishops, through the *Coordenação Nacional* (which included administrative staff and technical teams), as well as its counterparts at the state level, until they reached the basic units of organization, the local *sistema*. Each local "system" consisted of a team (*equipe*) of teachers, supervisors, and radio staff. It also included the rural poor who were being taught, and in particular, the natural leaders of each group. These were the *monitores*. At the peak of the MEB there were fifty-nine such *sistemas*.

The *monitores* were "one of the most essential cogs in the MEB machine." Although they were at first appointed from above, lay leaders soon began to be chosen by the persons they served and to whom they belonged. They gradually began to be valued as community leaders who could be entrusted with more and more responsibilities. This change in MEB outlook took place within the framework of a gradual shift in emphasis. *Conscientização*, rather than literacy, became the principle objective.

This change in orientation was closely related to the evolution in the self-image of the movement. Though it eventually became an autonomous entity, the MEB had begun as an organ of the CNBB. Despite the fact that they were not always in full harmony with one another, the ambiguous relationships with local bishops served as a buffer between the MEB and the increasingly nervous establishment (de Kadt: 143–48; Libânio 1979b: 3).

Two years before the 1964 coup, the MEB cadres met to rethink their goals. From this point onward they began to advocate sweeping changes in the social structures of Brazil. A growing number of *sistemas* became active in rural agrarian unions. In 1963 an allegedly subversive MEB training manual became a cause celèbre after it was confiscated by the governor of the state of Guanabara. This was "the straw that broke the camel's back" (de Kadt: 149–71).

After the 1964 coup, a number of MEB staffers were arrested or harassed. Forced to step in and take control of the movement, the bishops began to change its orientation. Although social justice continued to preoccupy the *equipes*, they were made to tone down the content of their didactic material. The general focus of the MEB gradually shifted from structural change to community development (de Kadt: 190–211).[82]

*Methodology.* Technical as well as ideological factors eventually made it necessary for the *Coordenação Nacional* of the MEB to deemphasize the directive pedagogy that was implicit in the radio schools and to rely increasingly upon local leadership. The long experience of the *equipes* with the *conscientização* methodology of Paulo Freire, and subsequent experiments in North American group dynamics techniques, would someday become useful in the lay-directed CEBs.

It gradually became clear to the MEB leadership that there was a fundamental contradiction between their desire to allow their trainees to exercise their full freedom of choice and their "strongly-held moral and political views about

'Brazilian reality' " bolstered by "philosophical views about human nature and society." For *equipes* impatient to achieve structural changes, nondirective techniques seemed wasteful, confusing, and inefficient. But the MEB slowly learned to live with this inherent contradiction (de Kadt: 212–20).

The contradiction still surfaces in the literature of the *comunidades*. Marins (1978c: passim) insists that the CEBs were not created as part of any ecclesiastical strategy but were spontaneous ecclesial responses to social reality, particularly at the grass roots (see also SEDOC 1975: 101); and Medellín calls upon the bishops to "encourage" and "favor the efforts of people to develop and create their own grassroots organizations in order to achieve true justice" (CELAM II: 2/27, 2/14). But these same documents emphasize the important role of the clergy in guiding these communities (CELAM II/11; Vallier: 107–8).

A SEDOC document quoted by Bruneau states:

In almost all the experiences described, the renovation is helped in its inception by the ecclesiastical institution. The institution takes the initiative; from the "center" the movement spreads to the bases. . . . But, to a degree in which this process takes form and begins to awaken the people, so it also begins to dismantle the traditional organization of the same institution which promoted it, and the particular priest, bishop, or religious enters an unlimited identity crisis [Bruneau 1979: 232].

Frei Betto is therefore on target when he observes that "there was a dialectical process in the development of the *comunidades*." The grassroots community motivation was channeled in CEB experiments by pastoral agents of the church. "Vatican II conceived the *comunidades*, Medellín baptized and confirmed them, but the people have given the CEBs their own particular personality" (Frei Betto 1980c).

## THREE ROUTES TO THE *COMUNIDADES*

Marins and J. B. Libânio point out that Catholics in Latin America have arrived at *comunidades* through various routes and from diverse starting points. Many grassroots communities, and in particular those who are far from parish centers, are completely new. Their link to the bishop is through the priest or through an authorized lay person. Such groups, Marins points out, put a strong emphasis upon the "celebration of the Word," particularly those that fit into the framework of the *círculos bíblicos*.

Grassroots Protestants can at times be found joining the *círculos* in prayer and Bible study. Together, "they discover in actual life-experience that the Word is neither a monopoly of Protestants, nor of the parish priest, but the collective property of the people, in the service of others" (Marins 1977a: 23; IRM 271: 251–52). The task of pastoral agents or ministers is to help these Bible-and-worship-oriented CEBs to incarnate their Scripture reflection into the socio-economic and cultural reality. Mesters states that the majority of the CEBs were born as *círculos bíblicos* (Libânio 1979b: 5).

Other grassroots communities took as their point of departure their new perception of socio-economic reality acquired through the *conscientização* process in the MEB *sistemas*, after they had been driven underground in 1967. The pastoral leaders who were sent out to implement the Combined Pastoral Plan of the CNBB gradually transformed these "natural communities" into "ecclesial communities" where Word and sacrament are celebrated (Libânio 1979b: 5). These, Marins comments, could be termed "liberation CEBs." They are more sensitive to social injustice than are other grassroots congregations.

A third route to the CEB experience is through attempts to revitalize the outmoded parish model of the church. They are encouraged by the more conservative priests and bishops. Often highly structured and sacramentalist in nature, they tend to be overdependent on the clergy. Their goals are largely church-centered; they help in parish revitalization activities.

The grassroots community movement did not get off to an easy start, says Marins. In a number of cases, he writes, they initially experienced "a complete failure." They failed because they attempted to arrive at "a new model of the church without a personal, communal, and structural conversion." The early communities were often organized with the technical and success-oriented approach of a consumer society, "leaving little room for the reality of the cross and its seeming inefficiency." Attempts to "outdo the Protestants" at their own game put the CEBs in danger of being infected with a fundamentalist and sectarian spirit (1977a: 8)!

Despite these initial setbacks, the grassroots communities began to proliferate as a growing number of bishops made them their primary goal (SEDOC 1975: 65, 69; Alicinio 1979: 21–23). By 1974 there were 40,000 grassroots communities in Brazil, according to the estimate of Marins (IRM 271:240; Concilium 104: 34; Marins 1977a: 30). By mid-1978, the estimate had risen to 50,000 (Marins 1978c). Less than a year later, *Time* magazine quoted an unnamed source to the effect that there were 80,000 *comunidades* in Brazil (May 7, 1979, p. 8). More recently, figures in the range of 100 thousand for Brazil and 75 to 80 thousand for the remainder of Latin America are being mentioned, but with no substantiating data. That the CEBs continue to proliferate, there seems to be no doubt.[83]

What is the reason for this rapid growth? The answer, I believe, can be found in the radical reorientation of Catholic belief and practice in one sector of the church (its option for the poor), which has found an echo in the lives of the oppressed peoples of Latin America. This reorientation can best be appreciated in the way that CEB participants understand the movement.

# Chapter 5

# The Self-Understanding of the Catholic Grassroots Communities

*He rescued the needy from their misery and made their families increase like flocks [Ps. 107:41].*

In order to appreciate the true significance of the *comunidades* for the life of the Latin American church, it is important to attempt to see the movement as it is viewed by its creators—the people—as well as by those who have identified with their struggles to establish an authentically human and Christian presence in the world.[84] Though most of the following insights are taken from the Brazilian experience, it is possible to generalize from them to the Latin American scene at large.

After five centuries of silent submission mixed with artful assertions of their own underground religiosity, the poor of Brazil are now being heard in the church. Let us listen to their own definitions of what the Christian church must be like, as expressed at a gathering of CEB leaders in 1975.

> We want a church that lives the problems, trials, and joys of the people . . . less concerned with the administration of the sacraments and with ministries than with promoting those who are "the least," those who suffer most. . . . A community that only concerns itself with prayer and worship is not concerned about others. . . . Let's go out and see what's happening around us and try to do something about it. . . . We need to move out from a religion of fear to a religion of salvation; from a religion of oppression to a religion of growth [SEDOC 1975: 22].

The theme of the Second Interecclesial Encounter of the CEBs, held in Vitória (Espírito Santo) in 1975, was "A Church Born of the People by the

Spirit of God."[85] Prior to the gathering, each *comunidade* was asked one basic question: What kind of CEBs do we need? The replies can be summarized under three general headings: (1) "We want mature Christian *comunidades* that are committed to Christ and to the people and its liberation"; (2) "We want *comunidades* that are led by the gifts of the Spirit, and that are integrated into the total church, along with other communities, in a spirit of free and fraternal intercommunication"; (3) "We desire communities that are in a constant process of reflection and of growth in-depth, under firm leadership" (SEDOC 1975: 23–24).

The CEB self-understanding moves along two converging axes: (1) "a return to God's Word; to christocentrism; to a personalized faith; to the mystery of communion; to the meaning of the people of God; to co-responsibility; to evangelical values," and so forth. This "vertical" axis intersects with (2) "openness to the signs of the times, to the reality of the world here and now, and to the meaning of the future; to secularization; to temporal commitment" (SEDOC: 14). In fact, the generic name of the grassroots communities says everything about them. The two axes—Christian community and solidarity (*comunidade*) and social commitment and solidarity (*de base*)—converge in the church (*eclesial*).

However, this convergence has not always been smooth or free from tensions. As I have shown in earlier chapters, the CEBs were born in an atmosphere of sharp ideological conflict within the hierarchy as well as between the Catholic Church and totalitarian governments in Latin America. In Brazil, the radical bishops' control of the National Conference of Bishops (CNBB) in the late 1950s and early 60s was checkmated by the conservatives soon after 1964. As a compromise, the majority moderates placed some of their own in power, only to become themselves increasingly radicalized in their struggle against right-wing totalitarianism (IDOC 1978: 44–45).

It is impossible to comprehend the complex way in which the *comunidades* understand themselves without taking into account the continuing existence of the same three ideological currents within the CNBB. As J. B. Libânio points out, "the members of the communities are experiencing a new situation of awareness in three areas: psycho-social, ecclesial, and political" (IRM 271: 231). These three areas are not unrelated to the varied origins of the CEBs, as Marins understands them: scriptural reflection in community, common socio-political ideals, and a concern for parish renewal. Today, though all CEBs are part of a common movement, they all tend to emphasize either the community, the ecclesial, or the grassroots dimension of that movement (LADOC 1981: XII/2: 8–12; REB 41: 287, 309).

Each of these three streams in the one movement is borne by a particular ideology and encouraged, as far as I can ascertain, by one or the other of the factions in the church. Though each stream in the CEBs may define the movement as base ecclesial community, each tends to perceive the threefold dimensions of the grassroots communities through the lens of the facet that is closest to its own ideological bias.

Let us now look more closely at the three approaches to the self-understanding of the CEBs in the expressions of their participants as well as in the writings of the theologians and pastoral ministers who identify with the movement.

## THE COMMUNITY UNDERSTANDING OF THE CEBS

The student of the abundance of published materials by CEB pastoral theologians will notice subtle differences between the various writers. Some of the grassroots community representatives are at pains to emphasize the *community* dimensions of the CEBs. One of them is Rogério Alicino, whose apostolate is in the Amazon region. His approach is theological. Ribeiro-Guimarães approaches the same theme from a mostly sociological perspective. José Marins and his team, more even-handed, seem to stress the community dimensions more than they do the other dimensions. By their more radical colleagues they are perceived as being more conservative in their approach to the CEBs.

The starting point of Alicino's treatment is Scripture and the contemporary documents of the Catholic Church. He frequently refers to the documents of Vatican II—in particular *Lumen Gentium* and *Gaudium et Spes*—to the documents of Medellín, and in particular to the Bible, for his analysis of the community dimension of the church.[86]

Alicino and Marins find the scriptural basis of community in the praxis of the New Testament church. Alicino points out that the New Testament community showed itself at three interrelated levels, which correspond to the three derivatives of the Latin cognate of *koinonia*: (1) *communio*—a union and sharing of ideas, thoughts, and sentiments, which requires intimate living together (*convivencia*); (2) *commune*—a union and sharing of goods, which requires meshing and harmonizing methods and efforts in concerted action; (3) *communus*—a union and sharing of responsibilities and tasks, which requires participation at the level of resources and responsibilities. This three-fold community awareness was demonstrated by the Jerusalem church where doctrine, liturgy, prayer, food, and possessions were all shared in common (Alicino: 46–53).

Marins adds that the Jerusalem community was both pluralistic (heterogeneous) and specific (homogeneous). He calls the New Testament churches *comunidades domésticas de base*, and cites this as one cause for their rapid multiplication throughout the empire. The strong community orientation of those house churches was the direct result of their christocentricity (1977a: 127–58).[87]

### Homogeneity and Heterogeneity

Medellín stated rather ambiguously that a CEB is "a community, local or environmental, which corresponds to the reality of a homogeneous group"

(CELAM II: 15/10). Alicino points out that the words "local or environmental" permit a broad range of interpretation. "Local" emphasizes geographic homogeneity, whereas "environmental" underscores a homogeneity based upon some specific social categories or community of interests. Medellín, Alicino concludes, chose to use mutually complementary rather than exclusive terms. Authentic communities arise in the same geographic locale where their members live, and these communities are thoroughly integrated into their physical, ethnic, and moral environment. Family and work are the homogenizing factors in the environment of Brazil, says Alicino (1977: 56–57; see CELAM III: 477). He adds categorically:

> When the Medellín document affirms that a community must correspond to "the reality of a homogeneous group" it is only trying to offer yet another element by means of which *comunidades* can be identified; it is not suggesting a method for the formation of a community [Alicino: 57; see also Delespesse 1973: 63].[88]

### "Natural" and "Ecclesial" Communities

Despite affinities with an Evangelical Protestant understanding of the nature and boundaries of Christian community, the CEB view is much more radical! The Medellín document also distinguishes between "natural" and "ecclesial" communities. The former is defined as natural groupings such as union shops, neighborhood or peasant associations, sports clubs, or any other variety of societal groupings where members partake of a common cultural or socio-economic reality.

"The ecclesial community," writes Alicino, echoing CELAM II, "is the same natural community that becomes the 'family of God' " (1977: 64; see CELAM II: 15/10). As a Catholic, Alicino recognizes the risks and difficulties in establishing clear-cut distinctions between both types of communities:

> There is the danger of emptying the former of many values which, though they belong to the natural sphere, do not cease to be profoundly Christian and implicitly ecclesial; there is also the risk of representing an ecclesial community on the basis of exaggeratedly structural elements, which cause it to be seen in terms that are disincarnate from human reality [1977: 63].

Because of this ambiguity, the pastoral efforts of the church should not be directed at "creating . . . new ecclesial structures, but at awakening, infusing, developing, sustaining the communal and ecclesial Christian spirit where it already exists in natural communities." Because a fundamental characteristic of an ecclesial community is its insertion in human reality, it should not extract persons from their natural social groupings in order to introduce them into an artificial "Christian-ecclesial environment." The *comunidades* are not a new organizational method but "a new way of being the church." Because of this, ecclesial community should not be reduced to Bible study groups or reflection groups, specialized service teams, or movements that aspire to a purely goal-oriented unity that fails to take "their environmental situation" into account (Alicino: 64–68).

Yet, the "community bias" of one stream of the CEBs does color to one degree or another the perception of these interpreters of the grassroots communities. For them ecclesiality turns upon the axis of community. It can also be perceived in the lifestyle of a number of the *comunidades*. For example, community-centered ecclesiality can be found in the *comunidades* of the parish of Our Lady of Help in Itarana (Espírito Santo). Only the children of parents who are members of grassroots communities or who have CEB godparents can be baptized there. Children's catechesis is done only in the *comunidades*, and marriages are performed by the priest only after consultation with the CEB leadership (SEDOC 1975: 40).

The CEBs within this "community stream" are also very conscious of their missionary responsibility outside the *comunidades*. Alicino's description of this community witness sounds almost evangelical in its terminology and methodological approach to evangelization (1977: 71–83). But probably the greatest weakness of this community orientation is that it fails to address itself sufficiently to the implications of the term *de base* in the three-part name of this grassroots phenomenon. Although Marins (1976b, 1977b, 1977e, 1979) and Guimarães do have a great deal to say about the "prophetic" dimension of the *comunidade* witness, they lack "historical concreteness," in the view of some of their colleagues. This is particularly true of the treatment by Alicino.

Alicino closely follows the strong Medellín emphasis on integral human development and promotion by the total community. But what is lacking is a sharper analytical perception of the root causes of the social reality that must be changed and of the role that community plays in the change process. As J. B. Libânio observes, community is "a maturing people, united and transforming the world in service and well-being for all." This "well-being . . . includes material values and all of the values which help people in their spiritual growth and which make their common life more human" (IRM 271: 247).

## THE POLITICAL DIMENSION OF THE CEBS

As I pointed out in the Introduction, the term *base* has psycho-social, sociological, and theological nuances. Dialectical sociology defines *base* at four interrelated levels: social oppression, economic manipulation, political disenfranchisement, and cultural alienation. This should be kept in mind in the following analysis.

### The Historical Roots of CEB Political Self-Understanding

Pablo Richard divides the emergence of the CEBs roughly into three historical stages:[89]

1. *The "revolutionary Christianity" stage* (1960–68) in which certain middle-class Christians became conscious of the underdevelopment, poverty, and misery of the masses, and "of the structural causes of this situation," coupled with the need for radical change (IDOC 1978: 116–17).

2. *The birth of the theology of liberation* and Christians for Socialism movement (1968–73). Although the radical critique of society was being made by members of an intellectual elite, they were rapidly making the lower classes the "social base" for this analysis. This experience "generated a renewal of the expression of faith, of the Christian symbols, of the reading of the Bible, of spirituality, and of theology" (IDOC: 118).

3. *The period of strong governmental repression* of movements of the left (1973–), during which the grassroots movements flourished, and a number of bishops began to identify with the aspirations of the people. The political commitment of a minority of Christians in the previous stages gave way to the radicalization of "the whole of the church's popular base . . . in its commitment to the poor and exploited." This was the birth of the "people's church. . .the *comunidades de base*." Richard is quick to point out what a CEB is not:

> . . .a church fragmented into small communities; it is not a division of one large community into smaller ones. The communities do not arise through a process of coming together of dispersed Christians who have made a conscious political option. In these communities the political work of the struggle for justice is not a supplemental or marginal task, but the very core of proclamation. *Faith is lived and expressed within the political practice without either confusing or reducing it to this* [IDOC: 119, emphasis added].

Richard recognizes that this "Christian dimension of political practice" is neither an automatic nor a spontaneous result of the development of the *comunidades*, but is generated in the ecclesial praxis of the grassroots communities. A CEB, as a popular movement, is the place where Christian activists "express, communicate, reflect upon, and celebrate their faith, hope, and charity." It is no wonder that the military dictatorships of Latin America look upon the CEBs as subversive (IDOC: 119).

Although Bruneau (1979: 233) suggests that the mainstream of the CEB movement in Brazil is politically conscious, J. B. Libânio candidly admits that the "political level" of the grassroots self-awareness is the weakest dimension of their ecclesial life. "The people discover themselves as a group, as persons, and as the church," but they remain "quite unaware of the political dimensions of such a discovery" (IRM 271: 249–50).

## The Grassroots Communities and the Poor

Alvaro Barreiro is one of the many writers who stress the *base* political approach to the *comunidades*—the so-called liberation theologians. In a brief introductory analysis of the Vatican II documents (1982: 4–7) Barreiro underlines the concern of the conciliar fathers for "the evangelization of the poor." Citing statistics, he then proceeds to demonstrate that "nearly all the CEBs in Brazil located in rural areas and, to a lesser extent, in poor neighborhoods on the outskirts of the cities, are communities of the poor" (Barreiro: 8). He supports his contention with statements by CEB members.

All the communities that were involved in the second *encontro* in Vitoria came from these two sectors of the poor. An IBRADES study in 1974 for the CNBB of more than a hundred reporting CEBs showed that 53 percent had sprung up in rural areas, 10.9 percent in rural-urban areas, and 16.8 percent in urban areas. But all the *comunidades* were located in the marginalized sectors of Brazilian society. A study made by CERIS of the participants in the Itaici bishops' conference tends to confirm this point (Barreiro: 8; REB 41: 303). Barreiro cites some statements by CEB members themselves.

Tacaimbó, a small (pop. 3,000) community about a hundred miles from Recife, lacks everything: work, housing, food, health facilities, and schooling. As *comunidade* participants in the village described the situation:

> The poor majority have no fixed work; they work for hire in the fields earning 12 cruzeiros a day [in April 1976 one U.S. dollar was worth 10.35 cruzeiros]. The fieldwork does not provide enough to live, but not only to vegetate. . . . There is meat for one day, but for eight days there is none. . . . Sometimes a father has five or six children and four die . . . of need, disregarded, because they cannot be treated. . . . Most of the people here in Tacaimbó reside in flimsy dwellings, in mud huts. There is almost no sanitation . . . they have no cesspools. All the children have swollen bellies, and are vomiting with dysentery, which is endless. The school facilities are very unstable. "I have a daughter who has been in school for three years, and she is just now learning how to write her name" [Barreiro 1982: 9].

In sum, concluded the CEB members of Tacaimbó, "the vast majority lead lives of deprivation, oppressed and afflicted in the vicious circle of poverty."

The situation of the parish of Imaculada Conceição de Barreirinhas in northern Brazil, where there are forty-four CEBs, was described in a report as "perhaps the most deep-seated impoverishment in all Brazil." Residents have been "deprived of all resources: cultural, social, economic, and political." Their food reserves have given out, their land is exhausted, and they are being slowly choked to death by the large landholdings that surround them (ibid., 9–10). In five *municipios* in this same state of Maranhão there are twenty-two *comunidades* located in small hamlets that are "connected with one another only by backwoods roads. . . . In 1963 there was no medical care or school in the region" (ibid., 10).

A report from the diocese of Goias in central Brazil states: "The vast majority of our 'baptized,' who are hence official members of the church, are poor and oppressed. The system becomes more burdensome for them every day, increasing their poverty and exacerbating their oppression" (Barreiro 1982: 10).

Despite their grinding poverty, *comunidade* members can be both generous and creative with the little they have. Poranga, in the large northeastern state of Ceara, is extremely poor. In order to raise money to restock their small communal medicine chest, they conducted "a fraternal fund-raiser" among the forty-five families in the community, the proceeds of which were used to buy the most urgently needed medicines. Their financial situation can be judged by the fact that thirty-five of them took out a loan of 200 cruzeiros (about $25 at the time) to be paid back over a 2-year period. The *comunidades* of St. Matthew's parish in tropical Maranhão attempted to support themselves after their beginning in 1973 with a monthly pledge of one cruzeiro, about 16.5 U.S. cents (Barreiro: 11).

Also very poor are the *comunidades* located in the peripheries of the large cities. This is the case with the *mucambos* surrounding Vitória, Recife, and in other northeastern cities. In João Pessoa (pop. 287,607), the capital of the state of Paraiba, not far from Recife, there is the *bairro* of Rangel (pop. 28,000), where there are over thirty *comunidades* of extremely poor persons who barely manage to subsist under subhuman conditions (Barreiro: 25-27). The reports of the CEB leaders who participated in the fourth *encontro* in 1981 contain similar stories of heroic struggles for existence in the face of the harassment and outright violence of local landlords and government officials (Barreiro: 12-13; REB 41:88-90, 285).

The reports to the 1976 CNBB general assembly from the twenty-nine dioceses of São Paulo, the richest state in the federation, make this revealing observation:

> The creation of the CEBs has taken place among the lower socio-economic classes. And, in the poor areas, it has been noted that the most underprivileged have been the ones most receptive to this ecclesial notion. The difficulties among the other classes are considerable, and when ecclesial groups come into existence, they often become closed and introspective [Barreiro 1982: 13].

### The Poor in Scripture and in the Perception of the CEBs

Although I shall analyze the role of Scripture in greater depth in chapter 7, it is important at this moment to make the point that the self-understanding of *comunidade* participants and pastoral agents is not a theoretical construct imposed upon the CEBs by Marxist agitators. This is a totally erroneous criticism; it reflects a condescending and contemptuous attitude. Involvement in the reality of the poor forced Catholic activists back to Scripture and to their own tradition in search of theological foundations and a liberating spirituality. Their Christian commitment, and not a political program per se, impelled them to identify with the struggles of the poor.

## ECCLESIAL SELF-AWARENESS OF THE CEBS

In a number of Spanish American countries the CEBs are called *comunidades cristianas de base*. The Brazilian church, however, has emphasized the *ecclesial* nature of the grassroots communities. It has even avoided the expression "popular church," which has come into vogue in some places. As Frei Betto explains:

> Every time that I speak of the popular Church in the context of Brazil, I run the risk of implying that the hierarchy or conservative sectors of the Church are the true possessors of the historical, constitutional, traditional Church, and that we must now create a kind of new Church. I think that the history of the Church confirms that only through an internal struggle is it possible to bring about changes in the Church. It would appear that the experience of the Protestant Church in this regard reaffirms this [LADOC XII/3: 1–2].

Whatever the theological starting point and ideological bias of the self-perception of the grassroots communities, CEB leaders in Brazil unanimously stress the ecclesial aspect. Libânio makes the point that there is an intrinsic relationship between this awareness of ecclesiality and the perception of community—the feeling of identity as a people. This, he says, is a "new ecclesial phenomenon" in the Latin American Catholic Church. He quotes the words of a *comunidade* participant: "Now I understand that we are the church" (IRM 271: 246). Frei Betto contrasts the centripetal potential of this ecclesial awareness with the fissiparous tendencies of historical Protestantism (LADOC: XII/3:2).

The structural side of ecclesiality is ecclesiastic. And in the *comunidades*, as Bruneau demonstrates, ecclesiastical legitimization is important. "All the primary and secondary studies show that the CEBs emerge and flourish only with direct support of the Church" (1979: 231–32). The danger, of course, is that the support can, and often has, become self-serving and manipulative. This is the case in a stream of CEBs that come close to being an aberration of true grassroots ecclesial community. It is an attempt to use the ecclesial self-awareness of the *comunidades* to further the ends of the traditional church. This could ultimately spell the destruction of the CEBs. Though it lacks widespread support in Brazil, the danger of this view of ecclesiality should not be downplayed: since Puebla, it has become the official policy of CELAM, with the apparent encouragement of the Vatican.[90]

Catholic traditionalists and some self-styled moderates who see the CEBs as a threat to their authority are nonetheless aware of their potential for parish revitalization. The *comunidades* could be made to serve as instruments of control over the Catholic popular sectors of Latin America that are being lost to secularism, Marxism, Protestantism, and spiritism.

A clear example of this "reinterpretation" of CEB self-awareness is the following analysis of the *comunidades* by the very conservative president and one-time secretary general of CELAM, Cardinal Alfonso López Trujillo. According to his view of the grassroots communities, they are "a special *form* of small community, by reason of their composition . . . rhythm . . . and perspective" (López Trujillo 1978: 5). The stress in this definition is obviously upon the *form* (structure) and *function* (usefulness) of the CEBs; it downplays their *meaning* for the institutional church.

The *comunidades* are not limited to the poor, says López Trujillo. They are open to "distinct sectors of the people of God, belonging to various groups." Acting as aids to the larger church, *they should not have their own agenda*, says López Trujillo, but should function in accord with needs and demands of the whole ecclesial community—the parish and diocese. Because of this, "they *should not limit themselves to one pastoral area*," such as social action, "or to one ecclesial sector, or a single group." The CEBs can be "a pastoral help" in large, urban parishes as well as in rural areas (1978: 5–6).

Addressing himself to the place of the poor in the CEBs, López Trujillo concedes that *comunidades* germinate most easily in "poor areas" because the "needy" feel a greater sense of solidarity among them than do the individualistic rich. But the latter also need to be benefited by the communities, for "would restricting the CEBs to given social groups," he asks, "not impoverish their real task?" (1978: 6).

The fundamental character and principal criterion for evaluating the grassroots communities, writes López Trujillo, is evangelization as it was defined in Medellín (CELAM II: 15/10). But it is an ecclesiocentric or centripetal evangelization that the president of CELAM sees as the role of the *comunidades*. He is emphatic about the centrality of the sacraments (1978: 7).

On the question of the basis of group homogeneity—economic or cultural?—López Trujillo comes down on the side of "common interest and relationship that serve as cementing factors." Central to his understanding of homogeneity is participation in a common faith that is practiced without equivocation and avoids being misused or trapped in "secondary objectives" (1978: 8). This faith, according to the CELAM president, is strongly centered in the institutional church. Though he recognizes that the *comunidades* are not so much a new pastoral strategy as "a new way of life," he points out that this new lifestyle is church-centered above all. "They are a way of bringing the church closer: their focal point is the Word and the Eucharist" (1978: 8).

The leadership of the CEBs, in the view of the cardinal-archbishop is primarily clergy-centered. The clergy and the lay permanent diaconate should work together as pastoral teams, avoiding the excesses of clericalism on the one hand and of "laicism" on the other. But "the responsibility of the laity, which must be recognized always, is regulated by the reality of the hierarchically constituted church" (1978: 9).

Finally, López Trujillo warns against the use of grassroots communities as instruments of political conscientization. "How can the identity of the CEBs be guaranteed," he asks, "while retaining the focus of conscientization properly understood, without leaving them open to being used for other purposes?" At the same time, he recognizes that the rediscovery of popular piety by pastoral agents in the *comunidades* can become "a major evangelizing instrument" (1978: 10, 91).

In sum, this traditionalist variant of the ecclesial understanding of the CEBs sees them as valid *forms* or structures within the church as institution. It values their services as useful functions or instrumentalities in the service of the church and among the poor in the church. But it fails to understand the real meaning or significance of the CEBs as the first truly "people's church" in the history of Latin American Catholicism (LADOC 1979: 48–49). Or is it perhaps that this meaning is understood only too well and is feared because of its implications for the authority of a church that is one of the richest, most powerful, and most densely structured institutions on earth?

## THEOLOGICAL ROOTS OF CEB SELF-UNDERSTANDING

The various perspectives from which leaders, supporters, and participants of grassroots communities understand the complex movement of which they are a part are rooted in different interpretations of their shared history, ecclesiality, reading of scripture, and ultimately in their different approaches to christology. Although each stream in what is undeniably one movement is conscious of the significance of the *comunidades* in terms of their potential for church renewal, they understand their contributions to their process somewhat differently in the light of their particular ideologically conditioned interpretation of the history of their church in each Latin American context (see Table 5).

One stream of the CEBs seems to be more impressed with the loss of Spirit-infused and dynamic interpersonal relationships in the traditional church and sees the contribution of the *comunidades* as a return to New Testament methods and community lifestyle. The Vatican II discovery of the church as the people of God is seen by them in the light of what could be termed the *prophetic koinonia* dimension, which is based upon passages in Acts and in several of the Pauline Epistles. For them the church is the sacrament or sign and instrument of ultimate union of God with alienated and divided humanity (Alicino: 50–54; Marins 1977e: 136–58).

A second stream perceives church history and the history of the Latin American peoples in terms of the *oppression-liberation* dyad. For five centuries, the church in Brazil has been an instrument of oppression in the hands of the state. Because of the action of the Holy Spirit in history, an "Abrahamic minority," in the words of Dom Hélder Câmara (Anderson and Stransky 1976: 78)—a "messianic community" (Vatican II: GS: 1)—has begun to live, reflect, and act as an instrument of integral human liberation. The CEBs are more than a return to early-church *koinonia*. They are a radically new kind of *prophetic diakonia* that has emerged from and identified with the poor and oppressed. They are concrete expressions of the church as "a sacrament of the poor." Their

## Table 5

### Self-Understanding of Grassroots Communities: A Typology

| TYPE | ORIGINS | VIEW OF HISTORY | VIEW OF CHURCH | SCRIPTURE FOCUS | LITURGY FOCUS | GOALS | DANGERS AND TENSIONS |
|---|---|---|---|---|---|---|---|
| *com-unidade* | *círculos bíblicos,* cursillos, charismatic groups, etc. | massification vs. community | people of God: a prophetic *koinonia* | Acts and Pauline Epistles; the church as a historical community acting under Christ its head | celebration of the Word and of the Eucharist in community | re-evangelization | turning inward, anti-clericalism, laicism |
| *eclesial* | dead parishes, cursillos, charismatic groups | attempts to re-gain lost influence and social control | people of God: the hierarchy; domesticating *leiturgia* | Scripture interpreted through church tradition in defense of the status quo | traditionalist; ecclesio-centric; celebration of the Eucharist | church revitalization and social control | manipulation and sidetracking of *comunidades* |
| *de base* | "natural communities," MEB *sistemas* | oppression-liberation | people of God: prophetic *diakonia*; messianic community, Abrahamic minorities, "sacrament of the poor" | Exodus, O. T. prophets, the Gospels; "epistemological privilege of the poor"; "hermeneutic of the people" | conscientization, the *marturia* witness of the church | re-evangelization, social justice, new socio-economic structures | rejection of ecclesial commitment; secularism |

Scripture reflection focuses primarily upon the exodus, the Old Testament prophets, and the Gospels.

But *comunidade de base* streams converge in their ecclesial awareness, which takes tangible form in *liturgia*—the sacraments. But in the liturgy of the official—though in fact deformed—version of the CEBs, "ecclesial" becomes a function of "ecclesiastical," within a modified-Christendom schema. No longer the unquestioned arbiter of religious dogma and social mores, the hierarchical leaders of this aberrant movement see in the grassroots communities a way to reestablish their control over the masses of nominal Catholics. The spokesmen for this movement, although recognizing that the church is all the people of God, cannot conceive of its existing apart from the clergy and the hierarchy (López-Trujillo 1978: 9). The basis of their understanding of the reality of the CEBs is rooted above all in church tradition.

### The Role of Christology

Self-understandings of the *comunidades* hinge ultimately on their christological focus. As Leonardo Boff has observed, "There is no such thing as a neutral christology" (1978a: 15). How is Christ worshiped in the Catholic Church? As head of the Body (Alicino: 26)? As suffering servant and liberator (Mesters 1981; L. Boff 1978a: 15–16, 21; idem,1978b)? Or as enthroned king of the church (López-Trujillo: 7; see L. Boff 1978a: 18–20)? Each of these christological images can be found throughout CEB literature, depending upon ideological bias. There is a clearly defined—or at times subtle—difference in the emphasis that is given in each case.

Popular expressions of this christology in the CEBs are best illustrated by two vignettes. A CEB member, a migrant worker in the booming construction industry in Brazil, answered my question, "What does Christ mean to you?" In his thick peasant accent he replied: "Christ means everything to me because he accompanies me in all my problems. . . . He helps me to bear my problems." He raised his hands in an eloquent gesture as if to say, "What more is there to say?"

After an entire *comunidade* in a small town was arrested and brought before the local police chief on charges of subversion, he demanded to be told who was behind them, guiding and manipulating them. They at first replied, "Nobody. It is all of us that you see here." The police, unconvinced, insisted, "Take me to your leader." They answered, "The one who encourages us and guides us is our Chief. It is our Lord Jesus Christ!" (REB 41: 293).

The christology of the *comunidades* is dramatized in the Eucharist, which is acted out in conformity with each community's understanding of its meaning. The Eucharist, which is at the heart of Catholic dogma, has in the CEBs both centripetal and centrifugal dimensions. Throughout its 500-year history, the Brazilian church has focused almost exclusively upon the centripetal dimensions of the Eucharist, using the Mass as a means of maintaining its control over the people. But in the CEBs the Eucharist is both a magnet that draws the community together for spiritual strength and a dynamo that energizes the people of God and sends it out into the world in service and in witness. In sum, the Eucharist can be seen as the axis of the unity of the Body of Christ—a sacrament of salvation and of liberation—or as a tool to maintain the *comunidades* under the thumb of the traditional church (Segundo 1974: 21–40).

## The Role of the Liturgy

The style of the liturgy reflects the particular focus of the CEBs. The liturgy of the Word and of the Eucharist, when it is opened up to the full participation of the entire community with active lay involvement, reinforces and gives meaning to the community dimension of the *comunidades*. When, in addition, the liturgy brings together communal reflection on the significance of the passion of Christ and on the witness (*marturia*) of the numerous *comunidade* members and leaders who have suffered and even died for their faith, then the liturgy gives vital meaning to the very existence of the grassroots ecclesial communities (REB 41: 298–300).

But when the liturgy reinforces the authority of the church through the use of traditional symbols and the exercise of priestly prerogatives, the *comunidades* cease to be "a hope of the church" (Paul VI: 58) and become just another movement that will be swallowed up by a static institution once it has served its purpose.

## PROBLEMS, TENSIONS, AND RISKS: THE VIEW FROM WITHIN

Emphasis on ecclesial community and emphasis on ecclesial praxis in solidarity with the poor and oppressed are not mutually exclusive, but rather inherently complementary. Both types of CEBs are committed to the poor, and both live out their commitment in community. If I have chosen to emphasize these two dimensions, it is not in order to prove that there are two kinds of *comunidades de base*. This would be a highly arbitrary and very artificial division. The typology I have used as a basis for this chapter (outlined in Table 5) is, at most, illustrative of tendencies and emphases that are the natural outgrowth of the different starting points of various *comunidades*.[91] Elements of both dimensions can be found in all CEBs because they are all part of an ecclesial whole. The strength of the communities is that they are all a part of one movement. This allows for cross-fertilization and integral growth.

Tensions in a dynamic and complex movement such as that of the grassroots communities are to be expected. But in contrast to the self-divisive tendencies of Protestantism, the Catholic Church has usually worked toward assimilating renewal movements, and in particular any grassroots dissidence that could threaten its control over its general membership. Those who labor with the grassroots church are not unaware of these tensions.[92]

## Theological Perspectives

J. B. Libânio summarizes some of the tensions and risks that he sees in the grassroots community movement: excessive clerical influence or, in reaction, an exaggerated anticlericalism; clerical attitudes on the part of lay leadership; an overconcentration of the liturgy and group reflection upon local or internal problems without reference to the overall reality of the universal church; the sidetracking of fundamental objectives of the CEBs into secondary issues; a premature "codifying of *comunidade* theology"; and a dichotomous perception of global reality (1980: 332, 337; LADOC XII/2: 13–16; 1979: 8–12; IRM 271: 254–57).

Marins warns of two great dangers to the *comunidades*. The "liberation" CEBs run the risk of "confusing the faith with political strategy, and of permitting themselves to be manipulated by groups that have better tactics and techniques for action." He adds, "they also find it more difficult to discover the way toward an ecclesial commitment." They tend to react, at times unjustly and unilaterally, Marins feels, against ecclesiastical pressures (1977a: 24; IRM 271: 252–53). Other CEBs, he continues, are in danger of "very quickly becoming little more than useful appendages to the existing structures instead of acting as live ecclesial cells (1977a: 24–25). These types of *comunidades* often are attracted toward the *cursillo*, charismatic, and neocatechumenate communities (IRM 271: 241). Marins brings these and other points of tension together within the following three dyads: (1) *renewal vs. tradition*, or the tension between an "evangelical" and a "traditional" church; (2) *community vs. mission*, or the tension between the centripetal and the centrifugal dimensions of *koinonia*; and (3) *institution vs. charism*, or the tension between unnecessary and necessary structures, between doctrine and experience, and between hierarchical center and popular base (1977a: 41–45).

Marins himself exemplifies these tensions. He can write that "the church does not exist without the hierarchy that the bishop represents, in an orderly continuity together with the college of bishops" (1977b: 51). But he is also capable of stating privately to a group of priests and nuns and a Protestant observer: "with a pope, or without a pope, be he married or celibate, the church will continue to be the church" (Marins et. al. 1978b; see *Pro Mundi Vita Bulletin* 62[1976] 9–10).

## Tensions between Forms and Meanings

Every social system (and religious systems are no exception) defines itself and defends its existence by means of distinct forms (signs or symbols) and by the specialized or peculiar meanings that are given to commonly held symbols. Symbols are not usually chosen arbitrarily. They generally develop as part of the complex process of institutionalization at the level of both socioreligious structures and systems of communication. Indeed, the meaning of any given symbol will almost certainly change over a long span of time, although its form may remain relatively inviolate. Problems in communication and in institutional integrity arise when static forms and dynamic symbols are confused.

Within the Christian Church there are many commonly held symbols, although the meanings that are given to them may vary considerably from one tradition to another. Baptism and the bread and wine of holy communion are two well-known examples among many of the symbols that are held in common in the Christian religion. They are also symbols that divide us.

Down through history, many of the great symbols of the early church gradually underwent a process of change in form, function, and meaning—or in some cases, in all three. Changes in form are usually prompted by historical circumstances; they are introduced in order to serve similar functions and to convey approximately the same meanings. Such changes went on during the early centuries of church history. But in time the process of historical accommodation congealed, and meaning was swallowed up in static form. In the end, it resulted in radically changed meanings and in self-serving rather than other-serving functions.

In the Catholic Church, even before Vatican II, there was a growing awareness of the stultifying results of centuries of hard-and-fast welding of form and meaning. From John XXIII onward—at least until John Paul II—there has been an accelerating motion in the direction of separating form from meaning. This is what was defined by the apt Italian word *aggiornamento* (updating) in the time of Pope John XXIII (Latorre Cabal 1978: 11–38).

Within the grassroots communities, this process has been even more rapid—and alarming to the Roman curia—because for the first time in more than a millennium and a half of Catholic history the church is being forced out of its medieval fortresses and gilded chapels into new and threatening situations where ancient forms and meanings no longer have any relevance.

The pristine simplicity of the Lord's Supper and of the *agape* love-feasts is being recaptured in some of the Catholic renewal movements. The original meaning of most of the old symbols was lost in the traditional church, although the form continued, often with spurious and highly questionable functions. The struggle to recapture the original meanings and to contextualize them within their own struggles for justice and freedom is a high priority in the theology of the grassroots church (LADOC XII: 3–6). In ways that are often profoundly disquieting to Evangelicals—we miss the holistic dimensions of salvation history—the "paschal mystery" is redefined as a paradigm of the continuing history of the socio-cultural oppression and liberation of the poor in Latin America (REB 41: 304–6).

The Catholic veneration of Mary, which shades into outright worship in popular piety, has long been a stumbling block to even the most open-minded of Protestants. Despite John Paul's attempts to reemphasize the traditional dimension of maryology, the *comunidades* are attempting to find contemporary applications of the meanings that are in Scripture. They are learning about Mary from "the underside of history," as they search for new action models. In this they have found support in the church fathers (Miranda 1974: 14–22; L. Boff 1978a: 115–28; Mugica 1978).[93] They are finding in the life of Mary, and in her socio-political milieu, a message for the grassroots communities of today (Leon 1978: 3–43).

Mary is closely identified with the self-image of Catholicism. Any reformulations of the doctrine of Mary in Catholicism should be seen as significant indicators of shifts in the Catholic understanding of the church, its theology, ideology, and mission. The Vatican reemphasis of Mary in traditional terms has a significance that goes beyond the purely doctrinal. It is also ideological. In the same way, this new identification of Mary with the poor in Latin American theology is but one expression of the "new way of being the church" that the CEBs exemplify.

The radical understanding of this new ecclesiality is synthesized in J. B. Libânio's provocative conclusion:

> Other churches may be richer in institutions, or talk more about the gospel. But the CEBs are more evangelical because of the evangelical notes of joy, hope, enthusiasm, joviality, largeness of heart, good news despite oppression, and certainty of victory despite evident obstacles. The new figure of the church is born when poor and unprepossessing groups of Christians gather together, even under a mango tree, to pray, to hear the gospel, to witness to their faith in Jesus, and to follow him [REB 41: 305].

The radicality of this witnessing to and following after Jesus will be appreciated all the more when we consider the four historico-theological coordinates that converge in the *comunidades*.

# PART III

# THE *COMUNIDADES* IN THEOLOGICAL PERSPECTIVE

# Chapter 6

# Fundamental Orientations of Grassroots Communities in Brazil

*The Lord says, "Do not cling to events of the past or dwell on what happened long ago. Watch for the new thing I'm going to do. It is happening already—you can see it now!" [Isa. 43:17–18].*

The CEB phenomenon resists facile definitions and explanations. It can be understood only from the perspective of firsthand involvement and identification with the historical praxis of those who make up these grassroots communities. Lacking this opportunity, the next best thing is to attempt to understand them, at first theoretically, by means of an analysis of the factors that have made the CEBs both possible and necessary in Brazil. We must be assisted in our study, however, by the insights of those who are intimately involved in the reality of the *comunidades*. And most important of all, we must approach our task with a willingness to let these grassroots communities speak to us and challenge us to practical involvement in their reality.

The purpose of the first five chapters of this research has been to help students of the CEB phenomenon arrive at their own connotative meaning (as opposed to a denotative definition) of the grassroots communities.[94] In this transitional chapter I shall attempt further to refine this connotative definition in terms of four fundamental orientations or perspectives shared by the *comunidades* in Brazil and in Latin America at large. These four orientations are: (1) a new way of seeing reality, (2) a new way of being the church, (3) a new way of approaching Scripture, and (4) a new way of doing mission.

These four orientations are, in fact, implicit in the subject matter covered in the first eight chapters of this work. In chapters 1 to 3 I have established the basis for the CEB understanding of cultural, socio-economic, and religious reality. Under the first fundamental orientation I shall attempt in this chapter to describe the process whereby those who are involved in the grassroots ecclesial communities have arrived at their new perspective of Brazilian reality. In chapters 4 and 5 I laid the foundations for an understanding of the radical nature of the new ecclesiology of the CEBs, the subject of the second fundamental orientation. The third and fourth fundamental orientations will serve as introductions to chapters 7 and 8, where I shall treat, respectively, the new hermeneutic and the new missiology of the grassroots communities.

Let us turn now to the first, and foundational, orientation of the grassroots communities.

## A NEW WAY OF SEEING REALITY

As stated in the Introduction, "reality," in the definition of Peter Berger, is "a quality appertaining to phenomena that we recognize as having a being independent of our own volition" (Berger and Luckmann 1967: 1). J. B. Libânio, following Berger, adds, "It would not be incorrect to say that man is a product of his environment. But, on the other hand, reality is socially constructed. . . . In a word: man is the producer and the product of social reality" (Libânio 1979b: 63,65). This reality has social, psychological, and religious dimensions.

This new way of seeing reality in the CEBs is more than a new point of view; it is even more than a new methodological approach—although it is both of these things, as we shall see. The new CEB way of seeing reality is an altogether new point of departure. Participants in the *comunidades* experience their *realidade* as poverty, injustice, political marginalization, cultural alienation, as well as religious inanition. *Comunidade* members have begun to discover that their reality is not a divine "given." They are seeking to understand it, not so that they can accommodate to it more efficiently or functionally in order to attract new followers, but in order to change reality as an integral part of their Christian witness. Scripture, along with critico-sociological and theologico-analytical tools, is used for questioning their reality and for setting in motion processes of change.

### The Role of Dialectical Analysis in Understanding Reality

"The dominant groups," says Leonardo Boff, "prefer the functionalist method of analysis . . . in which order and equilibrium are valued and in which society is represented as an organic whole with mutually complementary parts." But:

> The dominated groups prefer to use the dialectical method that has at its heart the idea of conflict and struggle and sees society as a contradictory whole. One view—historically articulated by the liberal tradition—sees society from the top down, from the point where [it] appears to be harmonious; the other view—historically articulated by the revolution-

ary and Marxist tradition—sees society from the bottom up, from where it emerges as struggle and confrontation [1978a: 22].

Marxist dialectical analysis of socio-economic reality is a tool—though not the only one—that is readily available to pastoral workers associated with the CEBs in Brazil. As a science of history it has helped them to understand and to unmask the mechanisms of socio-economic control that undergird the unjust and repressive state capitalism in their country. However, most, if not all, would reject the determinism and atheism of Marxist dogma (Comblin 1977: 56; Libânio 1979b: 72–73; C. Boff 1978a: 35; LADOC Keyhole 13: 54–55).[95]

As we have seen, the use of Marxian insights by *comunidade* pastoral theologians is mediated, particularly in Brazil, by their interaction with a number of philosophical theories. This has made possible the integration of non-Marxist tools of analysis with some of the insights provided by Marx. One such sociological instrument is the sociology of knowledge.[96] It is used by Clodovis Boff, together with French structuralism, in his development of a "political theology" (1978a: 69; 1978b: 41–42, 57–62, 273–389), as well as by J. B. Libânio.

Libânio uses sociology of knowledge schemata in order to clarify the role of ideology, both as an instrument of domination and liberation, and as a critical and change-inducing tool for the analysis of social reality. It can also help to understand the socializing processes at work within the *comunidades*. Libânio first describes, then analyzes, the basic components of an ideological structure. He then shows how hidebound ideological perceptions can change into new understandings of social reality. Though he uses concepts borrowed and adapted from Berger, the framework is the Catholic Action methodology— see, judge, act—which was used by Medellín.[97]

### 1. Seeing—a Descriptive Analysis of Social Structures

"Every group, insofar as it is constituted as a group, is conscious of its own identity, of what it was, what it is, and what it expects to be" (Libânio 1979b: 67). This self-identity is fully achieved as part of a process that includes: (1) *exteriorization*—the group becomes conscious of its own identity through such distinctives as language, values, and beliefs; (2) *objectivization*—the group acquires a consistency of its own that is independent of its creators and with which the group members may at times even be in conflict; and (3) *internalization*—the objective elements of the structure become subjective, an integral part of the self-understanding of each person in the structure. At this point the process begins anew, with modifications. Each time around, group identity is further reinforced until, for some reason, the structure begins to fall apart. But the process is not deterministic. At the ontological level there are priorities that will determine the order in which the constituent elements in the social structure interact in each step of the process.

In order for the group to maintain its self-identity it needs to feel that it is socially plausible. This "plausibility structure" is composed of several elements: (1) *legitimization structures*—such as the national security doctrine in Latin America—that explain and justify the social order for all concerned; (2) *therapeutic measures* (sport events, carnivals, religious pageants, spurious nationalism)—to keep the public mind off the real issues when socio-economic plausibility structures begin to fall apart; (3) *social control*—rigid laws that often are enforced by coercive measures; and (4) *communication structures*—propaganda directed at those who are judged significant to the group. Governments in Latin America, in desperate attempts to stem the tide of popular dissatisfaction, have used all these structures to maintain the plausibility of their social order. Significantly, the only institution that has so far managed to escape the control of these structures has been the Catholic Church in a few countries of Latin America. Therein lies the significance of the CEBs for unmasking the false "plausibility structures" of oppression in Latin America.

When dissatisfaction with "plausibility structures" reaches a certain point, *the dissident structure begins to redefine its identity,* and the entire process begins anew (Libânio 1979b: 109–14). Libânio cautions, however, that this sociological analysis must also take into account two factors that escape our capacity for analysis: "The free and voluntary action of God, which is grace; and unforeseeable human action, whether it be heroism or perversity." These two factors aside, predictable "plausibility structures" are in evidence in the structures of oppression, as well as in the growing self-awareness of grassroots communities as they begin to internalize the biblical vision of the kingdom of God. [98]

Libânio notes that persons, *opinion leaders* in particular, are the keys both to the redefinition of group identity and to the maintenance of a new identity. Their ideas and beliefs are important because opinion leaders interpret reality for the group. It is important, therefore, to understand the hermeneutic of the human knowledge of reality. It is not enough to be able to describe reality or to understand how it functions. Reality must also be judged or interpreted critically so that it can be changed (1979b: 103–4; IRM 271: 253–54). This is the role of the *agentes de pastoral.*

## 2. Judging—toward a New Understanding of Reality

"Reality is *given,* but," says Libânio, "it exists for us only insofar as it is known and interpreted." On the other hand, he adds, our interpretation, being imperfect, is not identical with reality. At best it is "an approximation of reality," which can be known only by human mediations:

> Only God's knowledge, because it is creative, totally penetrates reality. In Him, to be and to know acquire the fullest accommodation. We will struggle forever to achieve that accommodation, avoiding the two extremes of ambiguity and uniformity [1979b: 11].

Libánio then goes on to show how the components of social reality—as one example, class structures—are sustained by self-serving human interpretations and rationalizations. "An ideology attempts to systematize coherently, giving an appearance of totality to interests that are partial, belonging to certain groups or classes. We are all within the ideological game" (1979b: 25). In the interrelationship between our praxis and the theory that explains it, a closed "ideological circle" is formed, in which praxis and sustaining theory interact in a dialectical and mutually reinforcing relationship:

> Since the theoretical elements do not criticize the praxis . . . but justify, explain, and legitimize it, we can continue [our praxis] and strengthen it through a series of spiritual exercises . . . as long as there is no serious questioning of this circularity . . . . In fact, as long as we continue within this circle, whenever we are confronted with new questions it so happens that we offer old answers to new questions [Libânio 1979b: 32].

The obvious question, Libânio points out after this analysis, is "How do we become aware of the existence of this circle and [begin to] perceive that it is so far removed from present reality that it gets in the way of our understanding of new problems and of their solutions?" He suggests two steps that, within a fundamental attitude of openness to change, can make a new understanding of reality possible. It is the responsibility of pastoral workers to help the *comunidades* take these important steps.

*Step A.* The awakening of an "ideological suspicion" begins to call into question our Christian praxis and its underlying explanatory theories and supporting spirituality. This is induced when we begin to be confronted by obvious social contradictions, and open ourselves to the disturbing action of the Holy Spirit at work through a variety of agents. We then begin to look at the Scriptures in a new light.

*Step B.* This perception of new realities that contradict our previous understanding builds upon the "ideological suspicion." It will begin to pry open our "ideological circle." Initially, the challenge may hit us only at the theoretical level, when a new theory appears to explain reality more plausibly than did our old theory. It may help us to discover why our present actions are no longer relevant to the demands of new realities. But, Libânio warns, not every new experience or divergent theory will awaken an ideological suspicion. Theory must reinforce praxis and vice versa if significant change of attitude is to take place. "For a new experience to be able to question a particular practice it is necessary that the experience not be lacking in theory and that the theory not be devoid of a minimum of praxis" (1979b: 41).[99]

The change agent must approach ideological closure in an attitude of openness, and in a spirit of prayer, fasting, and prophecy, because:

> Prayer places us in solidarity with the closed person when we call on the loving presence of God. When we fast, we wish to bear this sin with our

sorrow. By means of prophecy we want to provoke, with the internal efficacy of the Word of God, the hardness of the human heart . . . . We cannot forget . . . the theological dimension of this opening up of the ideological circle . . . in the light of Revelation, as the presence and sign of sin in self-sufficient man. Seen from this perspective, the solutions belong, also, to the universe of faith, and of the mysterious action of God [ibid., 33–55].

### 3. Acting—the Methodology of Understanding Reality

In order to break the "ideological circle" that binds a community in a constricting view of reality, one must move beyond description and interpretation to concrete actions. But to project viable action, the same process must be continuously repeated, because action, is inseparable from theory. While we act, we continue to describe and critique the *structures* relating to this action, the *theory* or ideology behind the action, and the *persons* who will be involved in it. And at each stage (description, interpretation, projection), the three-step dialectic will continue to interact. Consequently, the actions of a community will consist of three dimensions:

*Descriptive Action.* Sharp questions need to be directed at each level (structure, theory, and persons) and along each step of the process. This should be repeated at the three fundamental dimensions of the life and mission of the church: its spirituality (which Libânio calls *evangelia*), its fellowship *(koinonia)*, and service *(diakonia)*.[100] A summary of this methodology can be found in Table 6.

True understanding of human actions—mission action included—must begin by describing ("seeing") the action-structures—their mechanisms, persons, and ideologies. But we cannot stop there. All too often, in our Protestant experience, we do not move beyond describing a situation, if we can even do that. We must also judge it in the light of Scripture and with hermeneutical tools such as the social sciences that God has placed at our disposal.

*Interpretive Action.* Interpretation requires critical analysis of the historical causes behind the objective phenomena. This means digging into the structural rationale of the action itself, which calls for a highly critical methodology that gets behind the theories to the vested interests and real ideologies that give them their true meaning. Needless to say, this can be very threatening to the persons involved.

*Projective Action.* Projection should follow description and interpretation, with a view to developing more viable or relevant structures. We are now in a position to formulate new theories for action, and the entire analytical process begins anew (Libânio 1979b: 119–42; L. Boff 1978a: 11–12).

This is, of course, the same "hermeneutical circle" that we shall apply later in this chapter to a new way of interpreting Scripture. But before doing this, we must look briefly at the new perception of the church that is a consequence of the new grassroots understanding of social reality.

## A NEW WAY OF BEING THE CHURCH

The International Ecumenical Congress of Theology that met in São Paulo in February 1980 pointed out that the social ferment and tensions, of which the *comunidades* are a part, "express much more than an economic grievance. They represent a phenomenon, new in our times: the massive irruption of the poor in every society":

These are the exploited classes, the oppressed races, people who some would hope to keep anonymous or absent from human history, and who, with increasing determination, show their own faces, proclaim their word, and organize to win by their own efforts the power that will permit them to guarantee the satisfaction of their needs and the creation of authentic conditions of liberation.

The document goes on to relate this to the emergence of the CEBs:

This Christian stream within the popular movement and the renewal of the church from the standpoint of its option for the poor constitute a unique and specific movement in the church. This movement takes shape in different types of basic ecclesial communities, where the people find space for resistance, struggle, and hope in the face of domination. There the poor celebrate their faith in the liberating Christ and discover the political dimension of love [Torres and Eagleson 1981: 232/9, 234/21; see also in *Occasional Bulletin* 1980b:4/3: 127/9, 128/21].

As these statements show, the new understanding of ecclesial reality that characterizes *comunidade* members is inseparable from their growing understanding of social reality. This is because the church is both the subject and the object of grassroots critical reflection on their social praxis. As part of a wider social reality, the church cannot escape being an object of the analytical process inherent in its own conscientization. But at the same time the church is the place where marginalized and oppressed Latin Americans have found breathing space, as well as the tools (divine revelation and sociology) to reflect in community upon the nature of an oppressive social reality and on the mission of the church—their own mission—in the midst of this reality.

How do CEB participants perceive themselves in relation to the church?

### The New Church from the Perspective of the Grass Roots

One of the clearest signs that something new is afoot in the Brazilian Catholic Church are the periodical convocations or *encontros* that bring together CEB leaders from all over Brazil. Significantly, they are not called "national" encounters but "interecclesial. . . in other words, it is the churches [not the hierarchy] that invite each other to attend, with one of them assuming

**Table 6**

**Questions to Be Asked in the Analytical Process**

(adapted from "Quadro geral para a análise," in J. B. Libânio 1979: 124)

| PROCESS | STRUCTURES | THEORY | PERSONS |
|---|---|---|---|
| Description: *evangelia* (spirituality), | What are the structures that sustain or express the reality being analyzed in its relationship to God? | What theory (philosophical, psychological, ideological, pedagogical, or theological) justifies or inspires the structure being analyzed? | What type of persons live within the structures being described, in the context of a relationship with God? |
| *koinonia*, | . . . in its interpersonal and communal aspects? | | . . . in the context of communal and human relationships? |
| *diakonia* | . . . as they relate to mission and apostolate? | | . . . in the context of mission and apostolate? |
| *kerygma* | . . . in the message that it proclaims? | | . . . in the context of preaching? |

| | | | |
|---|---|---|---|
| **Interpretation:** *evangelia,* | | | How do you explain that it is precisely these persons who live within these structures? |
| *koinonia,* | What are the historical reasons that explain the existence of such structures? | What critique would you make of the above theory? Of its presuppositions, elements that are ideologically used? What are its historical explanations? What are its limits? | . . . who have this particular communal type of lifestyle? |
| *diakonia,* | | | . . . who practice this kind of mission and apostolate? |
| *kerygma* | | | . . . who respond to this kind of preaching? |
| **Projection:** *evangelia,* | What structures should continue? | | What kind of persons could adapt to these new structures? Or what changes would they have to make in order to adapt? |
| *koinonia,* | Which should be abolished? | What theory should inspire these new structures? | How can this be achieved? |
| *diakonia,* and *kerygma* | What new structures should be created? | | By what means? |

the responsibility for overall coordination" (REB. 41: 283). Libânio adds that the concept of a grassroots *encontro intereclesial* does not fit into any of the standard meeting formats:

> It is not a council, or a universal or diocesan synod, or an assembly of bishops. It is simply an *encontro* [a meeting]. Who meets? Not the top of the church, but its bases, some of them supported by their respective bishops, others backed by the baptismal legitimacy of their members, with the explicit blessing of their bishops, and none against their [bishops'] will [REB 41: 279, 305].

Participants in CEBs may not always understand the technical terminology of the pastoral theologians who are in the process of formulating a new ecclesiology based on their involvement in the *comunidades*, but they are not unaware of the fact that something new and exciting is afoot in their ancestral church.[101] After studying the reports of many CEB regional assemblies, Libânio sums up this grassroots perception with the following brief insights:

1. "There is the consciousness of being called *ekkletoi*, an essential experience of being the church. . . ."

2. This ecclesial awareness is "intrinsically linked to being the people," concerned about each other's material and spiritual problems. This is the true meaning of "community."

3. The participatory dimension is the characteristic that distinguishes the *comunidades* from the old church. In the words of one participant, "Today the church belongs to everybody; all are owners of the church."

4. The new ecclesial community now perceives that the priest "is not a superior being but rather, a friend." In the new church "everyone has the rights that the priest had (including distribution of the communion bread); all together are responsible for the church."

5. The CEBs have discovered the long-dormant biblical dimension. "The Bible is no longer the book of the Protestants; it is accessible to all the people." Libânio quotes a comment by a *comunidade* participant:

> Earlier if one went about with the Bible under one's arm the person would be ridiculed; now the Bible has become part of the household and has even helped to overcome divisions among believers; now since we have begun to learn how to read the Bible, we find it speaks of our daily life; it has been popularized and entrusted to the laity; the Bible, when it is read and not hidden, makes the people feel more liberated, freer, and closer to the priest even though they have not studied as much as he [IRM 271: 248].

6. The new liturgy is neither the traditional Roman Catholic liturgy nor the "stylized liturgy" of post-Vatican II specialists. Religious festivals are no longer the domain of the landlord; they belong to the persons who reinterpret them within the context of their daily struggles.

7. The concept of God and of religion is reinterpreted. As a CEB member testifies, "From a vindictive God who was up in the clouds, God is now understood as being present with each person, inspiring and changing our lives; from being distant, now God is known as one who accompanies us and Jesus is our brother" (IRM 271: 246–48).

The starting point of the theology of the *comunidades* is their new perception of the presence of God in their midst. They know and understand God out of their ecclesial experience and in the context of their harsh reality.

### Theological Reflections on the New Ecclesial Awareness

José Marins offers us the following summary of "what the basic ecclesial community means for us":

> *It is not a movement*, an association or religious congregation. . . . *It is not a method* (or the only method) of building up the church; it is the church itself. *It is not a miraculous recipe* for all the ills of society and the church. It is the church renewing itself. . . . A pilgrim people and perhaps a sinful one, yet on the move with Jesus and the Spirit. . . . *It is not a Utopia*: it is a sign of the Kingdom, though it is not the Kingdom. . . . *It is not messianic*, but it can be prophetic and produce prophets like the church should. *It is not a natural . . . community . . .* identified with a race, language, people, family. . . . It is the church . . . in many countries . . . a force for unity between different races, languages, cultures. *It is not a protest group*, although its life is a protest against the mediocrity, sloth, and inauthenticity of many. . . . *It is not a special group* for special people. It is the church committed to the ordinary man, to the poor, to those who suffer injustice, which announces the kingdom, while denouncing all idolatry . . . and all injustice. *It is not closed*. It is open to dialogue with all. *It is not a reform of anything* in pastoral work: it is a decisive pastoral option made in order to construct a new image of the church.

Marins concludes:

> It may appear quite harmless to say that the CEB is the church. But precisely because it is the church itself, *it is a very dangerous thing*, because the church is dangerous: it is a revolutionary leaven in history, reconstructing the world with Christ's values and standards [IRM 271: 242; Concilium 104: 36; LADOC Keyhole 14: 7].

As Libânio points out, the church historically saw itself first as *church-as-society*; during the millennium and a half when Christendom reigned supreme, the accent was on "juridical visibility." Subsequent to the Council of Trent it began to perceive itself as *church-as-sacrament*, guided as it was by "sacramental visibility." Vatican II was the tangible evidence of a gradual shift to an awareness of *church-in-mission*—or *church-as-praxis*—of which the principal characteristic is the visibility of its actions (quoted in C. Boff 1978a: 54). Juan Luis Segundo would call this most recent stage the emergence of *church-as-sign* (1973: 81).

*From Church-as-Instrument to Church-as-Sign.* The Catholic Church today continues to see itself as a sacrament. But an influential sector in the church understands this in terms that are radically different from the pre-Vatican II perception. Whereas the Catholic Church had perceived itself universally as the "instrumental medium" (*medium in quo*) through which the kingdom of God is manifest, the post-Vatican II church, and in particular the grassroots church, understands itself as the "spatial medium" (*medium quo*) in which the kingdom of God is manifest. The emphasis is more on "sign" than on "sacrament," on meaning than on form (C. Boff 1978a: 26–29).

This change in perspective has far-reaching implications for the Catholic Church and for its concept of mission. Clodovis Boff comments:

> If we consider the church as a sacrament-sign (rather than a sacrament-instrument) then its function is not to save but to make salvation explicit. . . . *Ecclesiality is a matter of progression along a scale of intensity*: the more a community expresses salvation, the more ecclesial it will be. Ecclesiality is a quality of a human community to the degree in which it is the conscience of the kingdom of God preached by Christ [1979a: 33, 54].

The implications of the sign-bearing nature of the church, as Boff points out, "reflects" back upon the very nature of the church as an explicator of salvation. This new understanding of the church has implications for its structures and lifestyles as well as for its witness in the world. The external implications will be dealt with later. Let us return briefly to the sign-bearing nature of the church as it reflects back upon the ecclesial community.

*Internal Implications of the Sign-bearing Nature of the Church.* 1. This new ecclesial understanding has a direct bearing upon the liturgy and institutional structure of the church. In chapter 5 we saw how many of the traditional structures in ecclesiastical religiosity are being reinterpreted. Segundo points out that throughout the history of Catholicism there has been a tension between *sacraments-as-rites* and *sacraments-as-signs*.

On the basis of Matthew 5:23–24 ("If you are bringing your offering to the altar and there remember that your brother has something against you. . ."), Segundo concludes that whatever efficacy there is in the sacraments it is directly related to their rootedness in human relationships. "In the Christian conception it is not possible to scorn the efficacy of authentic human relations for the sake of some loftier efficacy. Any and all sacred magic is completely rejected." In the grassroots communities—which Segundo calls "creative communities"—the sacraments have the possibility of being restored "once again to the finality which Christ gave them" (1974: 23, 32).

2. The *institutional structure of the church* is also seen in radically different light from the perspective of the *comunidades*. Leonardo Boff asks the question, "Did the historical Jesus desire only one institutional form for the church?" (1977: 52). He concludes, after twenty pages of tightly reasoned arguments:

> [Jesus] desired, and continues to desire [the kind of church], that the apostolic community, illuminated by the Holy Spirit and confronted by the demands of the situation, decides to responsibly assume. Evidently, the episcopacy, the presbytery, and other functions will remain. The important fact does not reside in this, because it is self-evident that these structures meet needs that are always present in the communities, such as unity, universality, and the relationship with the larger testimony of the apostolic past [1977: 70].

But, Boff continues, it is more important to consider the lifestyle that these functions should assume *within* the communities than the function of structures *over* the communities. This is the alternative lifestyle that best expresses the praxis Jesus desired for the messianic community (1977: 70–71).

3. Libânio touches upon the fundamental challenge of the CEBs to the traditional view of the priesthood. He observes that the new ecclesial community awareness poses the problem of what to do with the clergy, because it is no longer considered indispensable by the *comunidades* (IRM 271: 247). Leonardo Boff argues at great length for the appointment of grassroots community leaders, including women, as ministers extraordinary of the Eucharist (1977: 73–108). This is, in fact, already taking place in a number of CEBs in Latin America, with the tacit support of some bishops, despite the fact that it contravenes canon law. As Marins makes clear, lay leaders now officiate at the sacraments of baptism, matrimony, and penance in many grassroots communities (IRM 271: 241; Concilium 104: 34).

Clodovis Boff adds that the hierarchy, which he calls the "ministers," are "each one *in his place*," a unifying factor: the pope at the level of the universal church, the bishop for the "diocesan-particular church," and the priests at the "parish-particular church" level. He goes on to point out that the traditional vertical relationship—bishop/priest/faithful—is now being challenged by a new triangular relationship in which bishop, priest, and faithful relate to each other (C. Boff 1978a: 45, 59; see also Libânio in IRM 271: 248).

In sum, what these Catholic pastoral theologians are saying is that the hierachical structure of the church must remain, for reasons of geographical proximity, theological unity, and historical continuity. But the institution should not inhibit the free action of God's Spirit, and of the apostolic leaders of the people of God, to discover new ways through which to express their common faith in each and every socio-cultural and historical situation. This is one of the most significant contributions of the CEBs to contemporary ecclesiology. It raises fundamental questions concerning their future within such a hierarchically structured institution. It also stamps large question marks on the doors of many of our sclerotic Protestant institutions.

This perception has not been forced upon the *comunidades* out of some theoretical construct of what the church in Latin America should be today. It is the result of the direct involvement of these pastoral theologians in grassroots communities. It is also the fruit of their reflection in community upon the nature of the church, in the context of their new perception of social reality, and in the light of Scripture and Catholic tradition. A new church—a new way of being the church—requires new forms in order to infuse new life and perhaps new applications into old meanings (L. Boff 1978a: 16).

4. This new ecclesial understanding evinces the age-old tension between *institution* and *community* in the Latin American church. But it is a creative tension. Although José Comblin predicted, early in the history of the *comunidades*, that the grassroots communities would eventually supersede outmoded parish structures, the facts—bolstered, says Leonardo Boff, by theology and sociology—indicated the contrary. Boff insists, on theological grounds, that "the CEBs . . . cannot be a total alternative to the church-as-institution" (quoted by C. Boff 1978a: 58). Community must remain in the church, but "as spirit . . . and not as an alternative to the church-as-institution" (1977b: 14). Futhermore, from a sociological perspective, Clodovis Boff adds, there is a dialectical relationship between *society* (in this case the institutional church, although he admits that the church cannot be equated with society except in a limited sense) and *community*. Each needs the other. "An organization can be renewed by a community but it cannot be transformed into a community" (C. Boff 1978a: 58).

5. A question raised by the community-institution dialectic is that of whether a "CEB is the church or does it only possess ecclesial elements?" (L. Boff 1977b: 21). Boff agrees categorically with the statement of José Marins:

> For us the basic ecclesial community is the Church itself, the universal sacrament of salvation, continuing the mission of Christ as prophet, priest, and pastor, and therefore a community of faith, worship, and love. The mission unfolds on the universal, diocesan, and local (*de base*) levels [L. Boff 1977b: 24; Concilium 104: 27; cf. *Omnis Terra*, 1978:LXXV/2: 110–11].

Both Leonardo (1977b: 30–32) and Clodovis Boff (1978a: 57–58) use arguments to defend the full ecclesiality of the grassroots communities that would strike a responsive chord in the ear of many a Protestant defender of the integrity of the local congregation. The "particular church" is not a part of a universal church that is identical with the church in Rome. "Rome is a locality where a local church can be found, even though it happens to be the church that has been charged with being the sign of the present unity of the universal church." It is not the local agency of a larger administrative body, nor is it made up of elements that are held in common by all the "particular churches."

Neither is the local church a constituent part of a confederation of churches.

On the contrary, says Leonardo Boff, the particular church is the "universal church in its phenomenal and sacramental manifestation"; it is the universal church made visible and incarnate in a particular spatial, temporal, cultural, and socio-economic context. The "particular church is all the mystery of salvation in Christ that is inherent in the universal church, but it is not the totality of that mystery. . . . It is all the church, but it is not all of the church."

### Spirituality of the Base Communities

When Gustavo Gutiérrez first broached the subject of "a spirituality of liberation," he observed that Christians who were participating in struggles "for the liberation of those oppressed by others" were "not always able to express in appropriate terms the profound reasons for their commitment." Christians who are identified with oppressed peoples find it difficult to articulate their religious motivation "because the theology in which they were formed—and which they share with other Christians—has not produced the categories necessary to express this option, which seeks to respond creatively to the new demands of the gospel."

Gutiérrez, a man of deep personal piety, warns, however, that to formulate this motivation in theological categories alone is not enough. "We need a vital attitude, all-embracing and synthesizing, informing the totality as well as every detail of our lives; we need a spirituality" (Gutiérrez 1973: 203–8; see also 4–78, 136, 287–88). One of the places where this new "spirituality of liberation" is maturing in Latin America is within the *comunidades de base*.

This challenge has been taken seriously by many "liberation theologians." Since the above statement was penned, a large body of material has been written on the subject in Portuguese and Spanish, much of it by persons who are closely identified with the CEBs, particularly in Brazil.[102] The concern for a totally liberating spirituality encompasses every dimension of ecclesial life: liturgy, Scripture reflection, prayer, the contemplative life, witness, pastoral work in society, and the struggle to overcome the ideological inwardness of the traditional church. We have seen an example of the last-named earlier in this chapter in Libânio's concern for fellow Christians who are bound by a closed ideological worldview.

But, as Frei Betto recognizes, it is not always easy to keep the tension between radical pastoral action and a life of prayer. It is much easier to let oneself become bogged down in a social activism that will end in frustration if it is not upheld by a life of prayer in community. He warns that "if the church wishes to rescue all of the church, it will inevitably have to restore, also, the essential elements of the Christian life and of ecclesial identity, such as liturgy and the mystical experience" (REB 1982: 42: 167, 447; Bonin 1982: 18):

Pastoral action works at the level of meaning—it allows us to understand history within the scope of the promises of God and, thus to cultivate the seeds of [the] kingdom. This meaning is personalized and historically fulfilled in Jesus Christ, to whose intimate fellowship the Spirit invites us by grace and through the prophetic witness of the church [REB 1982: 42:450; Bonin: 22].

A "spirituality of liberation" as it is experienced at the grass roots does not separate the "sacred" and the "secular" into separate spheres of experience and action. They are integrated in such a way that those moments of overt spirituality can, to the uninitiated, appear very secular. Conversely, secular activity should never lose sight of its profoundly spiritual content, which is what differentiates it from the secular struggles for liberation by non-Christians.

Frei Betto points out that the pastoral action of the church within the ecclesial community and Christian militancy in the political sphere must be two sides of the same coin. One is incomplete without the other. Within their ecclesial communities Christians find the spiritual energies for their political struggles. What makes the church "politically necessary" is not a superior political undertaking; that is the sphere of political movements per se. The essential contribution of the church to politics is the "spiritual" motivation—hope, strength for the struggle, christocentric evangelization and conversion, and "space" for critical analysis of reality in the light of the Word of God—that it alone is capable of imparting (REB 1982: 42:449-55; Bonin: 21-26).

This is a timely warning, as well, to "progressive" Protestants who at times give the impression of having thrown out the healthy baby of biblical piety and of a concern for evangelization with the dirty bathwater of a conservative ideology. Unfortunately, this has helped to discredit peace and justice movements in the eyes of more conservative Christians.

## A NEW WAY OF DOING THEOLOGY

"Every theology," Leonardo Boff asserts, "is constructed with two locations in mind. The place that is given to faith and that which is given to the social reality within which the faith is lived out." He adds, "Theology always works within a certain type of analysis of social reality" (1978b: 9-10).

The understanding that the CEBs have of their social and ecclesial context is the starting point for a new "hermeneutic of the people" or "theology of the base." In other words, the point of departure of this theology is not a corpus of abstract dogma but the material—as well as spiritual—reality of the persons who belong to grassroots communities. The reflection that is one at the grass roots is not the traditional theologizing that "sees society from the top down, from the point where [it] appears to be harmonious" (L. Boff 1978b: 22). It is "the view from the base"—Scripture reread in community "from the bottom up." From this perspective, social reality appears in all its crudeness, struggle, and confrontation (ibid.).

The church has always reflected upon Scripture in the context of the reality that it experiences and interprets through ideologically conditioned eyes:

> Sooner or later a group of people living in a specific situation, in a concrete place, on a certain date, will necessarily ask itself what these [Scripture] passages are saying to them; what they offer in the way of "good news," "hope," and "faith"; what they point out to them as the requisite new lines of conduct [Segundo 1974: 33].

The kind of questions that an ecclesial community will ask of Scripture will depend upon its ideological perception of reality. When the "ideological circle" is broken, biblical themes that were traditionally interpreted from the optic of the rich and powerful are now seen through the eyes of the poor and oppressed. Theology thus becomes a "reflection upon praxis" by both the oppressed and their former oppressors, leading to concrete actions toward their own liberation and toward the liberation of their fellow human beings.

The grip of the "ideological circle" can be broken only when the ecclesial community approaches Scripture along the lines of a "hermeneutic circle."[103]

The most succinct—and perhaps best known—contemporary description of the process is by Segundo:

> *Hermeneutic circle* is the continuing change in our interpretation of the Bible which is dictated by the continuing changes in our present-day reality, both individual and societal. "Hermeneutic" means "having to do with interpretation." And the circular nature of this interpretation stems from the fact that each new reality obliges us to interpret the Word of God afresh, to change reality accordingly, and then to go back and reinterpret the Word of God again [1976: 8].

The operation of this "hermeneutic circle," Segundo is careful to point out, depends upon two factors: (1) "profound and enriching questions and suspicions about our own real situation," and (2) an equally enriching new biblical interpretation.

The circle has four decisive moments: *First*—our new way of seeing reality leads to ideological suspicion. *Secondly*, we apply our suspicion to "the entire ideological superstructure in general and to theology in particular." *Thirdly*, we begin to experience reality differently. This generates an "exegetical suspicion": we begin to suspect that the traditional biblical interpretation has failed to take important scriptural data into account. *Finally*, we arrive at a new hermeneutic—that is, at a new way of interpreting the Bible with the elements we now have at our disposal (Segundo 1976: 9).

When the poor begin to read the Word out of *their own* experience of marginalization, they find new hope in hopeless situations. But they also help us to see Scripture in ways that were previously hidden to our eyes. In the following chapter we shall see practical application of this "from-the-bottom-up" methodology in the praxis of grassroots communities.

## A NEW WAY OF UNDERSTANDING MISSION

According to Segundo, the essence of the ecclesial community is its knowledge—through revelation—of God's plan of salvation (1973: 24). This knowledge, adds Clodovis Boff, is revealed in a political context (1978a: 77–78). The First Epistle of John "tells us that the revelation of the Word is summed up in the clear expression: *God is love*:"

> This is how we know what love is: Jesus Christ laid down his life for us. And we ought to lay down our lives for our brothers. If anyone has material possessions and sees his brother in need but has no pity on him, how can the love of God be in him? Dear children, let us not love with words or tongue but with actions and in truth [1 John 3:16–18; Segundo 1973: 25–27].

Reflection of the CEBs on their own social and ecclesial reality in the light of Scripture has led to a new understanding and practice of mission. This has set in motion a ferment of creative reflection by the pastoral theologians of the Latin American church. The proclamation of the gospel, in word and action, is both the *announcement* of salvation and liberation in Jesus Christ and the *denunciation* of the structures that oppress and alienate humanity. It is both reevangelization of the masses of nominal Christians and prophetic confrontation with oppressive "powers." As Marins observes:

> We describe evangelization as being the announcement, by actions and gestures (sacramental or not) and by words, of the presence and action of Jesus Christ the Savior in the history of men. As an event that converts and engages them personally and communally with him and with his community, in the service of the total liberation of man, until all shall become truly brothers, shall live the gift of divine sonship in Jesus and shall take the world upon themselves as heirs [1977c: 84; see also 1976b: 28, 37 and 1977e: 28–29].

As in the ecclesiology of the grassroots communities, the CEB christology is a fundamental key to understanding the mission practice of the grassroots communities. In the words of Comblin, who has worked with the *comunidades*, "the content, import, and underlying norm of mission is Jesus himself" (1977: 28). An important aspect of this christological dimension is the way in which the *comunidades* understand salvation and conversion. Comblin addresses incisive questions to our understanding of salvation:

Salvation is something new, a happening, a new reality in the world. What exactly is this reality? In other words, what is the context of salvation? Salvation is also action. What sort of action is it? Finally, salvation is something lived by the person who is saved. What does it really mean to be saved? [1977: 53].

Ultimately, the significance of the grassroots communities for the Catholic Church in Latin America—and their challenge to Protestantism—will depend upon the relevance of their understanding of mission to their historical situation and their faithfulness to God's Word. But before we can go deeper into the *comunidades'* understanding of mission, we must look more closely at the way in which they approach Scripture.

## Chapter 7

# The Hermeneutic
# of the Grassroots Communities

*He has filled the hungry with good things and sent the rich away with empty hands [Luke 1:53].*

Dom Hélder Câmara, in a talk given at the University of Chicago, posed an intriguing question: "What would Thomas Aquinas do about Karl Marx?" His conclusion: the greatest of Catholic scholastics would probably deal with Marxism today with the same spirit of creative criticism and accommodation as he did with the philosophical challenge and menace of a monolithic Aristotelian system in the thirteenth century:

The Aristotelian view of reality was enough to frighten away any Christian thinker who lacked the keenness of perception and the thoroughness of a St. Thomas. Thomas first identified the Aristotelian principles. Starting from them, he probed deeper . . . and went further than the Stagirite himself—who might well have gone that far, had he been illumined by Christian inspiration and followed out his principles [LADOC Keyhole 13: 10–11].

Archbishop Câmara adds that "it is fascinating and instructive to watch St. Thomas grappling with Aristotle's philosophy and rediscovering Christian values that had been contaminated by certain aspects of Platonism. . . . " In the same way, "Marx challenges our courage because he is a materialist, a militant atheist, an agitator, a subversive, an anti-Christian. Yet he too has in his system (why deny it?) certain truths that undoubtedly advance the development of human thought" (ibid., 10, 12). The attitude revealed by Câmara is illustrative of the willingness of the Catholic Church throughout its long history to grapple with new philosophies and, more often than not, to come to terms with them (Câmara 1971 and 1976b; 1976: 77–83; see IDOC 1978: 173–76).

However, there is a fundamental difference between Thomas's creative grappling with Aristotelianism within the secluded cloisters of the University of Paris or the ivory towers of the court of Pope Urban IV, and the equally creative interaction with Marxism on the part of grassroots pastoral theologians of the 20th-century Catholic Church in Latin America. The challenge of Aristotle to Augustinian Platonism was an intellectual battle with scant connection to the sub-Christian world of the European peoples, or to the social reality of feudalism that subjugated the masses to totalitarian princes, not the least of whom was the pope himself. The current challenge of Marx to the Aristotelian worldview is the direct result of the involvement of the church, through the *comunidades,* in the struggles of the poor.

Nonetheless, Archbishop Câmara's parallelism is apt to the degree that it points out a significant historical precedent for "a new way of doing theology." Forced to deal initially with the threat of Marxism to the millennial hegemony of the church, the grassroots theologians in Latin America—not without some reservations (Segundo 1976: 57–62)—have turned Marxism from a nemesis into a hermeneutical tool and a missiological challenge (Gutiérrez 1973: 9).

The use of Marx, or of any scientific instrument for that matter, is not unprecedented in the history of Christian thought. It is, in fact, inevitable. The rabbinical worldview, Platonist idealism, Aristotelian rationalism, Baconian empiricism (Scottish realism), Puritan individualism (the Calvinist work ethic), logical positivism (linguistic analysis), and existentialism, among others, have throughout the history of Christianity informed the approach of the church to Scripture. The hermeneutical locus has, of course, shifted continually, not without relation to historical events. It has moved from the realm of ideas to that of reason, and in this century to both scientifically verifiable "truth" and subjective experience. And since Medellín, society has become the hermeneutical *locus theologicus* in Catholic Latin America (Gutiérrez 1973: 8–12).

Each of these hermeneutical tools has made important contributions to a biblical search for truth and each in its own way has weakened the faith when the center of authority has shifted from the Word of God to the instrument itself. The result is syncretism. As Libânio aptly comments, a scientific instrument is never neutral; it is always altered ideologically by its designer and by its users (1976: 178). For this reason, it becomes very important for us to try to learn the place that Scripture has in the hermeneutic of the *comunidades.* This chapter will limit itself to an internal analysis of the hermeneutical method, which was summarized in chapter 6. I shall interact with this methodology from a Protestant perspective in chapter 9.

## THE USE AND AUTHORITY OF SCRIPTURE IN THE CEBS

The theology of the grassroots communities is, of course, not a fully developed, all-inclusive, systemic theology, as are the elaborated moral and dogmatic treatises that enjoy the blessing of our churches. The theological reflection of Latin American liberationists focuses on key biblical themes that have come out of their interaction with their own secular and ecclesial history (Gutiérrez 1973: 11-13). As might be expected, ecclesiology and missiology are important themes in this theological reflection. And there is, as well, a growing corpus of literature in Portuguese and Spanish liberation theology on the doctrine of God, christology, soteriology, hamartialogy, and eschatology. All these themes are developed in relation to the church and its mission in the midst of the poor and oppressed. But for the most part, the doctrine of Scripture in contemporary Catholic theology must be deduced from the way the Bible is used in the grassroots communities and in the heavy theological works that have grown out of pastoral involvement in the grassroots communities.[104]

Carlos Mesters is the only Brazilian *comunidade* theologian to give a lengthy treatment to the authority of the Word of God in the theology of the grassroots communities. Scripture is indeed taken seriously by all those who are involved in the *comunidades*. Their interest is not speculative. But the interpretive tools are different. Whereas philosophy is the "handmaiden" of traditional theology, sociology—the science of the development, structure, interaction, and collective behavior of organized groups of human beings—is the inseparable companion of a "theology from the underside of history" (Gutiérrez 1983: 30ff.). There are two levels to this sociological approach: (1) formal inputs from several schools of critical sociology by intellectuals who have placed their expertise at the service of the poor, and (2) the intuitive wisdom of the downtrodden that enables them to see behind the facade of oppressive subterfuges while maintaining their own sense of personhood.

### Two Approaches to CEB-related Biblical Hermeneutics

The fundamental role of Scripture in the CEBs is emphasized by Frei Betto:

In the measure in which the base ecclesial communities begin to have contact with the Word of God, I would say a true cultural revolution will occur within the interior of the church. The people discover that the Word of God is the story of their lives.

He goes on to admit:

The difference between the reading that we traditional priests make of the Bible and that which the communities make is that we look at the Bible as though we are looking through a window, curious to see what is happening outside, while the people of the communities look at the Bible as one looks at a mirror, to see a reflection of their own reality. Thus our reference to the Bible is. . . . to bygone things all very nice, wherein God was present. . . . What happens in the CEB is completely to the contrary. The people feel as though they are seeing their own lives revealed in the accounts of the Bible. . . . The primary task would seem to be one of returning the keys of the Bible back to the people [LADOC 1982: XII/3].[105]

To return the keys of the Bible back to the people is what the *comunidade* theologians are trying to do. In the process, they are using two intersecting approaches—"higher" criticism and the "wisdom of the people."

*"Higher Criticism" at the Service of a "Theology from Below."* When Leonardo Boff attempts to answer the existential question, "How can we know Jesus Christ?" he turns first to historical or "higher" biblical criticism (1978b: 34–37). But "history" for Boff is not only past history, biblical or secular. Because he sees the present and the past in dialectical relationship, he can make use of an "existential hermeneutics," which from the perspective of a Protestant Evangelical weakens the authority of Scripture, and ends in a diffuse christology.[106]

The essence of the hermeneutic circle, says Boff, is to reconstruct a history of Jesus while interpreting it in the light of our own experience of reality. "There is not, nor can there be, a single biography of Jesus" (1978b: 4–5). To be able to comprehend Jesus, we must see him as he relates to us and to our situation. "Defining Jesus, we are defining ourselves. The more we know ourselves, the more we know Jesus." This awareness, says Boff, has produced a "hermeneutic of political existence" wherein we are not only exegeting ancient texts but attempting to understand every aspect of life and "how to relate this to the evangelical message," and how it applies both individually and corporately (ibid., 41).

This approach allows Boff to apply the historico-critical method not only to Scripture exegesis, but also to the ongoing reflection of the church—that is, to tradition and contemporary theology. It is what he aptly, though disturbingly, describes as "the primacy of interpretation over bare facts" (ibid., 7). Consequently, he can be critical of his own tradition, question the factuality of some of the historical data in the life of Jesus and of the early church and, in their place, hypothesize alternative "facts" in the interests of furthering "a critical christology for our time" (ibid., 158–77).

Theological considerations aside, the question that must be raised at this point is methodological. Is there not an inherent contradiction between the use of the categories of an erudite "higher" criticism and the development of a "theology from below" based on the popular wisdom that informs much of the *comunidade* reflection?

*Returning the Keys of Scripture to the People.* Mesters is perhaps the Brazilian Catholic pastor-theologian who is most compatible with a Protestant Evangelical theology. He approaches Scripture reverently. A biblical scholar of Dutch origin and a philologist, he is not interested in constructing a theological critique of traditional dogmas, even from a grassroots perspective. His aim is to reestablish *"contact between the Word of God and the people for whom the Word was intended."*

In the first book of the two-volume development of his exegetical methodology—*Por tras das palavras* ["behind the words"]—Mesters makes clear that his concern is preeminently pastoral and people-oriented. He wants to "open a new window in the closed walls of the rooms of our lives in order to offer us a possibility of observing, with new eyes, the old and well-known vistas of the Bible and of life" (1974: 23). In order to do this, we will have to permit our shared realities to interact with the demands of revelation as expressed in the Bible itself and in the faith of the church (ibid., 21).

Mesters is wary of following the path of historical criticism to achieve these ends. He does avail himself of the insights of textual criticism (ibid., 91–102), but he qualifies their relevance to the concerns that are being expressed by persons at the grass roots (ibid., 23–24):

> The people do not exist for exegesis but exegesis for the people. . . .The ultimate purpose of the Bible is not scientific research of its literal and historical meaning, but rather to prepare men for the struggle that is before us (Hebrews 12:1) and to help them to live life to its fullest [ibid., 85].

In his vivid and earthy style, Mesters observes:

> Exegesis at times is like the gardener who took a famished man to his apple orchard! But instead of giving him some fruit right away so he could eat, he began to talk about the fertilizer and about the roots that would produce the fruit. When he had finished talking he looked around and couldn't find the famished man. Tired of waiting, [the man] had left to go and find another orchard where he began to eat the fruit that the owner gave him. . . . The hungry man wasn't interested in the roots nor in the fertilizers. He wanted to satisfy his hunger. Our people are hungry and thirsty, and before anything else, they ask for food for their dwindling hopes. [ibid., 85].

Mesters's hermeneutical *locus theologicus* is society, as is Boff's and that of other grassroots pastoral theologians. However, it is not society in the abstract that they are dealing with but concrete persons, the poor and oppressed.

Mesters in particular seems to be genuinely concerned about the existential questions that persons are asking as well as their pregnant silence—a silence that from the grass roots accuses the system that has condemned them to ignorance and threatens to destroy all their cultural values. He has a profound respect for the "wisdom of the people," for its religiosity, and the capacity to understand biblical truth. "The masses have their antennas hooked up in order to pick up the message of the Bible. They already have a door open to enter into the world of the Bible" (ibid., 31–36, 65, 78, 161–64, 175–78). His primary concern is not for a better methodology, merely because he perceives a gap between scientific exegesis and pastoral action. Instead he believes that the lack of a meaningful relationship between exegesis and lifestyle of faith is related to the exegete's inattention to the voice of the people:

> It has to do with what is termed *sensus fidelium.* Among the complex of vehicles of divine revelation that exist within the church, the *sensus fidelium* is a legitimate mouthpiece of the will of God and occupies its own place beside the Bible, tradition, and the magisterium. It has greater value than the conclusions of theologians. . . . Divine revelation itself bids us listen to the Voice of the People, so that we can discover what God has to say to us [ibid., 22].

This statement is the key to understanding Mesters's hermeneutical approach. The authority of Scripture becomes a fact only in a historical context. This context is interpreted and applied in a creative interaction between the hindsight of official tradition, the present authority of the ecclesiastical magisterium, and the understanding of the people of God—the true locus of a "theology of the base." The authority of the Word of God, then, is the product of the interaction of each of these elements: Scripture, tradition, magisterium, and the *sensus fidelium.*

Yet this is not to say that social reality as such is the arbiter of scriptural authority, as some of Mesters's colleagues seem to be saying. He warns against falling into the trap of attributing too grand a hermeneutical privilege to reality. It is equally important for Scripture to question the demands of reality:

> It is not enough to ask questions of reality. Not every human desire and aspiration points to God. Those who let themselves be guided by the exigencies of reality run the risk of fabricating a God in their own image and will end up being guided by their own shadow, thus becoming a victim of the "tyranny of the present" and reducing the Bible to an ordinary book. Reality in itself is ambivalent. It requires and demands that we turn to revelation in order to eliminate this ambivalence [ibid., 86].

Mesters's lofty view of the authority and inspiration of Scripture is indisputable, although his belief that "the Bible contains the Word of God" would leave many Protestant Evangelicals unsatisfied. He does not attempt to define scriptural authority denotatively. He simply takes it for granted, as does the Bible itself: "We accept it simply as the starting point of our study" (ibid., 160). But he does define it connotatively. Rather than give it a precise meaning, he will arrive at scriptural inspiration inductively, from the bottom up. He will describe inspiration as the product of the growing awareness on the part of the people of God of the mighty deeds of God down through history. It is a process that is the result of the interaction of measurable external historical forces and the incommensurate internal action of the Holy Spirit.

The *sensus fidelium,* says Mesters, began in the Old Testament in the form of oral tradition: celebrations, liturgy, institutions, art, laws, popular wisdom, and credal statements. This informal "prophetic tradition" was in continual tension with the formalizing and institutionalizing forces of the official tradition of the priesthood and nobility. The search for identity on the part of God's people, particularly in times of crisis, created a need for a written record of the divine actions in the past to give meaning to their present. Over a long period certain of these records were recognized as "canonical" because they met the needs of the people more adequately.

A new element was introduced after the resurrection. The Old Testament Scriptures began to be perceived as authoritative in a special sense because of the light that they shed upon the person of Jesus Christ. St. Paul recognizes them as divinely inspired (2 Tim. 3:16). Scriptural inspiration was "discovered" at the end of the New Testament as an awareness of something that had existed from the beginning but was only now fully perceived. In the Christian sense, says Mesters, inspiration connotes the fact that the Word was being borne toward Christ through the power of the Holy Spirit operating in human lives (ibid., 160–83). But Mesters is more specific:

> When it says that what *is written* is inspired by God, the Bible recognizes the divine authority and origin of itself, not only as it has to do with *content,* but also in regards to *the means that communicate the content.* That is, it is not only a man who writes things that God commanded to be done or said, nor is it only a man who writes things that God commanded to be written, but it is God himself who is considered to be responsible for the *act of writing.* It is as if the people kept following the course of the river upstream and found in the God of the people its fountain. . . . This is until today the faith of the church which looks at the Scriptures, as the Hebrew people did, from the inside, reading them with the same eyes of faith and with the same awareness that they are the people of God. The Word and the Spirit of God are also present in the origins of the Scriptures. [ibid., 180].

In this way, Mesters's belief in inspiration, in accordance with Catholic teaching, broadens to encompass the reflection of the church and of God's people at the grass roots. All these sources contain the Word of God. It broadens even more when he expresses the, for me questionable, conviction that the reflection on God's deeds that many persons of good will engage in *within the different world religions,* in the context of their respective historical situations, is even now forming the "Canon of the Bible of the Universe which will be manifest at the end of history" (ibid., 184–204).

### A "Hermeneutic of the People": Two Approaches

In chapter 4 the different sources of the CEBs were detailed, and in chapter 5 the three kinds of self-understanding that are a consequence of these different roots. Here once again it is possible to perceive subtle differences in the views of the *comunidade* theologians who approach their tasks, whether out of an involvement in a politically conscious *de base* situation, as with the Boff brothers, J.B. Libânio, and Frei Betto, or out of a long-term interaction with the community reflection of *círculos bíblicos,* as has been Carlos Mesters's experience.

For both Mesters and Leonardo Boff the oppressed are the "interlocutor" in biblical hermeneutics. They are the ones who address the questions to the theologian. Yet there is a subtle difference between these two approaches to a "theology of the base." For Boff—one gets the impression—it is the reality of the oppressed (i.e., the poor as a sociological category, verified by a critical sociology) that radically questions the categories of traditional theology; in Mesters it is persons at the grass roots who ask the questions and are helped to find their answers in the Word. This is not to say that Boff is either unaware of or out of touch with their questions. But whereas Mesters helps them to reach their own theological conclusions in the Word, Boff is more concerned with developing a coherent theology based on the concerns of the people that will serve as the theoretical framework of community praxis. But, curiously, he turns to an ivory-tower European theology for his tools!

Again, both theologians are at one in viewing human history as past and present in a dialectical relationship and in understanding salvation history as "the salvation of history." However, in the writings of Boff, human history seems to swallow up divine history. The questions that the reality of the poor poses to Scripture seem to have more weight than the critique that the Word directs to reality. This is what has been called the "epistemological privilege of the poor" carried somewhat to an extreme.[107] Not so with Mesters, as we have seen.

The utopian element in Teilhard de Chardin's theology is strong in both Boff and Mesters, as it is in most of the young Catholic radicals of the 1960s who became involved with the Brazilian *comunidades* in the 1970s. In Leonardo Boff's theology, the "christic structure"—which he calls the essence of Christianity—antedates the historical Jesus of Nazareth who, having lived its essence to the fullest, gave Christianity its name. This "structure" will culminate "when we achieve communion with God to the point of forming a oneness with him . . . when we have attained our maximum degree of humanization." When this goal is reached, says Boff, "God is humanized and the human being is divinized. . . . The end of anthropogenesis resides in Christogenesis."[108] This universalist vision of salvation he calls "Christian pantheism" (1978b: 247–63; cf. 1978a: 27–28).

Mesters's utopianism expresses itself in another dimension: his open-ended view of inscripturation. The main difference between the two at this point is that *Boff seems to build his premises arbitrarily upon categories of the European theological apex,* whereas Mesters attempts to free himself of these categories in order to listen to the voice of the people. The people is, in a sense, an added dimension to the Word of God, even as it becomes the subject of its own history.

*Examples from the Círculos Bíblicos.* Mesters opens the mysterious and recondite pages of Scripture for his Brazilian readers in a popular and eminently readable style. Thanks to his peasant roots, he knows their vernacular language and is familiar with their thought-patterns and idioms. Mesters's popular writings are full of words, expressions, and images drawn from the language of the people and from their day-to-day struggles to exist. He likens the study of the Scriptures to "eating rice and beans every day; a fellow doesn't even realize that he is repeating the same dish. It is the seasoning that makes the difference" (1974: 25).

Mesters is not so much interested in recounting past biblical history as he is in making it live for his readers today in order for them to be able to apply it in their own particular situations. A lengthy excerpt from the opening pages of his Bible survey, *Deus, onde estás?* ["where are you, God?"] will illustrate this point:

> The Bible is like a family album that preserves every kind of photograph: important pictures of our wedding day, of our children's christening, and of the new house. It even contains some seemingly unimportant snapshots of a relaxed picnic on some long-forgotten weekend. The criteria for deciding which photos are important and which are unimportant are relative. The snapshots that we took of our baby (all dirty and smiling!) with a cheap camera can be more important than the expensive studio portrait. But both are just as useless for our employment papers. They're no good for that. But for the album, everything is important, everything is useful; the album contains everything. In a kind of orderly disorder, following the rhythm of our family life, it offers a faithful portrait of the family. What a joy it will be for our children and grandchildren to leaf through those pages! As a matter of fact, because of this, all the photos are important, even those that don't seem to be.

Mesters then makes his point:

> The album is the Bible. It has everything: official and formal photographs and relaxed snapshots of insignificant episodes that don't even have a date anymore. Some of them were taken for the purpose of documenting a happening, but the only reason for including others is to bring a smile to the lips of those who look at them. It is the faithful portrait of a people that has been preserved in a sort of disorderly order in those ancient pages. It is an album that children and grandchildren continue to leaf through in order to find out who they are and so as to make them more aware of their belonging to a particular people.

But, Mesters concedes, some persons are asking, "What has all this to do with the history of the Brazilian people?":

Isn't the history of Brazil—that varied and complex album of ours—enough? Certainly it is enough. But it so happens that we (perhaps not all of us but many) walk through life with questions in our heads to which our album doesn't have all the answers: *Where are you, God?*

Mesters then goes on to ask, "In what way does this, our Brazilian history, have something to do with God? If God is in the midst of all this, what are the criteria we have at our disposal to help us discover God?" How do we find the right direction for the Brazilian history that we are all constructing? Different persons have different ideas about what is best for our future: "Where can I find a way to discern the spirits and to know that I'm betting on the right future?" Such are the questions that real-life persons are asking. They are serious questions: "From the answers that we give to them will depend the direction that we will take in life." This is why "the Bible is crucial in the reflection of the Brazilian people":

> The people of the Bible, within its own time and particular situation, raised the same questions and tried to answer them. . . . There are many—we Christians—who believe that the road that was followed by that people is the right road, the way of God. That is why Christians . . . read the Bible as an indispensable contribution to their reflection; to help them in their analysis of reality and in their search for answers to the questions that life itself raises. They see the history of the people of the Bible as a kind of model for action that hit the mark and that has God's warranty. That is why Christians study the Bible; not just to learn what happened way back then, but also, and above all, in order to know, through the information received from the Bible, in a better way, the meaning and importance of what's happening today, all around us, in our own history [Mesters 1971: 1–3].

From this angle of vision, Mesters goes on to answer some of the questions about the Bible that are being asked by the people:

> *Paradise:* Myth or Reality? *Abraham:* A man in search of the absolute. *The Exodus:* God in the history of the liberation of men . . . *The Prophets:* Where is the God in whom we believe? *Jeremiah:* To run away is never a solution. *The Parables:* They reveal the divine meaning of human reality. *The Miracles of Jesus:* A free sample of the future that awaits us. *Christian Freedom:* Pluralism in the way we live out our common faith in Jesus Christ. *Faith in the Resurrection:* "If God be for us, who can be against us?" [ibid.].[109]

The purpose of the *círculos* is to help CEB participants find viable answers to their existential questions. They are applying to their Brazilian reality the inscripturated reflection of the people of God upon the divine acts manifested in the history of Israel. The questions that are asked of *círculos* participants are brief, contextual, and to the point. Let us consider a few examples.

In a reflection on friendship, the question is asked: "What was lacking in Geraldo's friendship in the introductory homily, and in the friendship of Judas and Peter, that led them to the point of denying and betraying a friend?" (1978: 1,6).

"Which sentence (in the Scripture reading) caused you to say to yourself: 'That hit the nail right on the head! That's what I've always believed! I'm sure glad to find that in the Bible!' . . . What sentence made you think to yourself: 'I wasn't expecting that one! I had a different idea of how it was!' Tell us how you felt" (ibid., 2, 10, 14).

The provocative questions continue: On "God's lottery" (about "the kingdom of God and the treasure that was hidden in a field"—Matt. 13: 44–45): "Where is that hidden treasure of the kingdom? In the ground? In heaven? Only in heaven? In this life? In our *bairro*?" (1973: 9, 5, 8). On "Jesus and good persons who don't have faith" ("You didn't know it, but it was me! I was walking and you gave me a ride!" [Matt. 25:35]: "If all the good people get saved, what's the use of being a good Catholic?"

On the resurrection ("the firstborn Son of the future"): "Jesus rose again in the morning, but for those two lads [on the road to Emmaus] the resurrection didn't take place until the next evening. Has the resurrection arrived for you? Have you found him? Tell us about it" (1973: 34, 11, 16).[110]

***Other CEB Examples.*** The collection of booklets entitled *Da Base para a Base* ["from the base for the base"], coordinated by the editorial team of Mesters, the Boff brothers, and Frei Betto, is a noteworthy attempt to contextualize theological themes in the language of the people.

*A Semente e o Fruto: Igreja-Comunidade* ["the seed and the fruit: church-community"], by Frei Betto, is a popular treatment of ecclesiology. Using vivid imagery from the lives of poor farmers, and supported by numerous Bible texts, he develops the theme that God entrusted the seed of community as a gift to the church. This seed took root in the early church and must continue to be sown by us. The fruit that we expect to gather is not the church but the kingdom of God. The important thing for us is always to keep in mind that the seed is being sown, not in heaven, but in the ordinary soil of this earth (Betto 1979a).[111]

The third and fourth books in the series are by the pastoral team of the prelacy of São Félix do Araguaia (Mato Grosso), where a radical Basque, Dom Pedro Casaldáliga, is the bishop.[112] These booklets deal with the rites of baptism and the Mass in a series of poster-type lessons. The first of this pair of contextualized catechisms begins with the warning:

ATTENTION! Don't baptize your child if you don't know what baptism is all about! He can get into hot water. ("What happened? Did baptism change? Ain't it what it used to be?") Baptism is the mark of the Christian. It is to be baptized by the Holy Spirit, in order to accompany

Jesus Christ, so that we can live as he lived. "Whoever accompanies Jesus and lives like he lived is gonna get into hot water like he did. But he will also rise again. He'll win!"[113]

*Missa, O que e?* ["what's the Mass all about?"] follows much the same approach. It relates the Mass to the simple supper where Jesus and his Galilean ("peasant") disciples ate out of a common dish. It applies this to the reality of the Brazilian peasants. The lesson explains the significance of the bread and wine in terms of commitment to Jesus Christ and to the poor and oppressed, and of a willingness to follow Christ even unto death if need be.[114]

**The New Hermeneutic in the Hymnody of the CEBs.** Much can be learned about the theology and ideology of a group of Christians from their hymnody. Music and lyrics are the expression of the deepest feelings of a people. This is certainly the case in the Catholic grassroots communities. Traditional Gregorian chants have long since given way to lively renditions in the everyday language of the people. The *comunidades,* of course, do not have a formal hymnody. Their songs have many origins. Some have been borrowed and adapted from other Catholic renewal movements, Negro spirituals, and even from a few Protestant chorus sheets. But most of the CEB songs are spontaneous expressions of the participants' deep yearnings for justice and love, and for a genuine experience of the grace of God.

The hymnodic themes encompass the whole range of liturgical needs—the liturgy of the Word, the Eucharist—and the other six Catholic sacraments, but they all relate specifically to concrete events in the lives of the faithful. There are songs to the God who identifies with their plight. A few laud the example of Mary, but most express the anguish of slavery or celebrate hoped-for liberation through Christ. The CEB hymnody differs radically from more traditional Christian songs, which can often be used as escape mechanisms to help the faithful forget their harsh reality. For CEB participants, singing has become an instrument of conscientization that helps them understand their reality, gives them strength to endure it, and the determination to do something to change it.

Several stanzas excerpted from CEB favorites here and there will suffice to make my point:

I want to hear the people's voice / and discover within their reality/that seed of truth is about to sprout./I want to see everybody on their feet,/ freeing themselves from their fear of sharks./Shout without fear, shout, my people!/He that dies quietly is like a frog/that has been squashed by an ox.

•

We're gonna smile at life./We're gonna live with a smile./For when a tree trunk has been pruned/new life is about to be born [REB 41:302].

•

You don't recognize him, but he's with you,/he's with you, his name's "the Lord."/His name's "the Lord" and he's hungry,/crying through the mouths of starving persons;/But many see him and pass him by,/in a hurry to get to church./His name's "the Lord" and he's thirsty;/(he's also with those who thirst for justice)./But many see him and pass him by,/too busy saying their prayers.

•

You're the God of the poor,/the human, unpretentious God;/the weatherbeaten God,/the One who sweats on the streets./That's why I can talk to you / in the language of my people,/because you're the worker God,/Christ the laborer-God.

•

A Peasant Creed:
I believe in You: architect, engineer, artisan and
    carpenter, mason and shipbuilder. . . .
I believe in You: the laborer Christ—light of light, and
    truly firstborn Son of God,
Who to save the world took human flesh in the pure and
    humble womb of Mary.
I believe that you were scourged, mocked, and tortured,
Martyred on the cross by the praetorian Pilate—
That imperialist Roman, merciless and cruel.
He washed his hands, trying to erase his mistake.
I believe in You, who walk with me by the way—
The human Christ, the worker-Christ, who conquered death.
Your tremendous sacrifice gave birth to a new man
And began his liberation . . . .
[Nicaraguan Peasant Mass]

*The New Hermeneutic at Work in Grassroots Communities.* Four examples should suffice to illustrate how this "hermeneutic from below" works in the *comunidades de base*:

1. James Pitt, a Catholic researcher from England, describes his impressions after a month-long visit to four Brazilian dioceses. In the summer of 1979, he attended a first-communion class in São Mateus, a *bairro* on the periphery of São Paulo. He called it "a practical lesson in liberation theology." Eight mothers—all of them poor—met twice a month to study one of 30 themes that had been developed to prepare *comunidade* children for their first commu-

nion. The theme: "Jesus was born poor and humble and shares in our lives—why?" These migrant mothers "could easily identify with a poor family on the move whose baby had been born in a stable":

Indeed, a one-minute reading of Luke's account of the nativity provoked a one-hour discussion (led by an American sister) on the injustices, humiliations and hardships that the mothers themselves experienced.

The discussions focused on the substandard health conditions in the *bairro* "and how a local woman's baby had been born while she was waiting in a queue to see the doctor [the baby died]. . . . They talked of the high price of food in the local shops." After the theme had been discussed for about an hour, the catechist asked:

"Why did Jesus *choose* to be born poor and humble?" "Maybe," said one woman, a mother of ten of whom three had died and only two were working, "maybe it was to show these rich people that we are important too." A ripple of excitement ran through the room. Was God really making such a clear statement about *their* humanity? About *their* rights as people? The discussion progressed, but with an electric charge in the air. Half an hour later, a young woman said, "I think that God chose his son to be born like us so that *we* can realize that we are important" [LADOC 1980: 10/5: 11–12].

This contextual hermeneutic had helped a group of downtrodden women to discover their true worth in the eyes of God—a small but significant step toward liberation.

2. Pitt also describes a *comunidade* in the parish of São João de Meriti (Rio de Janeiro). They met in a chapel that is "more of a community center and meeting place than a church." On this particular occasion one of the twenty couples in the grassroots community was celebrating their twenty-fifth wedding anniversary. The special occasion called for a Eucharistic celebration in a "joyful, informal, and very spiritual" atmosphere. About half of the two-hour meeting was dedicated to discussing marriage. "People shared experiences both good and bad, and began to analyze the causes of marriage problems: the struggle for decent housing, the impossible cost of doctors and medicines." Throughout the dialogue, the priest, who never preaches a sermon, "very gently deepened the discussion" (LADOC 1980:/X/5: 14). The hermeneutic of the people relates to every dimension of human life, guiding *comunidade* members into new understandings of the totality of the Christian faith.

3. The Canhema *favela* sprawls over a red clay hillside overlooking Diadema, in the industrial suburbs of São Paulo. It was a chilly Sunday morning and the *favelados,* mostly Catholics and one or two Pentecostals, were busily staking out an arrow-straight street over the rough terrain. They were beginning to erect sturdy brick buildings in the place of the jerry-built

shanties that had previously been thrown up in total disarray. This is a necessary measure, I was told, in order to assure their permanence upon open lands that, in fact, belonged to a wealthy family that refused to sell to the CEB-sponsored cooperative.

After overseeing the work, Fr. Rubens Chasseraux, a Brazilian who coordinates some thirty CEBs in the area, gathered the faithful in the little brick chapel. He and his team then led a reflection upon the Scripture that was assigned in the weekly diocesan bulletin:

> Thus says the Lord Yahweh Sabaoth: Now go to this steward, to [Shebna] the master of the palace. . . . See, Yahweh hurls you down, down with a single throw. . . . I dismiss you from your office, I remove you from your post, and the same day I call on my servant, Eliakin son of Hilkiah. I invest him with your robe, gird him with your sash, and entrust him with your authority . . . [Isa. 22:15, 19, 20, JB].

The passage could not have been clearer in its contemporary application. In fact, the name of one of the more prominent ministers in the current Brazilian cabinet was substituted for that of Shebna, the corrupt and ambitious steward. The context of the *comunidade* reflection during the liturgy of the Word was the current scandal over the bankruptcy of the social security system (allegedly because of the graft of government officials) and the announcement that the massive deficit would be made up out of the paychecks of workers.[115]

Following a very simple and brief sacramental celebration, the entire *comunidade,* and other *favela* dwellers, discussed some interpersonal frictions in the CEB-coordinated food and building materials cooperative. That resolved, the pastoral team moved on to another *favela.* Each aspect of the morning activities merged into the other without visible lines of demarcation between the "secular" and the "sacred."

If the hermeneutic of the poor is disturbingly political, it is, of course, because their oppression in Latin America is unashamedly political. Refusing to keep the struggles of ancient Israel against their oppressors safely inside the aseptic wrappings of traditional theology, the poor in Latin America are capable of making exact applications to their situations today.

4. In a small village about an hour's jeep drive from a major Central American city, an ecumenical team began in the 1970s a base community for worship, Scripture reflection, and community social action. In time this aroused the opposition of the local bishop and was greeted with threats of violence from local authorities. As a precaution, it became necessary for the *comunidade* to meet at unscheduled times. Typically, the team would arrive unexpectedly, and in short order a group of Catholic and Protestant villagers would gather on rude wooden benches. The service would consist of a simple liturgy—combining elements of Catholic and Protestant worship—and, on this occasion, a lively discussion of the parable of the ten lepers.

Despite the threat of death that lay upon all of them, the discussion was unhurried and filled with the canny wisdom of a downtrodden people. The little group readily identified with the one thankful leper, and roundly condemned the unthankful nine. They saw in this a paradigm of the attitude of so many of their compatriots who, despite God's goodness to them, had turned their backs upon the mission of Christ, out of fear, indifference, or hope of material gain. The grassroots community members saw much for which to thank God, in spite of the violence around them and the seeming hopelessness of their existence. They proceeded to enumerate their blessings, then huddled to discuss in lowered voices one of their community projects. After agreeing upon the time of their next meeting, the team hurried back to the relative safety of the big city, racing to beat the oncoming dusk.

Scripture reflection of the *comunidades* in Central America is Christian in its motivation, as well as in the attitudes and graces that flow from it. Despite this, in a number of countries, to read the Bible in this way is considered just as subversive as if the object of study were Mao's little red book. In Guatemala, rural church workers with Bibles under their arms have been stopped and the bibles checked by army patrols. Maybe the verses that they have underlined may provide a clue to their ideology! Some have been asked under torture to give their interpretation of the exodus event, or questioned outright concerning liberation theology—an unfamiliar term to many of them.

## TWO FUNDAMENTAL CHARACTERISTICS
## OF GRASSROOTS HERMENEUTICS

### Prophetic Contextualization

From the above selective summary of CEB-related materials it is possible to appreciate both the degree and the kind of contextualization that is being achieved in the Brazilian grassroots ecclesial communities. Similar examples could be cited from elsewhere in Latin America.

As the pastoral guides of the *comunidades* see it, this is not merely contextualization at the level of language and of biblical imagery in order to achieve a better culture adaptation. It is what has been termed a "prophetic contextualization:"[116] it translates traditional biblical theology into political theology. This is not to say that the language of the Bible was apolitical and has now been changed into political language by the CEB leaders. Every human discourse— and the Bible as the Word of God in human language is not excluded—is political—that is, it is the language of the *polis,* the city-state, the people. Therefore, language is a reflection of human interaction with political reality. The Bible has always spoken a political language, whether or not we have understood it as such, simply because God's revelation became human language in numerous social and political contexts.[117]

Because of this fact, the proclamation of the Word by an ecclesial community cannot escape being a political medium of communication. It is very much of a political communication—albeit alienative—even when it is totally unrelated to the social context of the communicators or of the message receptors. The Christian message always passes through the ideological filter of the gospel witness. This is an inescapable fact of communication (C. Boff 1978a: 66–67).

But "prophetic contextualization" has an even deeper meaning for *comunidade* pastoral guides. As we have seen in the writings of Mesters, the Bible is the written record of God's dealing with the people of Israel in numerous historical contexts. It is an account of their reflection upon the great acts and pronouncements of God in each of these varied contexts and applied to other situations. A faithful remnant, a prophetic stream in Scripture, was repeatedly forced to live out the consequence of faith in God in the midst of oppressive socio-political and cultural realities.

Elijah's confrontation with Baalism and the related unjust landholding system in connection with Naboth's vineyard and on Mt. Carmel and at the court of a greedy Ahab; the unequivocal statements concerning human rights by so many of the prophets; the social awareness of Luke, of Mary in the Magnificat, of Jesus at Nazareth, and of St. James—these are just a few examples of the "prophetic contextualization" of the Bible (Marins 1977e: 37–80, 93–106).[118]

Unlike the functionalist contextualization of the gospel that is much in vogue in one stream of present-day North American Evangelicalism, the "prophetic contextualization" of the *comunidades* is highly dysfunctional for the dominant structures of Latin American society and for the international system that they represent (ibid., 8–35). In fact, this kind of contextualization is not even immediately functional for the grassroots communities themselves, because its consequences are often persecution and on occasion torture and death! The only functionality in the new structures that the CEBs strive to implement is their capacity to provide justice for those who have never known justice and hope for a better future in their lifetime.

The disruptive characteristics of "prophetic contextualization" are implicit in the accusation that was hurled at the Pauline pastoral team in Thessalonica: "The people who have been turning the world upside down have come here now. . . . They have broken every one of Caesar's edicts by claiming that there is another emperor, Jesus" (Acts 17:7, JB). To fully proclaim the lordship of Jesus Christ is to put the forces of evil on the alert. It may mean social disruption: "Do you think I came to bring peace on earth? No, I tell you, but division" (Luke 12:51).

## The Centrality of Orthopraxis

Leonardo Boff sketches his vision of the christology that is developing within the grassroots Catholic Church in terms of the "primacy" of the anthropological, utopian, critical, and social elements of the gospel over the ecclesiastical, factual, dogmatic, and personal dimensions of the faith. Although some of his arguments are open to question, the last point in Boff's outline is particularly significant for our understanding of the CEBs. It is what he calls *"the primacy of orthopraxis over orthodoxy"* (1978b vi):

> [In classic christology] orthodoxy, that is, correct thinking about Christ, occupied primacy over orthopraxis, correct acting in the light of Christ. . . . We know, nevertheless, that for Christ and for the primitive church the essential did not consist in the reduction of the message of Christ to systematic categories of intellectual comprehension but in creating new habits of acting and living in the world. This praxiological moment of the message of Christ is especially perceptible in Latin American theological reflection [ibid., 46–47].

It is important to note that the CEB pastoral theologians *are not saying that correct knowledge is unimportant, or that it is less important than correct action,* but that truth—efficacious truth—does not exist outside concrete history. In other words, truth is not an abstract concept, composed merely of statements that we must believe, but a reality that comes home to us in the midst of concrete historical situations. Unless divine truth is incarnate in our own histories, it will be meaningless to us. *God is truth because God exists, but we perceive God as truth because of our experience of God's actions in history*—that is, in our lives and in the lives of our fellow human beings. In the same way, God's Word is truth, but not as a proposition that lies outside human history; it is true for us because it is validated by God's actions in our lives.

This is why it is impossible to separate orthopraxis from orthodoxy, as conservative Christianity has tended to do down through history. Correct action is not only the validation of correct belief, it is the only way to arrive at correct belief. It is impossible for us to conceive of a correct doctrine in abstract terms. We can discuss it only in the context of its application to concrete situations. In Latin America these situations are, unfortunately, the facts of poverty, marginalization, oppression, and death.[119]

Truth in the First Epistle of St. John is always active (1 John 1:6). To know truth is to practice it. Specifically, it is to live in fellowship with God, to love God and one's fellow human beings, to do good to one's neighbor, and so forth. Taking this a step further, knowledge of divine truth in Scripture is also related to justice. "To know God is to do justice" (Gutiérrez 1973: 194–96). This does not mean merely that justice is the logical consequence of knowing God. It is the proof that we know God: "He defended the poor and needy. . . . Is that not what it means to know me?" (Jer. 22:16, NIV). In fact, so closely related are knowledge and action that the verb *to be* can also be said to establish an equivalent relationship between the two parts of the sentence: *Knowing God is the same thing as doing justice.* Conversely, *not to do justice is the equivalent of turning our backs upon God.*

In sum, from the perspective of the *comunidade* pastoral theologians, truth is not verified rationalistically but ethically. Theology—the study of divine truth—is a reflection upon the historically rooted praxis of the people of God

(Libânio 1976a: 29). Orthodoxy and orthopraxis must always remain in dialectical tension. The hinge is praxis, for praxis is not raw action, disconnected from truth. It is action that demands reflection and in turn reflects back upon action (Gutiérrez 1973: 6–11).

It is this praxis that will concern us in the following chapter as we turn to the missiology of the grassroots communities.

# Chapter 8

# Mission in the Grassroots Ecclesial Communities

*Look, I send you out as sheep among wolves; be wary as serpents, innocent as doves. And be on your guard, for men will hand you over to their courts, they will flog you in the synagogues, and you will be brought before governors and kings, to testify before them and the heathen [Matt. 10:16–18, NEB].*

The object of this final chapter in our study of the theology of the Catholic *comunidades* is to analyze the praxis—that is, the mission practice and the mission theory—of the CEBs. My point of departure will be mission as it is practiced by the CEBs, including its basic orientations and grassroots pastoral planning. Given the abiding dialectic between practice and theory in CEB theology, it is important for us also to study the missiology of its pastoral guides before returning to mission in and by the *comunidades*, which will engage us at the close of the chapter.

The practice of an ecclesial community often says more about it than does its theory. But the way in which this community interprets its practice is also crucial. The problem becomes more complex when the interpretation is mediated by an elite corps of theologians, even when—as is certainly the case with the CEB theologians—they are deeply involved in the practice of the community. Inevitably, the following questions will arise: How valid are the interpretations of the theologians? How much of the praxis of the church is being filtered through the ideological and theological presuppositions of those who have learned how to handle recondite hermeneutical tools? These questions, of course, apply to any missiological reflection, including this one. The issue should be dealt with before we move on to a summary of the missiological perspectives of a prominent CEB-related pastoral theologian in Brazil who has addressed himself specifically to mission and evangelization (J. B. Libânio).

## THE RELATIONSHIP OF HERMENEUTICS TO PRAXIS
## IN GRASSROOTS MISSIOLOGY

The mission practice of the *comunidades* is an integral part of their approach to the study of Scripture. Put another way, *Latin American Catholic catechesis "from below" is a function of the ecclesial life of the CEBs within an oppressive social reality, as well as an expression of its mission outreach*. Mission in the CEBs is not a separate activity primarily directed outward to the unchurched or non-Christian, but the very lifeblood of a church that is all too conscious of the merely nominal and uncommitted adherence of the majority of those who bear the name of Catholic Christians—the majority of Latin Americans.

Mission and reflection upon Scripture relate to each other continually within the action-reflection-action process that takes place *within* and *out from* the community of faith. Mission-evangelization is the very essence of the church. This is the conviction expressed by a group of Latin American theologians at a gathering where the CEBs were the main topic:

> A community is Christian because it evangelizes; this is its task, its reason for being, its life. Evangelizing is a diverse and complex action; a Christian community is called upon to evangelize in all that it does: by words and by works. To evangelize is to announce the true God, the God revealed in Christ: the God who covenanted with the oppressed and defends their cause, the God who frees his people from injustice, from oppression and from sin [Torres and Eagleson: 237–38; IECT 1980: 39–40, in *Occasional Bulletin* 1980a: 4/3: 129].

From this perspective, mission is both the hermeneutical approach of a Fr. Geraldo—who is involved in a pastoral ministry for street urchins whose livelihood is earned by scavenging a city dump for a recycling industry—and the steps that the youths themselves take in order to change their social environment. Using the Freire method, Geraldo identified the "creative themes" of the street-urchin culture, starting with their own perceptions, in order to help them reflect creatively on their own reality as the first step toward change. Among other things, this meant taking positions counter to municipal authorities who were attempting to wall off the unsightly dump, denying them access to their means of livelihood (LADOC 1980: 10/5: 29–30).

The inseparability of hermeneutics and mission is evident in Dom Hélder Câmara's *encontros de irmãos* ["meetings of brothers"] movement. These grassroots communities, which are also called *grupos de evangelização*, meet regularly for singing, reading of the gospel, discussion, and prayer. Several of these groups are engaged in resolving ecclesial problems; others address community needs.

In the rural town of Jacarú in Paraíba (northeastern Brazil), a team of sisters and lay workers under the leadership of the local auxiliary bishop have organized some thirty-five *canteiros* ("seedbeds") or free schools for children. They are primarily aimed at conscientization and at teaching basic skills (LADOC 1980: 10/15: 15–17).

Mission in the grassroots church goes beyond hermeneutics as a catechetical tool to concrete involvement that takes the form of denunciation and an explicit identification with the grievances of the oppressed. The church, from the CEBs to national episcopal conferences such as the CNBB, has spoken clearly on such issues as freedom of worship for peasants whose *comunidades* are being harassed, illegal moving of boundaries between large plantations and small peasant plots, and the eviction of peasants from their hereditary lands by powerful *fazenda* and multinational interests. In recent years—most notably in Brazil, but also in Chile and in other places throughout Latin America—the church has begun to speak out in defense of the rights of urban laborers (SEDOC 1979a 12/125: 257–95, 310–11, 319–59; 12/126: 429–42).

Street theater was used as a hermeneutical tool to help twenty-five thousand inhabitants of a Recife *favela* stand up to land speculators who were attempting to evict them from their seaside shacks. Hélder Câmara, who invited me to accompany him on one of his pastoral rounds, gathers CEB members in local *assembleias populares* where he addresses and exhorts standing-room-only audiences. Afterward, the participants joined in a communal meal in the parish house, to which Protestant visitors were heartily welcomed.

In a rural municipality in northeastern Brazil, the CEBs have been the spiritual force behind a long and partially successful struggle to defend their village from forced eviction by a land development company. This company happened to be owned by the general who was also the head of the government land reform agency that has a statutory duty to intervene in such cases and, if necessary, expropriate the land and sell it back to the villagers (LADOC 1980: 10/5: 19–21).

In the Chimborazo province of Ecuador the praxiological training of grassroots leaders at Bishop Leonidas Proaño's center at Santa Cruz and the Scripture reflection of the (Amerindian) Quechua base communities have enabled them to discover their own worth as creatures of God, and to stand up for their rights in the face of abuses of the Law of Agrarian Reform. Much the same is taking place in Bolivia and Peru. It is the Bible, not Marx, that is putting steel into the backbone of the resistance of the urban laborers of Chile, turning once passive Guatemalan Indians into canny resisters of Ladino oppression ("wise as serpents"), and fanning the flames of hope in the seemingly hopeless morass of El Salvador.

Thanks to grassroots communities in large urban areas, the trade union movement is once again very much alive in Brazil, despite sometimes brutal police repression. This fact is attributed to the active involvement of the church in a small but very effective "workers' pastoral apostolate." It has been called a "kindergarten" for future labor activists in the Trade Opposition Movement, which has recently resurfaced after years of underground activity.

I referred in chapter 7 to my experience in the Canhema *favela* of greater São Paulo. I was able to observe firsthand the creative way in which Fr. Chasseraux brought together contextualized Scripture reflection and specific mission action, from a Catholic perspective. I also saw grassroots hermeneutics at work on a Sunday evening in August 1981 at the incipient *Amigos de Cristo* community, which meets in a parish house basement in a swank neighborhood of Rio.

The little group was composed of two disparate subcultures, both of which belong to two of the most despised categories of urban workers in Brazil. The migrant construction workers spend part of each year back home in the harvest with their families, and the rest of the time as underpaid and unprotected workers on the luxury skyscraper apartment buildings that were mushrooming all around us. A smaller group of shy live-in maids has recently been added to the evolving CEB. Both kinds of persons are exploited and both have been uprooted from their rural or small-town cultures and feel lost and homesick in the big city. The community-in-process has gradually begun to provide the convivial atmosphere that they need.

It took over two years for the small FASE pastoral team, *Programa Nuclar*, to dissolve suspicions and break down natural reticence in a nonnatural community such as this.[120] The transitory character of participant involvement worked against them. In all, some one hundred fifty persons had passed through the group. Despite these drawbacks, they eventually reached the point of being able to freely discuss a name for their group and to vote on it—an exercise related to the church program of teaching democracy to the grass roots in preparation for national elections in 1982, and which doubtless continues with future elections in mind. The group was not considered a real *comunidade*, because the participants were, as yet, too dependent upon the FASE team. At the time of my visit in August 1982, a natural leader was only just beginning to mature and to inspire the confidence of the group.

The activities that evening consisted of songs, poorly and haltingly sung. Their content was religious, with very clear applications to current problems in Brazil. After a time of problem-sharing and prayers for those in need, the Scripture texts for the week were read. The group then began to discuss their application to their problems as workers in a strange and hostile environment. At this stage in the development of the group, the methodology was quite directive. Leading questions were addressed to specific persons. They were answered hesitatingly. Someone suggested that the construction workers involve themselves in the labor union protest against the projected social security increase. There was not much response. Apparently most of them considered themselves much better off than their rural relatives and had no desire to "rock the boat." The meeting closed with a brief Scripture meditation by the visiting Protestant pastor and a benediction by the priest-leader of the team.

Although the reflection was frankly political, concern for a Catholic spirituality was not lacking. It was, in fact, so closely interwoven with the sociopolitical dimensions of a base ecclesial hermeneutic that it was impossible to separate them. This, I believe, is the key to understanding the mission praxis of the CEBs. For Protestants, myself among them, steeped in generations of neatly compartmentalized secular and sacred areas of life, this is very difficult to understand—and to accept.

## Basic Attitudes of Grassroots Mission

The missionary praxis of the Catholic Church, most noticeably in Brazil, is characterized by five basic attitudes that I have observed in grassroots communities.

1. *Centrality of the gospel.* The central place that is given to the study of Scripture in the thousands of *comunidades*, as also in the more formal liturgical celebrations, is the driving force of the involvement of the base church in mission.

2. *Option for the poor.* Reflection on Scripture by CEB participants and their lay leaders, by the clergy, pastoral guides, and bishops, focuses on the reality of the poor. But the rich are not excluded from this reflection. They are invited to participate in building a just society. But it is firmly believed that their salvation "will come through the witness of the poor."

3. *Liberation and conscientization.* Working for justice and educating for justice are two sides of the coin of evangelization from a Catholic perspective. They are inseparable.[121]

4. *A missionary approach to ecclesiastical structures.* Church structures exist to serve the world and must be adapted to meet the needs of the world. Ecclesiastical structures are viewed as administrative devices that should not be allowed to get in the way of mission. When, for example, an urban parish structure is deemed inappropriate to a given urban situation, that structure is allowed to atrophy and new, flexible, grassroots structures and interparish teams take its place. Flexibility is today one of the most noteworthy characteristics of Catholic mission in Brazil.

5. *Respect for others.* Being "harmless as doves"—even toward opponents of the new social activism of the church—is the hallmark of a true base ecclesial community spirituality. As James Pitt observes:

> This refusal to overcome domination through outmaneuvering and application of strong force seems to be a significant dimension in the reorientation of the Brazilian church, in which people at the fringe have become leaders of the center, despite their absolute minority and the "outrageousness" of their ideas.

But, we must not lose sight of the fact that a significant factor in this "reorientation" is the process of pastoral planning that has evolved, in Brazil, since 1965 (LADOC 1980: 10/5: 31–32). This is perhaps the most revolutionary contribution of the CEBs to mission—all the more significant because of where it is taking place: in the most hierarchical of churches.

## Pastoral Planning: Mission Strategy from the Bottom Up

Ivan Vallier makes the point that, despite the vertical or hierarchical organization of the Catholic Church, it is, in fact, horizontally structured in its approach to problem-solving. The Catholic Church does not have a unified and centralized system all the way down to the grass roots, though since Vatican II the organizational mode of the church is characterized by a combination of "national unity and coordinated micro-units" (Vallier 1970: 7-8, 12). But a number of dioceses in Latin America have moved well beyond this point, thanks to the CEBs.

In Brazil, which is the most outstanding example of this new approach, combined pastoral planning takes place at every level of the church, not from the top down, but from the grassroots communities right up to the CNBB. Frei Betto calls the pastoral plan "the compass that guides God's canoe" in the faraway dioceses on the headwaters of the Amazon (1977: 245-50). The basic ingredients of this process are reflection, decisions on priorities, construction of a plan, and the plan itself. During the first step sharp questions are asked at each level of the church concerning the work of the people of God in the context of each particular reality.

The questions that the diocesan pastoral coordinators ask of the CEBs fall basically into four categories: What is your *comunidade* doing that is good . . . that could be done better . . . that it should not be doing? What is it not doing that it should be doing? The questions turn upon the priorities chosen in the previous pastoral plan: which priorities should be retained, which should be dropped, and which modified. The questions also have to do with intraparish and interparish relationships.

At a fairly typical all-day diocesan assembly, grassroots community leaders will debate and refine priorities for the next biennial period on the basis of the replies to a questionnaire. The assembly in Nova Iguaçu (Rio de Janeiro) consists of lay delegates and one priest to represent the clergy. The recommendations of the assembly are presented to a diocesan meeting by a commission of three lay persons and a priest. The bishop and his priests will add their suggestions to the list. Soon afterward, at a second diocesan assembly, priorities are narrowed down to the three or four that will guide the diocese during the next period. The general objective of the Nova Iguaçu diocese for the next two years remained:

> To announce the good news of the people of Baixada Fluminense in their real life situation, bringing them to a greater communion with God, and to a conscientization so they may participate in the process of liberation, both personal and communitarian [LADOC 1980: 10/5: 3].

This same process will take place at the parish level as well as in the general assembly of the CNBB. The national conference of bishops chose the following priorities for 1977/78: CEBs, family pastoral ministry, and urban pastoral ministry. All three were put into effect (CNBB 1977a). The four priorities in the

São Paulo diocese were CEBs, human rights, urban laborers, and "missionary actions in the periphery of the city" (LADOC 1980: 10/5: 5).[122]

When the objectives and priorities have been established at each level, it is the responsibility of each part of the church to determine the implementation of the pastoral plan. After the diocesan coordinator has been informed, his team draws up a list of activities for each priority. As researcher Pitt observes:

> Each activity is part of a program which has an explicit objective and which was voted upon as a priority for a diocese. *Yet no one at any stage has told anyone what to do*. This is a crucial part of the dynamics of this pastoral plan.

The important thing is not the plan itself—which serves primarily as a point of reference at all levels—but the planning process, which involves the continuous flow of action-reflection-action:

> It is a never-ending cycle of conscientization and formation that is rooted in the gospel, in the reality of people, that is always correcting itself, that foments unity and at the same time encourages diversity [LADOC 10/5: 6].

## THE THEOLOGICAL BASIS FOR
## GRASSROOTS COMMUNITY MISSION

The *comunidade* approach to mission and evangelization cannot be divorced from its own theological understanding of the nature of mission and evangelization. This definition of mission and evangelization is inseparable from scriptural hermeneutics at the grass roots. The study of Scripture from their own perspective of socio-political subordination has enabled the CEBs to gain new insights into the meaning of mission in the Bible and in their own tradition.

Similarly, grassroots missiology is interwoven with grassroots ecclesiology, because the way the *comunidades* understand the church strongly influences the way they do mission. Ultimately, the CEB understanding of the reality of the world in which the mission of the church is to be acccomplished determines their approach to mission. Mission is the active dimension of the action-reflection-action process. Thus it both follows and precedes reflection. The reflection of the grassroots church is directed first of all to social reality and then to its mission in the midst of this reality, at the behest of the Word of God.

This process of action-reflection-action is, in a sense, not new to the Catholic Church. Without having recognized it at work until but recently, it has, in fact, been the road along which the understanding of mission and evangelization has undergone modifications throughout its long history.

Catholic reflection on mission in contemporary Latin America flows from the bottom up. Much of the published work of the liberation theologians comes out of their experience with CEBs. But not all these theologians relate closely to the CEBs. I dare say that the more they are involved with the grassroots, the closer their writings are to the Bible, and vice versa. Doubtless because of the healthy state of its grassroots communities, Brazil is the nation with the largest and most creative body of missiological reflection in all Latin America. Unfortunately, only a fraction of it has reached the English-speaking world (in fact, only a relatively small portion of the Brazilian production is available even in Spanish).

Two of the best-known missiologists are Fr. José Comblin, who has worked with *comunidades* in Brazil and Chile, and J. B. Libânio, a Jesuit on the staff of the John XXIII Institute in Rio who spends much of his time interacting with CEBs. One of Comblin's mission-oriented works is available in English (Comblin 1977), and has much to contribute to our understanding of a theology of mission that proceeds from the praxis of the poor. But Libânio's several works are all but unknown to monolingual Anglophones—only his work on spirituality has been published in English translation (Libânio 1982). It is to him that I turn in the following section, summarizing his major contributions to a CEB-oriented missiology.

### Evolution of the Concept of Evangelism in Catholic Missiology

Libânio points out that the term "evangelization" has experienced a progressive amplification of its meaning as the Catholic Church has confronted new situations. Nonetheless, there is a core meaning that remains unchanged throughout:

> Evangelization speaks to us of a process of transmitting a reality pertaining to a supernatural order that has already been appropriated and must now be communicated to others. . . . There is the underlying perception that this announcement is meta-historic—for all time and cultures, meta-geographic—for all geographic regions. It is not a particular reality for the private use of one group, but universal in its scope. The one who knows is not a uniquely favored person. On the contrary, he is responsible for making it known [1976a: 14].

The successive stages in the amplifying awareness of the meaning of evangelization in the Catholic Church, as Libânio interprets them for us, move out in ever-widening circles from this central core.

1. In the early church, evangelization was understood as "*the first announcement* of the reality of salvation accomplished in Jesus Christ *to those who have never heard*" [emphasis added]. "To evangelize is an obligation that flows from the certain knowledge that Jesus Christ is Savior and that apart from him there is no other gospel." This biblical consciousness eventually narrowed to a postbiblical *extra Ecclesiam nulla salus* as the missionary horizon broadened from the Roman empire outward to new peoples and unknown lands. Vestiges of this narrow view still remain, says Libânio. Church planting and growth were specifically singled out as goals of evangelization by Vatican II in the Decree *Ad Gentes* (AG: 6–7; see Abbott 1966: 16–20).[123]

2. Because of this, "evangelization" broadened gradually to include "every *spoken announcement* of salvation through Christ *to those who have never heard and to those who have already heard*." This broader definition was also born out of an awareness that much of the early evangelization had been shamefully superficial. Slowly the perception grew that more than a catechesis for the already evangelized was needed. A "real evangelization" was called for. The crisis caused by the tension between evangelization and sacramentalization—at the root of which was a deficient understanding of the relationship between Word and sacrament—once again amplified the meaning of evangelization (Libânio 1976a: 20–24).

3. Little by little, evangelization came to be understood as "*every announcement of salvific reality in Jesus Christ, by either words or sacramental gestures*." This new approach became clear in a Vatican II decree that aimed at doing away with false dichotomies by making the liturgy of the Word an integral part of the Eucharist (Abbott: 149–50, 156–58).

The contradictions in this view did not take long to appear, resulting from the growing awareness by the church of the socio-political world. It became apparent that faithfulness to Word and sacrament did not necessarily produce Christians who were sensitive to the needs of their fellow human beings:

> To speak of the freedom of the children of God, and of the infinite love of a Father God, to talk of the maternal love of the church, of the Eucharist as the sacrament of union and fellowship within a context where every evidence is shouting just the contrary, is nothing but a cruel falsehood [Libânio 1976a: 24–28].

This awareness of a dissonance between theology and practice led to the final circle of meaning and to the present understanding of evangelization in the Catholic Church. This fourth and broader meaning of evangelization came to a focus in the CEB experience.

4. Evangelization is *every announcement, by word or deed,* whether sacramental or nonsacramental, *of the salvific work of Jesus Christ so as to accomplish the liberation of "all men and all of man."* In this way, says Libânio, faith "discovers a political dimension without denying its fundamental theological reality" or core meaning.[124] At this point in the development of the meaning of evangelization, liberation becomes an integral part of evangelization—though not identical with it, as we shall see.

This broader definition was explicated in the document of the third general assembly (1974) of the Catholic Synod of Bishops entitled "Evangelization in the Modern World":

> We experienced profound unity in reaffirming the intimate connection between evangelization and liberation. . . .The church does not remain within merely . . . social and political limits (elements which she must certainly take into account) but leads towards freedom under all forms— liberation from sin, from individual or collective selfishness—and to full

communion with God and with men who are like brothers. In this way the church, in her evangelical way, promotes the true and complete liberation of all men, groups, and peoples [Gremillion 597/12].

### A New Point of Departure for Mission: The CEBs

The mission praxis of the grassroots communities in Latin America is perceived by pastoral theologians as a logical extension of the new self-perception of the CEBs in the midst of Brazilian social and political reality. It is the product of grassroots reflection on the Word of God in the context of this reality:

The universality of the Christian message has moved beyond an extra-worldly approach that takes faith (i.e., dogma) as its starting point in the direction of an inner-worldly concern for the non-persons everywhere who somehow manage to exist in a sub-world; or what Gustavo Gutiérrez has called, "the underside of history" [L. Boff 1978a: 78–84; Gutiérrez 1983: 169–221].

The point of departure of Catholic mission, says Libânio, shifted in mid-Council from the church to the world. It moved away from the world seen through the eyes of the apex of the church—as was the case in the early Vatican II documents[125]—toward the "church-for-the-world" or the "church-in-mission."[126]

This new understanding is not without its tensions and risks, as Libânio readily admits. In his opinion, *two tendencies* have clouded the issue. A *conservative reaction*, from synodal bishops on downward, is attempting to force evangelization into the earlier "spiritualizing" and "vertical" mold. At the same time, the Christians for Socialism movement has insisted too peremptorily on a *revolutionary option*, although not divorced from the Christian faith. According to this second view, faith does not precede revolutionary praxis but grows out of one's involvement in this praxis.

Between these two extremes Libânio sees *two other alternatives* that were strongly supported in the Synod of Bishops: (1) the *integration of evangelization and of human promotion*, though the latter is subordinated to the former, an alternative strongly espoused by Paul VI and by the majority of the synodal bishops; and (2) a *dialectical relationship* "between faith and political commitment, announcement and socio-political liberation."[127] It would be risky, Libânio believes, to abolish the dialectic, whether in terms of the theoretical element, leading to a reactionary traditional position, or in terms of praxis, which would result in a radical revolutionary dead end (Libânio 1976a: 30–32).

## DIMENSIONS OF EVANGELISM—A HOLISTIC PERSPECTIVE

Following is a summary of Libânio's analysis of the conversion process using theological, sociological, and psychological tools. His view of "conversion" is of course different from the prevalent Protestant Evangelical understanding. We must keep in mind that the conversion he discusses is a process taking place in persons who are already Christian in a sacramental sense. But before they can become efficacious witnesses for Christ, they must undergo, personally and in community, a conversion process that encompasses a dimension of conversion that Evangelicals consider very important. But they do so from a different perspective, which we must make every effort to comprehend.

### Internal Dimension: Conversion

For Libânio, evangelization itself is a process (see Table 7) that "expresses itself in three profoundly interrelated "movements": *conversion*, a *"diaconate of faith"* (announcement), and a *"diaconate of liberation"* (denouncement). By his use of the word "diaconate" for both the announcement of the good news and the denouncement of socio-political "bad news," Libânio is stressing that there must be a profound service dimension to both evangelization and liberation. When he puts conversion on the same level as evangelism and liberation, he is showing that it is not only the first step in evangelization, but an element that permeates every aspect of mission.

"At the source of all evangelization there is a continuous conversion that the evangelizer must undergo," Libânio insists. Conversion is the internal dimension that "is fundamentally an announcement (faith) and a transforming action (liberation) with the fulfillment of the kingdom in mind" (1976a: 9, 91). Conversion, says Libânio, "presupposes a movement toward oneself [reflection] . . . so as to understand one's own way of thinking, desiring, and acting." It "speaks of a change in direction in life, leaving old ways for the newness of another life" (see 2 Cor. 5:17). This means that a new significance has been given to our existence because a new direction has been imposed upon our lives. Conversion does not come upon us like a bolt out of the blue. We are converted only when we are questioned by someone else, by a reality different from our own, which causes us to become aware of and confronted by that reality (ibid. 55–56). Ultimately, that Someone is the Holy Spirit who continuously interpolates us through numerous someones and the social contexts of which we are a part.

The process of conversion takes place at *three interrelated levels*: the level of the conscious, of the unconscious, and of a change of mind.

1. At the *conscious* level there is (a) a *theological dimension* to conversion when a person abandons the idols of magic—"the eternal desire to manipulate God," of materialism, eroticism, and the domination of one person by another, and turns to the only and true God. There is also (b) a *christological dimension*—the "new creation" of which St. Paul speaks—transforming our egocentric religiosity into a Christ-centered, open-ended, and other-directed lifestyle. Meanwhile (c), the *ecclesiological dimension* of conversion is at work, moving us out from church-centered toward mission-oriented ecclesial action. The *"religious" or vocational dimension* (d) is a call to an even more "radical evangelical witness," particularly for those who have taken religious vows. Our

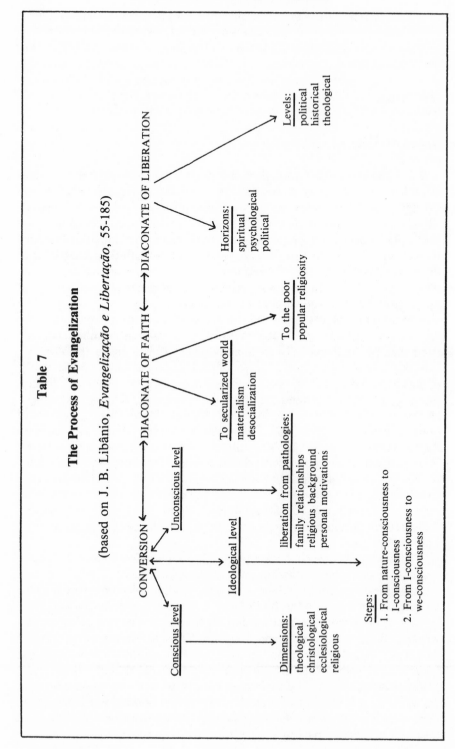

**Table 7**

**The Process of Evangelization**

(based on J. B. Libânio, *Evangelização e Libertação*, 55-185)

CONVERSION

Conscious level

Unconscious level

Ideological level

Dimensions:
theological
christological
ecclesiological
religious

liberation from pathologies:
family relationships
religious background
personal motivations

Steps:
1. From nature-consciousness to
   I-consciousness
2. From I-consciousness to
   we-consciousness

→ DIACONATE OF FAITH ← → DIACONATE OF LIBERATION

To secularized world
materialism
desocialization

To the poor
popular religiosity

Horizons:
spiritual
psychological
political

Levels:
political
historical
theological

conversion becomes *radical* (from *radix*, "root") because of our Spirit-rooted faith. It is *evangelical* in its commitment to others because it is ready to face, if necessary, the *marturia* consequences of *witness* within the oppressive situation of Latin America.[128]

2. At the *unconscious* level conversion means the overcoming of the various "pathologies" or hang-ups from our past and present experience that hinder us from becoming fully converted to God and neighbor. Unfortunately, it is at this point that many of our affluent brothers and sisters become mired. They do not perceive that Christian conversion must go much deeper than a mere psychological "inner healing," however important this may be at one stage.

3. Conversion is incomplete until there has been a *change of mind* that affects all our points of reference. At this *ideological* level conversion follows two steps: from *nature-awareness* to *I-awareness*, and from *I-awareness* to *social awareness*. Grassroots persons take the first step in a change of mind when they move from a sphere where they were dominated by the fear of the elemental forces of nature to an awareness of themselves as persons who have the possibility of overcoming these forces. They move from being an object unable to control their own destiny toward becoming a subject of their own personal history.[129]

*Real conversion* takes place, says Libânio, when subjects become aware of others who share their history. They are no longer satisfied with maintaining structures that serve their own personal needs. They begin to be aware of the need to interact with their own communities in order to form new and better structures (1976: 55–90). Leonardo Boff clarifies this point further when he says that "the conversion postulated by Jesus is not only a change of conviction (theory), but principally a change of attitude (practice)":

[It is] not merely something that happens to me as an absolutely free personal agent (the heart), but as something that takes place in man as a concrete being who is involved in a living and active network of relationships that have been modified at every level of personal and social reality in such a way that liberations become concrete anticipations of the Kingdom. The personal and social dimensions are in dialectic tension [1978a: 32].

From personal observation and interaction with the CEBs, I conclude that the process of conversion in the understanding of *comunidade* participants begins at baptism (if not earlier, with the commitment of a child's parents) and progresses along a continuum as each Christian is confronted with new challenges and options during the course of an action-reflection-action process. Although in a sense the process is never complete (and in Catholic theology continues in Purgatory; see L. Boff 1980), there is implicit in the analysis by Libânio the belief that the "conversion process" comes closer to its final goal to the degree in which the Christian enters fully into the social dimensions of the faith—that is, into solidarity with the struggles of the poor and oppressed.

**External Dimension: "Diaconate of Faith"**

"Evangelization is fundamentally an announcement (faith) and a transforming action (liberation) with the fulfillment of the kingdom in mind." This calls for a double diaconate in the evangelization process: a "diaconate of faith" and a "diaconate of liberation" (Libânio 1976a: 91).

The "*diaconate of faith*" is directed to two social realities. It is aimed at persons who, though belonging to the underdeveloped world, live out their lives within the "secularized and technical-scientific cultures of the developed nations." But it has a special mission to accomplish among those who exist in the midst of marginal and popular cultures (ibid., 91–92). Libânio discusses the problems of witnessing to the first social group: decline of religious experience, conformity to the natural world, and decreasing concern for the supernatural. This is verified by the increasing number of dropouts in this social sector from the public forms of religious expression. The resulting crisis of faith poses a challenge that Libânio insists cannot be ignored by pastoral theologians in the Catholic Church (ibid., 92–115).

But a "diaconate of faith" for the grass roots of Latin American society confronts the church with entirely different challenges. It requires a deeper appreciation of the positive, genuinely Christian, and intrinsically Latin American values in popular religiosity, coupled with a more critical awareness of its alienating elements and ambiguities (ibid., 115–22). A grassroots diaconate of faith eschews any paternalistic desire to "own" and manipulate popular religious symbols for the benefit of whatever interest group in the church. A CEB approach to popular religiosity can be party neither to indiscriminate and undiscerning tendencies to do away with religious rites and symbols, nor to a reactionary and uncritical maintenance of popular religion. Libânio comments with considerable irony, "Secularists take away the anesthetic and let the patient die of pain"; traditionalists "prolong the period of stupor" (ibid., 125).

A genuine evangelization of popular religion is threatened from three directions: (1) from a bourgeois secularization that substitutes popular rites such as religious *festas* with tourist-oriented "shows" that are easily manipulated for gainful or ideological purposes; (2) from "utopic materialistic revolutionaries," who would like to do away with all religion; and (3) from the culturally insensitive initiators of post-Vatican II liturgical reforms (ibid., 128–31). In sum, a genuinely Christian evangelization within Latin American Catholicism will take the valid elements in popular religiosity as its point of departure rather than ignore them, gloss over them, or manipulate them.

Evangelization, says Libânio, must be both critical and historical—because it knows the dynamic of events. The efforts of evangelizers should not be directed to changing symbolic forms until they have taken into account the causes of their deformation that have to do with the economic sphere. This approach, says Libânio, does not overlook the dialectical relationship between form and meaning, but rather tries to restore a lost balance. He concludes:

We . . . have been so badly contaminated by a purely spiritualizing and idealistic analysis, and accustomed to dealing with the solution of problems at the level of ideas, wills and desires and of conscience, that we forget to look at the concrete economic, daily, social, and political reality, and to ask ourselves if our solutions are really working out in actions. A materialistc analysis—not in the sense of denying the force of the spirit, but in the sense of observing the material conditions of life—will serve as a counterbalance to an exaggerated spirituality [ibid., 128].

### External Dimension: "Diaconate of Liberation"

"To proclaim the liberating faith of God who saves us in Jesus Christ in a continent that is submerged in a situation of oppression cannot but lead to gestures that fulfill this liberation" (Libânio 1976a: 136). As a frame of reference for his discussion on this third dimension of evangelization, Libânio returns again to the documents of the 1974 Synod of Bishops.

This Roman synod chose the term "liberation" rather than "human promotion" because of the greater depth of its meaning and profound biblical content (EMW: in Gremillion: 597/12). The source of liberation is Christ and its object both personal and corporate sin. Corporate sin, the synod stated, is manifested in the colonialist socio-economic structures of the Third World. Similarly, in the Second World liberation has to do with freedom from communism and its oppression at spiritual, ideological, religious, and moral levels. Liberation calls the church to a personal and corporate conversion, to an austere lifestyle. It requires that it consciously take a stand in opposition to anything that militates against human dignity and the radical transformation of social structures. The basis for a diaconate of liberation, said the synod, is faith in humankind, in its dignity and possibilities as a creature of God, as well as in the announcement of the redemptive work of Christ.

A "synthesis" of evangelization and liberation is necessary, insists Libânio, in order to avoid the four pitfalls of "a loss of faith, the political instrumentalization of the church, the ideologization of faith, and the temptation toward violence." He clarifies his mediating position further: "Salvation is not reduced to the process of human liberation, but it includes it, because every human who has Christ fully as his model, is the permanent criterion":

Consequently, liberation, as the saving work of Jesus Christ, is that process by means of which man is admitted into full communion with God and with his brethren. It overcomes, through the truth of Christ, and by the ministry of the church, everything that impedes human fulfillment, whether it be sin which dwells in man's innermost being or its social implications. In no way is a purely psychological liberation sufficient [Libânio 1976a: 147–48].

Using two interrelated paradigms, Libânio shows how salvation-liberation interacts at three intersecting planes or "horizons"—theological, psychological, and political (see Gutiérrez 1973: 36–37, 235–36).

*1st Plane: Liberation is freedom from a world of sin (errors, evils, vices) in order to live in a world of grace and truth.* In the New Testament, liberation is Christ's victory over the prince of this world. In the Gospels this meant, specifically, freedom from sickness, death, the law, as well as from demons and sin. Because of his cultural and historical sensitivity, Jesus did not combat Roman oppression. The people, says Libânio, probably felt the oppression of Pharisaic legalism more than they did the Roman domination, which was more galling to the religious elite.

As the vitality of the church diminished, this horizon of liberation was ultimately narrowed to two distinct realms. At the level of ideas, sin would be the equivalent of theological heresy and dogmatic error. At the level of conduct, sin would be reduced to vice and immorality. Henceforth, orthodox Christianity would interpret liberation exclusively as freedom from error and from vice (Libânio 1976a: 157–64).

*2nd Plane: Liberation is the process of freeing oneself from subjective hang-ups—of psychological, moral and religious nature—in order to find fulfillment in life.* This horizon of liberation, which has been studied by both atheistic as well as theistic schools of thought, places a great deal of emphasis on therapeutic techniques (ibid.: 164–71). Although Libânio recognizes important values in each of these "horizons," he insists that they do not plumb the depths of the significance of liberation for the poor and oppressed in Latin America. Consequently, a third dimension must be added to liberation.

*3rd Plane: Liberation is the process of becoming free from a world of oppressive structures in order to enter into a new and nonoppressive world.* This is, of course, the dominant horizon from which the theologies of liberation view liberation. It is an important key to understanding the missiology of the *comunidades*. Libânio calls this a broader and more profound way of understanding sin and liberation. It results from the new way in which this missiology views reality:

> Sin, from which we were liberated in Christ (Rom. 6:18, 20, 22), is revealed in this lack of power to live under the covenant of God in Christ. It is sin, whether it is personal selfishness or conditions in society resulting from unjust structures, which hinders us from taking on the form of the people of God [IRM 271: 244].

Libânio is emphatic: "Evangelization, if not done with a view to modify history—which is where salvation and condemnation take place—is useless. . . . Consequently, evangelization and the concrete liberating project can never be two parallel things" (1976a: 181–82). In fact, the interrelationship of these two dimensions of evangelization will make possible a liberating vision that transcends a particular political project. Political liberation alone does not get to the root of sin in the human heart. "The manifestations of sin will continue to appear, in other forms, in the liberating forms that have been implanted. This is why the liberation process is greater than the political project" (ibid., 183).

## THE METHODOLOGY OF GRASSROOTS MISSION

Such an understanding of mission, Libânio warns, will not necessarily provide us with clear-cut solutions or prepackaged methods. We must learn to rely upon the Holy Spirit:

This is the privileged field of discernment. How to live a Christian life, how to evangelize, so that the means chosen can, in fact, accomplish that for which we have fundamentally opted? We cannot avoid the risks nor the possibility of mistakes [1976a: 191].

### Evangelization Groups: the CEBs in Mission

In the prelacy of Acre and Purus, which is located in the western rim of the Amazon jungle close to the Bolivian border, the majority of Brazilian coloniz-ers who have moved into the territory over the years struggle to maintain their very existence. Rubber-tapping and Brazil-nut gathering have been replaced by a habitat-destroying lumber industry and by large cattle ranches. Once-prodigal nature no longer provides for the basic needs of the rural poor and aborigines. Nor are the owners of enormous tracts of land inclined to be concerned about anything but their own interests.

There are so many CEBs in the prelacy that they have become the principal object of its pastoral plan. They are coordinated by various lay parish councils. In an interesting variation, which reminds one of early Methodism (see chap. 10), each *comunidade* is made up of a number of *grupos de evangelização*. They function as grassroots cells for the specific purpose of evangelization. The *grupos* meet regularly under the leadership of lay *monitores* who value this privilege almost as though it were a "second chrism." This serves as an incentive for the multiplication of grassroots cells, because only those who have themselves initiated a *comunidade* or a *grupo* can become CEB cataly-zers. The evangelization groups meet once or twice weekly for singing, sponta-neous prayer, and the presentation of new members and visitors. They also review each participant's problems and achievements, and discuss possible solutions. The lengthy discussion period is followed by a reading of the gospel from the *Good News Bible*, with an appropriate commentary. (Almost every CEB member in the prelacy, which subsidizes the purchase of scriptural texts, owns at least a New Testament.) The meeting of a typical evangelization group will close with short spontaneous prayers and the Lord's Prayer (Betto 1977: 243–44, 252–53, 273–77).

### Pastoral Priorities in Mission

Much can be learned about an ecclesial community from its mission priori-ties. Alicino discusses the priorities of the CEBs in two dimensions. *Comun-idade* leaders need to focus first upon the *internal* dimension of evangelization, recognizing the need for a progressive conversion of CEB participants, in order to involve them more integrally in the evangelization of the Brazilian masses. This dimension also includes helping the *comunidades* to grow in truth, in openness to new ideas, in their capacity to resist the crises of faith, and in their ecclesial lifestyle.

*Externally*, evangelization will require that the *comunidades* be missionary communities, in word and deed, "taking the gospel beyond the frontiers of the church." This concern was voiced by a CEB participant who is cited by J. B. Libânio: "There are thousands of persons outside; in the parish there are hundreds of persons who do not know Christ. This is why we should meet together" (IRM 271: 246). But this concern for winning persons to Christ, the grassroots pastors insist, cannot be divorced from a concern for liberation and human promotion (Alicino: 71–105; Guimarães: 223–48).

Though he expresses it differently, Marins has the same concerns when he outlines the pastoral priorities of the *comunidades* for the coming years:

(1) Building up a living church rather than the multiplication of [church edifices]. . . . (2) Vital participation of the people instead of inert masses of . . . passive Christians. . . . (3) Training leaders and increasing the number of well-chosen ministries and ministers. . . . (4) Integration into the life of the people and its reality [which runs counter to] individualistic, alienating, and alienated faith in Christ. . . . (5) Sharing in a vital liturgy, which should be in real contact with life, directed toward God and the life of all, in Jesus, through the Spirit. . . . [IRM 271: 241; Concilium 104: 35].

Marins then sums up his vision of the Catholic Church of the future in the perspective of the mission of the *comunidades*:

The future will require of the church a more effective and evangelizing presence in the world. It will not be present as a great, powerful, and imposing society, but as a communion of communities of human beings who love one another in Christ as sons of the same God and Father; who are in vital contact and dialogue with all men to make them critically aware in order to shape history in the service of all [IRM 271: 242; Concilium 104: 37].

If the CEBs continue with this vision, the Catholic Church in Brazil may indeed become the first church in the history of Christianity to achieve revitalization—internal evangelization—"from the bottom up" without rending asunder the fabric of the church. Will they be able to do so?

# PART IV

# GRASSROOTS COMMUNITIES AND PROTESTANT MISSION

# Chapter 9

# Protestant Dialogue with the CEBs

*. . . and the Good News is preached to the poor. How happy are those who have no doubts about me! [Luke 7:23].*

We come at last to a critical and dialogical analysis of the theology of the *comunidades* from the perspective of one who is committed to the theology of the Reformation. The object of this critique is not to downplay the significance of the CEBs for Christian mission, or to set up Roman Catholic straw men for Protestants to knock down. I have no interest in "attacking" the theology and social doctrine of the Catholic CEBS, but rather in offering what I hope are constructive observations from a Reformation perspective—while pointing out areas where Protestants can profit from creative interaction with the CEB phenomenon. This is what I mean by a dialogue with the Catholic *comunidades.*[130]

Fundamental differences aside, Protestants have a Christian obligation to stop, look at, and listen to what the Spirit is saying to the churches through the instrumentality of the Catholic CEBs. We are obliged to do this for at least four reasons, each of which is based on Scripture:

1. *The imperative of a holy inquisitiveness.* From earliest times God enjoined the people of Israel to "enquire, probe, and investigate thoroughly" (Deut. 13:14,NIV) all human phenomena, particularly those that might have an important bearing on their life and mission.

2. *The injunction to read the signs of the times in socio-ecclesial events—* and, as we are reminded by Comblin (1977: iii,1), in the persons who are the living embodiments of these events. Our Lord scathingly indicted the Pharisees for being more apt at interpreting signs in the sky than at reading the signs of the times (Matt. 16:1-4). We are asked to discover God's work in human history by means of a discerning comparison of the revealed Word with historical events and social movements.

147

3. *The requirement to recognize God at work in others, even in those with whom we heartily disagree.* Jesus warned against a too hasty and sectarian consignment of human actions to the forces of evil. "Do not stop him!," Jesus said of the man who was driving out demons, though not in his name. "No one who does a miracle in my name can in the next moment say anything bad about me, for whoever is not against us is for us" (Mark 9:39, NIV). He asks us to broaden our vision of his work in the world.

Using the opposite argument in Luke 11:23, Jesus roundly rejects any attempt to attribute his prophetic ministry to Satan, whose destructive and divisive work is the very antithesis of the communitarian or gathering orientation of the kingdom of God: "He who is not with me is against me, and he who does not gather with me scatters." We are told to discover where and when God is at work in human actions and social movements, and to be wary of attributing to Satan what may be of God, and vice versa.

4. *A willingness to let history and the God of history be the ultimate judges of ecclesial movements and events.* Our attitude toward the CEB phenomenon should be that of wise old Gamaliel: "If the purpose or activity is of human origin, it will fail. But if it is from God, you will not be able to stop these men; you will only find yourselves fighting against God" (Acts 5:38–39, NIV).

Therefore, we should not try to evaluate the *comunidades* according to our affluent Protestant perception of Latin American Catholicism. The grassroots communities cannot be fully appreciated or objectively critiqued from our own comfortable ivory towers. Only incarnation into the reality of the CEBs, with all that this implies, can give us both the experience and the right to make critical observations.

Having said this, however, there are critical questions that should be asked by a Protestant evangelical student of the movement. Accordingly, I have chosen what seem to me key questions from each of the four fundamental orientations of the *comunidades* (chapter 6): (1) the adequacy of the new understanding of *reality* in the worldview of the grassroots communities; (2) the scope of *liberation* in their religiosity; (3) the normativeness of *Scripture* in the CEB hermeneutic; and (4) the meaning of *conversion* in CEB missionary praxis.

## THE CEB INTERPRETATION OF "REALITY"

We should be profoundly grateful to the Catholic CEBs for making us aware of the existence of a reality altogether different from that which most of us have experienced. As Christians who believe in the historical fact of the incarnation, we cannot deny the right of other Christians to work out their allegiance to Jesus Christ in accordance with their particular historical contexts; to interpret their own reality in the way that they are experiencing—or suffering—it; to read the Bible in the light of that reality; and to contextualize their ecclesial lifestyle, structures, and ways of communicating the gospel in political as well as socio-cultural categories. To do otherwise would be to undermine a foundational pillar of the Christian faith, and to deny to others what we do ourselves.

We can also be grateful for the Word of God that comes to us in a new way out of the life and witness of the poor of the earth. "The hermeneutical privilege of the poor" is more than a demagogical catch phrase. It is solidly grounded in Scripture. It cannot be wiped away by pious theological rationalizations if we have never experienced real poverty and if our definition of oppression comes out of a totally different socio-economic reality.

All this notwithstanding, I am obliged to address the following questions to the *comunidades* from a Protestant perspective. Is the Catholic CEB understanding of reality complete? Does it deal with the personal dimensions of sin as adequately as it does with institutional sin? In other words, does it give as much weight to sin as transgression against God as it does to sin against neighbor? In what way does the "lostness" or "fallenness" of humanity before God relate to our intrapersonal and interpersonal alienations? Finally, does oppression have only social manifestations, or are there not also personal manifestations of Satanic domination that have not been taken sufficiently into account by the grassroots communities? Let us consider these questions one by one.

1. Throughout this entire argument, I am assuming the impossibility of divorcing personal experience from its historical context. But a very real dimension of this context for the overwhelming majority of Latin Americans is the luminous world that provides meaning to every other dimension of their reality.

Table 8 attempts to illustrate the totality of human Latin American reality. Gospel incarnation must take into account every dimension of reality, although it is only natural to want to focus primarily upon the dimension that is most familiar to us. There are four poles and two intersecting lines of tension in total reality as illustrated here: personal-impersonal and earthly (empirical)-otherworldly (transempirical). The forces of secularization pull us vertically toward the empirical pole (squares 5 & 6), while they push us horizontally toward the dehumanizing "impersonal" world (sqs. 1 & 5). On the other hand, the forces of reaction propel large numbers of persons toward opposite extremes, moving them vertically in the direction of otherworldly escapism (sqs. 1 & 2), or horizontally toward socio-empirical reductionism (sq. 6). But between these two extremes, there is a world the pure empiricists reject because it cannot be proven scientifically, but is no less real and tangible for untold millions of persons (sqs. 3 & 4).

This is a dimension of human reality in which millions of Latin Americans are seeking for answers to their existential problems. It is the world of the various forms of spiritism and of popular religiosity. While the elite try to find answers in the impersonal forces of magic, astrology, and parapsychology, the masses are attempting to forget their alienation and marginalization (sq. 6.3) in the comforting veneration of saints or communing with African tribal gods. Increasingly, this "intermediate" world is also becoming an escape hatch for an

**Table 8**

**The Dimensions of Reality**

(adapted from lecture notes, Paul E. Hiebert, Fuller Seminary, 1978)

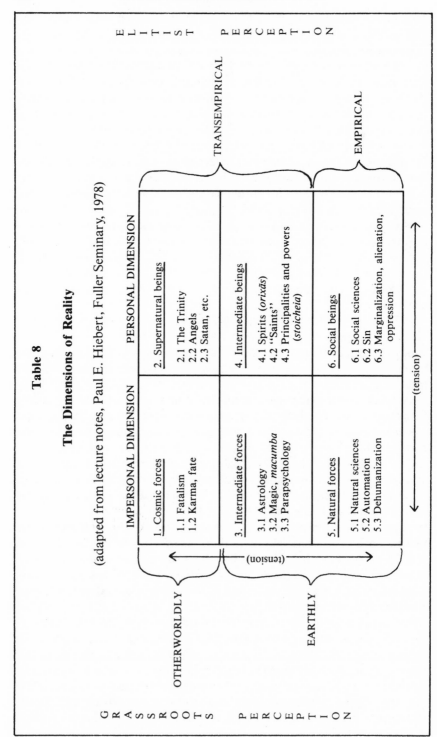

| IMPERSONAL DIMENSION | PERSONAL DIMENSION |
|---|---|
| 1. Cosmic forces<br><br>1.1 Fatalism<br>1.2 Karma, fate | 2. Supernatural beings<br><br>2.1 The Trinity<br>2.2 Angels<br>2.3 Satan, etc. |
| 3. Intermediate forces<br><br>3.1 Astrology<br>3.2 Magic, *macumba*<br>3.3 Parapsychology | 4. Intermediate beings<br><br>4.1 Spirits (*orixás*)<br>4.2 "Saints"<br>4.3 Principalities and powers<br>(*stoicheia*) |
| 5. Natural forces<br><br>5.1 Natural sciences<br>5.2 Automation<br>5.3 Dehumanization | 6. Social beings<br><br>6.1 Social sciences<br>6.2 Sin<br>6.3 Marginalization, alienation,<br>oppression |

ELITIST PERCEPTION

TRANSEMPIRICAL

EMPIRICAL

(tension)

OTHERWORLDLY

EARTHLY

(tension)

GRASSROOTS PERCEPTION

alienated middle class (sqs. 5.2 & 5.3). The "intermediate world" is, in short, the sphere of influence of the demonic "powers" behind all the oppressive structures of this *aeon*.

If we truly believe in the incarnation, we must take all these dimensions of total reality into account. Unfortunately, however, each stream of Christianity in Latin America moves within its own limited view of reality. Many conservative churches—both Catholic and Protestant—are involved only on the fringes of Latin American reality, while millions of Latin Americans are trapped within dehumanizing and impersonal systems or are bound by the shackles of spiritism. But other churches are so involved in secular concerns that they seem to neglect transcendent realities.

The important point here is that neither extreme takes the spirit world seriously. Unfortunately, the Pentecostal and charismatic communities, which often lack a clear perception of the true dimensions of social reality, are virtually the only ecclesial movements that accept this "intermediate" world at face value and attempt to do something about it. Despite their ideological myopia, their concern is valid and can be gainsaid only at tremendous loss to the totality of the gospel. The CEBs and their pastoral guides would do well to take this dimension of total reality more seriously than they do, integrating it into their belief in the demonic nature of structural evil. The abandonment of a magical worldview to which Libânio alludes (1976a: 56-57, 83-85), in the Pentecostal experience is often accompanied by a dramatic confrontation ("power encounter"), or with demonic forces at a personal level. A biblical understanding of confrontation with "the powers" should lead us to practice exorcism at both the personal and institutional (structural) levels.

2. We should therefore ask whether the CEB perception of reality, as interpreted by its pastoral theologians, is totally faithful to a grassroots view of reality. As I have pointed out earlier, the church will always have need of theological interpretation and prophetic guidance by intellectuals who are both committed to the reality that they are interpreting and have the hermeneutical tools to do so. These tools are the property of the universal church. Theory is indispensable to practice, and vice versa. Nonetheless, it is fair to ask whether the Bultmannian, Chardinian, and Marxist presuppositions that are the theoretical frame of reference of the theology of one or another of the committed CEB pastors may not at times unwittingly distort the worldview of their grassroots communities, hindering them from comprehending their reality in their own social and cultural terms. By the same token, the pagan Platonic dualism that infuses much of our Protestant theology has also contaminated the understanding of many of our Evangelical grassroots communities.

3. Libânio, Comblin, Marins, and other CEB pastoral theologians do not reduce sin merely to its social manifestations. They are very careful to insist also upon its personal manifestations. But doubtless because the personal dimensions have been for centuries overemphasized and its structural dimensions largely overlooked, personal sin is almost invariably discussed by them as sin against fellow human beings. This is understandable, and it is an important

dimension of what the Scriptures call sin. As Evangelicals we need to learn that personal sin, whether against God or against neighbor, is always socially defined. This cannot be otherwise, because, as social beings, we are the products as well as the producers of social structures.

But does not sin have another dimension that is largely missing in the theology of the grassroots communities? *Sin,* which is the central fact of our fallen human condition—fully taking into account the mediation of social institutions—*is not merely sin against humanity; it is also transgression against God.* There is an awareness of this dimension of sin in the CEB liturgy, but I do not find it explicated in its theological reflection.

But first a word of caution to my fellow Evangelicals. If sin is transgression against God, the knife cuts both ways. This strong evangelical conviction must first judge us before we can aim it at Catholic grassroots theology. Our shameful unconcern for the poor and oppressed who surround us—except as objects of pity and charity—is not only a sin against our fellow human beings; it is transgression against a just and loving God.

Indeed, even so-called personal sins are socially rooted and have social consequences for which we are accountable to God, as well as to our fellow human beings. Unless we are ready to admit this, we cannot insist upon an equal accountability before God, "who does not show favoritism" (Rom. 2:1, NIV).

Catholic theologians are not, of course, unaware of the divine accountability of human beings. But, because of the social locus of sin and grace of which they have recently become aware, divine justice is for them mediated through social relationships. It could not be otherwise! The God to whom we are accountable is the one who from the beginning has gambled on the side of humanity. Jesus Christ, and through him the church, is the culmination of divine identification in human history. But this truth should not be carried to extremes. The doctrines of the incarnation of God into human reality and of the growth of the Christian into full humanity are seen, at least by Leonardo Boff, as convergent lines in a historical process that finds fulfillment in the "humanization of God" and the "divinization of man" (1972: 248-56).[131] This would seem to make our accountability to God and to humanity indistinguishable one from another. Whereas Boff is correct in reminding us that God's self-revelation is always historical (Exod. 20:20), and that our perception of God in response to God's Word always takes place in social contexts, we are given little encouragement in liberation theology to feel awe and reverence in the presence of a unique, transcendent, and holy God against whom all sin is ultimately directed.

Quite understandably, the CEB theologians are reacting against an unapproachable God who for centuries had been identified with the power of earthly sovereigns who used religion as an instrument to dominate the people. Like human sovereigns, God was a distant monarch unconcerned with the sufferings of the masses. God could be approached, and perhaps persuaded to act on behalf of their spiritual and physical needs (but never their social needs), only through the mediation of a hierarchy of celestial court functionaries. This pantheon of celestial beings was felt to be more ready to listen to those who had money and influence than to hapless wretches who possessed nothing in this world but desperate physical, material, and spiritual need.

A theology from below would inevitably reject such a god. The very idea of accountability to a divinity on these terms is understandably abhorrent. The masses of Latin America cry out for a God who identifies with the sufferings of the people and is capable of exclaiming:

> I have indeed seen the misery of my people in Egypt. I have heard them crying out because of their slave drivers and I am concerned about their suffering. So that I have come down to rescue them from the hand of the Egyptians and to bring them up out of that land into a good and spacious land [Exod. 3:7-8, NIV].

However, it must be added that the God of the exodus is also the one who demanded a paschal blood sacrifice in anticipation of him who would one day shed his blood for the redemption of humanity. God is the unapproachable Presence of Mount Sinai and of the holy of holies in the desert tabernacle, wherein no sinner could approach.

The absolute otherness of God is a thread that runs through Scripture. It is not contradicted by the mystery of the incarnation. On the contrary, the very depth of Jesus' humanity, as Leonardo Boff has put it, caused the disciples to conclude that "only God himself could be so human" (1978b: 179). The humanity of God does not negate the holiness and love of God and the possibility of sinning against God by transgressing God's law and rejecting God's love. The indisputable fact that God's law and love—their acceptance and rejection—always come to us through human mediations and have social consequences does not in any way diminish the fact that all sin is ultimately transgression against God.

4. According to Scripture, *humanity is innately and fundamentally in rebellion against God*. In words that were used by our Lord Jesus Christ, humanity is "lost," "gone astray." This fallen human condition results in a reality that is composed of intrapersonal and interpersonal alienation, and in evil actions and oppressive structures. Human sinfulness is the cause, not the result, of this reality. This is a crucial distinction with important implications. It means that the salvation process begins, not when we become aware of our infrahuman reality and make a decision to become subjects of our own history, but when God in Christ, and through the power of the Holy Spirit, becomes the subject of our history. When we, the objects of God's love, choose to identify with divine history, we then can become the subjects of our history, which is also God's history.

In other words, we become subjects of our own history when we recognize the fact that, but for the grace of God, we are incapable of taking charge of our history. We confess our sinfulness before God, recognizing that we have not sinned in a social historical vacuum. We accept God's forgiving love, see this love manifested in the community of God's people, and take on concrete, socially mediated responsibilities as agents of God's kingdom. As the grassroots communities have shown us, sin and the forgiveness of sins, although personal realities, are also community-related and society-oriented.

5. As the theology of the CEBs makes clear, evil is not abstract. As has been well said, "Sin has names and surnames." Evil is personified in persons and in structures. Evangelicals readily perceive the personification of good and evil in persons. But in the *comunidades* evil is more often singled out in its institutional forms—governmental structures, transnational corporations, the *fazenda* system, and so forth. Both perceptions are, I believe, correct. But beyond that, the Scriptures tell us that evil is personified in supernatural beings, or at least in socio-cultural institutions and systems that are manipulated by demonic beings.

In every one of St. Paul's epistles except Philemon, he alludes to forces at work behind the movements of human history—forces that struggle with God for dominion over the universe. He calls them by such names as principalities *(arches)*, powers *(dymanis* and *exousias)*, dominions or lordships *(kuriotetos)* and rulers of this world *(kosmokratoros)*. In Romans 8:37–39, Paul lists a number of personal beings (angels, demons), time-space dimensions, life-and-death powers, all of which were created by God, and to which the apostle ascribes quasipersonal qualities (Berkhof 1977: 16–17).

Paul also uses the intriguing word *stoicheia,* meaning "ranks," "orders," or "series", which was used by astrologers to signify the ranks of the stars that influenced human destinies, and in philosophy to refer to the primeval elements of the world and the rudiments of knowledge (cf. similar usages in Heb. 5:12 and 2 Pet. 3:10).

But Paul gives the word a new twist. He relates it to tradition and seems to equate it as well with the constituent elements of our human existence—that is with, what today we call the structures of culture and of society (Col. 2:8, 14ff.; Gal. 4:1–11). As with the terms we have seen above, he endows the *stoicheia* with a personality of their own. They seem to be, in fact, synonymous with the "powers" (Kittel 1978: 1:482–83; 2:571; 3:1096; 7:684–85). Berkhof says, "Paul sees them as structures of earthly existence, " created by God to serve humankind but, as the result of the fall, in rebellion against God. "Propaganda, terror, and artificial ideologizing of all life are inseparable concomitants of the rule of the powers since Christ" (Berkhof 1977, 18–35; 57).

The ultimate confrontation with the powers took place at the cross, where Christ forgave our sins and freed us from the bondage of the law, having "disarmed the powers and authorities" and "made a public spectacle of them, triumphing over them" (Col. 2:13–15). The image that Paul uses is that of a triumphal procession. Discerning the spirits and confronting the powers, the church today continues the mission of Christ (Berkhof 1977: 36–52). Its point of departure is not human reality, but Christ, because he is both the source and the point of convergence of all creation.

## LIBERATION AND THE RELIGIOSITY OF THE CEBS

The most attractive dimension of the *comunidade* phenomenon to many Protestants is the new way in which these communities are being the church. It rings responsive chords among Christians of small-group orientation, social activist Protestants, and "radical" Evangelicals who have chosen to live out their Christian commitment through a service-witness or a more simple lifestyle. But when the grassroots communities are studied in the First World as a model for life and action, we need to be reminded of the precise nature of their ecclesial challenge.

The Catholic CEBs are not, to begin with, the product of conscious decisions taken "from above"—even by persons who, reacting against the values that characterize the top of the social pyramid, decide to start a countercultural ecclesial community. Their roots are in the response of those who are already poor—who in the eloquent and alliterative words of a Brazilian expression (*Não têm voz nem vez*) "have neither voice nor opportunity" vis-à-vis the seeming hopelessness of their socio-economic reality. As de facto groups of persons, they already existed. Then, through Word and sacrament and the instrumentality of pastoral guides, they gradually acquired an ecclesial identity. In the *comunidades,* the poor of Latin America find not only spiritual and psychological liberation, but the possibility of socio-cultural liberation as well. Through the CEBs, the Catholic Church has become the only "space" where oppressed Christians can begin to be truly human in the biblical sense.

What this means is that the precise CEB experience cannot be duplicated just anywhere, because of the unique historical circumstances of a powerful church in solidarity with the poor. What we can do, however, is identify with the struggles of the *comunidades* and seek to apply their insights to other situations of oppression, of whatever kind, even among middle-class communities. Wherever and however men and women are oppressed and manipulated, there is an opportunity for a grassroots community expression of the church. But in order for this expression to be complete, there should be solidarity between more affluent communities and communities of the poor.

### The Catholic CEB Challenge to the Protestant Search for Community

Small communities are ecclesiastically "in" in North America and northern Europe—house churches, "the church in the home," group encounters, group Bible studies, sharing groups, *koinonia* groups, mission action cadres, base groups, prayer groups, task forces, cell groups, base communities. As Charles M. Olsen, the author of *The Base Church,* has observed, these small groups are responses to three human needs: "the need to be"—that is, to feel authentically human; "the need to belong" to some group; and "the need to have and to do"—the human need for a sense of destiny and purpose (Olsen 1973: 34–40; see Clark 1977).

These needs have become particularly acute in contexts where economic prosperity, social mobility, urbanization, rapid change, and specialization have resulted in anomie and identity loss. Evidences of this phenomenon can be seen in the counterculture movement, or where hitherto segregated and marginalized groups have begun to demand their own identity (Olsen 1973: 41–49; Clark 1977: 1–20).

However, the significance of the *comunidades* for Protestant mission is not to be found in their response to social pathologies that are more characteristic of an affluent lifestyle, but in the prophetic nature of their *koinonia*. Their existence is a sign of the kingdom of God, and therefore a threat, not so much from the fact of *community*, but from their social origins at the *base* of society and from their identification with the cry of the poor and oppressed. Whatever theological criticism we might care to make of the *comunidades* from a Protestant perspective, the prophetic nature of their ecclesial lifestyle is, I believe, an incontrovertible sign of the kingdom in our midst. This renewal stream within a worldwide ecclesial movement of marginalized peoples who are demanding their place in the sun constitutes a unique movement within the church that cannot be ignored (IECT: 21 in *Occasional Bulletin* 1980: 4/3: 128; Torres and Eagleson: 234).

The meaning of the CEB option for the poor must be clarified still further. It is not to be found in the *fact* of the material poverty of the *comunidades*. There are many poor Protestant churches whose aspirations and values are those of the dominant system. Nor are the CEBs conforming to a poverty lifestyle for the sake of a congruent Christian witness, or as a countercultural reaction against middle-class values. As Santa Ana points out, there is no particular virtue in becoming poor. To make a poverty lifestyle a Christian imperative is tantamount to subjecting the gospel of grace to the demands of the law (1977: 15).

The unique fact about the *comunidades* is that they are a counterculture movement that is part of their own culture. They have no need to identify with the poor: they are often the poorest of the poor. Their identification transcends a poverty lifestyle to become active involvement in changing their own reality.[132]

## Cultural Identification and Confrontation

Culture is ambiguous. It has both liberating and oppressive dimensions. There is need, then, for prophetic discernment. CEB pastoral theologians are the first to recognize this ambiguity and to critique it from a christological perspective. The fundamental problem in popular religion, says Galilea, is its off-centered christology—its worship of a "dehumanized Jesus" (1978: 61–68; see Libânio 1976: 115–22). From this perspective, grassroots theologians tend to view the negative aspects of popular religiosity socio-politically. They are more aware of the manipulation of religious symbols by socio-economic powers in history than of the ultimate manipulation of historical forces by the suprahistorical "principalities and powers" of which St. Paul speaks. As Christians, we must be alert to both levels of manipulation.

Christian witness is able to deal with the historical manifestations of this cosmic "power encounter" because the ultimate confrontation took place at the crux of human history—the cross and the resurrection. It is this historical fact that gives the ecclesial community the authority to confront the powers, because, in effect, they have already been disarmed (Col. 2:13–15).

The historical fact of the cross and the resurrection leaves us no alternative but to accept the historical concreteness of the powers, particularly as they are manifested in the reality of the poor. For almost two millennia popular symbols have been twisted and manipulated by religious, political, and socio-economic interests. Indeed, an integral dimension of the present mission of the church is to accompany the people in a joint unmasking of false "isms," and in their place to rediscover genuinely liberating and socio-culturally relevant forms.

Because of their sociological and anthropological training, most of the *comunidade* theologians whom I have met have a profound, if critical, respect for every kind of popular religion—Catholic, Pentecostal, or spiritist. They are sensitive to the fact that gospel communicators must always make the reality of receivers their point of departure. True Christian communication is never a one-way street. It is dialogical and incarnational. Christian communicators must also be receivers, open to assimilating truth even from those to whom they have been sent with the truth.

Communication is not exhausted in dialogue, as CEB pastoral guides well know. There is such a thing as confrontation: political denunciation of the powers. But the focus of the *comunidades* on socio-political denunciation is only one side of the coin of confrontation. What is lacking is an equal concern to confront the demonic forces in popular religiosity and spiritism. These forces act at a structural level in social and religious movements, and they are also present in the actions of individual persons. These are two aspects of the same demonic reality.

The CEBs should take this "intermediate world" with the utmost seriousness. They must understand that spiritism is not merely an escape mechanism from socio-economic oppression. It also is a manifestation of demonic power at a core level of the worldview of grassroots peoples. They can learn from the Pentecostals, whose growth is not just a function of socio-economic factors, but the result of their "naive" belief in the reality of the spirit world, and of their everyday confrontation with satanic powers in their personal manifestations. Because of this key fact, they are a challenge to all levels and traditions of the church (see Johnson 1969: 120–25).

## Marxism and the Theology of Liberation

In any discussion with the majority of critics of base community theology, the bone that sticks in their throats is not, if the truth were honestly stated, theological (i.e., doctrinal), but ideological. It does have to do, however, with theological methodology—the choice of Marxism as a hermeneutical instrument of analysis of Scripture and social reality. Although I have attempted to address some of these objections at different points in preceding chapters, our dialogue with the CEBs would be incomplete without the following considerations.

1. As was emphasized in chapter 7, no one can escape "the ideological game." No one is neutral. The important thing is to be able to recognize this fact and to be capable of self-criticism in order to avoid absolutizing any methodology, no matter how coherently it may seem to respond to our basic questions and needs. Whatever criticism we level at any ideology must be made, first of all, while standing in front of a mirror! Only after we have faced up to the self-interest that often motivates our dogmatic defense of an ideology—no matter what its political coloring—are we in a position to point the finger at an opposing system. As Christians, we need to go beyond our pious protestations and theological rationalizations and get to the root of the problem.

2. Responsible criticism of "liberation theology" requires that we become aware of its complexity. Latin American theology is not one but several streams ranging from that which tends to absolutize the Marxist analysis to others that make use of it as one tool among many, and may even, in fact, be critical of the evidences of Marxist absolutism in other parts of the world.[133] The common denominator is their capacity for systemic criticism and their activist theological reflection from within the struggles of the poor for survival and freedom to be human as God intended them to be.

3. It is more accurate to speak of the approach used by grassroots theologians and social scientists as "critical structuralist," which borrows concepts from Marxism and a number of other critical sociologies. Some of these systems were conceived in opposition to Marxism. These thinkers subscribe to variants of the so-called dependence theory of economics. As mentioned earlier in another context (note 95), it would be difficult to find responsible social scientists today, of whatever persuasion, who do not in some way avail themselves of a Marxian insight. As someone in Latin America has observed, "One can be for Marx or against Marx, but in our modern world, it is impossible to avoid Marx!"

4. It is not necessary to be a Marxist to speak out against social injustice. As Christians, we can appeal to a much higher authority, the Word of God—from which Marx, the Jew, is reputed to have derived his prophetlike ire against systemic exploitation. CEB theologians are, for the most part, judicious in their use of Marxian analysis, while critical of it as a philosophical and political system. One Latin American theologian has, in fact, turned Marxist analysis into a critical tool against contemporary Marxist systems.[134] Before we train our guns against those who use Marxist critique, we should ask ourselves how effective our own systems of analysis are—if indeed we have any—in the face

of the inhuman global systems—communism and capitalism—that exploit two-thirds of humanity.

5. North Atlantic theology and social sciences (and their offspring, missiology) by and large subscribe to the functionalist school that pretends to be "impartial" and "apolitical" while it supports the status quo. It is understandable that we should feel very much threatened by any analytical methodology, whatever we might want to call it, that digs beneath surface appearances of normality and unmasks the root causes of social sin in which we are all implicated. The Marxist label, irresponsibly used, becomes a convenient way of dispensing with uncomfortable truths! In many places in Latin America this accusation literally pronounces a death sentence on anyone who dares to criticize social and ecclesiastical oppression. It is quite understandable that those with vested interests in totalitarian political systems should react in this way. But it is unpardonable that so-called Christians would resort to dishonest and unethical tactics in order to silence the truth.[135]

6. A final point must be made. The CEBs appeared, it should be remembered, as a response, in part, to the challenge of Marxism already at work in grassroots organizations. They are attempting to present a radical Christian alternative to two false political utopias—the one promised by Marxist-Leninism and the one that already exists in most of Latin America. Because of this, Marxist-Leninists have tended to scoff at the CEBs. They cannot accept that the masses have the capacity to throw off the yoke of oppression without the centralized top-downward leadership (so foreign to the CEBs) of the "vanguard of the proletariat." At the other extreme, the more radical elements in the *comunidades,* far from being attracted to communism, object to what they see as too much interference from outside elements, including their own pastoral theologians (see Mainwering 1982). They have been radicalized by the leaven of Holy Scripture, not by *Das Kapital* or Mao's little red book.

## THE CEB APPROACH TO SCRIPTURE

One of the most challenging dimensions—for Protestants—of the CEB experience is their new approach to the study of Scripture. Traditional religious pedagogy can profit much from the grassroots theologians' concern for letting the text speak to believers out of their own experience of reality. And among Evangelical Protestant missiologists there is also a growing awareness of the importance of allowing every people, group, and culture to approach the Scriptures out of the wealth of its own particular experience.

Someone has observed that the universal church will not fully comprehend the breadth and depth of the meaning of Scripture until every culture, tribe, and people possesses the Bible in its own tongue and thought-patterns, and until each has the opportunity to reflect upon Scripture within its own sociocultural categories to formulate its own theology.[136] If this is true, then the universal church is immeasurably enriched by the CEB hermeneutic.

But there is considerably more to the theological reflection of grassroots cells than just one more contribution to the pool of universal biblical knowledge, coming from yet another segment of society. The poor make up the overwhelming majority of the population in all truly Third World nations, and Latin America is unique in that its predominant culture is at least nominally Christian. In this context, we must seek to understand what it means for grassroots communities in Latin America to "discover" long-forgotten Christian truths and to apply them in new ways to their own reality.

### The Challenge of a Hermeneutic of the Poor

The specific contribution of the *comunidades* to our Protestant Evangelical understanding of Scripture is their "prophetic contextualization." The challenge of this more profound approach to contextualization comes to us not so much from their theologians, who have sometimes developed complex theologies out of the simple "wisdom of the people," as it does from the people. The closer one gets to the grass roots, the closer one seems to get to the world of the Bible.[137] Theological differences should not blind us to the new insights from Scripture that come to us from grassroots reflection. It is indeed possible that the apprehensive Evangelical Protestants reaction to liberation theology comes not only from theological conviction, but from a fundamental ideological bias. The starting point of theology is indeed crucial.

Our Protestant Evangelical answer to the theologies of liberation will be found not in the ivy halls of our theological institutions or in our missionary councils and consultations, but in solidarity with the poor and oppressed wherever they are found in the world. However, when we attempt to theologize in solidarity with the poor, we are hard pressed to find Protestant communities that can serve as centers for grassroots reflection and as generators of a liberating and holistic missionary action. Somehow, we must find ways to relate pastorally (not paternalistically) to popular religiosity in the spirit of the Suffering Servant. Might not identification with the struggles of the poor open the way to a mutually enriching interaction between orthodoxy and orthopraxis?

### The Source of Scriptural Authority in the Grassroots Hermeneutic

Once we have recognized the challenge that the *comunidades* pose for Protestants, we are left with some vital questions that we should ask concerning the grassroots hermeneutic. What is the ultimate source of authority in the theology of the CEBs? Is it the church, the reality of the poor, or the Word of God? Or, to put the question in a different way, is tradition, or the *sensus fidelium* of the grassroots church, or Scripture the source of authority?

In a sense, these questions are irrelevant because we all approach Scripture from the perspectives of our own theological traditions and from within our own socio-cultural context—as did the Scripture writers themselves. Yet we are still left with the question of who is to be the ultimate arbiter of revelation. How are we to determine what is truth and what is falsehood? Or should we be satisfied with the *consensus fidelium* that arises out of the awareness of reality by a majority of the ecclesial community? But then we would have to ask in what measure the grassroots hermeneutic is a consensus and to what degree it is imposed from the outside, albeit indirectly, through the kind of questions that theologians bring to the text. Do we not have just as much of an obligation to exercise our "ideological suspicion" on these questions as on the concerns of traditional theology? This is an obligation that theologians such as J. B. Libânio of course recognize (1976a: 30–31; 1979: 25, 115).

The preceding statement does not question the validity of the issues that are being raised by the *comunidades*. But from a purely rational standpoint, their questions are neither more nor less valid than the existential concerns that are being expressed in other social classes. We must look for validation elsewhere than in social reality alone.

The CEBs are not just "natural" communities; they are also "ecclesial," which implies that the questions they are posing have a certain degree of theological substance. And because the CEBs are, specifically, *grassroots ecclesial* communities, they can ask questions that are both sociologically and theologically more concrete. However, ecclesiality alone does not provide the requisite validation for their concerns. It lacks social specificity.

So a fundamental problem remains: Are the questions of the CEBs any more valid than those that other ecclesial communities are asking out of different social and ideological perspectives? If the answer is yes—as I believe it to be—it can be so only if the fundamental issues that motivate the CEB concerns find their basis in a higher authority than social reality and the church. This authority is Scripture.

Protestants, of course, have always insisted that sacred truth can be found only in Scripture. Yet this Reformation doctrine will remain a theory until we understand the meaning of "truth" in Scripture, and how it relates to the teaching ministry of the Holy Spirit.

*Truth in Scripture has a very dynamic meaning.* When Jesus promised his disciples the Holy Spirit (John 14:26, 16:13), who would teach them "all things" and guide them into "all truth," he did not have in mind a fixed body of doctrinal propositions. The order of the Greek words *(ten aletheian pasan)* in John 16:13 signifies "truth in all its parts."[138] Truth, this phrase implies, is multidimensional, and its communication must be holistic. The absolute "all" *(pasan)* refers back to the "many things" *(polla)* in verse 12, which Jesus had left unsaid, but which he would, by implication, reveal to the church, in each age and particular context (Kittel 1: 238–49).

The word "to teach" *(didaskeo)* was infused with a powerful new meaning, without setting aside the obedience-centered meaning of the Septuagint. Jesus was probably aware of the Greek approach to learning as an open-ended process by which both practical and theoretical knowledge is absorbed. But Jesus made *himself* the focus of sacred "teaching," and not, in the first instance, a body of revealed or empirical truth. Unlike the rabbis and philosophers, he could make specific demands upon his disciples on his own authority (Kittel 2: 133–34).[139]

After his ascension, Christ's teaching was continued by the Holy Spirit, and the Spirit's hermeneutical tool was *hypomnesei,* "to bring remembrance." Repeatedly, the Holy Spirit reminded his disciples of (1) the preresurrection words and actions of Jesus (Luke 24:6–8), (2) the Old Testament Scriptures in the light of the resurrected Christ (John 2:17), and (3) the apostolic teaching and example that centered on obedience to Jesus Christ (1 Cor. 4:17, 11:2). *Hypomnesei* is what we today call "theological reflection" or "doing theology." In each historical context the church "brings to remembrance" the same three elements: the historical Jesus, his life and teaching; the "christic structure" of the Old Testament; and the apostolic, as well as the postapostolic, theology and praxis, and we apply them to our particular situations.

We can conclude, then, that an important aspect of the Spirit's teaching of truth to the church in all times has to do with the total witness of the church from the Old Testament period until the present. The Spirit brings to our remembrance, not a past, static tradition or hermetic body of truths, but specific applications that can serve as guidelines for new contextual applications. We can observe this principle already at work in the early church. When Peter was called on the carpet by the Jerusalem presbytery for baptizing Cornelius, a gentile (Acts 11:16, NIV), the essence of his defense was: "Just as I was starting to speak, the Holy Spirit came on me as he had come on us at the beginning. Then I remembered *(amnesthesen)* what the Lord had said, 'John baptized with water, but you will be baptized with the Holy Spirit' " (Kittel 4: 675–78).

Although divine revelation is open-ended and requires constant reinterpretation and application, it is by no means relative. This is because "truth" in the Johannine sense is not conceptual, it is personified in Jesus Christ (John 14:6). The person (truth) of Jesus is manifested to us in manifold ways. In Latin America he is being manifested in new and, for some of us, unsettling ways, in the midst of the poor and the oppressed.

**Hermeneutic of the Poor: Final World or Mediated Word?**

The most momentous fact of our time is the emergence of the poor at center stage in history. Both the Catholic *comunidades* and the Pentecostal churches that are proliferating among the Latin American poor have dramatized this fact to a complacent Christianity. But only the CEBs and the related Latin American theology have taken the poor and their socio-economic context as the point of departure for an entirely new way of "doing theology." How does this square with a Protestant understanding of Scripture?

There is abundant evidence in Scripture to force us to look at the Word of God through the eyes of the poor. Their privileged position in Scripture, which is forcibly documented in Miranda's and Santa Ana's studies, among others, demands that we take the issue seriously. The Mosaic code made provisions for the protection of the poor, and the prophets denounced Israel's disobedience of these laws. But they did more than denounce; they also unmasked the social causes behind the inhuman condition of the poor (Amos 5:7; Jer. 5:28) and scoffed at a religion that piously pretended to nurture spiritual growth while practicing injustice and oppression (Isa. 58; Amos 5:21-24; see also Hanks 1983: 3-40).

Jesus defined his ministry as "good news to the poor" (Luke 4:16-21), and he carried out the major portion of it among the poor. Startlingly, he did not ask the rich young ruler to believe in him in order to attain eternal life, but rather to sell what he had and give to the poor. Saving faith is never abstract. It always focuses upon concrete human sin. When Zacchaeus proclaimed his intention to restore what he had stolen and to give half of his goods to the poor, he may or may not have been responding to a specific challenge by Jesus. In any case, our Lord places Zacchaeus's decision within the framework of a full-orbed "plan of salvation" when he says, "Today salvation has come to this house, because this man, too, is a son of Abraham. For the Son of Man came to seek and to save what was lost" (Luke 19:1-10). This one-time oppressor's identification with the poor in response to the call of Jesus identifies him fully with the family of Abraham, the "father of the faithful." The opposite condition, according to this statement by Christ, is equivalent to being "lost" (see Santa Ana 1977: 1-35; Miranda 1974: 77-104).

We Evangelicals are being challenged to take another look at our Bibles from the perspective of the poor. Salvation and conversion, as we shall see in the final section of this chapter, are much more profound than we have been taught to believe.

However, a basic question remains to be answered: Does the social reality of the poor determine our hermeneutic in an absolute sense, or does it mediate our understanding of Scripture relatively, particularly in the historical circumstances in which we live in Latin America? Does the "hermeneutic circle" pass only through the reality of the poor, or are there not also other way-stations that should be taken into account?

The CEB theologians believe that Scripture becomes the Word of God through the mediation of the official teaching and tradition of the church and of the *sensus fidelium* in concrete historical situations (C. Boff 1978b: 244-245). Protestants in the Evangelical stream would prefer to say that Scripture, *the* Word of God, becomes contextually meaningful to us through the illumination of the Holy Spirit. The Spirit uses both the theological tradition of the church and the ongoing reflection of the community of faith to apply the Word of God to concrete situations. *Scripture is the Word of God* first of all *because of its divine origin and* then *because it is so perceived by the community of faith as God is revealed to us through it in concrete historical situations.* These are the two poles of a hermeneutical dialectic. We accept the first by faith, but only after we have experienced the second in our everyday lives.

Clodovis Boff is correct when he says that the "hermeneutic circle" operates in a dialectical relationship between the past and present history of humanity and of the church (ibid., 247–48). But this should mean not only that we reflect back upon biblical and ecclesial history from out of our present identification with the poor, but also that we permit the always valid kingdom message of Scripture to speak to us and to judge us today.

Clodovis Boff is also helpful when he points out that biblical truth becomes meaningful to us midway in the dynamic interaction between the written Word and the historically rooted reflection of the ecclesial community. It speaks to us in the midpoint between the encoding of divine meanings by the biblical authors of the past and the continual decoding of Scripture meanings by the church in each historical present—that is, between word-forms and message-meanings. This process was also at work when the Word of God was put down in written form (ibid., 244–47).

But it is the Holy Spirit, whose role in this process has not been sufficiently appreciated in grassroots Catholic theology, who provides the dynamic link between the dialectical relationships that are at work in the "hermeneutic circle." Because the process is dynamic, it cannot be encapsulated into the neat theological formulas of either a conservative or a liberal theological approach. Yet, faith in God's Word establishes for us parameters beyond which we cannot go—a fact that Clodovis Boff is quick to recognize (ibid., 249).

There is a limited parallel between the incarnation of the Son of God (the divine *logos*) and the inscripturation of the Word of God. Both are divine, both became human, and in both instances the two dimensions are fully integrated in ways that elude human reason. It follows that there is a close relationship between christology and theology, as also between christology and ecclesiology. Any tendency toward heresy in the one—whether it be neodocetic or neoadoptionist—will be reflected in the other. The church is challenged in every period of its history to keep the divine and human elements of all theology in creative and enriching tension.

For the CEBs there is just as much a danger of overemphasizing an open-ended ecclesial reflection pole of the hermeneutical dialectic that grassroots theologians practice, as with our conservative Protestant "freezing" of the divine encoding of the verbal forms of Scripture at the opposite pole.

This same dialectical tension is at work in God's actions in transforming peoples and communities into the image of Christ. How should we respond to the *comunidade* perception of conversion?

## CONVERSION IN CEB EXPERIENCE

Whereas the traditional Protestant view of conversion could be described as a point-in-time event, in the CEBs it is experienced as a lifelong process. Borrowing a comparison from Greek grammar, classic Protestantism would describe conversion in the aorist or punctiliar tense, whereas grassroots Catholics experience it in the imperfect or progressive tense. For the Evangelical Christian, conversion enables one to state confidently: "I was converted (or saved) at such and such a place and time." In contrast, the *comunidade* participant would simply assert, "I am being converted. . . . " Before we look for the source of both emphases in Scripture, it will help us to summarize very briefly the theological definitions of conversion in Protestantism and Catholicism.

### The Order of Salvation in Classic Protestantism

The classic Protestant theologies coined the term *ordo salutis* to describe the process by means of which divine salvation takes place within persons. Because the "order" is not so much a chronological order as it is a logical way of describing the process, it varies within the Reformed and Lutheran traditions. The process begins with divine calling (illumination) and regeneration, and moves on to faith (conversion), justification, adoption, sanctification, and glorification.

In recent years there has been considerable debate in Protestant circles on the meaning of conversion. As Christian communicators have learned to dialogue with persons of non-Christian faiths and secular ideologies, they have been forced to reassess—with a biblical perspective—what in many cases was a too-limited and static definition of conversion.

Eric Sharpe has pointed out that "there are at least three ideals of conversion that can be traced" in recent debates: (1) individual conversion as a transaction between God and the soul, (2) incorporation into the church as the Body of Christ, and (3) conversion into a secular "concerned community" (1969: 224). Paul Loffler has done us a great service by showing that the biblical concept of conversion does not necessarily support the traditional overcircumscribed view of conversion (1965: 93–101). In an attempt to bridge the gap between theological liberals and conservatives, Arthur Glasser attempts to move the debate on to new ground by suggesting that in conversion to any religion "the question is not superiority but truth." He proposes the concept of "paradigm shift" (following Kuhn 1970: 152–53), which he defines as faith that a new "truth configuration" answers existential questions more satisfactorily than do other paradigms (1981: 399–407).

### The Catholic Doctrine of Conversion after Vatican II

In its decree on the missionary activity of the church, Vatican II defines conversion in the following terms:

> All must be converted to Him as he is made known by the church's preaching. All must be incorporated into Him by baptism, and into the church which is His body. . . . Through baptism as through the door, men enter the church. . . . Conversion, to be sure, must be regarded as a beginning. . . . By the workings of divine grace, *the new convert sets out on a spiritual journey.* . . . This transition . . . brings with it a *progres-*

*sive change* through its social effects, and should be *gradually developed* during the time of the catechumenate [AG: 7, 13 in Abbott: 593, 600; emphasis added].

In conciliar Catholic theology, conversion could thus be said to be a process that includes turning to God (in faith), to the church (by baptism), and to the world (in service). But the emphasis is on the church.

## A Liberationist View of Conversion

The CEB theologians hold to what could perhaps be called a spiral model of conversion, which is closely related to the "hermeneutic circle" we have considered earlier. The point of departure in each is social reality. Gustavo Gutiérrez describes the workings of this spiral in his well-known "three levels of liberation." The Christian moves centripetally from an awareness of oppression, through an assumption of one's role in history, to an inner spiritual liberation (1973: 33, 37). He applies this model to conversion when he states categorically:

> A spirituality of liberation will center on *conversion* to the neighbor, the oppressed person, the exploited social class, the despised race, the dominated country. Our conversion to the Lord implies this conversion to the neighbor. . . . Conversion means a radical transformation of ourselves; it means thinking, feeling, and living as Christ—present in exploited and alienated man. *To be converted is to commit oneself to the process of the liberation of the poor and oppressed* . . . generously . . . with an analysis of the situation and a strategy of action. To be converted is to know and experience the fact that, contrary to the laws of physics, we can stand straight, according to the gospel, only when our center of gravity is outside ourselves.
>   Conversion is a permanent process in which very often the obstacles that we meet make us lose all that we have gained and start new. . . . But it is not a question of a withdrawn and pious attitude. Our conversion process is affected by the socio-economic, political, cultural, and human environment in which it occurs. Without a change in these structures, there is no authentic conversion [Gutiérrez 1973: 204-5, emphasis added].

In terms of this definition, conversion to Christ is neither different from nor temporally prior to conversion to neighbor and to the historical process of human liberation. They are indeed identical, because Christ is to be found in the neighbor and at work in the midst of the poor and oppressed. The center around which this spiral revolves is Christ, who is encountered in the neighbor.

How close are any of these three interpretations—classic Protestant, post-conciliar Catholic, and Latin American liberationist—to Scripture? Is it possible to find a mediating position that is firmly grounded in Scripture and takes human history seriously?

## Conversion in Scripture: An Exegetical Study

In an article entitled "Conversion as a Complex Experience," Orlando Costas analyzes the biblical language of conversion in the context of Latin American experience. Relying on the insights of several exegetes, he briefly summarizes the meanings of four words in Scripture that relate to conversion.

The Hebrew word *shub* signifies "to return" and has to do with the prophetic admonition to Israel to "turn from" its sins in order to "return to" Yahweh and renew its covenant vows. The word is also linked with the acts and demands of God vis-à-vis Israel and the nations, through the covenant and the manifestations of God's kingdom. Conversion, then, is an event that is inseparable from human involvement in God's historical acts, which are signs of God's rule in human affairs (Loffler: 95, 97–98).

The Septuagint translated *shub* by the Greek word *epistrepho*. Costas and Gabriel Fackre emphasize the prominent place that "to turn, bring back, or return" occupies in the New Testament. *Epistrepho* is most often applied to the first-time turning of unbelievers to God. Another New Testament word, *metanoeo* ("to change one's mind"), can also mean "to adopt another view." The word is applied both to an apostate church and to a rebellious sinner. *Metanoeo* is often used in conjunction with *epistrepho* or *pisteuo* ("to believe, to trust"). Costas then proceeds to make his point: conversion in Scripture is multifaceted and complex:

> These different words and their various usages in Scripture underscore several aspects about the various biblical *concepts* of conversion. First, conversion means a turning from sin (and self) to God (and his work). Secondly, this act involves a change of mind, which implies the abandonment of an old worldview and the adoption of a new one. Thirdly, it entails a new allegiance, a new trust, and a new life-commitment. Fourthly, it is but the beginning of a new journey and carries implicitly the seed of new turns *[sic]*. Fifthly, it is surrounded by the redemptive love of God as revealed in Jesus Christ and witnessed by the Holy Spirit [Costas 1978b: 32–33; cf. Castro 1971: 164].

"Conversion," says Costas, "is both a distinct moment and a continuous process." This twin fact of conversion appears clearly in 2 Corinthians 3:16, 18:

> Whenever anyone turns *(epistrepho)* to the Lord, the veil is taken away. . . . And we, who with unveiled faces all reflect the Lord's glory, are being transformed *(metamorpheo)* into his likeness with ever-increasing glory, which comes from the Lord, who is the Spirit.

Conversion is both a volitional turning to Christ and a gradual transformation into the likeness of Christ, a process accompanied by a hermeneutical unveiling of the will of God for the people. Conversion, adds Loffler, is a gift of the Holy Spirit, and to manipulate it for either church growth or "spiritual authority" would be a "flagrant violation of the Lordship of God over his Kingdom." Conversion, he adds, "bears the eschatological tension. . . . It shares in 'the already.'. . . It lives towards the 'not yet' " (1965: 96, 98–99).

When John the Baptist calls the people of Judah to repentance and announces the imminent arrival of the kingdom, he is announcing, Costas writes, "a new order of life which the Father offers in Jesus Christ through the enabling power of the Spirit. It is a future reality, which is, nevertheless, anticipated in the present . . . a reality that we experience both personally and in the community of faith." Conversion thus implies a constant turning from the idols of self, which dehumanize our existence, to "a humanized and humanizing life . . . from death and decay to life and freedom" (1 Thess. 1:9). Conversion, Costas concludes, is not a static once-and-for-all event but a new and dynamic life that "implies new challenges, new turnings, and new experiences" (Costas 1978b: 33–34; 1979: 9–12; cf. Castro 1971: 164–68; Fackre 1975: 84–85; Loffler: 94).

### The Biblical Dimensions of Conversion

*Conversion is a social reality,* Costas stresses: it does not occur in a historical or socio-cultural vacuum. The particular contexts in which conversion takes place influence and are affected by a person's conversion to Christ. This means that the manifestations of conversion will vary according to the context. This explains why, in the CEBs, conversion is seen primarily in terms of commitment to the poor, whereas in affluent classes and nations conversion is appreciated largely as a very personal and interior turning to God (Costas 1978b: 35; Castro 1971: 164; Loffler: 94).

Conversion is both "a break with and a new commitment to society." Even if society is no longer important in our scale of values, it is primary in our Christian commitment. Christians, like Peter when faced with the challenge of the gentile Cornelius, will always be in need of "new turnings" in relation to society. Evangelization requires discernment on the part of the evangelizer as to the application of the "ethical minimum" to be included in the gospel message in each social context (Costas 1978b: 35, 38–39). It requires from each Christian and from the ecclesial community a creative, and critical, involvement in society:

This leads Christians to fully identify with and participate in the joys and hopes, the values and life struggles, of their society, and at the same time, to maintain a critical distance so as to be able to detect any form of idolatry or any attempt to absolutize a given practice, person, group, institution, or vision [Costas 1978b: 38–39].

*Conversion is an ecclesial reality* because it is the fruit of the witness and commitment of "a visible, concrete community, and leads to incorporation into that community," with all its implications for life and mission. Conversion is the genesis as well as the constant renewal of the church down through its history. The church cannot minister to others unless it is ministered to by others; "In order to call others to conversion, it must be converted itself" (ibid., 35-36, 39-40).

*Conversion is also a commitment to mission.* The great commission in Matthew 28:19-20 makes clear that conversion to Christ—outwardly demonstrated through baptism as a sign of incorporation into the body that is his church—advances through a process of discipleship toward the goal, which is to place men and women under obedience to Jesus Christ in the service of God and humanity (Costas 1978b: 36-37).[140]

Fackre suggests that Christian conversion implies a fourfold turning: to God, to the Word of God, to the church, and to the world. Each "step" in this process is symbolized by a concrete action: we turn to God in *repentance,* to God's Word in *faith,* to the church through *baptism,* and to the world in *commitment.* But the problem, he adds, is that Christians in the church often become sidetracked or bogged down at some stage in the conversion process. The result in each case is a heresy, a stultifying "ism," be it mysticism and false pietism, legalism and biblicism, "groupism" and ecclesiasticism, or secularism and materialism (Fackre 1975: 75-108).

What is missing, however, from the CEB conversion experience and understanding of evangelization, from an Evangelical Protestant perspective, is the invitational dimension of the gospel. As the WCC *Ecumenical Affirmation on Mission and Evangelism* (EAME) puts it: "The proclamation of the gospel includes an invitation to recognize and accept in a personal decision the saving lordship of Christ" (EAME: 10). Emilio Castro points out that "The proclamation of the gospel is not a disinterested story-telling. We tell the story of the gospel with the public hope that decisions will follow." When we open the Word of God and seek to interpret it to a human community, we are exercising "hope in the action of the Holy Spirit" who is capable of provoking the "miracle of a response of faith even to our very limited testimony of Jesus Christ" (IRM 72: 287, 305). Though conversion is, indeed, "a dynamic and ongoing process" (EAME: 12), it also calls for an overt commitment to Jesus Christ.[141]

But evangelization, as Castro and the EAME insist, should not be distorted by our innately individualistic worldview: "The Christian gospel is an offer, an invitation, a call to people to respond personally and socially to God." The moment of conversion thus becomes "the moment of conscientization, of awareness, of a personal relationship to God in Christ, an invitation to enter with him in the actual task of transforming this world according to God's will" (IRM 72: 287, 305). It is this awareness of the potential of evangelization and of the conversion process for structural transformation that imbues the *comunidades de base* and should spur Protestants, as well as Catholics, to reexamine their evangelism praxis.[142]

From these reflections we can conclude that conversion-as-a-process is not foreign to the biblical worldview. Nor is conversion-as-a-point-in-time. Both are complementary dimensions of the same phenomena.

## Conversion from an Anthropological Perspective

Professor Paul Hiebert of Fuller Seminary uses "set theory" to explain the various ways of approaching Christian conversion from an anthropological point of view. "Set theory" is a paradigm borrowed from semantic analysis. It organizes linguistic symbols, concepts, and thought-patterns into categories or "sets" along a denotative-connotative axis. Every people or ethnic group tends to order its conceptual categories into some kind of distinct "set." At least three kinds of groups have been isolated by semanticists: clear-cut "bounded sets," ambiguous "fuzzy sets," and goal-oriented "centered sets."

In the first category there are no ambiguities. Objects are either black, white, blue, or red, and persons are either "good" or "bad," in or out, on the basis of well-defined specifications of color, values, beliefs, conduct, and location. Similarly, many Protestants feel more at home when they can speak of persons being either Christian or non-Christian, "saved" or "unsaved."

The problem with this categorization is that it is static, permitting no room for gradations either toward or away from our own fairly fixed definition. We have problems with "bounded sets" when we are asked to define borderline cases. We are forced then to make hard-and-fast and often arbitrary categorizations with regard to persons who do not fit into our culturally, ideologically, or theologically prescribed definition of "Christian" or "saved." Fortunately, the grace of God refuses to be straitjacketed, and Christian communities have always found it necessary to adjust the parameters of the "bounded set," even if only slightly, according to any number of criteria. When this happens, we are forced to relate "conversion" to a more flexible "set."

The so-called fuzzy sets into which certain cultures order their concepts allow for a much wider latitude of definition. We have such categories in our own language as well. When we say that an object is large or small, that a person is fat or thin, or that he or she is Christian or non-Christian, our meaning will depend upon a subjective scale of values or upon comparisons with other persons. But it is impossible to set any standards, or fix meaningful goals, on such ambiguities.

A third type of category may help us more in our understanding of the CEB view of conversion. Certain concepts belong to "centered sets" on the basis of their orientation *toward* or *away from* a commonly agreed-upon goal, in the way a boy's growth might be evaluated with reference to a statistical average or by comparison with his father's height. The statement "I feel sick" belongs in a "fuzzy set"! But "You are headed toward a heart attack" belongs to "centered sets" when it is evaluated by another person, although, from the perspective of the unhappy person who has made the statement, it could well fit into a "bounded set"! But "You are headed toward a heart attack" belongs to the "centered sets" when the statement is that of a doctor who knows the patient's medical history and present condition.

The statement of CEB Christians, "I am being converted," belongs in just such a "centered set." They are converted when they make an about-face *and* they are being converted as they move toward Christ. There is room here for a wide variety of gradations within the one basic christocentric orientation. There is also room for both "conversion-as-a-definite-turning" and "conversion-as-a-process." Persons are "unconverted" when they are moving away from Christ, who is the center.

This does not, however, take into account the attitudes of persons in non-Christian religions for whom the "center" is not Christ, or for whom the "center" is relative, as in Hinduism. In order to clarify our understanding, we would need to "add a dotted line" around those who are Christ-oriented so as to avoid a different kind of "fuzziness" (Hiebert 1980: 4–12; see Kraft, 1979: 239–45).

As useful as this model is in helping us to conceptualize the complexities of "conversion," it has one fundamental weakness. The act of "turning" is probably much more a part of the actual process than is a straight-line orientation to or away from Christ. In other words, "turning to Christ" is composed of many small turnings to secondary or mediating centers, in which Christ is also present.

## Toward an Integrated Model of Conversion

Orlando Costas suggests that conversion can best be illustrated by a spiral that has its origin in our fundamental conversion to Christ but moves in successive conversions to the various dimensions of our socio-cultural reality (1978b: 31). Fackre's conversion model could be superimposed upon Costas's if we heed Emilio Castro's warning against making clear-cut distinctions ("bounded sets") between each "step" in the process (Castro 1970: 167). In the words of Costas, "The complexity of conversion does not lie in a fixed number of experiences, but in the fact that it is a plunge into an ongoing adventure. Christian conversion is a journey into the mystery of the Kingdom of God which leads from one experience to another" (1978b: 31; 1979: 9–10).

Latin American theology, as I have noted, also defines conversion in terms of a spiral. But the direction is different. In both Costas and Gutiérrez, the "center" is Christ. But for Gutiérrez, conversion is centripetal: the community moves inward from its insertion in the world toward Christ (1973: 204–5). In Costas, conversion is a centrifugal movement outward from Christ, whom I meet in my neighbor, toward ever new awarenesses of total reality. Costas warns, however, that the fundamental reference points of conversion, though always christocentric, will change as we follow Christ along the pathway of his identification with the sorrows and struggles of humanity (1978b: 31; 1979: 9).

In sum, there is a dialectical tension in conversion between the human and the divine, with Christ at the center. When we are converted to Christ, we are converted to God *and* to humanity (Matt. 25:31–40).

This explains why Jesus replied to the only two persons who came to enquire about eternal life with demands that were surely more ethical than they were religious (Mark 10:17–29; Luke 10:25–37). Similarly, the Baptist's reply to the question of the multitudes that he was calling to repentance is very specific in its ethical instructions to them, as well as to the tax collectors and soldiers. Luke makes the interesting observation that "the people were on the tiptoe of expectation, all wondering about John, whether perhaps he was the Messiah." Evidently this was the kind of message they had learned to expect from the Christ! Then the account adds, "In this and many other ways he made his appeal to the people and announced the good news to them" (Luke 3:1–19, NEB).

To evangelize is also to make ethical demands upon the hearers of the "good news," and the salvation that comes after a person receives the gospel of Jesus Christ has ethical implications (Luke 19:1–10). Even the Philippian jailor's query cannot be reduced to merely spiritual concerns. It is the anguished cry of a man who has just survived an earthquake and who fears for his life at the hands of his superiors. The apostles' reply ("and thy house") again underscores the social dimension of salvation (Acts 16:25–34). And the jailer's solicitous attention to his prisoners, presumably at some risk, is further evidence that salvation-conversion cannot be neatly packaged into a once-in-time, purely vertical, event.

To be "saved," in Scripture, is to become a whole person. Salvation is holistic; it involves the totality of human existence. We can indeed be grateful to the *comunidades* for bringing to our attention a forgotten dimension of salvation, even though as heirs of the Reformed tradition we miss more specific responses to the transcendental dimensions of the conversion experience.

The totality of Christian mission, and its relationship to a socially and divinely mediated experience of salvation and liberation within the Reformation tradition, will concern us in the concluding chapters of this book. We shall attempt to discover the significance of the grassroots communities for Protestant mission in church history and in the concrete experience of a segment of Latin American Protestantism.

## Chapter 10

# Historic Patterns in Protestant Grassroots Communities

*All these things happened to them as examples for others, and they were written down as a warning for us. For we live at a time when the end is about to come. Whoever thinks he is standing firm had better be careful that he does not fall [1 Cor. 10:11–12].*

The significance of the Catholic *comunidades* cannot be fully grasped until they are seen within the sweep of church history. They are not isolated phenomena. And Protestants need to consider the *comunidades* against the background of the numerous Protestant community movements that have appeared from the time of the Reformation onward. What similarities are there? What differences? Does the presence of grassroots communities in contemporary Catholicism have anything to say about the absence of grassroots communities in much of the history of Latin American Protestantism?

These are important questions. We shall begin to answer them as we attempt to understand some of the socio-historical processes that have contributed to the appearance of base community movements in history. We shall search for historical precedents—particularly Protestant ones—for what is currently taking place in Latin America. This is important, given the virtual absence of a historical perspective within Latin American Protestantism.[143]

### HISTORICAL FACTORS IN THE APPEARANCE OF GRASSROOTS COMMUNITIES[144]

The historiographer who attempts to study the church "from the underside of history"[145] must be aware of the following factors related to the emergence of the ecclesial community movements.

173

### Reaction against Institutionalism

In the context of the *institutional model of the development of social movements*, basic communities tend to appear at the beginning of the process, as well as in later attempts at revitalization, or in breakaway movements.[146] Indeed, every socio-religious movement can be seen as a reaction against an earlier situation that is perceived by the reactors as institutionalized, or its religious equivalent.

Thus, from a sociological perspective, the grassroots communities of the early church were a reaction against the deadening institutionalism of rabbinical Judaism. The early Old Testament community of the *qahal Yahweh* (the assembly of God's people) degenerated into a lavish and impersonal temple-centered religiosity. Even before the end of the Old Testament, community revitalization by the "faithful remnant" had turned in upon itself and would become the hypocritical Pharisaism Jesus condemned. But the grassroots church that Christ founded took only three centuries to become an institutional church under Constantine the Great.[147]

Even before Constantine, grassroots revitalization movements had begun to appear. The process accelerated during the "Dark Ages" and climaxed in the Protestant Reformation. The second-century Montanist communities were an early popular reaction to the inexorable drift away from an oral (i.e., prophetic) tradition. That Montanism itself became institutionalized can be deduced from a comparison between its early meeting places in private "houses of prayer" and its "temples" just before the movement was wiped out in the fifth century (Grant 1970: 14, 248–49). A closer look at North African Donatism in the fourth century, and at the related radical cells of Circumcellions who harassed the empire for several centuries, might also show the existence of grassroots communities in a movement that was characterized both by rejection of creeping institutionalism and reaction against Roman cultural and political imperialism.

The successive waves of monastic communities were another expression of dissatisfaction with the sterility of the institutional church. But each of these movements was in turn co-opted by the institution. A creative modality of monasticism provided the infrastructure for the vigorous missionary outreach of the Irish church. The Poor Men of Lombardy and of Lyons—the Waldensians—were unsuccessful grassroots attempts to put life into a decadent early medieval church that rejected them.

On the other hand, Francis of Assisi and his little band of Brothers Minor consciously chose to demonstrate a genuine grassroots community lifestyle inside the church. They were a prophetic voice in a society where disenfranchised poor, the artisan class, and the lower middle class were attempting to shake off the yoke of foreign domination allied with feudal overlordships (Petrie 1964: 51–52). A fourteenth-century example of a moderately successful revitalization community was Gerrit Groote's Brethren of the Common Life in the Netherlands.

## Centripetal-Centrifugal Polarities

Gurvitch's three-part typology of social groupings is a helpful way of explaining the place of Catholic *comunidades* within the social and ecclesial movements of contemporary Latin America.[148] *Community-type* groups are usually found at the beginning of the institutionalization process—as well as in the revitalization attempts that react against institutional fossilization. Institutionalism at the other end of the process is often characterized by individualist *mass-community* values and of personal identity.

Curiously, the closer we get to the Reformation period, the more we find ecclesial revitalization movements pulling away from open *community* toward closed *communion*. One significant difference between communions and communities in Protestantism is that the former are very often clones of other *communions* against which they are reacting, and not fresh and creative new *community* beginnings. The Unity of Czech Brethren during the Hussite revolution, and the later Hutterites and Mennonites, began as grassroots communities and soon became closed communions.

## Paradigm Shifts

Communitarian movements of whatever type have proliferated during times of severe social stress that have often accompanied transitions to new social orders. Thomas S. Kuhn has written extensively on a phenomenon in science that he calls "paradigm shifts." He defines it as the *conversion* on the part of the scientific community *from one accepted pattern of thought or theory to another*. At the level of socio-political phenomena a paradigm shift "proves to be a choice between incompatible modes of community life." The process of conversion from one pattern to another begins with "the awareness of anomaly"—that is, with the recognition that the expectations aroused by one paradigm have somehow been violated.

In a society, as well as in a science, "failure of existing rules is a prelude to a search for new ones." But "the proliferation of versions of a theory" that had for a long time been useful in integrating and explaining the facts of existing institutions "is a very usual symptom of crisis." Out of this proliferation of patterns comes a theory or integrating principle that explains reality better than any other known theory. This may take place in the form of a return to an earlier principle (traditionalism) or as the adoption of a radically new principle (conversion) that will displace most other principles (Kuhn 1970: 68–71, 77, 84, 94, 150). Historian Michael Walzer makes the same point in connection with the appearance of radical movements: "All forms of radical politics make their appearance during times of rapid and decisive change, moments when customary status is in doubt and character or 'identity' is itself a problem" (1976: 310, 315, 317).

There have been a number of such paradigm shifts in human history, during which many grassroots community movements have made their appearance.

They accompanied attempts to repudiate an order that was perceived to be no longer valid. Very often they became the prelude to a new order.

A 500-year-long shift from a voluntarist to a sacralist understanding of the church began about the middle of the second century. It followed in the wake of the gradual transformation of Rome from a republic to a despotic empire. As the self-understanding of the church gradually shifted from *Corpus Christi* to *Corpus Christianum*, the rebellion of many true believers against the status quo found its most cogent expression in dissident communities. Numerous sodalities, small lay communities, blossomed within traditional Catholicism during the breakup of the "medieval synthesis," which took place between roughly the twelfth and the seventeenth centuries: the confraternities, the Beguines and Beghards, and the medieval "singing guilds."

Other periods of social and religious paradigm shifts that coincided with the appearance of dissident communities (e.g., the Taborites and the Lollards) took place during the breakup of the feudal social order and the rise of urban centers that preceded the Reformation. Dissident communities also appeared during the Industrial Revolution in northern Europe. The seventeenth-century Levellers, Diggers, and Ranters, early Quakers and Congregationalists, the Lutheran and Dutch Reformed *collegia pietatis*, as well as the Methodist "classes," happened during periods of social paradigm shift and of acute stress. The same forces are at work today in the crisis and uncertainty caused by the demise of Christendom, the advance of secularism, the bankruptcy of the classic captialist social order, and the failure of communist utopias.

### Cultural Self-Assertion and Social Protest

Radical contextualization, which often grew out of *an innate need for cultural distinctness*, or *served as a sign of social protest*—as also because of religious factors—played an important role in the birth and development of ecclesial communities in the history of the church. It can be perceived as an important factor in the Montanist and Donatist communities, and was clearly present in the establishment of the monastic villages in sixth-century Ireland.

Eschewing the highly formalized asceticism of Greek and Roman monasticism, and studiously avoiding formal relationships with established churches, St. Patrick and his successors developed grassroots communities that fitted neatly into the village organization of Celtic tribes. Whether consciously or not, this was a typical assertion of Irish cultural and political independence in the face of the encroachment of the Germanic peoples who professed the Roman faith.

A little-known example of cultural self-assertion, with strong socio-political overtones, came out of the mountain fastnesses of Armenia, beginning around the fifth century. According to the definitive study of Armenian scholar Nina Garsoïan (1967), the obscure Paulicians in their undocumented beginnings were probably not the "Manichean" villains that they were subsequently made out to be by Byzantine chroniclers and by historians who based their conclusions largely upon later Paulician writings. The early movement seems to have consisted of fairly orthodox communities of "Old Believers" who had been driven underground because of their tenacious resistance to the byzantinization of the Armenian Apostolic Church, beginning in the fourth century.[149]

This was an amazingly long-lived movement. A sect with a Paulician name and original beliefs surfaced during the Radical Reformation (Williams 1962: 317, 678). In the nineteenth-century they reappeared in Armenia as the small Throndrakeci sect (Conybeare 1898). A Greek-speaking and militantly heretical spin-off of the original Armenian Paulicians harassed the Byzantine empire for centuries, and much later may have interacted with the Bulgarian Bogomils. This eleventh-century Balkan sect is yet another example of heretical grassroots communities born out of cultural dissimilarity and socio-political protest. The Bogomils may have passed their beliefs on to yet another dissident movement, the heretical Cathars or Albigenses of medieval Europe.

The political dimensions of base ecclesial community contextualization can be perceived in the revolutionary attitudes and actions of the Lollards in fifteenth-century England, as well as in the Taborite community in Bohemia at a slightly later period. Both communitarian movements were taking to their logical conclusions the radical preaching of the great prereformers, Wycliff and Hus (Leff 2: 598, 604–05, 690).

### Ecclesiola in Ecclesia

The concept of *ecclesiola in ecclesia*, the little church of true believers within the larger body of nominal Christians, found its full expression after the Reformation. It had been present very early in the thinking of Luther and Zwingli but was discarded by them as unworkable. Their germinal idea came perhaps from the attempts of medieval monastics, as well as the Waldensians and Franciscans, to revive the church from within. The concept may have led to the formation of the Unity of Bohemian Brethren in the fifteenth century. An eighteenth-century reincarnation of the *Unitas Fratrum*, the Unity of Moravian Brethren, in a sense wanted the best of both worlds. Zinzendorf conceived Herrnhut as a Pietist *ecclesiola* within a Lutheran *Landeskirche* as well as an *ecclesia* in its own right. The most notable examples in Protestantism of this ecclesial modality were Spener's *collegia pietatis* and Wesley's "classes." Most of these *ecclesiolae* came to an early end, either because they were co-opted by the *ecclesia*, or because they opted out of the *ecclesia* due to opposition or impatience.

A strong case can be made of Leonard Verduin's contention that this ecclesial model is in fact unworkable in the long run because it combines "two irreconcilable views of the church," borrowed from the Old Testament "holy remnant" and the New Testament "believers' church" (1964: 82n). Verduin may well be correct; if so, this raises significant questions regarding the future of the Catholic *comunidades*, which are, of course, *ecclesiolae in ecclesia*. It may be, however, that the sacralist world of an Old Covenant-type national church structure such as Latin American Catholicism should be approached, at least initially, from an Old Testament perspective.

### Missionary Zeal vs. Institutionalization

Social groupings exist in constant *tension between institution and charismatic community*, or, in theological terms, *between idolatry and heresy*, between dogmatism and outright rejection of dogma. Within every human being there is a yearning for stable institutions and predictable structures. Because of human sinfulness and the natural tendency to dominate, institutionalism is the norm and community the exception to the rule. Because of this, basic communities are seldom seen with approval by those holding institutional power. They are perceived, correctly, as threats to the established order, and in consequence, have often been branded subversive, outlawed, and driven underground.

During long centuries, both the ability and the power to chronicle ecclesiastical history has been carefully kept in the hands of representatives of the establishment. It should not surprise us, therefore, that most dissident movements have been branded heretical for posterity by champions of orthodoxy who desired nothing less than their destruction! At least some of these movements were heretical. But as John Moore has put it, "The more remote the report becomes from the heretics themselves, the more elaborate and comprehensive become the doctrines which they are alleged to have held" (1946: 10). And the closer these communities were to the grass roots of their society, the more heretical they seem to have been. But theological heresies of the left were usually reactions against praxiological heresies of the right. And they often served as prophetic calls back to a more biblical balance between orthodoxy and orthopraxis.

Grassroots dissidence appeared both inside and outside established Christianity. Despite its monolithic structure, Western Catholicism was often more creative in channeling dissent toward its own revitalization than was Eastern Orthodoxy—at least until massive dissidence threatened to destroy the very foundations of the papacy in the Middle Ages. As the number and intensity of dissident movements grew, the Roman See became increasingly more harsh and inflexible in imposing its authority. Gordon Leff expresses it well:

Initially at least, heresy was a deviation from accepted beliefs rather than something alien to them: it sprang from believing different about the same things as opposed to holding a different belief. . . . Whatever its forms, medieval heresy differed from orthodoxy and mere heterodoxy less in assumptions than in emphasis and conclusions. It became heresy by pressing thus too far. . . . What ultimately turned it into heresy was the failure to gain ecclesiastical sanction. . . . In that sense, *heresy was born when heterodoxy became, or was branded, dissent* and more specifically when the appeal to the Bible and to evangelical virtues of poverty and humility became, or were treated, as a challenge to the church. It was then that the protest became uppermost, conceived henceforth in directly anti-sacerdotal terms. This point was the culmination of the conflict between group and authority [1967:2: 1-3, emphasis added].

Leff's perceptive commentary should be kept in mind whenever Protestant missiologists ponder the relevance of the Catholic or Protestant CEBs to Christian mission and ecclesiology. It is pertinent also to the current debate in the highest circles of Catholicism regarding the future status of the *comunidades.*

*Grassroots communities are inherently proselytistic,* no matter how clandestine their existence. It seems to be a characteristic of small group movements, particularly those that have arisen as a reaction against an oppressive institution or in an attempt to revitalize a dying one, that they have an inner compulsion to enlist others in their cause. Indeed, one of the evidences of institutionalization is the demise of proselytizing enthusiasm. Evangelism, of course, was of the essence of the life of the early church, and of all its grassroots manifestations throughout history.

So succcessful was the spread of the Christian faith across the Roman empire that, at the close of the second century, Tertullian could boast of the places where the gospel had reached: from Armenia and Persia in the east to "the manifold confines of the Moors" and "the limits of Spain"; and from "beyond Cyrene" in northern Africa to "the places of the Britons inaccessible to the Romans." Of these far-flung localities he could flatly state, "In all of these places the name of Christ who has already come now reigns" (*Ad Judeos* 7). Then, in a burst of pardonable pride, Tertullian gloats:

We are but of yesterday, and we have filled every place among you—cities, islands, fortresses, towns, marketplaces, the very camps, tribes, companies, palace, Senate, and Forum. We have left you only the temples [*Ad Gentes* 37 in Ayer 1952: 52-53; see Grant 1970: 145-46].

Heretical sects such as the Paulicians broke out of their isolated valleys in Armenia into the eastern provinces of the empire, where, because of their missionary zeal, they were "discovered" by official theology. This same zeal took them across the northern boundaries of the empire into the Balkans, and along the trade routes into western Europe. In the Middle Ages, contemporary reports, perhaps exaggerated, speak of the Cathars as being "infinite in number" and "like the sands of the sea." In any case, by the close of the twelfth century, a knowledgeable Dominican heresy-hunter estimated the number of Cathars at 4 million. Still another chronicler recorded that there were Catharist communities in a thousand cities! What was alarming, from the perspective of the hierarchy, was the missionary zeal of the Cathars. They "sent out emissaries like locusts" (see Schaff 1950:5: 473-74).

The early Waldensians and Franciscans, the Lollards, Brethren of the Common Life, and early Anabaptists, the Ranters, Diggers, Congregationalists, and Quakers, the Pietists, Moravians, and Methodists, all went about earnestly enlisting others of their own kind into similar communities—until they lost their grassroots community nature and spiritual vitality. Even now, the churches that came out of the Radical Reformation know of no other ecclesial structure but the basic community or "believers' church." The Catholic CEBs seem to be an exception to the rule. They have not yet shown much of a concern for evangelization *ad extra*, for reasons we have already considered.

The above factors, demonstrably related to the appearance of grassroots communities in history—(1) the tendency toward institutionalism, (2) the centripetal-centrifugal pull in basic community, (3) periodical "paradigm shifts" in the social order, (4) cultural self-assertion and social protest, (5) the short life of *ecclesiolae in ecclesia*, (6) the loss of missionary zeal, as it interacts with institutionalization—should not be overlooked as we consider some outstanding grassroots community movements in Protestantism. They should also be kept in mind as we search for grassroots community models in Latin American Protestantism.

## BASE COMMUNITIES IN THE HISTORY OF PROTESTANTISM

Because "Protestantism recognizes within its own history the Christian theme of resurrection," the number of grassroots communities that have appeared in the relatively short history of the Protestant movement are legion. "That history is marked with recurrent dissatisfaction with dead ends, with 'orthodoxies' and conventionalisms." This spirit of prophetic criticism and of creative protest is what has been called the "Protestant principle" of continuing reformation: *ecclesia reformata et semper reformanda* (Dillenberger and Welch 1954: 313–14, 325).

Our present interest is only in those community movements that attended the birth of the principal Protestant confessions that can be found today in Latin America and, in particular, in Brazil.[150] By reason of number of adherents, the principle Protestant churches in Brazil are the Pentecostals, Lutherans, Baptists, Presbyterians, Adventists (who are not a part of this study), Methodists, and Congregationalists. All but two of these movements began in Europe as base communities or experienced a period of grassroots dissidence early in their history. Lutheran immigrants were the first to appear on the Latin American scene, followed by Methodist and Congregationalist missionaries. The last to appear were the Pentecostals. The arrival of Mennonites and of a number of small churches within the Pietist tradition is a more recent phenomenon.

What follows is a comparative analysis of the base community origins in Europe of the Protestant churches that are now in Brazil, for the purpose of establishing certain comparisons between these early movements and the Catholic CEBs. A number of these religious groups eventually became institutionalized state churches. Their linear descendants were revitalized after being brought into contact with each other in the crucible of the North American frontier. Such was the case with Scotch-Irish Presbyterianism, which was strengthened by New England Puritanism (Congregationalism) and revitalized by the Dutch Pietist *ecclesiolae* during the Great Awakening. I shall deal with this North American transition period in the next chapter, along with the fairly recent U.S. and European roots of Pentecostalism.

A brief history of the base community origins of the various Protestant movements should suffice for our purposes. We shall then focus our attention on the common social and religious factors that were present at the time of their birth, and on the ideology that informed them, before noting some of the base ecclesial characteristics of each movement.

### The Emergence of Base Communities in European Protestantism

Verduin reminds us that grassroots dissidence at the time of the Reformation was but a continuation of the discontent that had smoldered and flared among the masses throughout a thousand years of Catholic history. This view is supported by a statement attributed to Martin Luther:

> In our times the doctrine of the Gospel, re-established and cleansed, has drawn to it many who in earlier times had been suppressed by the tyranny of Antichrist, the Pope; however, they have forthwith gone out from us . . . for they were not of us even though for a while they walked with us [Verduin 1964: 14–18].

*The Anabaptist Movement.* The Radical or Anabaptist Reformation was, in fact, a protest against what its participants understood to be a traitorous and cowardly turning back on the part of Luther and Zwingli. Virtually all the Anabaptist positions had been espoused earlier by these two reformers, who would later reluctantly conclude that the Reformation could not succeed without support from civil power. Upon being challenged by their grassroots supporters, the reformers responded with increasing conservatism and violence, turning back to positions that were, in several respects, very close to that of Catholicism (Verduin: 12, 18, 38, 49, 72ff., 127–30, 157, 183, 198–209, 231).[151]

Although the reformers had encouraged small *collegia*, they soon found them to be a threat to their view of the church. They then labeled them seditious, blasphemous, and heretical (Littell 1964: 10–12; Williams 1962: 121–22), thereby releasing a groundswell of popular dissidence with a variety of manifestations. In time, Anabaptist communities coalesced into larger movements, such as the Swiss-Dutch Mennonites, the Bohemian-Moravian Hutterites, and the lesser-known Dutch English Familists.

*Congregationalism.* By the time Anabaptism had reached England, the history of grassroots dissidence in England had a very long pedigree. And from another direction Calvinism had instilled in dissident groups—such as the

Brownists and Barrowists, forerunners of the Congregationalists—a religious zeal, a strict code of ethics, and (later) a revolutionary fervor that would eventually overturn the monarchy. Although Congregationalism may owe something of its early basic community structure and antiestablishmentarianism to the Radical Reformation, by the time of the English revolution it had become largely a middle-class movement (Williams 1962: 787–88; Dale 1907: 101–2; Escott 1960: 3–10; Cowen 1976: 78–79).

The Anabaptist Familists merged into the strong current of grassroots dissidence (Hill 1972: 26–28), but another Anabaptist movement began in Amsterdam and in 1612 established itself among the working class of England.[152] These were the Particular (Calvinist) Baptists who became the forerunners of the principal Baptist bodies of today (Latourette 1975:2: 818).

*Presbyterianism.* Presbyterianism had a broad popular base during the years when Scotland fought for its independence from England. Sixty thousand persons, most of them peasants, shepherds, and weavers, signed the National League and Covenant in 1638. But when the Scottish clergy and nobility made their peace with the English crown, grassroots Christians were forced to worship in outlawed conventicles, meeting in houses and in remote fens and glens (Smellie 1975: 256–95).

Those who are conversant with the present "troubles" in Northern Ireland may be surprised to learn that the militantly anti-Protestant United Irishmen began, at least partially, as a joint *Presbyterian-Catholic experiment in grassroots community*. According to Irish historian A.T.Q. Stewart:

> During the last quarter of the 18th century, the northern Presbyterians played a leading role in the drama of Irish history. Yet it was an enigmatic role, and one which may have been profoundly misunderstood by later generations. At the zenith of the political achievement of the so-called "Protestant nation," there was formed, among the middle class Presbyterians of Belfast, the radical society of United Irishmen, whose threefold aim was Catholic emancipation, the reform of Parliament, and the independence of Ireland.

Stewart goes on to show that "the United Irishmen had the view that no reform or political progress was possible in Ireland until dissenter and Catholic united to isolate the Irish executive and overthrow the power of the Anglican Ascendancy." Stewart concludes, "There can be no doubt that the Presbyterians were deeply implicated in the United Irish movement" (1977: 101). As we shall see, this movement was undergirded by grassroots political groups and religious sects.

*Pietism.* Meanwhile, discontent with the spiritual and moral condition of Lutheranism in Germany gave birth to a renewal movement under the leadership of John Arndt. In Stoeffler's words, he "transformed the doctrine of the Word, as Luther understood it, into an ethical doctrine, and thereby changed the experience of justification into one of sanctification" (1965: 202–3). Pietism revitalized a sterile orthodoxy with a vibrant orthopraxis.

It was Philipp Jakob Spener in 1670 who found the way to make Pietism come alive in Lutheran churches when he initiated the *collegia pietatis*, an idea he may have borrowed from the Dutch Reformed churches. These *ecclesiolae in ecclesia* were small intrachurch conventicles in which clergy and laity studied the Word and prayed for mutual edification. Spener envisioned them as bodies that, he hoped, would assume in local churches the Presbyterian functions lacking in Lutheranism. Though Spener himself was hindered from giving greater breadth to his vision, the *collegia* spread rapidly into several regions of Germany, most notably in Swabia (Württemberg) where they sparked a notable revitalization movement (Stoeffler 1965: 229–37; Schattschneider 1975: 24).

An early seventeenth-century "second reformation" in the Dutch Reformed Church was relatively short-lived (Bosch 1980: 126–27). But later the preaching of the mystic Jean de Labadie sparked a religious revival that was buttressed by Reformed conventicles (*Gezelschapen*). The concept of the *collegia* was taken to North America by Theodorus Frelinghuysen, who used them to nurture his converts in the preaching missions of the Great Awakening. Similar basic communities contributed to the revitalization of Presbyterianism in the New World (Tannis 1967: 8, 22, 36, 59–60, 149, 158–60; see NIDCC 1974: 392, 428).

*Methodism.* The initiator of one of the most unique grassroots movements in Protestantism remained an Anglican clergyman until his death, John Wesley. Intimations in his eventful childhood provide some clues to his later actions as the founder of the Methodist societies. His father Samuel, a somewhat headstrong Anglican rector and one-time Nonconformist, organized a short-lived Society for the Promotion of Christian Knowledge (SPCK) in his Epworth parish—an experiment that he defended as a kind of renewal monasticism. During one of his enforced absences, John's mother Susannah conducted parish services in the rectory kitchen. She spiritedly defended her actions in the face of Samuel's outrage (Cameron 1961: 32–33; Durnbaugh 1968: 132, 137; Snyder 1980: 15–17, 168–69).

An Oxford fellow and a frustrated missionary to the American colonies, Wesley experienced his famous "second conversion experience" at Aldersgate. It transformed his life. His contact with the Pietist Moravians, as well as with Dutch Reformed *collegia*, "classes," not only influenced his spiritual pilgrimage but may have informed his radical rethinking of church structures (H. Davies 1948: 67–68; Cameron: 35–36; Durnbaugh: 137).

Wesley himself tells us how he came to initiate the unique ecclesial structures within Anglicanism that in later years became the Methodist Church. Toward the end of 1739 some eight or ten persons, "being under deep conviction of sin," sought him out in London to ask for spiritual counsel. They were joined by several others the following day. So "that we might have more time for this great work, I appointed a day when they might all come together. . .every week" (Simon 1937: 100). Thus, in response to a need that was forged in the heat of a widespread evangelistic thrust, was born the first of a unique family of holiness grassroots ecclesial communities. It would be the forerunner of a phenomenon that would become generalized in evangelical churches, in particular during the "Awakenings" in Britain and the United States.

Wesley himself defined the movement that he had set in motion:

> A company of men having the form, and seeking the power, of godliness: united, in order to pray together, to receive the word of exhortation, and to watch over one another in love, that they may help each other work out their own salvation [Simon: 100–101].

Methodism spread rapidly throughout Britain and into the American colonies. Gradually the movement defined its identity as a church in its own right. The final break with an unsympathetic Anglican Church came shortly after its founder's death (R. Davies 1963: 123–41; Cameron: 37). In retrospect, the strength of the Methodist movement was in its unique blend of Pietist life and witness with an aggressive program of social involvement that set the stage for profound reforms in behalf of the working class during the Industrial Revolution.

This was due, in part, to Wesley's unique organizational gifts, and to his knack for discovering natural talents and spiritual gifts in others and putting them to work in new base ecclesial community structures, even if this meant breaking with established ecclesiastical practices. Many of his class leaders and a few of his lay preachers were women. Snyder estimates that up to one in five of the Methodist membership was put to work by Wesley in significant ministry (1980: 63). Within Methodist societies leaders from the popular sector were trained who might otherwise have never made a contribution to society or the church. This leadership was a significant force in evangelism and in the organization of industrial trade unions. The Methodist "classes" may have, in fact, inspired the structure of communist cells, "possibly mediated through Socialism which had a strong linkage with Methodism" (Durnbaugh: 140).

**The Social and Religious Context of Protestant Base Communities**

A comparative study of the socio-economic, political, and religious contexts in which the several base community movements that concern us were born will show a large degree of similarity between them, despite differences in time and place. In many respects, the factors we shall summarize are not unlike those that we find in Latin America today.

1. Medieval Europe, at the time of the Reformation, was little more than a Roman fiefdom. The populations of the principal nations were heavily taxed in order to support the luxurious lifestyles of Roman functionaries. But alone among these peoples, the Germans could not keep tax revenues within their territorial boundaries, even if only for the benefit of local princes.

The crazy quilt of hereditary and ecclesiastical principalities, in what would later become Germany, owed allegiance to even more powerful princes, not the least of whom was the Roman pontiff. In consequence, the not inconsiderable wealth of its mines and the fruit of its trade flowed into foreign coffers. If this was inconvenient for the German nobility, and a factor in their support of the Reformation, it was a tragedy for the general populace (Kautsky 1966: 90–102).

The peasants and the workers of Germany eagerly supported the reformers in the early days of the movement because they hoped to find in the Reformation redress for socio-economic ills. In support of this thesis, Robert Crossley singles out the fundamental changes in the sixteenth-century that had a profound effect upon the workers and peasants of northern Europe and prepared them for revolt. Much of what he says would apply to Britain a century later as well.

(a) It was a time of *fundamental economic changes*. An agricultural economy was gradually being superseded by a mercantile urban economy as a new merchant class had begun to compete in the marketplace with the products of the labor of the rural population. The ensuing change from barter to monetary exchange put the already hard pressed peasants at an acute disadvantage. Meanwhile, the nobility was also feeling a financial pinch—and responded by appropriating the lands that from time immemorial had been held in common by villagers, making serfs out of one-time freemen. Having nowhere else to go, the dispossessed moved into the fast-growing cities where they became part of a large, discontented, and unskilled labor force.

(b) The nobles were able to justify their actions by having *recourse to Roman law*, which was gradually superseding Old Germanic, or Native Common law, in the rural areas of the Holy Roman Empire. From earliest times the poor had been judged by their local lords and by a jury of peers. They were now obliged to face an impersonal royal functionary. And, if they could afford it, they could be defended by an equally impersonal defense counsel. More devastatingly for the peasants, Roman law recognized private property and knew nothing about common ownership. Nor was it bound by oral tradition. Of this fact, unscrupulous landlords were not slow to take advantage, so that soon the benevolent image of the paternal landlord changed to that of a robber baron.

(c) Meanwhile, *the self-image of peasants was also changing*, as they began to see that they were an important, though oppressed, cog in the system. With growing conviction, they demanded equality with other segments of society.

(d) This change in the peasant self-perception was in part the result of the *widespread use of the recently invented printing press*. Humanist scholars became champions of the poor, using the new medium to disseminate their ideas, which also reached the more literate peasants. It was these factors, says Crossley, that precipitated the Peasants' War, 1524–25 (1974: 24–30).

Peasants, workers, and a number of parish priests turned against the magisterial reformers when they perceived that it would not break their alliance with the temporal powers. Fr. Thomas Munzer, a one-time follower of Luther, began to take part in the cloth-makers conventicles that were led by the "Zwickau prophets." These working-class men were influenced by the Waldensians and radical Taborites of Bohemia. In time, Munzer too became a prophet of radical reform and actively supported the Peasants' War.

2. Much the same kind of socio-economic situation obtained in England in the seventeenth century. British historian Christopher Hill documents in minute detail the bitter class antagonisms that were rife before 1640. These feelings were exacerbated by the deep economic depression of the years 1620 to 1650, for which the people blamed the government. During the civil war, Royalists and Roundheads alike were haunted by the nightmare of a popular uprising. The people had begun to protest the enclosure of common lands and fallow fields, the cutting down of forests, and the draining of marshes. The marshes were the traditional haunts of the so-called masterless men: free peasants, runaway serfs, thieves, cutthroats, and Protestant sectaries. They were the greatest threat of all to the social order, says Hill, because "the essence of feudal society was the bond of loyalty and dependence between lord and men," and these men owed allegiance to no one (1972: 25–59).

Meanwhile, the brisk trade in wool and textiles between Holland and England provided a natural bridge for the transmission of radical religious beliefs into Britain from other parts of Europe. For a while England also became a haven for persecuted dissidents. They found a soil that had been well watered by a long history of grassroots dissidence. The earliest recorded official contact with "heretics" (*publicani*, "men of the people") dates from 1160. But one suspects that grassroots ecclesial movements had existed in England from long before that date—feeding perhaps upon the vestiges of the Celtic independent church that Rome had only recently managed to totally absorb—because of the surprising rapidity with which popular heresy spread throughout the kingdom. From the twelfth century onward, we find frequent references to grassroots sects, until their full flowering in the time of Wycliff and the Lollard movement (Dale 1907: 48–58; Whiting 1931: 111ff.).

Gradually authorities became aware of the threat that this influx of alien beliefs posed to the social and religious system, and began to hunt them out with increasing violence. After the fall of the radical communitarian experiment in Münster (1535), the trickle of Anabaptist refugees became a flood, and persecution intensified apace. Public executions of captured expatriate heretics only served to make the populace more aware of their existence and to attract supporters to their cause. A Dutch Anabaptist group called the Familists (*Familia Caritatis*) emigrated to England where it joined the welter of grassroots dissident movements that erupted during the Puritan revolution (Williams 1962: 401–3, 479–81).

3. There was considerable fear in Scotland that the people would revolt in the wake of the signing of the first Covenant (1638), which was ratified by nearly sixty thousand representatives of the people. As one cultured Scotsman expressed it, the question now was whether "peasants, clowns, farmers, base people all in arms, may not swallow the nobles, invest their possessions, adhere together by a new Covenant and follow our example" (Hill: 24).

Indeed, popular protest did come in the form of grassroots conventicles. Thousands of the common people gathered in the open air, as well as in small groups, to listen to eloquent preaching from Presbyterian divines. Outlawed and hunted down by the king's soldiers, the Convenanters did not always take their harsh treatment peacefully. At Drumclog the people fought back and dealt the royalists a humiliating defeat (Smellie 1975: 256–95).

4. From the time of Henry VIII onward, the native Irish were subjected to a series of oppressive measures aimed at subjugating them to the total power of England. During the reign of James I (1603–25), small colonies of wealthy English Anglicans and large groups of Scottish Presbyterians of small means were settled in the "Ulster Plantation," as well as in other sectors of Ireland. The former became the nobility of the new British fiefdom; native Catholics made up the majority of the very poor of the land. Between the two extremes were the thrifty Presbyterians, many of whom had been landless peasants who had come to Ireland in search of a better life. But it was long in coming.

During the first three-quarters of the eighteenth century, increasingly discriminatory penal laws were enacted by the Irish Parliament, "which effectively excluded the entire Catholic population from the political and private life of the country and . . . interfered with their rights to worship, or educate their children as they pleased, or bequeath their property in the normal way."

And Presbyterians in general were put off by their treatment by the Episcopalian minority, who granted them the status of second-class citizens. Inspired by the example of the American Revolution, to which Northern Ireland was contributing so many of its native sons, Presbyterians joined Catholics in grassroots political movements, which in time became exclusively Catholic or polarized into conservative Protestantism (Barkley 1959: 6–18; Moody 1974: 10–11; Stewart: 101–3).

5. The Pietist movement in seventeenth-century Germany was born in the wake of the series of conflicts that convulsed Europe for a century after the Reformation. The causes of the conflicts were political and economic, as well as religious.

Then came the Thirty Years' War, which rapidly engulfed a sizeable portion of northern Europe. The conflagration had a devastating effect upon the German people. Entire villages and towns were obliterated by rapacious armies. Whatever was not burned, destroyed, or consumed was abandoned by the fleeing populace. Hordes of displaced persons roamed the countryside, begging, robbing, and destroying everything they found in their path. All social organization and restraint broke down; money became worthless; famine and disease decimated the population.

Inevitably, the moral fiber of the people was destroyed. The rapacity and immorality of the rich was matched only by the cruelty and vice of the poor. Observes Stoeffler, "The defenseless peasantry was depressed to the level of beasts of burden. . . . Class consciousness reached unprecedented proportions." The nobility shifted the tax burden onto the sagging shoulders of the defenseless populace. Family values evaporated and witch-hunts abounded. In one city a jurist boasted that he had sentenced twenty thousand witches to death (Stoeffler 1965: 181–82; Schattschneider 1975: 18, 198).

In the midst of all this, the condition of territorial churches had declined to an all-time low. The opportunism and rapacity of princes and the cruelty of the soldiery was but a reflection of the general state of affairs in Lutheranism. The cause of this malaise takes us back to Luther's decision to place the church under the authority and protection of the princes. This fatal mistake prevented his movement from ever attaining the ecclesial and missiological significance of the Reformed and Anabaptist churches. No presbyterial government was allowed to assert itself in Lutheranism because of its subservience to princes who were "often dissolute and seldom devout." Even if Luther had taken the time to develop a system of church discipline, it would not have stood a chance under the ecclesiastical system that he left behind.

Luther failed to foster the believers' church ideal that he had at first considered. This was the fundamental weakness of Lutheranism. Nor did the system permit this to develop later, as it would in the Reformed churches where the believers' church ideal had earlier been rejected by Zwingli. The Lutheranism of the day was rigidly orthodox and viciously intolerant. Although lip service was paid to biblical authority, real authority, Stoeffler points out, was vested in a particular interpretation of doctrine with little or no thought for its ethical implications. Intolerance led to heated controversy, first with Catholics and Anabaptists, then with other Reformed churches, and in the end with fellow Lutherans (Stoeffler 1965: 182–87); Stoeffler concludes:

> The rise of the Pietistic movement within Lutheranism must be seen against this background. It is not surprising to find that its early representatives continually insisted that the Lutheran Reformation had unfortunately been only partial, that it was their task to add to the reformation of doctrine a reformation of life. In this endeavor they appealed to Luther, who did not divorce faith from its fruits [1965: 187].

6. In many respects, conditions in eighteenth-century England were similar to those in Germany, with one major exception. England was not wracked by a debilitating civil war. On the surface, as Richard Cameron observes:

> It was an age of relative stability at home and peace with other nations. The ruling oligarchy was quite satisfied with things as they were, the writers gave literary form to their complacency, and the thinkers elaborated theoretical justification for maintaining the blessed equilibrium free from change. But this imposing superstructure was built on a foundation of poverty and wretchedness which was nonetheless real for being inarticulate. Insofar as the governors and thinkers took the masses into account, it was to say that the prosperity of the nation presupposed a permanent pool of poverty to sustain it, and that it was a providential government which had decreed that the many poor should serve the interest of the few rich [1961: 27–28].

Two significant revolutions—agricultural and industrial—were rending the social fabric of England. The agricultural revolution was similar in its causes and effects to that which had precipitated the Peasants' War and other popular revolts in other parts of Europe in the sixteenth century. It also has striking resemblances to what is currently taking place in industrialized Third World nations such as Brazil. Large-scale farms were swallowing up smaller holdings and common lands were being rapidly enclosed for grazing privately owned cattle. The net result was to force landless peasants and agricultural laborers into the new manufacturing and mining centers where the Industrial Revolution absorbed them and degraded them into faceless cogs in an impersonal machine (Cameron: 28). High prices, low wages, and grinding poverty exploded in the Bristol riots, 1838–40. These were also the years of the beginning of Methodism in Bristol and London (Snyder 1980: 32; Halevy 1971: 69; Semmel 1973: 13).

The populace drowned its hopelessness in drunkenness and promiscuity, and sought to ameliorate its poverty by thieving and gambling. The rich, no less intemperate, immoral, and dishonest, differed from the poor only in that they "could afford to drink brandy from France and were carried home by servants to bed, " whereas the poor got drunk on cheap English gin and had "clean straw on which to lie for nothing in the public houses." Crime was so rampant that it was seldom punishable, but when petty thieves were caught, for them it was the gibbet. And in government the Walpole administration was cynical and opportunistic, and George I's court was notorious for its immorality and corruption (Cameron: 29; Davies 1963: 24).

A century had passed since the Puritan reformation, which had accompanied the English revolution. And once again, religious conditions were appalling:

> The Baptists and the Independents had maintained their Calvinist orthodoxy firmly enough; but that orthodoxy was devoid of religious feeling or social passion. The English Presbyterians, on the one hand, had suffered from the inroads of the low theology of Deism, and the low Christology of an 18th century form of Arianism. As for the established Anglicanism, being closely connected with the state, it suffered the defects of the governmental outlook. If the government cared not a whit for the sufferings of the poor, how should a state church do better? [Cameron: 21, 30].

The Anglican Church lacked the machinery and the strength of leadership to set its house in order. Paradoxically, there were more than enough clergymen to fill the available benefices—which were often sold to the highest bidder—but an insufficient number of priests to meet the spiritual needs of the new industrial towns in the north and midlands. These regions, according to Hill, were precisely the places where grassroots dissidence had been rife a century earlier (1972: 73–86). As a consequence, thousands of the poorest Englishmen grew up unchurched. It was also where Methodism had its greatest appeal.

Within the camp of the Nonconformists, chapels had been allowed to reopen, provided they were properly registered and their doctrine was acceptably trinitarian. Nonetheless, they had lost their pristine evangelical zeal, as well as their grassroots identity. As Davies points out, they "gained the restricted ends of religious and commercial freedom for themselves by abstention from proselytization and by the quiet practice of their religion" (1963: 25–27).

It was in this kind of milieu that the Methodist grassroots communities were born.

### Ideology of the Early Protestant Communities

As we have had occasion to observe of the Catholic *comunidades,* a key criterion in establishing their grassroots nature is their ideological orientation. Are they inward-directed or outward-directed, and if the latter, in what way? One should not, of course, apply to the base community movements of the past exactly the same criteria as we have done in the case of Latin America. Each geographic and historical context is unique, despite some socio-economic similarities that we have noted. Our object is to show that within their own situations several of these communitarian movements can be, in a real sense, *comunidades de base,* and that all of them were involved to one degree or another with the grass roots of their church and society.

1. The ideology of the grassroots communities that arose during the Radical Reformation can be deduced, in part, from the epithets that were pinned to them by their enemies. The very term Anabaptist *(Wiedertaufer)* "rebaptizer," had radical connotations, because to reject infant baptism was to reject the Christendom model of the church and society on which the entire medieval order stood. In this same vein, the dissidents were sneeringly called *Sacramentent schwärmer,* because of their opposition to the sacramental hegemony of the state churches and in recognition of the threat to the establishment that was posed by the insectlike "swarming" of the radicals. The Anabaptists were indeed ardent proselytizers, and were dubbed *Leufer* ("runners") because of their ceaseless itinerant evangelism.

They were also called *Catharer* ("pure ones") in reference to their blameless lifestyle as well as in allusion to what were perceived to be their ideological predecessors, the austere and heretical Cathars of the Middle Ages. Like the Cathars, the Protestant dissidents worshiped in clandestine conventicles, which also earned them the sobriquet *Winkler* ("out-of-the-way gatherers"). They were dubbed agitators, heretics, and schismatics *(Rottengeisteren).* Because a number of the radical Anabaptists practiced community of goods, they were called *Kommunisten.* But they were also avowed pacifists, joining the grassroots sects that for centuries had carried staffs instead of swords, symbols of their rejection of conversion by coercion and of all other forms of violence (Verduin 1964: 21–22, 63–64, 95–96, 189–90, 221–22).

Yet, except for their ecclesiology, most Anabaptists could be classified within the mainstream of the Reformation faith. But it was at the crucial juncture where the great truths of the Reformation took on flesh and bones in the ecclesial community and in its relationship to the social order that Anabaptists could truly be called "left-wing" or "radical." They believed that the church, from the era of Constantine onward, had fallen. In time they came to apply the epithet "fallen" to the Reformation churches that refused to turn their back upon the Christendom understanding of the social order (Verduin 1964: 29–31, 35–43, 45, 66–67).

Luther's attitude toward the Peasants' War is illuminating. Though he had earlier sympathized with their cause, he was repelled by the violence he had observed firsthand, and turned against the peasants—whose very stimulus for revolt came from his teaching. He stated his position clearly:

> My sympathies are and always will be with those against whom the insurrection is made, however wrong the cause they stand for, and opposed to those who make the insurrection, however much they may be in the right. For there can be no insurrection without the shedding of innocent blood and wrong done to the guiltless [Crossley 1974: 96–99].

Luther's socio-political conservatism, which perhaps may be traced back to his relatively prosperous peasant roots, is expressed in his theological dualism—the doctrine of two kingdoms—and vice versa. At the ecclesial level this conservatism evidenced itself in his slowly evolving opposition to all forms of grassroots ecclesiality (Sider 1978: 5, 16).

Though Ulrich Zwingli, the leader of the German-Swiss Reformation, was less conservative than Luther, he too was unwilling to follow his convictions to their logical conclusions. In the words of Arthur Gish, he chose to "work within the system" (1970: 52). When his disciples launched a grassroots protest movement, Zwingli found himself retreating into positions he had previously condemned (Estep 1973: 9–15).

John Calvin came upon the scene when the battle had been joined with the Anabaptists. An advocate of "accommodation" between Christian individualism and a rational ideal of society, as well as in the interpretation of Scripture, he believed that church and state had a constructive and mutually supportive role to play in civic life. Civil government was divinely appointed to work for the common good, whereas the church was responsible for giving spiritual support to just government, defending the poor against oppression, motivating magistrates toward justice, and warning them when their authority became unrighteous and unjust. But, unlike his fellow reformers, Calvin was suspicious of the wealth and charity of the powerful princes who supported the Reformation (Graham 1971: 67, 74).

And Calvin was no stranger to dissident ecclesial communities, having perhaps attended Huguenot conventicles during his student days in Paris. Troeltsch shows that Calvin adopted the "sect-ideal," or the Christian "holy community," along with the Anabaptist methods of enforcing ecclesial purity, but he "applied this ideal to a whole national church, instead of to small groups of genuine Christians within the church" (1960: 694). In the end, however, Calvin was forced by socio-political realities, his authoritarian personality, and his ideological mind-set, to oppose leaders of the Radical Reformation with all his might when they appeared on his own turf (Williams: 580, 614; Troeltsch: 628; see also Verduin: 51, 58, 82, 131–57, 230). Nonetheless, the base community ideal did not die out in the Reformation churches; it would reappear in later centuries, and under different circumstances, in Europe, Scotland, and the New World.

2. The dissident groups that appeared in England during the seventeenth century were variously and indiscriminately called Lollards, Anabaptists, and Familists by their enemies, regardless of their relationship to the original movements. What they had in common was a rejection of magisterial authority and of sacramentalism, which, as the establishment rightly perceived, threatened the very foundation of the social order. Of not a little significance is the frequency with which these movements used the expression found in Acts 17:6 (AV) to "turn the world upside down" (See Hill: 13, 19, 107). These grassroots movements found much support among the populace. Hill documents numerous cases of popular iconoclasm that demonstrated the unpopularity, in every sense of the word, of the established church and social order. In at least one recorded instance, clergymen were sneeringly dubbed "dumb dogs, greedy dogs, which can never have enough" (1972: 25–31, 354, 356).

As they observed what appeared to be "a death grapple between Protestant and Catholic" in the Thirty Years' War on the Continent, some prominent British Protestants had begun to see themselves as a chosen people in Christ's imminent kingdom. But:

> What turned out to be especially dangerous was the wholly traditional view, repeated by many of the preachers, that the common people had a very special role to play in this crisis, that they were somehow more chosen than the rich and the powerful.

This became a dangerous doctrine when the Puritan Parliament began calling upon the people to participate politically and martially for the first time in their history. The masses took the millenarian preachers and the politicians at their word and began to demand an equal voice and a share of socio-economic resources (Hill: 33–38).

What energized the sects, says Hill, was "the spiritual experience of conversion . . . a break-through to a new life of freedom." The Protestant Christian's "burden rolled off his back and he acquired a sense of dignity, of confidence in himself as an individual." Conversion also gave strength "through oneness with a community of like-minded people." Hill adds, "This double sense of power—individual self-confidence and strength through unity—produced that remarkable liberation of energy which is typical of Calvinism and the sects" during this period (1972: 151–54).

The other side of the religious coin is what Hill calls the ideological "brainwashing" that was carried out by the Puritan divines, using the symbols of the Calvinist religion to keep the masses in their proper place. The emphasis of the

Protestant ethic on "the religious duty of working hard in one's calling, of avoiding the sins of idleness, waste of time, overindulgence in the pleasures of the flesh," however worthy in themselves, were often used against the general populace, Hill claims, as instruments of social oppression.

But the "True Levellers," as the most radical communities of that period were called, refused to play this game. As one of their leading representatives, Gerrard Winstanley, a commoner, observed:

> Free is the man that will turn the world upside down, therefore no wonder he hath enemies . . . . True freedom lies in the community in spirit and community in the earthly treasury, and this is Christ the true manchild spread abroad in creation, restoring all things unto himself . . . . Rich men receive all they have from the laborer's hand, and what they give, they give away other men's labours, not their own . . . . There cannot be universal liberty till . . . universal community is established [Hill: 107, 324–32].

When Congregationalist and Presbyterian preachers assailed the grassroots sects with Scripture, the sectarians responded with the inner witness of the Spirit, and with an appeal to ongoing revelation and socio-economic orthopraxis over theological orthodoxy (Hill: 366–70).

The early Congregationalist communities did include sizeable numbers of persons from the marginalized class. In fact, they were given the name "congregationalists" because all their decisions were made by "popular suffrage"; and they were called "independents" because they believed in the autonomy of each local community. Autonomy was, in fact, a self-protective measure against persecution, although they also developed "county associations" of churches, under the supervision of one minister, for purposes of mutual support (R.T. Jones 1962: 80–83).

Congregationalist worship was simple, spontaneous, and lengthy. As Jones observes, "People who had come together at some risk to themselves were in no mood for skimpy services or sermonettes." The key leadership consisted of a lay ministry, which gradually became professionalized. Though their sermons were directed primarily at spiritual needs, they attempted to make their preaching relevant to the conditions of the times (Jones: 84–85, 127).

Walzer observes that "the Puritan ministers provide, perhaps, the first example of 'advanced' intellectuals in a traditional society" (1976: 121). In this respect they were similar to the pastoral theologians in the Catholic *comunidades*. Walzer adds that "the Jesuits especially resembled the Puritan ministers, both in their impatience with episcopal control and their willingness to experiment politically." But the Puritans had a motivation that the Jesuits of that time lacked—a radical ideology. This prompts Walzer to call the early Puritan movement, "The Revolution of the Saints" (1976: 131).

Still, these "saints" were becoming middle class in their ideological orientation, despite their radical grassroots beginnings in Brownism and Barrowism

(Dale: 101–2; Williams: 707f, 187, 302). By the end of the seventeenth century, it would be said of the independents that "socially, Congregationalism was very much the religion of the economically independent." There were, adds Jones, a solid core of "gentlemen" and "tradesmen" in both town and country churches, along with the closely-allied "farmers" and "yeomen." As Jones points out, business success became a way in which the discriminated-against dissenters could find their place in a social order where the universities and the liberal professions were closed to non-Anglicans.

3. Grassroots dissidence was also present in Scotland at a very early date. Brownism appeared in 1583, and Quaker, Anabaptist, and other sectarian preachers remained in Scotland after the victory of Cromwell's very politicized New Model Army. Persecution from the Kirk was forestalled by the tremendous surge of nationalism that erupted in the 1630's in opposition to the uniformitarian policies of Charles I. It was after the reversal of the establishment to British royalism that the conventicles began to be harshly persecuted (Shaw 1967: 178–88). The radicality of their beliefs has been well documented (Hill: 57–72).

4. Since the early 1760s, Irish peasants had been venting their grievances against the pro-English establishment in intermittent violence against magistrates and landlords. These acts were organized by clandestine societies, such as the Protestant "Peep-of-Day Boys" and the Catholic "Defenders." There were also a number of dissident sects, "great levellers or republicans, " who called themselves by names such as "Old Light, " "New Light," and "Seceders" (Stewart: 107). A number of these grassroots communities, secular and religious, forming the Radical Alliance of Dissenters and Roman Catholics, became the popular expressions and real strength of the United Irishmen. They supported the Catholic emancipation movement.

But in the classic "divide-and-conquer" maneuver, the Catholic and Protestant agrarian dissident groups were goaded into turning against each other by an Anglican aristocracy that dreaded "the results of union between Saxon and Kelt." They successfully diverted "the attention of Presbyterian farmers from their civil and religious bondage," and stirred up "their hatred against the Roman Catholics who suffered from the same laws." As a result, the Protestant Orange Order was organized in opposition to Catholic Irish republicanism (Barkley: 36; Moody: 11–12; Stewart: 105–6). Both movements would soon polarize into militant extremes.

5. Though it was not politically radical in the same sense as the English grassroots sects, neither was German Pietism exclusively a middle-class movement. As Stoeffler points out, "the rural sections [of Germany] especially were open to its message, so that in time few villages were untouched by its influence" (1973: 121). This was especially the case in Württemberg, where the movement manifested "a remarkable vitality":

While it may be said that in other sections of Germany it often appeared to attract especially the nobility, this was not the case here. In Swabia it became a genuine grass roots movement, in which the butcher, the baker, and the candlestick-maker had a real stake. There were a few villages and towns, indeed, in which one or more pietistic cells did not function either within or without the Lutheran church [Stoeffler 1973: 129].

Pietist communities took a number of forms: *ecclesiolae in ecclesia,* dissenting para-ecclesiastical groups, closely knit communions many of which practiced community of goods, and heretical sects (1951: 55–56). Contrary to the present stereotype of "pietism, " the Pietist movement was not, as one detractor has described it, "stuffy, pretentious, and anemic." Despite—and in fact because of—its strong emphasis on holy living, Pietism was not a quietist and otherworldly movement (Schattschneider 1975: 24). Ernest Stoeffler's four fundamental characteristics of early Pietism (1965: 12–23) make this point clear:

(a) The *experiential dimension*—what is often called "spirituality" today—for the Pietists of Spener's day signified a profound awareness of the historical context of their faith: a corrupt social order at almost every level.[153] This was Spener's concern when he wrote the "Conspectus of Corrupt Conditions" in the first part of *Pia Desideria* (Spener 1964: 39–75). Another vital dimension of the Pietist dimension, particularly in Swabia, was joyful communal worship. God, for the early Pietists, was the Sovereign of history, a fact to be celebrated (Stoeffler 1973: 121–29).

(b) Although the early Pietists were fully aware of the corruption of their world, as children of the Reformation they also believed in the possibility of change. Stoeffler calls them perfectionists because they believed that true Christians could not sit by while "Rome burned" all around them. They were, in a sense, optimists—utopians—because they believed that they could change the church from within. That is why Spener could dedicate the second part of his work to "the possibility of better conditions" (1964: 76–86).

(c) Pietists have always turned to *the Bible as the source of their faith and ethical conduct.* This was the object of their gathering in *collegia pietatis* to study the Word together and to discuss its applications to their everyday lives (Stoeffler 1973: 121).

(d) Finally, the early Pietists were not passive when it came to confronting ecclesiastical as well as social evils. They believed in applying the *"reform principle" of Protestantism* to every area of life, and not exclusively to doctrine and polity, as had been largely the case with the magisterial reformers. Spener wrote about the duty of Christians to share their goods in community with those who were in need (Spener 1964: 61), and under August Francke, Spener's successor, notable works of social concern, enlightened for their time, were undertaken at Halle (Stoeffler 1973: 52–57).

Pietism would later develop unfortunate sectarian tendencies, and its vitality would be stultified by a legalistic and otherworldly approach to the Christian life. Yet, a vital modality of the movement, the Dutch *Gezelschapen,* would also have a profound effect upon religious life in the United States—in evangelism, Christian nurture, and social action—during the Great Awakening (NIDCC: 392, 428).

6. The English Methodist movement is indebted to Pietism through Wesley's contacts with the Halle movement, as well as with the Moravian Herrnhut community. Methodism is also, as Snyder points out, within the tradition of the Radical Reformation (1980: 28–29, 169, 171n).

John Wesley was profoundly motivated by his divine call to proclaim the gospel. When he was not allowed to address the upper classes, he instinctively turned to the masses, in spite of his high church training and Tory ideology. As in the case of the Catholic *agentes de pastoral,* his identification with the poor, taken at first out of "strategic" considerations, had a profound effect upon his missionary praxis. Early Methodism was, from the beginning, a working-class movement, although it did attract a few upper-class supporters. A random sampling of early "class" leaders reveals:

> a poor peddler, an impoverished widow, a family servant, a carpenter, a schoolmaster-shepherd, a retired soldier, an upholsterer, a tailor, a tanner, a piecemaker, a handloom weaver, a cordwainer, a cooper, a grocer-breadbaker, and a brazier [Cameron: 41].

H. Richard Niebuhr confirms that "the weavers of Bristol, the miners of Kingswood, the colliers and keelmen of Cornwall and Staffordshire and Wales—these were the groups whence Methodism drew most of its converts." In the eyes of the rich, early Methodists were, indeed, a "rag-tag mob" (1957: 60–62). After studying the biographies of sixty-three Methodist preachers, Cameron concludes that they came from the social stratum located between "unskilled labor" and the "middle class." Most of the preachers worked to support themselves, until they were forbidden to do so in 1768.

Methodism stepped into the vacuum that had been left by the upward mobility of the seventeenth-century Congregationalists (Jones: 147ff.). Bristol, a center of great social unrest, was also the center of early Methodist activity. But Methodism itself did not take long to begin its social climb, a fact that certainly troubled Wesley. "Wherever riches have increased the essence of religion has decreased in the same proportion," he wrote. "The form of religion remains, the spirit is swiftly vanishing away." Wesley's solution to the conundrum posed by the Puritan ethic was: work all you can, gain all you can, save all you can—"that is, in effect, to grow rich"—then give away all you can (Niebuhr: 28, 70–71).

E. R. Taylor makes the point that "the Bible was the greatest political weapon as well as the greatest religious dynamic of the seventeenth century." Their interpretation of Scripture is what made Whigs out of Puritans and provided the theological rationale for the Tory convictions of Anglicans (1935: 10). Methodism was no exception. Yet it was unique in that it underwent a metamorphosis from political conservatism to liberalism, and did so while it was moving up the social ladder from a movement of the poor to a church of the middle class. This split personality may be due, in part, to the curious fact that Wesley, although ideologically a Tory and theologically an authoritarian High Anglican (some of his detractors dubbed him "Pope John") was in practice a liberal and in ecclesiology a pragmatist. Despite his strong commitment to helping the poor, Wesley was convinced that they were incapable of governing themselves. His communities, therefore, functioned under a very rigid hierarchical organization that was relaxed only a little after his death (Cameron: 42–43; Snyder: 70–71).

Paradoxically, the increase in Methodist political involvement—which had considerable influence upon the founding of the Socialist Party in Britain— was accompanied by a loss in grassroots community lifestyle as well as in spiritual dynamic. One suspects that these factors are not totally unrelated. Meanwhile, in the populist American frontier, Methodism was managing, at least until the Civil War period, to keep its evangelical fires burning while maintaining an active involvement in movements for social justice (T. Smith 1977: 74).

## Types of Base Communities in Early Protestantism

There were probably as many kinds of base communities as there were sociocultural and ecclesiastical contexts in early Protestantism. However, it is possible to group them into at least four general types:

1. *Countercultural communities* or movements of socio-religious protest. If we keep in mind that the culture of the periods we are studying was based upon the Christendom model of society, most early Anabaptist communities were indeed countercultural, although their dissidence was couched in religious terminology. Like the Catholic *círculos bíblicos* in Brazil, they began as Scripture-reading groups that met in houses (they were called "schools for agitation" by their detractors) in the environs of Zurich, and quickly spread throughout northern Europe (Littell: 12). Having attempted unsuccessfully to reform the Reformation churches from within, they broke with them and began forming loose fellowships of "brethren" (Estep: 10–11). At first dynamic in their witness and prophetic in their message, the years of hostility against them and their enforced wanderings over the face of Europe transmogrified many of the Anabaptist communities into closed ethnic "communions" such as the Amish and Hutterites.

Their English successors, the Familists and similar dissident groups, were in some respects like the more politically conscious *comunidades* in Brazil. The Levellers, Seekers, and Ranters (wandering "prophets" with loosely structured popular followings), were similar to the messianic movements in early Brazilian popular religiosity. The Ranters and the "Children of Light"—"Shattered" or sectarian Baptists—coalesced into the Quaker movement. In their earliest history, Quakers, under James Naylor and before George Fox, were apparently a very radical movement (Hill: 107–150, 184–250). Some of these popular movements never became institutionalized and their dynamic continued, providing the support for grassroots political movements in following centuries (Jones: 147ff.).

2. *Puritan communities* maintained a grassroots identity and lifestyle during their inception and as long as they were struggling to maintain their identity in

the face of violent official persecution. They met secretly in woods, in caves, private homes, mud cottages, and barns and took every kind of novel precaution to protect their preachers from the royal police (Jones: 77–80). But once the pressure let up and they were granted recognition, an inner drive compelled them to achieve their place in the sun—and to abandon their grassroots community origins. Such was the case with the Congregationalist meetings and with the Scottish Presbyterian conventicles. Similarities are immediately noticeable here with the early experience of Protestantism in Latin America.

3. *Liberation communities* consisted of Christians who banded together primarily for political purposes in contexts of socio-economic and cultural oppression. Such a community were the seventeenth-century English "Diggers" (True Levellers), led by Winstanley. They set about plowing up wastelands in symbolic gestures of protest against land enclosure by the rich and, says Hill, thumbing their noses at the Puritan work ethic (1972: 14–15, 107–27). The Irish Catholic "Defenders," a secret agrarian society, and the Presbyterian "Peep-of-Day Boys" also belong in this category.

4. *Planned communities* appeared within the Pietist stream as a conscious attempt to revitalize dead ecclesiastical structures and to provide a prophetic witness within society. The outstanding examples are the *collegia pietatis* of Germany and Holland, the Moravians at Herrnhut and, above all, the early Methodist movement.

The Methodist societies were very large groups, which Wesley subdivided into various kinds of base communities, to meet a variety of needs and purposes. The "classes" *(collegia)* were the true base communities of Methodism, which eventually swallowed up the other groups. All society members were obliged to belong to a class, regardless of their commitment to Christ. They enabled the class leaders to help members along in their Christian pilgrimage. The "bands," which preceded the classes in time, were of specialized classes for those who were maturing in the Christian life. Different bands were organized for evangelization and discipleship. And for those who showed evidence of unusual growth in piety and conduct, Wesley created the short-lived "select societies," a kind of lay religious order, the special rules of which included community of goods (Cameron: 35–40; Snyder: 34–38, 54–62).

There is some similarity here to the structure of Catholic and Protestant renewal communities, which have great appeal for middle-class Christians around the world—with one fundamental difference. The original Methodist societies were a church of the poor. It is this fact that prompted Ralph Della Cava to liken present-day grassroots Catholicism in Brazil to early Methodism (LADOC 1978: 50).

## Common Features in the Early Protestant Communities

The Protestant communities we have surveyed have several points in common. These characteristics they also share with the Catholic *comunidades* in Latin America.

All these movements arose during *periods of acute social stress,* which usually included structures of injustice or of institutional violence. They were reacting against some form of *religious and political, institutionalized and social, entropy,* but in time, they themselves followed the path of institutionalization (Hill: 373–74). They often appeared at a time when the poor were beginning to break with the magical and fatalistic worldview of their past and to discover that they could take a hand in shaping their own destinies (Hill: 87–90, 142–43, 151–52, 163–64, 287–300, 383).

Though some of the community movements were more spontaneous than others, their structures, however loose, and their ultimate impact depended to a great deal upon the *quality of their leadership.* The grassroots communities provided opportunities for leadership growth, often under the guidance of mature and enlightened leaders. As often happened, the base community milieu brought to the fore numerous "prophets" who belabored the established order.

Inevitably, the base communities ran into *opposition* and *persecution* from the establishment. It happened even with the Pietists and Methodists who attempted to "play ball" with the system. *With perhaps one exception, none of these community movements could survive within the system.* Those that did not effect a radical break at the beginning (the Anabaptists and English sects) either became part of the establishment (the Congregationalists and Presbyterians), were forced out (the Irish dissidents), were suppressed (some of the Pietist cells), or became a church (the Methodists). Perhaps because of their lack of organizational structure, the Pietist *ecclesiolae* have continued to crop up in different contexts and periods of history. Yet, despite their short-lived character, every one of these community movements—as well as most of those that can be found throughout the history of Christianity—have had a profound impact upon the church, and in many cases upon the social order.

No less can be said about the Catholic *comunidades* in Latin America. For this reason, we must now attempt to assess the challenge of the CEBs in the context of the Protestant movements that have developed out of the base communities we have considered in this chapter.

# Chapter 11

# Grassroots Communities
# and the Protestant Predicament

*You say, "I am rich and well off, I have all I need." But you do not know
how miserable and pitiful you are! You are poor, naked, and blind [Rev.
3:17].*

In the previous chapter I analyzed the history, context, and ideology of six
Protestant confessions from their beginnings in Europe until they became
established in the New World. The same religious groups—Lutheran, Methodist, Congregational, Presbyterian, and Anabaptist—established themselves
in Latin America. In the intervening years, each of these confessions experienced, to one degree or another, the influence of Pietism, another movement
with basic community roots. We shall also confront a uniquely Latin American
phenomenon, homegrown Pentecostalism, whose roots, to a degree, are also
European and North American.

In the first part of this chapter, I sketch the history of these movements in
their new environment, pointing out the exogenous forces that impinged upon
them. My object is to establish the presence or absence of a base community
ethos with all that this implies. This should enable us to assess the significance
of the Latin American Catholic CEBs for Protestant missions, and vice versa.

This analysis is written from the perspective of a concerned Evangelical
Protestant with many years of involvement in programs of evangelization in
Brazil as well as in other Latin American countries.

## A PROTESTANT FOOTHOLD IN BRAZIL

The arrival of Protestantism in Brazil was, in many respects, similar to its
arrival elsewhere in Latin America. Because of this, my analysis of the Protes-

tant movement in Brazil should be applicable to other contexts in Latin America. Yet there are differences, sufficiently marked to give Brazil a certain uniqueness in Latin American Protestantism.

One characteristic that should be noted is the strong presence of the historical denominations and the relatively unimportant role of the independent faith missions in establishing Protestant Christianity in Brazil. The result has been that in Brazil, more than in most other Latin American nations, Protestant ecclesiastical institutions are very strong and have been relatively influential in national life. Another characteristic that differentiates Brazil from the rest of Latin America is, of course, the kind of Catholic Church that developed there at one time—Jansenist and suspicious of Rome. This meant that early Brazilian Protestants did not find themselves as acrimoniously opposed to or by Catholicism as were Protestants in other Latin lands.

### The First Protestant Colony in the New World

Fifty-two years before the founding of Jamestown, and a little more than a half century after the discovery of Brazil by the Portuguese, French Huguenots established a tenuous foothold on an island in Guanabara Bay, across from what is now the city of Rio de Janeiro. The ill-fated experiment ended in 1560, destroyed by treachery and bloodshed.

Seventy years later the Dutch established a "benign" Protestant theocracy at Olinda, near Recife, on the northeastern "hump" of South America. Despite its religious overtones, the pragmatic goal of this colonial venture was to wrest the profitable African slave monopoly from Portuguese hands. Salvador, to the south, was at that time the largest slave emporium in the Americas. A small Dutch Reformed missionary outreach to the native Amerindian population had barely gotten under way when the colony was retaken by the Portuguese in 1654 (Hoornaert 1979: 137–41). Not until the nineteenth century would Protestant colonists be allowed again to settle in Brazil.

### Protestant Immigrant Colonies in Brazil

Brazil and Spanish America were effectively insulated from Protestantism and other "heresies" for a century and a half by means of royal protectionist policies and the wrack and screw of the Inquisition. However, the politics of power and the mercantilist interests of the nations of northern Europe were soon to make a crack in the solid wall of Portuguese and Spanish American resistance to religious innovation.

*British Mercantilism and Expatriate Anglicanism.* In 1807, when Napoleon invaded Portugal, the royal court fled to Brazil under the protection of the British navy. Britain urgently needed to find new markets to take the place of those it had lost to Napoleon. A commercial treaty signed in 1810 between Prince John and Lord Strangford included a clause that authorized the erection of the first Anglican chapel (in 1819) exclusively for the representatives of

British interests who were residing in Rio. Other chapels were soon built in several of the principal port cities along the Brazilian seaboard (Hahn 1970: 78–84; van der Grijp 1976: 4–5).

Not all British immigrants were happy with the liturgy of the Anglican Book of Common Prayer. Some preferred to worship God in the quiet of their homes as part of small Nonconformist cell groups. They prepared the way for the Congregationalist communities that would be begun by Kalley several decades later (Hahn: 100–101).

*German Colonies and Protestant CEBs.* Napoleon's defeat and banishment opened the gates for the first trickle of immigrants to the New World—persons searching for a new home away from war-ravaged Europe. A royal decree in 1808 offered free land and initial subsidies to acceptable immigrants to Portuguese lands in South America. Acting on it, the first group of German and Swiss-German Lutherans arrived in Brazil. The constitution of 1824 guaranteed freedom of worship for all inhabitants of Brazil. Later, representatives of Dom Pedro I scoured Europe looking for immigrants and encouraging them to bring their pastors, with promises of royal subsidies for their upkeep.

The same year the first German colony was established in Friburgo in southern Brazil and a Lutheran church was organized. Over the following decades new German colonies were founded in the southern and southeastern regions of Brazil. The worship of these Lutheran communities was rudimentary, reflecting both the trials of a wild frontier and the low spiritual ebb of Lutheranism in the homeland. A shortage of pastors encouraged the ministry of lay pastors, a practice that had no precedent in German Lutheranism, except in the Pietist movement Hahn: 102, 11; van der Grijp 1976: 5–7; Altmann 1980: 1). The practice may, however, have provided a precedent for future Lutheran CEBs.[154]

In time, many German immigrants in southern Brazil prospered, transforming their rude colonies into small replicas of their ancestral lands. But in recent decades the developmentalist model of the so-called economic miracle of Brazil has induced stresses that began to radically alter the social fabric of the German colonies in Brazil. This fact has presented new challenges to the *Igreja Evangélica de Confissão Luterana no Brasil,* the unified body that in 1949 brought together the Brazilian expressions of the various German territorial churches (van der Grijp: 49–50).

Except for a minority that has managed to make the adjustment and maintain a prosperous middle-class style of life, most Brazilians of German descent are presently unable to meet the increasing demands of mechanized agriculture and complex financing systems, or to make the change from monocultural subsistence agriculture to the varied demands of the export market. Consequently, many Brazilians of German descent have been forced to follow one of three roads: sell their small holdings to owners of large landholdings and (1) join the ranks of the rural working class, or (2) move to the large cities to become part of the urban work force, or (3) migrate to recently opened areas of colonization in the interior of Brazil.

This context "has been propitious for the gradual awakening of social consciousness and for the beginning of grassroots community experiences" among Lutherans. The experiences have taken a variety of forms: (1) defense of dispossessed small landholders near the giant Itaupú (Paraná) hydroelectric dam; (2) interconfessional (Catholic, Pentecostal, and Lutheran) CEBs and a community center in a working-class suburb of Porto Alegre, the seat of Brazilian Lutheranism; and (3) CEB projects, guided by seminarians, on the outskirts of São Leopoldo, which minister to the displaced original residents of a one-time large *fazenda,* now an industrial park, and to a group of more recent immigrant workers.

Another grassroots Lutheran project is a "pastoral ministry for Indians" in the new state of Rondônia near the northern border of Bolivia. But instead of founding CEBs, a missionary couple has made every effort to integrate completely into the existing Amerindian community. Eschewing the Wycliffe method of language study, they have learned the local dialect in the give-and-take of everyday tribal life.

In an ecumenical experiment, two students left the seminary and joined forces with a Catholic priest to serve a number of CEBs in the distant interior of Brazil (Altmann 1980: 4–7).

The most unique Lutheran experience deserves special mention. A colony of German immigrants settled many years ago in the isolated tropical valleys of the present seaboard state of Espirito Santo. They managed to eke out a peasant existence while hanging on to their ancestral customs and dialect (Pomeranian), though without the benefit of the official ministrations of the Lutheran faith. They were "discovered" by fellow Lutherans in the twentieth century who began to minister to them in the traditional way.[155] More recently, the German peasants of Espirito Santo have become the focus of a Lutheran CEB pastoral ministry (Altmann: 2–3; IECL 1980: passim).

The history of the Swiss-German colonies was slightly different. Although they came from the same kind of religious background as their German counterparts, a number of the Swiss pastors seemed to have been influenced by the Pietistic awakening in Europe (Hahn: 124). Even today a small number of Lutherans evidence Pietistic concerns that are akin to those of their evangelical brethren in other Protestant denominations. Unfortunately, it is not always easy to find in Brazilian Lutheranism instances of creative interaction of the Reformation concerns for personal regeneration and for community-based social involvement.

## THE PROTESTANT RETREAT: FROM BASE COMMUNITY TO PROSPEROUS ESTABLISHMENT

The extraordinary geographic expansion and material growth of the Protestant churches began with the avowed intention of accomplishing a "Brazilian reformation" of the Catholic Church. This ambition, in the heyday of Jansenism, was never realized, although the support that the Reformation message had in the beginning from representatives of the Brazilian elite paralleled the princely support during the Magisterial Reformation (Léonard 1963: 71, 89-90, 99).

The Reformation in Europe failed to fulfill all its tremendous promise. It shied away from the full implications of the doctrine of the priesthood of all believers, and from its grassroots community manifestations. Enter the Radical Reformation. Similarly, the Protestant mission in Brazil should be assessed in terms not only of its notable triumphs, but also its failures, not the least of which was its gradual retreat from the relative simplicity of its early witness, and its virtual ignorance of an even earlier history in which the counterparts of the CEBs of today played an important part.

We recognize the enormous contributions of the Protestant churches to the life of the Brazilian nation (including, probably, the inspiration for certain inputs in the Catholic CEBs), and thank God for the zeal of many in giving evangelical witness where for centuries the living Christ was all but unknown. But the Savior that was proclaimed in Brazil and in Spanish America by Protestants down through the years was not in every case the suffering servant of Scripture. For this reason, the analysis of this chapter will take a different tack. It will attempt to trace in certain key church bodies in Brazil the same downward trend we were able to detect when we studied the origins of the Protestant movement in the previous chapter. This retreat from simple— though not always "grassroots"—beginnings to the "successful" and respected institutions they are today, I believe, is deflecting Brazilian evangelicalism from a holistic gospel witness and is contributing to a slowing down of its vaunted numerical growth. As we shall see, the roots of this "retreat" can be found in the early history of each church, not excepting the historical forces that were at work at that time in the lands of their origin.

Though the context was different in almost every way, the founders of Brazilian Evangelical Protestantism nearly unanimously made the same fatal choice that Luther, Zwingli, and Calvin made in their respective worlds. In both cases it was a political choice, having to do with the use of power in the service of the church. They sought the support of earthly powers even as they proceeded with the important task of witnessing to the transforming power of Jesus Christ (Verduin 1964: 36ff., 63ff.). Brazilian Protestantism, of course, never became a territorial church and has never consciously desired to supplant Catholicism as the state church—except, perhaps, in its early dream of a "Brazilian reformation." The Brazilian counterpart, however, was a consciously sought-after upward mobility that, spurred on by the Puritan work ethic, forgot the subordinated classes it sprang from.

Many things have changed in the religious world of contemporary Brazil. The same Catholic Church that was once part and parcel of the power of the state has lately become a thorn in its flesh. Protestants, though rarely persecuted with any degree of violence, were nonetheless always outsiders, second-class citizens at best. Paradoxically, they were suspicious of the state while attempting to win adherents within the state bureaucracy. Today, Protestants are courted by the state; some of their number wield some authority within the state and, until recently at least, gave their almost overwhelming support to the state.

These facts should be kept in mind as we consider the ways in which the *ideology* that the first Protestant missionaries brought to Brazil, *interacting with* the natural forces of the *institutionalization process* in a particular socio-economic milieu, brought the principal churches in Brazil to the point where they are at present.

## Igreja Metodista

*The North American Connection in Brazilian Methodism.* English Methodism was characterized by a vigorous opposition to the institution of slavery. The "General Rules" written by John Wesley in 1743 included a prohibition against "the buying and selling of the bodies and souls of men, women, and children, with an intention to enslave them." Wesley taught that the slave traffic was the greatest of all evils because it was "the spring that puts all the rest into motion." Just a few days before his death, he wrote to encourage Wilberforce: "Go on, in the name of God, and in the power of his might, till even American slavery (the vilest that ever saw the sun) shall vanish away before it" (Dayton 1976: 73-74).

Timothy L. Smith, historian of nineteenth-century North American evangelicalism, says, "evidence has multiplied that holiness preaching was an important catalyst to Methodist participation in movements for social justice from Francis Asbury's time onward." But he adds:

Methodists tended to link that holiness doctrine as much with loyalty to a credal past as with concern for a revolutionary future. Some of them preached and wrote about Christian holiness without any reference at all to the social crisis of the 1830s, the Abolitionist movement, and the impending Civil War for which their message was newly relevant [Smith 1977: 7, 10].

Perhaps it was a lack of contextualized theological reflection that caused American Methodists to retreat so soon from this fundamental conviction of Wesleyanism. Donald Dayton reminds us:

The 1784 founding conference of the Methodist Espicopal church had called for the expulsion of any member engaging in the slave trade, but with the growth of Methodism into the largest American denomination, this stance was gradually abandoned. When faced with the alternative of growth into a national church or maintaining discipline on the slavery issue, Methodism chose growth and prosperity. By the 1820s the Methodists had largely accommodated to the institution of slavery, maintaining a most nominal disapproval preserved in the *Discipline* [1976: 74].

Slavery was a prime issue in the secession of the abolitionist Wesleyan Methodists (the early founders of Wheaton College) and of the proslavery Southern Methodist Episcopal Church, both in 1845 (Dayton: 73–84). It was while these issues were still boiling that the Methodist Church embarked upon a missionary venture in Brazil.

*Methodist Beginnings in Brazil.* The modern era of Protestant evangelization in Brazil began in the mid-nineteenth century with the journeys of the American Methodist colporteur, Daniel P. Kidder. He was not, however, the first North American missionary to step on Brazilian soil.

In 1828, the General Conference of the Methodist Episcopal Church U.S.A. recommended that research be undertaken concerning the advisability of initiating a mission in South America. In 1835, Fountain E. Pitts was commissioned to visit several South American cities. He preached in Rio, where he began small Methodist societies for the English-speaking community, before returning home the following year. Encouraged by Pitt's reports, the Methodist Church lost no time in commissioning Justin R. Spaulding and, shortly thereafter, Daniel P. Kidder. By mid-1836, a Sunday school and a daily school were operating at the imperial court. It included a few noble Brazilians and a handful of slaves.

The peripatetic Kidder's untiring efforts in the distribution of the Scriptures in Portuguese won him the approval of the civil and religious authorities, who at that time were strongly sympathetic to Jansenism (van der Grijp: 7–8; Léonard: 28–45; Hahn: 345–50; Reily 1982: 4.3.1 to 4.3.3). Not everybody was happy with the missionaries' work, however. In 1838, a priest wrote an anti-Methodist treatise in which he hinted darkly that Spaulding's literacy classes for blacks might be some kind of a revolutionary plot (van der Grijp: 8).

Another facet of the Methodist mission was directed at the colony of disgruntled Confederates who, after the Civil War, had emigrated to Brazil where slavery was still permitted (Reily 1980: 103–4). Nonetheless, the greater part of the Methodist endeavor was bent upon witnessing to native Brazilians.

Loyal to their Wesleyan heritage, Methodists, more than any other group that came to Brazil, were conscious of their responsibility to *the poor and disenfranchised.* After Spaulding's early experiments in literacy classes for blacks, Methodists did not, in fact, initiate any work among slaves. But Duncan Reily observes:

Though there may not have been any Methodist work among slaves, and after emancipation, no specific work directed to blacks, there is evidence of a significant number of blacks in the Methodist congregations, which suggests a close relationship between color and poverty [1980: 105–6].

Though from time to time a wealthy landowner would embrace the Evangelical faith, on the whole, Methodist congregations consisted of working-class persons who worshiped in very humble surroundings (Reily 1980: 106–7). This situation could not, of course, continue indefinitely.

When Methodists little by little became interested in winning the upper classes, they found that their emphasis upon "protracted meetings" as an evangelistic strategy no longer worked for them. Increasingly, Methodists turned to education as a method of witness. Today, a relatively large number of prestigious secondary schools and universities bear the Methodist label.

Sunday schools also came into prominence as an evangelistic tool. Gradually, the number of Methodist children who were converted was larger than the influx of Catholic children. Reily examines statistics from the years 1890 to 1930 and concludes:

Until more or less 1920, "direct" evangelism (with "protracted meetings," personal evangelism, etc.) was what produced the most growth, but between 1920 and 1930, growth became more internal (from the influx of the children of members) and from Sunday school [1980: 108–12; see also van der Grijp: 25–26, 40–42].

Early Methodism placed a great emphasis on *lay leadership*. Reily observes:

[Methodists] have a curious mixture of clericalism and laicism in their paunch, which they inherited from Wesley and North American Methodism. The *Ecclesiolae in ecclesia* at the local level were directed by the laity, and their preaching was permitted. But if there was lay leadership at the local level . . . the conferences, where policy, doctrine, and the great administrative questions were determined, were totally in the hands of bishops and itinerant preachers [1980: 113].

*Factors in the Decline of Methodism in Brazil.* The significance of all this, of course, is that with the gradual demise of social classes in Methodism—which had already begun to disappear by the time Methodist missionaries came to Brazil—*the laity became less and less an important factor in the Methodist church*. Despite its "believers' church" roots, Methodism was in fact moving toward what the Catholic Church would at a later date begin to move *away from*: a church that, for all practical purposes, was concentrated in the clergy.

In the meantime, as Methodism strove for its place in the sun, devoting larger and larger portions of its budget to institutions of higher education as part of a strategy of evangelization, *it lost not only its spiritual vitality, but contact with its grassroots origins*. Indeed, both losses may be two sides of the same coin!

A third factor, implicit in what was just stated, is *the creeping loss of community in Methodism,* an inverse course to what Reily calls its "search for maturity." My contention is that it is to these three factors and not necessarily to any change in "evangelistic strategy" that the poor showing of the *Igreja Metodista* in church growth charts can be attributed (see Table 9; see also Read, Monterroso, and Johnson 1970: 48).

## Table 9

## Comparative Statistics of Seven Brazilian Protestant Churches, 1960-70

### (adapted from Read and Ineson 1973: 77-78, 80)

| CHURCH | 1960 MEMBER-SHIP | % BRAZIL TOTAL | 1970 MEMBER-SHIP | % BRAZIL TOTAL | AVERAGE ANNUAL GROWTH DURING DECADE |
|---|---|---|---|---|---|
| 1. *Congregação Cristã* | 178,250 | 11.7 | 357,800 | 13.6 | 7.2 |
| 2. *Assembleia de Deus* | 376,800 | 24.6 | 746,400 | 28.5 | 7.1 |
| 3. *Convenção Batista* | 186,900 | 12.2 | 330,500 | 12.6 | 5.9 |
| 4. *Ig. Evangélica Congregacional* | 26,200 | 1.7 | 46,100 | 1.8 | 5.8 |
| 5. *Ig. Evangélica de Confissão Luterana* | 366,150* | 24.0 | 433,000 | 16.4 | 1.7 |
| 6. *Ig. Presbiteriana do Brasil* | 210,900 | 13.8 | 244,050 | 9.5 | 1.5 |
| 7. *Ig. Metodista* | 55,850 | 3.7 | 62,500 | 2.4 | 1.1 |

* Includes baptized infants

Numerical growth, of course, is not the only index of ecclesial vitality, just as height or girth is not a necessary concomitant of health in humans (though the opposite—stunted growth and an emaciated physique—should alert one to the probability of fundamental illness in the body!). The *Igreja Metodista* seems to be following somewhat the same course that its British and North American ancestors tracked in an earlier period, with variants caused by historical forces and by *Metodista* dependence on influences from outside Brazil. Evangelism has decreased, and with it a basic community lifestyle. But social and ecumenical concerns have increased, at least at the official level.

Certain sectors of Methodism in Brazil, as elsewhere, have opened themselves to the refreshing breezes of charismatic renewal. But it has been accompanied by a turning inward and a shunning of urgent problems in the very communities where these churches are located.

More recently, the Methodist Church in the large urban centers of Brazil, and particularly in its theological institutions, has "discovered" the Catholic CEBs (Leite 1981: passim). Methodist seminarians are working as apprentices with Catholic CEB guides in the working-class suburbs and *favelas* of São Paulo and Rio. The problem, of course, in the words of a Catholic theologian, is that these kinds of concerns "were parachuted into the Methodist Church by Catholic liberation theology." They have not risen out of the lived experience of the *Igreja Metodista* as a church of the poor.[156]

The lack of theological coherence and depth in the theology of the *Igreja Metodista* has exposed it to the inroads of "foreign" ideologies, which it has ingested but not digested. In consequence, Brazilian Methodism is at present a congeries of liberal, fundamentalist, introverted, socially concerned, traditional, and neo-Pentecostal beliefs, all fermenting in the same pot. The root of this acute problem, I believe, is the almost total absence of the kind of grassroots community theologizing that, after allowances have been made for historical factors, was the driving force of Methodism during the life span of Wesley. One gets the impression that the CEBs are all right as a strategy to win the poor and to fulfill one's Christian duty toward them. But they are not permissible as a means of renewing the church!

Ironically, the Methodist leadership in Brazil today seems to fear the same basic community structure that gave it life. This may be because *Metodista* leaders remember their history too well! What happened when grassroots communities began to proliferate within a sterile Anglican church could well repeat itself today, as the numerous Pentecostal schisms within Brazilian Methodism testify.[157]

### Igreja Evangélica Congregacional Cristã do Brasil

Scottish immigrants, involved in the mercantile ventures of the British empire, settled in the commercial centers of Brazil, but not in ethnic colonies, as did the German and Swiss Protestants. As we have noted earlier, they brought with them the ecclesial lifestyle and liturgical practices of their native land, including Congregationalism. By this time, the persecuted conventicles of "the revolution of the saints" had given way to the prosperity of the hard-working Calvinist Congregationalists.

*The Beginnings of Congregationalism in Brazil.* Robert Reid Kalley, a colorful Scottish doctor, arrived in Rio in 1855 with a group of persecuted Madeiran Portuguese Protestants (Hahn: 176–211). To Kalley and the Scottish Congregationalists belongs the honor of having founded the first Portuguese-speaking Protestant church on Brazilian soil. Today, the staid *Igreja Fluminense* continues to meet in an imposing old building in the heart of Rio.

Among the first full adherents of this congregation were two imperial courtiers (Léonard: 49–54; Reily Documents 1981a: 3.3). Indeed, one notable characteristic of early Brazilian Protestantism is the relatively large number of adherents it attracted from the aristocracy and from the landholding classes. Léonard, the French historian of the early Protestant period in Brazil, comments:

> The adhesion to Protestantism of a relatively large number of members of the Brazilian aristocracy, during the last thirty years of the 19th century, is such a surprising happening, at first glance, that it deserves to be studied in detail . . . . Brazilian Protestantism found in these aristocrats . . . the same kind of support and example that the manorial families who became converts of the Reformation had given to Europe in the 16th century. Their fortunes . . . were fundamentally rural in origin . . . . The names of *fazendeiros* are numerous when we study the origin of the Protestant churches of Brazil; and it can be stated that the majority of these communities were born on the very *fazendas* [1963: 95, 99 and 125–354 passim].

Dr. Kalley, a layman, "had helped to institute a pattern of lay preaching in the molds of *family worship*—a pattern that was spreading over the vast hinterland and being effectively used for the evangelization of the nation." The style of worship was dour, its basic content the study of Scripture. The singing tended to be slow and "unspirited, reflecting the struggles of 'Pilgrims' through a very difficult land beset with temptations, and persecutions, yet with a duty to share [their] faith with the pagans around [them]" (Hahn: 211).[158]

But Hahn adds that what the first Brazilian congregation "lacked in love, joy, and devotion, it made up in courage, heroism, and disciplined faithfulness." This discipline was eventually to make Brazilian Protestantism "one of the most 'rapidly growing Evangelical churches' in all mission lands" (1970: 211).

Yet because Congregational churches were founded in widely separated regions of Brazil, the *Igreja Evangélica Congregacional* has remained small by Brazilian standards (see Table 9). It was never able to form a lasting fellowship of congregations (Read and Ineson 1973: 25). Nonetheless, Congregationalism has had a lasting influence on church life in Brazil. As historian Hahn observes:

The churches established by Dr. Kalley took the name Congregational. They were Calvinistic and Presbyterian in local government and doctrine, but the sovereignty of each local church was retained. In liturgy they had begun with the simple service Kalley had defended as "family worship" which later . . . assumed the Baptist mold without any Book of Church Order. This became, and still is, the dominant pattern of Evangelical worship throughout Brazil [1970: 443].

*The Pros and Cons of Congregationalist "Base Community."* At the heart of Congregationalist policy, as we have seen in chapter 10, is the local congregation or community of those who have made a voluntary commitment to Jesus Christ. Unlike its sister Presbyterianism, Congregationalism knows no other form of the church. In this sense—as small local cells of believers—the Congregational (and Anabaptist) churches in Brazil can be called *basic* ecclesial communities. This understanding of the church would become the norm for Brazilian Evangelicalism no matter what the church polity (Hahn: 443). And it was precisely this dimension of Protestantism that inspired one of the earliest experiments in Catholic CEBs in northeastern Brazil (IRM 271: 273; Concilium 104: 30-31).

But if, for the sake of consistency, we sharpen our definition of "basic," if we define the term as we have used it in reference to the Catholic base communities, we are forced to admit that there are few evidences of grassroots ecclesiality in Congregationalism. In its origin it was upper-class, and in its present aspirations it is middle-class.

This is not to say that communities of Congregationalists do not exist at the grass roots. I myself have worshiped on more than one occasion in a rustic chapel on the prairies of central Brazil with peasants and missionaries who had adopted a quasi-peasant lifestyle. But this kind of Protestant church, though probably quite numerous in the interior of Brazil, even in mainline denominations, does not lay down the ecclesial norm in Brazil. The orientation of these *congregações* comes from and moves toward middle-class ecclesiality. The point of this entire study of the CEBs is that quite the opposite is becoming the case in an influential sector of the Brazilian Catholic Church.

### Igreja Presbiteriana do Brasil (IPB)

*The North American Heritage of Brazilian Presbyterianism.* The mainstream Protestantism that came to Latin America cannot be understood apart from its North American socio-cultural origins. As Emilio Willems observes, the attempts of North American missionaries "were, to a large extent, continuous with the evangelization of the American frontier. Indeed, the early South American missions may be conceived of as an extension of the frontier" (1967: 10).

The missionaries who brought the gospel to Brazil were influenced by American civil religion, voluntarism, denominationalism, and the so-called Methodist era. The latter was characterized by Franciscanlike circuit riders, class meetings, Sunday schools, and camp meetings. This supercharged religiosity, for all its notable accomplishments, was theologically impoverished— that is, reductionist, with a paucity of reflection on the crucial issues that had wrenched the nation for more than a generation. Of crucial concern to Christians was the slavery issue, which in the end polarized the gospel into evangelism and social concern. The fact that the majority of the early missionaries came from the American south, and that several of the Old School Presbyterians in the north had southern sympathies, is not without significance for the kind of ideology that would inform the infant Protestantism that was beginning to develop in Brazil (Reily 1982: 6–15).

*Charles Finney vs. "Old School" Calvinism—a Necessary Excursus.* None of the historians whom I have read has commented on the historical coincidence between the "great reversal" in North American Evangelical theology that took place immediately after the Civil War and the arrival of the first missionaries in Brazil. Evangelicals today overlook the fact that the greatest evangelist of the pre–Civil War period, Charles G. Finney, was also an outspoken social activist. In the unexpurgated version of his *Lectures on Revivals of Religion,* Finney argues that "revivals are hindered when ministers and churches take wrong ground in regard to any question involving human rights."[159] Finney insisted, in effect, that "the spiritual vitality of the church is sapped, not by her involvement in social questions, but rather by her failure to embrace reform" (Dayton 1976: 15–19; see Smith 1977: 10).

Finney was radically opposed to the "Old School Calvinism" championed by Charles Hodge of Princeton Seminary. The Presbyterian missionaries who went out to Brazil were products of the Old School. Finney denounced Hodge's position because he believed it supported and gave divine endorsement to slavery and other sinful institutions. Dayton shows convincingly that the Princeton doctrine of sin and grace "came perilously close to making the sinful state a normative one." In contrast, Finney emphasized the doctrine of redemption and exalted the power of God's grace to transform sinful persons and social structures. In a significant passage, Dayton writes:

> Finney's emphasis on redemption provided that utopian edge necessary for a theology to support major social change. The importance of this theologically grounded utopianism has again become clear in recent discussions between the South American theologies of liberation and the school of Christian Realism that has dominated much recent American theology . . . . By analogy, Hodge was in his time a very conservative "Christian Realist" whose theology served as an "ideology of the establishment." Though accused of perfectionism by the Princeton theologians, Finney and his followers found in the doctrine of redemption the utopian vision that enabled them to press toward a society free of slavery and the subordination of women [1976: 131–32; see Smith: 11–13].

After the Civil War, Christian Realism and "a common tendency toward a pessimistic worldview" as reflected in the premillennialist prophecy conference movement coalesced into modern fundamentalism (Dayton: 132–34). Social concern and evangelism went their separate ways. Fundamentalism was the emerging ideology out of which the first Presbyterian missionaries came to Brazil in the second half of the nineteenth century.

*The Beginnings of Presbyterianism in Brazil.* The first Presbyterian missionary, Ashbel Green Simonton, arrived in Rio in 1859. He was joined the following year by Alexander Blackford, his brother-in-law. During the eight years before Simonton's death he "left behind an impressive series of accomplishments" as a pioneer in personal evangelism, local church planting, Christian journalism, leadership development, and theological education. Simonton was an intellectual trained in "Old School" Presbyterianism, whereas Blackford came from Ohio frontier stock. "He demonstrated the rural, frontier spirit which would be typical of most of his future colleagues" (Pierson 1974: 19–20; see Hahn: 212ff.).

As Professor Hahn sums it up:

The early Presbyterian missionaries brought the traditions of the West with its camp meetings, evangelism, and intellectual freedom of outlook. They inherited Kalley's emphasis of *worship in the home of each believer, shared with the entire household, and with the neighbors* —a system which easily adapted itself to the natural capacity of the people of the Brazilian hinterland and to the environment [Hahn: 444, emphasis added].

After the schism in U.S. Presbyterianism occasioned by the Civil War, southern Presbyterians began, in 1861, to send their own missionaries to Brazil. The first thrust of this sending was motivated in part by the spiritual needs of the ex-Confederate colony that had settled in Santa Barbara. When they began to work with Brazilians, the emphasis of this new group of missionaries from the beginning was on the education of the children of the elite (Pierson 1974: 26). In contrast, documents of the period show that northern Presbyterian congregations were being established among illiterate peasants. The speed with which the peasants learned Scripture and their simple eloquence when witnessing amazed the missionaries—an indication, perhaps, of their paternalistic attitude toward folk culture. Professor Reily also documents the involvement of some of the northern Presbyterian missionaries in behalf of the abolitionist movement (Reily 1982: 4.5.3.1, 4.5.3.2, and 5.8).

Meanwhile, Blackford was focusing his tremendous energies on evangelism and church planting in the interior of São Paulo state. His most outstanding convert was Father José Manoel da Conceição who, after years of attempting unsuccessfully to reform his several parishes from within, would eventually become the first Brazilian Protestant minister. Conceição's tireless itineration and winsome speech brought many to the Protestant faith. Unfortunately, Conceição lacked the patience to remain long enough in one place to make disciples of his converts and to establish them firmly into new congregations (Léonard: 56–67; Pierson: 19–21; Hahn: 256–69).

Presbyterian historian Paul E. Pierson likens Conceição to a "modern St. Francis" who lived simply, "often giving away money or the gifts that he received, healing the sick with home remedies, and communicating the gospel through preaching, conversation, and life." Unfortunately he was hindered from imparting a Brazilian quality to the *Igreja Presbiteriana* because of his restless spirit, policy disagreements with his missionary colleagues, and his premature death. Instead the IPB has remained strongly marked by the individualistic and moralistic ethos of the North American frontier (1974: 21).

Pierson singles out *four personal traits in Conceição* that, if there had been the opportunity to share them through thoughtful dialogue with his missionary and national colleagues, might have helped avoid the "more formal and rationalistic Protestant orthodoxy" that came to characterize Brazilian Presbyterianism in all its later manifestations. (1) Conceição did not entertain the harsh polemical attitude toward Catholicism that was characteristic of his North American counterparts and their converts. He freely recognized his spiritual debt to his mother church. (2) He had an unusual spirit of understanding vis-à-vis the popular religiosity of his fellow Brazilians. He was sensitive to the danger of destroying the worthy elements in their beliefs when bringing them to a true faith in Christ. His prayer is a classic:

Oh my God, I will respect the religion of the ignorant, the faith of those who had few opportunities of knowing and worshipping Thee in a worthy way. I will never allow myself to be dominated by vanity and presumption in such a way that I might shatter the pious faith of others by inconsiderate words and actions [1974: 22].

(3) Conceição's christocentric piety echoed that of the medieval Catholic mystics, yet (4) his faith was neither passive nor quietistic. His concern for the ethical implications of the gospel transcended both traditional Catholic "good works" and the largely individualistic ethics in North American Protestant morality. It is unfortunate, says Pierson, that this kind of Christian faith, which had in it elements of the best Iberian Catholicism mediated by a latter-day Jansenism, was not translated into living communities in Brazil (Pierson: 28–31). Conceição's one great fault was his activism, which left him no time for reflection or for life in community.

*The Liturgy of the Early Presbyterian Churches in Brazil.* There is a clue here to the dynamics at work in these communities. On the one hand, the liturgy was as unstructured as it had been on the U.S. frontier, prior to the acceptance of the Book of Common Order. On the other hand, says Hahn, Presbyterian services were sterile and lacking in a truly communitarian spirit. This seems to have reflected the state of affairs in North American Presbyterian churches at that time, if we are to believe the criticism of Professor Charles Shields of Princeton Seminary. The following observation was written not long after Simonton and Blackford had departed for Brazil:

With all our boasted Protestantism, we have in the heart of our communion the essence of the Roman ritual, a *"vicarious service,"* of which the people are but auditors, and in which, sometimes, they can no more individually participate than if priests and choir were praying and singing for them in a separate performance [Hahn: 236-37].

Over the years the IPB continued to grow and to extend itself along the Atlantic seaboard and into the hinterlands, albeit slowly. This *lack of growth* in comparison with Baptists and Pentecostals (see Table 9; Read and Ineson: 19), who arrived later on the scene, Pierson attributes to "a more rigid, centralized structure."[160] Newly organized groups were usually maintained "in the dependent status of unorganized *congregações* longer than the Baptists, who established autonomous churches with smaller constituencies" (Pierson: 124).[161] This practice also contrasts sharply with the large measure of autonomy the Catholic CEBs enjoy in a number of dioceses in Brazil.

*Control Maintained through the Educational System.* This hierarchical approach persists today. It is a mentality similar in some respects to that of traditional Catholicism, but strikingly different from what obtains in the grassroots congregations of contemporary Brazilian Catholicism. Pierson points out that one result of the Presbyterian policy of "sharply limiting the number of pastors and elevating those who completed seminary into the middle class" was to restrict numerical growth.

Another fruit of this policy was the isolation of urban pastors "—culturally, economically, and spatially—from the poor":

There were no Presbyterian pastors who were also shoemakers or industrial workers, living in the poorest sections of the cities among those who had recently arrived from the North or the hinterland. Yet Baptist and Pentecostal preachers were living and working among them. And it was usually in that stratum, the largest segment of Brazil's population, that Protestantism grew most rapidly. Even though Presbyterian ministers delivered a message with better theological content because of their seminary training, the uneducated often found it abstract and difficult to understand. The isolation of many pastors from the humble made it difficult to state the message in terms meaningful to the poor [Pierson: 125].

Upward social mobility, always present in Protestantism, was more than an "Evangelical predicament," to use the phrase of Presbyterian William Read (1965: 222). It was "a conscious goal" of Brazilian Presbyterianism, as Pierson shows in the following excerpt from an official report submitted in 1925 by a missionary working in Brazil:

If society consists of superimposed strata, then the Evangelical Church in Brazil will not be a vertical section but a funnel, widening as it rises. This is due to two causes: (1) the ignorant classes cannot easily understand the full gospel or study it. . . . (2) Protestants educate their children, hence such families tend to rise gradually higher in the intellectual scale [see Pierson: 125].

To this Pierson replies that by concentrating upon the 15 percent of the population that was literate, Presbyterian policy effectively condemned itself to perpetual stagnation (ibid., 125–26). Elsewhere he asks:

Why [did] the missionaries . . . not attempt to discover a pattern of ministry and preparation capable of meeting the urgent need for workers which at the same time could have laid a foundation for serious theological study in Brazil? Could the tradition of lay piety and leadership in Brazilian Catholicism, combined with brief intensive courses and some type of apprenticeship, have provided the basis for such a new pattern? [ibid., 25].

The problem with the Presbyterian approach to ministerial training became more acute in the impoverished northeast and the far western frontier. The wealthier churches of the south and southeast drained away the promising leadership from the regions where it was most needed.

Acre, tucked into a remote corner between Peru and Bolivia in the Amazon basin, is a territory of recent colonization. Today there is a thriving Catholic pastoral ministry there with numerous CEBs serving the needs of Amerindians and *camponeses* who are being crushed under the steamroller of "land development" (Betto 1977: passim). Pierson observes that Presbyterians were the first Evangelicals on the scene in Acre. "But their traditional insistence on a well-trained ministry made it impossible to place a pastor there for any length of time and led to disappearance of the work by 1960." By that time, Pierson shows, the Pentecostal *Assembleias de Deus* had five churches in the territory with an approximate membership of two thousand, and the Baptists four with 621 members (1974: 133).

In 1903, after a decade of animosity over the issue of the Brazilian identity and control of the church, the IPB suffered a debilitating schism out of which was born the *Igreja Presbyteriana Independente* (IPI). Ironically, as Pierson points out, "the nationalism of the new *Independente* church was limited to ecclesiastical independence from the missions. Never did it involve theology or the relationship of faith to the Brazilian culture." Not long afterward, with the Brazil Plan of 1917, control of the IPB was turned over to national leadership (1974: 39; van der Grijp: 23–24).

During the decade of the 1960s both Presbyterian denominations—as well as Methodists, Congregationalists, and Baptists—were rent by divisions over the issue of "charismatic gifts." But the fundamental problem was the institutionalization of the life of the church. The "renewal" churches have not, however, been able to overcome the basic causes of this institutionalization.

Another issue was the IPB relationship to social issues. Theologian Zwinglio

Dias observes that "the identity of Brazilian Protestantism was built and historically consolidated in opposition to Catholic identity. This has profoundly influenced the Protestant communities no matter what their denominational color" (Dias 1982: 9). That this is precisely what has happened to the IPB is borne out by Pierson's research. The virulent anti-Catholicism of conservative Presbyterians and the social activism of their more liberal members were caused by their *respective reactions to two streams in Catholicism.*

The Catholic nationalist movement and a resurgence of Catholic clericalism, centering around the Centro Dom Vital (see chap 2, above), from the last quarter of the nineteenth century until the 1930s, had two effects upon the Presbyterian Church: "It gave impetus to development of a social and political ethic, *mainly as a defensive measure.*" Paradoxically, it also brought about among Presbyterians *"a more introverted and defensive stance"* (Pierson: 148, emphasis added; Hahn: 328). From the other side, it should be noted that Catholic opposition to Protestantism, although ostensibly theological, probably had strong ideological and political motivations as well, encouraged at the beginning by the Protestant friendship with the anticlerical emperor and his court.

The threat of a revitalized Catholic clericalism served to unite a heretofore divided Protestantism and sparked a new interest in politics and social change. But Pierson warns, "The newly awakened interest in politics was primarily a reaction to Roman Catholic clericalism. With a few exceptions it did not reflect a serious attempt to understand the role of the church in society."

Therefore, when the church and the state reached a modus vivendi during the Vargas regime, "Presbyterians again moved to an introverted position, their political viewpoints on most issues determined more by local and personal factors than by theological principles" (Pierson: 150–51). In the 1960s, as the IPB adopted ultraconservative positions, local congregations and entire presbyteries seceded or were expelled over issues of theology and polity. The majority of these churches became part of the *Federação Evangélica Nacional de Igrejas Presbiterianas* (FENIP) which has recently organized as the *Igreja Presbiteriana Unida* (IPU). Others have joined the IPI, which began to back away from its earlier ultraconservative isolationism.

In general, Presbyterian and Protestant suspicions of the Catholic Church have made it difficult for Evangelicals to respond in a positive way to changing attitudes in Brazilian Catholicism (Pierson: 148). In consequence, the several Presbyterian churches and their sister Evangelical denominations have become increasingly isolated and stagnant; they are in dire need of a renewal affecting every aspect of church theology and practice (Pierson: 175–241; van der Grijp: 39–40). Renewal can come to Presbyterianism—and to Protestantism as a whole—only as the leadership and the rank and file of the churches of Latin America open themselves to a Spirit-directed dialogue with Scripture, in concert with their rich tradition and culture, and in an attitude of openness to Brazilian society at large, of which, until now, they have been largely an aberrant subculture.

## *Convenção Batista Brasileira* (CBB)

The largest Evangelical, non-Pentecostal church in Brazil (see Table 9) was a relative latecomer to the missionary scene. After the U.S. southern defeat in the Civil War, Baptists did not come to Brazil with the same kind of "manifest destiny" that impelled their northern co-religionists. But this did not hinder them from engaging in aggressive evangelism.

*Baptist Roots in the U.S. South.* The first Baptists to come to Brazil were searching for a land with features similar to their own, in which to perpetuate the slavist plantation economy that had supported the U.S. south for over a century and a half. An English-language Baptist church was organized on the good red soil of Santa Barbara do Oeste by members of the same group of Confederate immigrants whom we have met previously in Methodist and Presbyterian circles (Crabtree 1953: 1–55).

*Early Baptist Congregations in Brazil.* Southern Baptist missions in Brazil began in 1881 when two young Texans, William B. Bagby and Zacharias C. Taylor, took charge of an English-speaking congregation in Santa Barbara. Aided by an ex-priest, they then founded the Brazilian Baptist Church in the old colonial capital of Salvador da Bahia far to the northeast (Crabtree: 39). Within two years of their arrival in Brazil, Bagby and Taylor had established six preaching points in the surrounding region.

By 1885, three new churches were founded in Rio de Janeiro and in Maceió, in the small northeastern state of Alagoas. Rio—the present center of the wealthy and prestigious CBB (which was established with eighty-five churches and five thousand members in 1907)—was the Baptists' hardest nut to crack. After seven months of steady evangelism, their first "convert" was a member of one of the four Protestant confessions previously located in Rio (van der Grijp: 17–18; Crabtree: 40–55).

The first church in the city of São Paulo—the second large center of Baptist work—was founded in 1899, taking advantage of the fact that an English-language congregation had met there briefly beginning in 1881. By 1907 there were ten churches with a total of three-hundred members in São Paulo state (Crabtree: 114–18). Indeed, as van de Grijp observes, the most obvious fact in the history of Brazilian Baptists is "their desire to *occupy,* as soon as possible, every state in the national territory, and their systematic efforts to attain that desire"(1976: 26).

*Christian Education and Theological Training.* From the beginning, Sunday schools and Christian education were emphasized in the local churches. Yet, probably because of their rural origins, Baptists took a long time to enter the halls of academia. When they decided to do so, they wasted little time in catching up with the Presbyterians and Methodists. But all their efforts were directed to the service of local congregations. Eschewing universities even today, they entered the field of primary, secondary, and theological education, principally as an adjunct to their aggressive evangelistic programs (van der Grijp: 27).

Although the Baptists' approach to theology continues to be rigid and dogmatic (van der Grijp: 43), there are signs in recent years of a willingness, among a new generation of Brazilian Baptists, to dialogue with fellow Christians and to learn, in some cases, even from Catholics.

*Baptist Growth.* Inasmuch as the Baptists, to a great degree, measure their success in terms of their numerical growth, it is only right that they should be evaluated, at least in part, by this criterion. There is a manifest concern among Baptist leaders with whom I have talked over what appears to be a slackening of Baptist quantitative growth. According to Baptist figures, their numbers have doubled every decade since their beginning. Although, as van der Grijp states (1976: 42), Brazilian Baptist expansion has never experienced a period of real stagnation, there are indeed signs that growth is tapering off, and indeed may have begun to plateau since 1960.

Although the Read and Ineson study of church growth (1973: 95) gives only five membership totals from 1955 to 1970, making it difficult to compare Baptist growth since 1960 with growth in previous decades, it is possible to derive some hints from the statistics available. Five-year growth for the periods in question was: (1955–60), 23.5 percent; (1960–65), 34.11 percent; (1965–70), 31.86 percent. These figures show that, after a significant increase in growth rate in the early 1960s, as compared with the previous quinquennium, Baptist growth began to taper off slightly, precisely during the period of greatest social change in Brazil.[162]

There are other indicators that all is not well in the Baptist fold. A study in which I participated in 1975, for the CBB Board of Evangelism, dealing with a random sample of the four-hundred churches in the São Paulo Baptist Association, turned up the statistics recorded in Table 10 (Cook 1977b: 3). Although migration factors probably have something to do with the uneven growth that the figures show, I suspect that the fundamental cause may lie elsewhere.[163] The poor in Brazil are concentrated in rural areas and in metropolitan centers. Baptist churches, which are concentrated in population centers of less than 100,000 inhabitants, are barely keeping up with the national population growth. Although the large metropolitan churches are growing several times faster, the same research turned up the information that over a third of the increase was due to transfers from smaller churches in the interior of Brazil (and a similar number transferred out!). Metropolitan Baptist churches are, I suspect, growing only among the steadily shrinking middle-class sector that is their "natural field of gravitation."

Despite their roots in the rural U.S. south, Baptists in Brazil have focused their attention on the cities, where more than two-thirds of the national population now reside. But in the cities, *upward mobility and increasing institutional respectability have,* in effect, *built an insurmountable barrier between most Baptist churches and the masses,* which make up 85 percent of the population of Brazil.

Another element in the loss of Baptist vitality may be the institutionalization of its ecclesial witness—*the loss of basic community in a denomination whose cardinal ecclesial doctrine is the sovereignty of the local congregation.* This is hinted at by the large number of Baptists who leave their churches.[164] The aforementioned survey also turned up the revealing fact that house meetings— once so much a part of early Baptist practice—had fallen into disuse, at least in São Paulo, whereas mass evangelism was on the increase. More significantly, concern for the social need of the wider community was placed at the bottom of a list of priorities by the pastors who were surveyed.

**Table 10**

**COMPARATIVE GROWTH OF FOUR TYPES
OF SÃO PAULO BAPTIST CHURCHES, 1965-75**

|  | Annual growth % | Decadal growth % |
|---|---|---|
| 1. Metropolises (400 thousand inhabitants +) | 5.2 | 66.0 |
| 2. Medium-sized cities (100-400 thousand) | 8.1 | 117.7 |
| 3. Small cities (10-100 thousand) | 2.57 | 28.9 |
| 4. Rural towns (10 thousand and under) | 1.02 | 10.7 |
| Total sample (average) | 5.32 | 67.9 |
| National average | 5.0 | 66.0 |

Thoughtful Baptists have cause to be alarmed. So long as they continue to focus their evangelism upon the shrinking middle class to which they belong, the trend will not be reversed. This is not only a matter of correct strategy; it is a *theological* problem, which should drive Baptists back to the Bible in search of correct priorities. Ultimately, it is an *ideological* problem that hinders Baptists from preaching the "good news to the poor . . . freedom for the prisoners," while they concentrate only in a spiritual sense upon "recovery of sight for the blind" (Luke 10:18). The rationale for this ideology has its roots in the New Hampshire Confession of Faith of 1833, to which the CBB subscribes—even though a good case could be made for civil disobedience on the basis of the same confession. [165] The problem, of course, is that the will of Jesus Christ, on social issues in particular, is always interpreted according to our own ideological criteria. Our ideology can trap us into justifying with biblical language even something that contradicts the spirit of the Bible.

The Baptist problem also has *historical* dimensions. The European ancestors of the Brazilian Baptists of today suffered death and ignominy because they refused to concede spiritual authority to any temporal prince. Yet this is what Baptists in Brazil are in danger of doing when they permit civil authority to define for them the limits of religious freedom.

## Brazilian Pietism and the Denial of the Grassroots Community Ethos

The Pietist movement did not evolve into a formal ecclesiastical institution, as did other communitarian movements studied in chapter 10, above. It became a religious ideology that far transcended the very brief periods in which it was energized by the *collegia pietatis*. Pietism gradually permeated major segments of North American Protestantism during the Evangelical Awakening through the Dutch Reformed churches, the Methodist "classes," and the Moravian movement.

Apart from the small, German-speaking *Cristianismo Decidido* in southern Brazil—a direct descendant of Lutheran Pietism—the most obvious practitioners of a pietistic way of life are the smaller U.S. denominations and "faith missions" that came to Brazil immediately after World War II. A Pietistic ideology also informed, to one degree or another, the several missionary movements summarized in this chapter. But what passes for Pietism today is only distantly related to the seventeeth-century phenomenon. Stoeffler's four fundamental characteristics of early Pietism (1965: 12–23), summarized in the previous chapter, do not now have the meaning they had in Spener's day.

Mediated as it was by its more recent rootage in North American soil, Brazilian—as well as Spanish American—Pietism, in a sense, turned its back on the world. It became dour and ascetic. The joyful community celebration of the early German Pietists degenerated into a personalized spirituality. By the time the first Protestants arrived in Brazil, the essence of Christian piety consisted in a rugged individualism and a stern set of ethical rules. Even though the faith of Latin American Evangelicals was mixed with a conscious desire to succeed in the here and now, the motivating force in their religious experience—paradoxically— was, in essence, otherworldly. Their involvement in the present social order was often more a function of personal needs and the needs of their churches than a response to the problems of society.

The Pietist missionaries who arrived in Latin America, beginning in the nineteenth-century, were "perfectionists" of a different sort from the activist Pietists of Spener's day. They were demanding of themselves and they demanded perfection from their disciples. They encouraged their converts to strive for individual holiness, believing this to be the only way to effect real change in the social order. Unlike Spener, they were, in a sense, pessimists in their attitude toward the institutional church and the world. Pietist perfectionism today evidences itself in a lack of charity toward Christians who differ from them on points of doctrine or conduct, or toward those who suffer momentary lapses in conduct. It is also evidenced in the general skepticism on the part of Protestants toward Catholic renewal movements. In the light of history, this in itself is a denial of the Pietist heritage!

Pietists have always turned to the Bible as the source of their faith and ethical conduct. Latter-day Pietists have seriously reduced the scope of the message of Scripture. Large segments are either ignored, reinterpreted, or allegorized, so that the Bible speaks only to the needs of individual Christians and offers pat answers to their problems. The biblical call to community holiness and social justice has been largely overlooked. Current Evangelical Pietism is confident of having "arrived," theologically speaking. It has failed to grasp the ongoing need for ongoing reformation within its own ranks, except as it applies to the kind of hairsplitting that provokes schism. This has contributed to the proliferation of new denominations in Latin America in recent years.

An overview of this analysis of the historical Protestant churches in Brazil yields an impression of tremendous zeal, unlimited sacrifice, steady and sometimes rapid growth, and amazing expansion throughout the entire national territory. This fact, added to the even more extraordinary Pentecostal phenomenon to be analyzed in the following sections, has made the Protestant churches in Brazil the object of numerous studies. Unfortunately, there are no studies of Protestant growth after 1973, and the facts on which such studies would be based are even older. It is impossible, therefore, to be certain whether the growth of Protestantism has continued at the same rhythm into the 1980s. I suspect that it has not. My suspicion is based on personal observations and on a brief study of seven churches in Paraná state in which I participated in 1976 (Cook 1977b: 1–13). The task of verifying this suspicion belongs to someone else.

Although the same lack of information makes my hypothesis unprovable at this time, I suspect that this slackening of growth is due as much to factors that are inherent in the kind of Protestantism that came to Brazil as it is to external social factors such as modernization, internal migrations, and social stresses. A comment by Professor Reily gives us a strong hint about *the ideology that motivated the early missionary efforts in Brazil:*

It is not possible to read the official reports of the early missionaries without perceiving that they were aware of the totality of the Brazilian population, including slaves (blacks and mulattoes) and the indigenous peoples. But the great concentration of efforts in the Protestant missionary work were directed toward free, civilized, and generally white human beings. There are exceptions to this rule, which should not be overlooked, but these efforts to evangelize black slaves and Indians never engaged the majority of the missionary force, and can be considered peripheral to the priority goal [1981: 1].

Amerindians, of course, were only a tiny minority, but the blacks made up a not inconsiderable proportion of the Brazilian population. The dilemma of Protestantism in all Latin America today is not a *strategic* problem—what evangelistic method to use in order to induce greater church growth. At bottom, it is a theological problem. Ultimately, it has to do with concrete options. *What will be the choice of the evangelical churches of Latin America—the dominant classes or the subordinated masses?*

One stream of Latin American Protestantism would seem to offer hope for the future. The Pentecostal movement, a popular religious phenomenon, may provide us with some guidelines for a Protestant grassroots movement. Let us examine the evidence in Brazil, the nation with the largest Pentecostal population.

## The Pentecostal Movement in Brazil

In 1910, barely six years after the Azusa Street Revival in Los Angeles, two young Swedish-Americans—Daniel Berg and Gunnar Vingren—received a vision that sent them on their way to Brazil. They arrived the following year in Belém de Pará, at the mouth of the mighty Amazon, and immediately began working with the local Baptist missionary. At a time when they were briefly in charge of the local congregation, they participated in a general Pentecostal outpouring. This Baptist congregation was to become the first "mother church" of the autochthonous *Assembleia de Deus* (Assembly of God), a movement that by 1970 would claim three-quarters of a million adherents, making it the largest Protestant denomination in Brazil.

The Pentecostal movement spread like wildfire. A number of other local churches now have large congregations numbering in the thousands. These "mother churches" oversee numerous branch churches throughout the country, with Sunday schools and grammar schools, as well as various social services—trade schools, clinics, and small factories that employ Pentecostals. Every year the number of baptisms in each mother church and satellite congregations will be in the thousands (Hollenweger 1972: 75–82; *Historia* 1960: 13ff.).

But the *Assembleia* was not the first Pentecostal church to appear in Brazil. In 1910, the *Congregação Cristã do Brasil* (CCB)—now the third largest denomination—was founded by Luigi Francescon. He was an Italian Waldensian by birth, an American Presbyterian by denomination, and a Pentecostal by experience. The CCB began as a true grassroots movement among immigrant Italians in the state of São Paulo (Italian was the "liturgical" language until the 1930s). The Waldensian heritage of its founder, Hollenweger believes, has produced a greater sense of "responsibility towards fellowmen, going beyond the individualistic understanding of the average Protestant, as evidence of faith in the Holy Spirit."[166] Social activities transcend CCB membership. Policy dictates that in "industrial undertakings" that focus on unemployment, "only a small proportion of those involved (about 6 percent) are to belong to its religious community" (Hollenweger: 90–91).

The Waldensian heritage of Francescon may also be manifested in matters of doctrine and polity. "The community passionately rejects any kind of legalistic ethic," including an explicit dissociation from the Anglo-Saxon observance of Sunday and the rejection of an enforced tithing system (Hollenweger: 89).

In 1970 this popular movement had almost 358,000 registered members (see Table 9; Read and Ineson: 23). Hollenweger observes that in the state of São Paulo "the *Congregação* can even stand comparison with the Roman Catholic Church," particularly if allowances are made for the fact that many Catholic parishes consist of largely nominal Christians, including infants—especially at the time when this comparison was made. In 1948 there were in fact more CCB churches than Catholic parishes in two out of ten dioceses in the state of São Paulo, an identical number in one diocese, and a little over half the number of Catholic parishes in another four dioceses. At that time the CCB was intrinsically a worker church, thriving in the industrial heartland of Brazil. But it also found its way to the rural poor as increasing numbers of unemployed began a reverse migration to the hinterlands (Hollenweger: 88).

Other Pentecostal groups have arisen since 1950. The most notable is the *Brasil para Cristo* Church led by the controversial missionary Manoel de Mello. A member church of the World Council of Churches, it is active in evangelism and social action, and carries enough political clout to enable its founder to add what for many is another grassroots Evangelical voice to the Christian call for social justice.

*Mainline Pentecostal Denominations: True Grassroots Communities?* No, says sociologist Carlos Brandão, to whose study of popular religiosity in a small rural region of Brazil I referred in chapter 3. Pentecostal denominations with a national following, he argues persuasively, make up the lower reaches of the Evangelical middle class. The very rustic character of some of the Pentecostal meeting places, and the cheap clothing that some members wear, should not be allowed to hide the fact that "the roots of the local group are in other worlds and in other social classes" (1980a: 78, 110).

But one could ask, Is this not also true of Catholic CEBs? Is not their ideological and theological framework of European (Catholic, Protestant, and secular) origin? I submit that the concept of *base* requires other criteria than Brandão's. The major difference between Catholic and Protestant CEBs is not so much a matter of roots as of ultimate goals. On this basis I agree that one might validly question the intrinsically grassroots nature of the mainline Pentecostal groups.[167] If the institutionalization model holds true, the CEBs are also destined to a similar upward mobility, but with certain differences (see note 132).

The objective of the Catholic CEBs is to establish *their own grassroots identity* as the people of God. This, ultimately, is what validates them in the eyes of their own members and protagonists. Sociologically, the goals of the large Pentecostal movements are oriented differently. They began as reactions against the overrationalized faith (or institutionalism) of Puritan Protestantism, because they wished to regain direct access to God without clerical intermediaries, and to experience God at work for them in their daily struggles for existence. For reasons of class and of culture, they attempted to recapture, within Evangelical limits, forms of practice and belief that were closer to their own grassroots origins.

But the heirs of the original Pentecostal dissidents—"changing their loyalties"—began to internalize dominant Protestant norms and middle-class values in their search for respectability (Brandão: 110-11). The process of institutionalization is gradually moving mainline Pentecostals away from the popular sector of society and may be slowing their numerical growth. Now it is the dissident sector of Pentecostalism that is growing, Brandão believes, because these sects find in their own popular religion the supernatural protection, community *identity,* and experience of *power* over the sacral world that mainline Pentecostals are leaving behind (ibid., 139–41).

The relative presence of the popular sector among Protestants, Brandão points out, varies from a *subordinate* presence in traditional Protestant churches, through a much more *participative* presence in mainline Pentecostalism, to *active* involvement and leadership in the dissident groups of grassroots Pentecostalism. The truly grassroots Pentecostal groups, Brandão's research shows, "are the very small sects with at most a regional radius of influence." They "are always under the imminent threat of takeover by the insecure mother churches" in metropolitan areas (1980: 109–10).

By 1970 the combined Pentecostal membership accounted for 49.4 percent of all Brazilian Protestants (presumably not counting the truly grassroots groups). If they have continued to grow at the same rate during the decade of the 1970s, Pentecostals in all probability now make up more than two-thirds of the Protestant population of Brazil (projections based on Willems: 65; Read and Ineson: 31–33, 64, 96–98).

*Factors Helping and Hindering Pentecostal Growth in Brazil.* In their studies of Protestant growth in Brazil, Willems, Read and Ineson, and Muniz de Souza place a heavy stress on *the role of social change in the rapid rise of Pentecostalism* among the masses (Willems: 12–13, 54, 57–58; Read and Ineson: 93–130; Read 1965: 159–79; see also de Moura in LADOC:1973 III/ 36a: 1–3). In his study of Chilean and Brazilian Pentecostalism, Willems's third "leading hypothesis" runs:

> Heavy concentrations of Protestants are correlated with changes strongly affecting the traditional structure of the society; conversely, Protestantism may be expected to be relatively weak in areas that have had little or no exposure to such changes [1967: 12].

He adds that the masses—the Brazilians most directly affected by these changes—find in Protestantism, particularly in Pentecostalism, one of several possible answers to their search for social identity (ibid., 123).

In his 1973 study of Brazilian church growth, Presbyterian Read uses the statistics furnished by the IBGE to show that it was during *the years of greatest social upheaval*—that is, during the large urban migrations between 1960 and 1970—that the most notable Pentecostal growth took place (Read and Ineson: 55, 103, 108, 125–127).

But Francisco Cartaxo Rolim disagrees with the conclusions of these researchers. His analysis provides us with a Catholic "structuralist" perspective that may prove helpful in understanding the phenomenon of Pentecostal growth in Brazil and elsewhere in Latin America. Taking as the object of his study *the period of greatest social change in Brazil*—the fifteen years between

1955 and 1969—he breaks it down to three 5-year segments, and then compares the growth figures in each period as provided by the IBGE. From 1955 to 1959, the relative increase in Pentecostal members was 78.9 percent; from 1960 to 1964, it was 44.9 percent; from 1965 to 1969, it was 38.8 percent. Although the rhythm of growth decreased from one 5-year period to the next, the urbanization and industrialization processes moved on unabated and, in fact, accelerated from one period to the next. Cartaxo Rolim concludes from this that probably other factors at work overruled those that have been posited in the more functionalist analysis used by Willems, Read, and Muniz de Souza (Rolim 1978: 83-84).

Rolim argues that a more satisfactory explanation for the growth of Pentecostalism among the masses of Brazil can be found in an analysis based on the concept of socio-economic "class." After studying a small sample of Pentecostal churches in several small towns surrounding a major city, he concludes that 82.6 percent of the Pentecostals he surveyed do not belong to the lower or working class, but to the lower middle class. They are, he says, neither directly involved in the struggle between bourgeois and elite nor totally excluded from it (ibid.: 85-86).

Rolim compares the Pentecostal religious structure with the structures of other religious groups. He concludes that, unlike traditional Protestantism, Pentecostalism, provides "direct access to the means of religious production." This fact permits Pentecostals to become the owners of the means of production and, at the same time, to relate to each other on the basis of their use of the means of production. In traditional Christianity there is a sharp difference between intellectual and manual religious labor—between those who plan and those who execute—but Pentecostals are simultaneously planners and executors of their labor.

As to Willem's hypothesis that Pentecostalism merely provided the organizational means to *adopt* an already existent popular Catholicism in the service of upward mobility (Willems: 21-25, 35-54), Rolim disagrees. He postulates that, on the contrary, Pentecostalism represents a *structural break* with popular Catholicism at the level of the "means of religious production" (Rolim 1978: 86-88). That is, in both traditional Catholicism and traditional Protestantism the production of religious symbols is clergy-controlled, but Pentecostals, in their assemblies, have become the producers—as well as the consumers—of their own religious world.

Instead of being the symbolic social protest that Willems postulates (1967: 12-15, 111-17), or an adaptation of the old model of the plantation lord (D'Epinay 1968: 111-17), both of which are replications of traditional social structures, Pentecostalism, Rolim insists, is *in fundamental opposition to the basic structures of society.* Pentecostalism does not duplicate class divisions. Instead, encompassing, as it does, great numbers of those who are not direct producers, it "transforms them into direct producers of their religious world" (Rolim 1978: 89).

The social significance of Pentecostalism in Brazil, concludes Rolim, is best expressed, not as a religious response to social anomie, but in terms of *class relationships*—relationships, however, that are *in tension*. On the one hand, Pentecostalism is capitalistic in its ideology, with all the class relationships that this implies. But on the other hand, Pentecostalists keep their religious distance from the larger society, without losing their dependence upon other social structures.

There may not be much difference between the final positions of Willems, D'Epinay, and Rolim. In essence, Willems is saying that Pentecostals *announce a new society*; D'Epinay that, nonetheless, Pentecostals *truncate liberation*; Rolim that they do so by *spiritualizing liberation and legitimating the dominant order*. All of this notwithstanding, the Pentecostal ideology, even as Rolim analyzes it, is potentially as radical as that of the CEBs because of its grassroots origins and fundamental opposition to social structures. Continuing interaction of the reformist-conformist tension within Pentecostal ideology may yet transform Pentecostalism into a force for social change.

The foregoing analysis by Brandão and Rolim should be taken seriously, but with an important caveat. As pointed out in chapter 9, the Pentecostals, more than members of any other Protestant movement, are in a position to challenge Catholic popular religiosity and Afro-Brazilian spiritism precisely because they take demonic powers seriously, as did the writers of the New Testament and their contemporaries. The Pentecostal confrontation with such powers is not entirely an otherworldly escape mechanism, nor is it a superstitious aberration. It is the Pentecostal way of confronting real-life social evils, though on a different plane from that chosen by others. The fact that they overlook the structural dimensions of social evil does not negate the fundamental fact of the confrontation they engage in—nor its potential for more significant social involvement of the type that Brandão postulates, as will be taken up shortly.

De Moura, in the respected Franciscan journal *Revista Eclesiástica Brasileira,* shares a pertinent insight:

> The established churches offer doctrine and the Afro-Brazilian cults offer experience, but effective evangelization requires both together. . . . It is only because they feel powerless to change the world with its injustices, that Pentecostals, often at great cost to themselves, create a world apart [LADOC 1973: II/36a; see Brandão 1980a: 117 n. 8, and 142].

What this means is that Pentecostalism should be taken seriously as a Protestant CEB movement, at least in *potentia*.[168] But it is such a movement with a difference. Unlike CEB Catholics, Pentecostals do not allow themselves to be placed structurally within the confines of class struggle—though they continue being members of an exploited class (Rolim 1978: 89; LADOC 1973 III3: 36a: 3). But here we must also take into account the "dissident" Pentecostal groups; Brandão has a different assessment of them.

*Dissident Pentecostal Communities.* Unlike traditional Protestants and mainline Pentecostalists, grassroots Pentecostals, Brandão believes, partake of the same community solidarity as do CEB Catholics. It is an integral part of their world. He shows that the discourse of Pentecostal grassroots religiosity is also, by its very nature, "political" in the sense that, as he seems to imply, it is at least as promising as the political discourse of Catholic CEBs. He elaborates on three basic reasons in support of this position:

1. The preaching of grassroots Pentecostals is political in its "them and us" attitude toward religious competitors and the great mass of "the idolatrous" whom grassroots Pentecostals have set out to conquer for their faith. They see themselves as participating in a holy combat against "the power of the world" under the domination of the Evil One. The significant point Brandão makes is that this holy mission, as grassroots Pentecostals see it, has been given not to the saints in general but *to them in particular as the poor of the earth*. Whereas the ancestral ideology of popular Catholicism was one of *cultural resistance* to domination, popular Pentecostalism has redefined this in terms of a *social conquest*. This is, of course, strikingly similar to the ideology of popular dissidence throughout the history of the church!

2. Brandão makes the telling point that Pentecostalism, in its beginnings, discovered the political radicality of the gospel that the traditional religiosity of every confession tried to ignore: that the saint is "a poor person who condemns riches and a dominated person who condemns domination." For Pentecostals in general, to give in to the work and the "power" of the "Evil One" is to lose one's saintly identity and character. But more recently, Brandão states, mainline Pentecostalism has lost this "saintly" quality in its quest for ecclesiastical acceptance:

> But among the ministers of the small sects, those who see themselves as "the poor and humble," as compared with "those believers in the churches," the feeling of a holy war is alive, together with the hope of a final struggle that will re-create a social order without "the power of the mighty of this earth," continues to be stronger than the hope of personal salvation [Brandão 1980a: 259; see the whole passage, 241–60].

3. Brandão concludes that, should it come about that the subordinated classes are given an opportunity to participate in the political process in Brazil, we would see a massive involvement of grassroots Pentecostal communities. If their leaders prohibited them from doing do, he is convinced from his long involvement with these communities, many grassroots believers would abandon their religious groups for other forms of popular struggle. The reason he gives for this conviction is worth citing:

> Because no one is better prepared than the small-sect Pentecostal—who lives, to use one of their own expressions, [in a social environment] "where Christ is stronger," and where the hardships of life are experi-

enced daily—to make the leap from radical religious labor in one sector to political labor in another [ibid., 251].

Something like this happened in the early 1970s in the hardscrabble mining and steel processing region of southern Chile. It helped bring Salvador Allende to power.[169] Whether or not it will happen in Brazil, the potential of popular Pentecostalism has often been recognized by Catholic *agentes de pastoral* and they are trying to involve Pentecostals in their projects.[170]

Because of their middle-class orientation, mainline Pentecostals face a different kind of challenge. They have not been able to break their dependence on the "reformist-conformist" religious ideology that Rolim postulates, even though they are being exploited by those who control the public flow of ideas, goods, and services. If Pentecostals are ever able to break this dependence, Rolim suspects, they will be forced to reformulate their understanding of the power of God vis-à-vis social structures, and thus alter the content of their conformism (dos Santos: 88–91). It is precisely at this point that Catholic CEBs, I believe, challenge the Pentecostal movement.

Conversely, the CEBs are challenged by the Pentecostal movement. It is probably the reason why Pentecostals have been the object of numerous Catholic studies! The growth of Pentecostalism, despite the weaknesses of the movement, cannot be explained solely by sociological factors, whatever the instrument of analysis. As a believer in the transforming power of the gospel and the energizing fire of the Holy Spirit, by faith I must accept the fact of God's sovereign work in Pentecostalism—even as I recognize it at different levels in Catholicism and other forms of Protestantism.

The quintessential message of Evangelical Protestantism—its theological and sociological oversimplifications duly recognized—is the biblical announcement of total liberation (redemption, forgiveness, sanctification, freedom) for persons who are being formed into "committed communities" by virtue of submission to Jesus Christ the Lord. This fact was sealed at the cross and the empty tomb. Protestant grassroots communities, too, have a significant role to play in the transformation of society. If they are consistent with their faith, they cannot avoid it.

Profound social change in Latin America is inevitable. It may be deflected for a time, or postponed, but it cannot be stopped. If this change is to be truly significant and avoid the trap of new totalitarianisms, there is a key role in the process for transformed and transforming Catholic and Protestant CEBs. It may be that grassroots Pentecostals, despite their theological aberrations, will point the way to fellow Protestants in the coming years. But for this to happen, Protestants will have to become aware of the underside of their own history. The Protestant churches will have to die to every social and religious pretension in order to be reborn in the image of him who, being God, took human nature as his vocation and became the suffering servant of the Lord.

# Chapter 12

# Conclusion

*You can predict the weather by looking at the sky, but you cannot interpret the signs concerning these times! [Matt. 16:3]*

As we reach the end of this lengthy study of the *comunidades de base* in Latin American Catholicism—within the context of the broad sweep of church history—we must now ask what significance, if any, the CEBs have for Christian mission. What are their implications for Protestant evangelization? What do they have to say to Catholicism in Latin America? I shall attempt to point out a few of the more important challenges that the grassroots communities hurl in the face of Christian mission today.

## THE CHALLENGE OF THE CEBS FOR PROTESTANT MISSION

The Catholic communities have profound implications for Protestant evangelization in Brazil and in all Latin America. The challenge is historical, hermeneutical, ecclesiological, and missiological.

### The Historical Challenge

As we have had occasion to observe in chapters 10 and 11, virtually all Protestant churches now working in Brazil and in many Spanish American nations can trace their roots to some kind of grassroots community movement. True, none of those movements was as conscious of the socio-political dimensions of the gospel as are the contemporary CEBs, nor were all of them identified with the socio-economically disadvantaged as are the *comunidades*—a fact that should be evaluated in the light of the evolution of Christian social awareness as it has interacted with a parallel evolution in secular socio-economic theory.

Most Protestant churches today are afraid of the very kind of church

**230**

movement that gave them birth or revitalized them along the way. Some churches seem to be more concerned about attaining and maintaining one or another type of respectability, even in the face of institutionalized injustice and violence, than they are about identifying with the masses whom they profess to be trying to reach with the gospel of Christ. Fearful of speaking out in defense of fundamental human rights, Protestants mistakenly identify "religious freedom" with "freedom to preach the gospel." They overlook the fact that a gospel that fails to be concerned about *every dimension* of human freedom is not worthy of being called the gospel of Jesus Christ (Luke 3:1-20, 4:4-21; James 2:1-12, 4:5-6).

The CEBs also challenge the Protestant churches at the level of their historical goals. The grassroots-oriented Catholic Church is exemplifying the unassuming simplicity of a poor and servant church, but the majority of the Protestant churches in Latin America either have achieved or are (consciously or unconsciously) moving toward the attainment of status and social respectability.[171] Furthermore, whereas CEB Catholics have as their "historical project"[172] to change alienative social structures, most Protestants prefer not to rock the boat. In the face of this contradiction—which goes against the seemingly irreversible populist trend in Latin America today—Protestant leaders might well ask themselves if there will be any significant role for their churches in the new social order that will, in all probability, appear sooner or later in Latin America.[173]

## The Hermeneutical Challenge

The historical pillars of the Reformation are *solus Christus, sola gratia, sola fides, sola Scriptura*. These are not, however, aseptic propositions dropped from heaven in one neat package into the hearts and minds of the great reformers. To believe this would be a denial of the very principles espoused, and tantamount to giving the same status to tradition as to Scripture. Just as the trailblazer reformers elaborated these great truths in the light of the challenges of their day, we are called upon to think them through in response to the urgent needs of human beings today.

*Christ: The Focal Point of the Theology of Mission.* The major currents of Christian theology of mission have as their point of departure one of the following four cardinal themes: God, Scripture, the church, the world. Traditional Reformed theology insists that God, the Trinity, is the true starting point of mission theology. Without exactly denying this, Fundamentalist Protestantism, in fact, makes Scripture its starting point. For traditional Catholicism, the church is the starting point of mission theology. And when Protestants overemphasize the institutional welfare of their churches or their numerical growth, they are saying—their theological disclaimers to the contrary notwithstanding—that their church is the starting point of their theology of mission. On the other hand, secular theology keeps reminding us, with some reason, that the world sets the agenda of theology and of mission.

Which viewpoint is correct? Taken exclusively, none of these perspectives is totally correct, but as the cardinal points of four converging lines of mission thought, all four contribute to a holistic theology of mission. Their *point of convergence* is *Christ,* at once Son of God, Son of Man, Word of God, and head of the church. Symbolically, where the four reference points of mission theology come together, they form the cross of Christian mission.[174]

To say that Christ is the focal point of theology of mission is to affirm that mission will find itself in a constant and dynamic interaction between God (the author of mission), the Word (its verbalization), the church (its instrument), the world (the sphere of mission action). Therefore, *solus Christus* is much more than a statement of faith; it is a unique expression of the *modus operandi* of mission. "As the Father has sent me, I am sending you" (John 20:21, NIV)—that is, we are sent *in the same way and with the same mission* as Jesus Christ. Earlier John had affirmed, "Even in this world we have become as he is" (4:17, JB). How was Christ? How was he sent? Jesus himself expressed it in his inaugural address at Nazareth:

The Spirit of the Lord is on me: therefore, he has anointed me to preach good news to the poor. He has sent me to proclaim freedom for the prisoners and recovery of sight for the blind, to release the oppressed, to proclaim the year of the Lord's favor [Luke 4:18-19, NIV].

In Matthew 11:5, after the Baptist had sent to inquire of Jesus if he were truly the Christ who had been foretold, Jesus let the messengers observe his works, then sent them back to John with this succinct statement:

The blind receive sight, the lame walk, those who have leprosy are cured, the deaf hear, the dead are raised, and *the good news is preached to the poor.* Blessed is the man who does not fall on account of me [NIV, emphasis added].

Good news to the poor is what the gospel is all about. It is also, as Jesus foresaw, the block upon which the church would stumble throughout its entire history. Most significant ecclesial movements, including the New Testament church, began with the poor but, forgetting their roots, moved up the social scale to become respectable and powerful. Today, after centuries of rigid institutionalism, traditional Catholic dogma is being reinterpreted through the eyes of the poor. Similarly, a Reformation theology for today must be redefined from below. This is what happened, to a certain degree, during the Radical Reformation and the English revolution, in English Methodism, as well as within one stream of the Evangelical Awakening in North America (Dayton 1976).

The Evangelical church in Latin America today could take the lead in this rediscovery of its "radical" roots. To do this, however, it will also have to "discover" the poor—who are everywhere around it—and find the true meaning of witness in community at the grass roots of Latin American society. Will the Evangelical Church in Latin America be able to do this? Probably not of its own volition. History seems to show that only when the church is forced, often in the interests of institutional self-preservation, to defend the oppressed in its midst, will it begin to rediscover the Word of God "from below." This is, indeed, what has happened to the Catholic Church in Latin America. It may be beginning to take place in some sectors of evangelicalism in Central America. This discovery is, in fact, an act of divine grace, sometimes painful, but nonetheless necessary.

*Revelation of the Ultimate Form of God's Grace: The Incarnation.* "Remember how generous the Lord Jesus was: he was rich, but he became poor for your sake, to make you rich out of his poverty" (2 Cor. 8:9, JB.) St. Paul is here equating divine grace with the mission of God, as it is expressed in concrete acts of identification with human poverty and misery in all its manifestations. The Son of God exchanged the unlimited riches of divinity for the poverty of our humanity (incarnation) so that humankind might exchange the poverty of its sinful condition for the riches of holiness (humanization; see Eph. 4:24; Col. 3:10). Through Christ, those who because of sin are living subhuman existences have the possibility of attaining the full humanity for which they were created by God (Ps. 8:3–9).

God's grace is manifested within us as social beings and exacts from us social responsibilities. As Leonardo Boff puts it, "Since the gift of grace is God himself, human beings will become a new creature, a new humanity. As the adopted children of God, they will enjoy eternal life and the Spirit will dwell in their hearts" (L. Boff 1979: 49–50). But the purpose of divine grace is to make human existence "gracious, enchanting, full of joviality and beauty"— adjectives that are implicit in the meaning of "grace" (L. Boff 1976a: 67)—so that "now we can live in the freedom of the children of God" (Rom. 8:14–21; Gal. 4:6), as "heirs and masters of the universe" (Gal. 4:1–3). Boff concludes:

> When we talk about the experience of grace, we should always remember it is an experience of the Holy Spirit and his activity in the world. It is part of all life and experience that contains an element of surprise and breaks down existing limitations and barriers. To experience grace means to allow ourselves to be overtaken by the presence of the Spirit. And that can happen only if we join with the Spirit [1979: 51].

If one were to judge only by the large Pentecostal movement, and by the smaller but influential charismatic renewal in Catholic and Protestant churches in Latin America, one could conclude that the Holy Spirit is alive and well in Latin America. But this view may be superficial. Not until we are willing to let the Spirit work freely—not only in our personal lives, but also in far-reaching ecclesial change—and not until we can make ourselves recognize that the Spirit is working within movements of social change (even those that do not bear a specifically Christian name), shall we begin to understand the vastness and complexity of the Spirit's work and attempt to be a part of it. This too is a lesson we are learning through the Catholic grassroots communities.

*Grace and Faith.* Though itself a gift of God, faith is the human response to the gospel, even as grace is its divine manifestation. Neither of them is merely an entry in a theological dictionary. As is true of all the positive content of biblical theology, grace and faith are dynamic and creative concepts, capable of ever new applications. By grace we receive eternal life, and by faith we accept it as a continuous and endless process through which we are brought face to face with the meaning of divine justice. That is what Paul means when he says:

> I am not ashamed of the Good News: it is the power of God saving all who have faith . . . since this is what reveals the justice of God to us: it shows how faith leads to faith, or as Scripture says: the upright man finds life through faith. The anger of God is being revealed from heaven against all impiety and depravity of men who keep truth imprisoned in their wickedness [Rom. 1:17–19, JB].

The meaning is clear: the process of faith ("faith leads to faith") takes us on a journey of constant discovery of the meaning of the two-edged justice of God. Faith in Christ is not sterile. Though salvation is not of works, it leads to good works (Eph. 2:8–10). The justice of God, which faith reveals to us, is not a passive attribute having to do with what God does or does not do. Divine justice acts *for* and *against*: *for* the sinner and *against* the sin of the sinner; *for* those who have been treated unjustly, and *against* those who act unjustly.

Faith in Jesus Christ leads to knowledge of God. But, "to know God is to do justice," as Gustavo Gutiérrez reminds us (1973: 196). "He defended the cause of the poor and needy, and so all went well. Is that not what it means to know me?" (Jer. 22:16, NIV). "Faith by itself," says St. James, "if it is not accompanied by action, is dead" (2:1–17; cf. 5:1–6). In this context, action is clearly related to Christian social ethics.

The end of faith is the total liberation of the human being in history and beyond history. As Leonardo Boff points out, faith is both a point of departure and the goal of Christian theology. We are saved by faith, and through faith "we witness and proclaim that God through his eternal Son intervened to liberate history from its perversion and take it to fullness of life and completeness" (1978a: 8).

The challenge of the CEBs to Protestant mission is their vital faith in a Christ who has called them to participate in the liberation of their own history. It is a challenge that Protestants will be incapable of taking up so long as they, by their silence and indifference, or by their active complicity, continue to be involved in the false histories of today. "The liberation of history"—that is, the holistic freeing of human existence in order to serve the purposes of God—is an undertaking that can be carried out only by those who have identified with the totality of human needs and, by faith, have undertaken to change history in the power of the Holy Spirit.

**Sola Scriptura.** The greatest hermeneutical challenge of the Catholic grassroots communities to Protestant mission comes from their use and application of the Word of God. How can Protestants, who profess to base their beliefs upon *the sole authority of Scripture*, deal with a hermeneutic that questions the very foundations of their present institutional existence? This, I believe, gets to the core of our problem with the hermeneutics of the CEBs.

In theory we recognize the great diversity of Scripture interpretations, even within the Bible, as a sign of the action of the Holy Spirit in different historical and cultural situations. But somehow we find it hard to recognize that *our* hallowed interpretation is also historically (i.e., socio-culturally) conditioned, and therefore can be questioned.

We fail to realize that a theological approach that, at one moment in history, served as a prophetic challenge to an entrenched theological system, may itself fall prey to similar evils and require the Spirit-inspired confrontation of a renewed perception of the action of God in history. As so often throughout church history, the poor and despised of this earth are the ones God is using today to call us back to a true and dynamic faith. The Reformation principle of *sola Scriptura* is not a sealed and impregnable box containing all the (changeless) truths that we ought to know about the life and mission of the church. Rather, it is a key that allows us to open any number of boxes in our day in order to discover new ways to participate in God's mission within human history.

**The Ecclesiological Challenge**

As noted in chapter 9, the most attractive dimension of the CEBs for evangelical Protestants is their "new way of being the church." However, this perception can be the result of a superficial assessment of the Catholic CEB understanding of the church. At one level the CEBs represent a return to what Protestants believe is a more scriptural model of the church, but at a deeper level the grassroots understanding of ecclesiality is far more radical than what many Protestants would be willing to accept. In fact, the Catholic communities challenge Protestant mission in Latin America at both levels: their present church-mission and their loss of grassroots identity. The challenge of the CEBs is, at heart, a very Protestant challenge, for the following reasons:

1. As we have observed in the final chapters of this work, *ecclesiastical institutionalization* has, in fact, produced a phenomenon in which Protestant churches and at least a segment of the Catholic Church are passing each other in the night. Whereas grassroots Catholics have rediscovered the doctrine of the "priesthood of all believers," Protestant churches are leaving it far behind—if some of them ever practiced it at all! Indeed, it was only the churches of the Radical Reformation that really put this doctrine into practice. They were in the stream of grassroots dissident movements throughout church history for whom anticlericalism was a cardinal tenet of faith. The principle

was rediscovered briefly in Protestantism in the Pietist and Methodist movements and resurfaces here and there today.

The CEB emphasis on a committed Christianity harks back to the believers' church concept which the magisterial reformers rejected as impractical. It was left to the radical reformers, and to their successors in subsequent centuries, to bring the believers' church into being and to keep it alive in the face of the onslaughts of nominalism. In view of the creeping nominalism in much of Latin American Protestantism today (even in the churches that came out of the Pietist tradition), the Catholic communities are a ringing call to Protestantism to return to their earlier commitment to Christ and to his mission in all its dimensions.

In an age when the virtues of life-in-community are being extolled as an antidote to the poisonous anonymity of secular materialism, the Catholic communities have a special appeal. And they challenge the superficial and often narcissistic Protestant understanding of Christian community even more profoundly by their active involvement in the world around them. This is where the grassroots communities begin to challenge Protestant churches at the level of Christian lifestyle.

2. *The CEBs,* in Brazil and elsewhere in Latin America, *are a challenge to our comfortable church life.* Thoroughly accommodated with the alien elements of Latin American culture, most, if not all, Protestant churches have some kind of stake in maintaining the status quo. Rocking the boat is not an Evangelical practice! We forget, however, that this is precisely what the early church and many of its grassroots successors down through history did: turn their socio-cultural and political world upside-down with the gospel (Acts 17: 1-9)![175]

The point was made in an earlier chapter that "upside-down" is a perception of those who are "on top." The view "from below" considers upside-downness to be right-side-up! (see note 145). The grassroots communities make us uncomfortable, they threaten us, and we call them "subversive" simply because they are questioning our "top down" values, which we have always assumed to be Christian and supported by Scripture. "Not so," the CEBs are telling us, and we had better listen. To fail to do so is to run the risk of being left out of a major dimension of God's renewal in the church today. But beyond that, not to heed the challenge of the "base church" is to deny that a sovereign God can work in history in ways that escape us, and that God has chosen to do so through the poor and despised of this earth.

3. *The spirit of prophetic criticism* against every kind of absolutism, whether religious, social, or political—implicit in the "Protestant principle"—is evident in the ethos of the *comunidades.* So is the positive side of the "principle"—creative protest, which is open to God's ever new dealings with humankind in changing historical situations (Dillenberger and Welch 1954:313-14, 325-26).

So it is that the CEBs challenge the Protestant churches of Latin America, many of which have forgotten, or were never taught, the "Protestant principle." When they close themselves to ongoing renewal and reject God's ever new workings in history, the Protestant churches are denying their Reformation heritage. Might it not be that in this respect, at least, the *comunidades* are more "Protestant" than the Protestant churches?

## The Missiological Challenge

At this point, all the other challenges of the CEBs to Brazilian Protestantism converge in the *witness of the church* in Latin America. How do the *comunidades* call our Protestant churches to reevaluate their practice of mission? Table 11 illustrates how a new hermeneutic, applied to a historical understanding of mission, will produce a new conception of the church and a new understanding of mission.

Writing to the dispersed and persecuted ecclesial communities throughout Asia Minor, the apostle Peter assures them:

> You are a chosen people, a royal priesthood, a holy nation, people belonging to God, that you may declare the praises of him who called you out of darkness into his wonderful light. Once you were not a people, but now you are the people of God; once you had not received mercy, but now you have received mercy [1 Pet. 2:9–10, NIV].

### Peoplehood, Participation in Community

Within the CEBs the alienated and marginalized peoples of Brazil are discovering, by God's grace, their own identity and, with it, the meaning of mission in their own context. In order to explain to the communities of the diaspora the nature of their mission, Peter uses the symbolism of the three historical ministries of Judaism—*king, priest,* and *prophet.* According to the Gospels, Jesus has assumed these three ministries; now St. Peter is applying them to the mission of the church. Each one of these ministries had been defined in the Old Testament (Deut. chap. 17 and 18), and had become, through the process of institutionalization, something else than what God desired for it. But new meaning was given to the royal, priestly, and prophetic ministries by Jesus. The meanings we should look for today are not the meanings that have evolved throughout the history of the church, but the meanings of Jesus Christ.

1. In Deuteronomy 17:14ff., the Israelites are told what to expect from *the kingly ministry*: the regimen of an autocrat, if not a dictator—though what God really wanted the kings of Israel to be was a shepherd, concerned for the welfare of the people. In 1 Samuel 8, the people of God is warned against the dangers of adopting pagan monarchical structures.

Significantly, *the king in Deuteronomy is also a person who can read and write.* He belongs to "erudite culture"; he is a member of the elite. The church quickly grasped, twisted, and sacralized the monarchic model for its ecclesial

**Table 11**

**Typology of Mission Lifestyles**

**(1 Peter 2:9-10)**

| TYPE | CULTURE | SOCIAL STATUS | ORIENTATION | CHRISTOLOGICAL RE-DEFINITION |
|---|---|---|---|---|
| 1. *Royal Mission*<br><br>Deut.17:14, 18-19<br><br>The king must know how to read and write. This is defined for him by the "priestly" communication. | Erudite | elites | From the top down; monologue; paternalistic; traditional | Christ redefines royal mission as SERVICE<br><br>Mark 10:42-45<br><br>from the bottom up |
| 2. *Priestly Mission*<br><br>Heb. 8:4, 5<br><br>Priests deal with "copies," "shadows," and "patterns" —symbols. | Symbolic | all, within their own culture and ideology | Sensory, ideological; total communication | Christ redefines priestly mission as SELF-SACRIFICE<br><br>Heb. 7:26-27 |
| 3. *Prophetic Mission*<br><br>Deut. 18:18-22<br><br>Prophets communicate via the spoken word. | Oral<br>or<br>Verbal | The poor and illiterate<br><br>*the majority* | From the bottom up; participatory lifestyle; dialogue; grassroots communities | Christ redefines prophetic mission as INCARNATION<br><br>John 1:14 |

life and mission. For centuries, its symbol was the papacy. Yet, in spite of our Protestant rejection of Roman Catholic monarchism, this same model, with modifications, has gradually been adopted by many churches in Protestantism. However, the model is not biblical: its orientation is "from the top down," its pedagogy is monolithic, and its mission institution-centered.

2. Hebrews 8:4-5 defines *the old priestly ministry* in terms of "copies. . . shadows. . .and patterns"—that is, images, signs, and symbols.[176] The Old Testament priesthood was a symbolic ministry that reached into every social level and every dimension of the lives of the people. It was given the awesome responsibility of handling ("manipulating") culturally comprehensible symbols in order to communicate divine truths. They were the religious media persons of their time. The symbols became indeed manipulative when they were mistaken for divine reality itself, in the interests of an aberrant royal authority. They then became idols. This is of course a problem not only for Hebrew or Catholic religiosity. Protestantism also has its symbols, which too often have taken the place of a true Christian experience, and which are sinfully manipulated. Evangelical mission requires that the church be forever knocking down its idols while it searches for dynamic symbols through which to communicate the living and liberating Word of God.

3. The *prophetic ministry*, according to Deuteronomy 18:18-22, is eminently oral. Though it was directed to the entire people of God, its cultural roots were often the semiliterate Israelites of the grass roots from whom many prophets sprang. God spoke through the prophets, using the symbols, images, and concerns of the people. God spoke in order to call the people back to full commitment to the kingdom ideal.

But even the prophetic ministry became distorted, as false prophets began to parrot the party line. In Davidic times, when the monarchy was still relatively unostentatious, true prophets were accepted as royal counselors, but by the time of Isaiah and Jeremiah they were hounded to death for speaking out against royal and priestly pride and rampant injustice.

4. Jesus radically redefined these three traditional ministries. He gave them a new content with powerful implications for a new, holistic model for Christian mission. He admonished his disciples who were squabbling over places of privilege in his kingdom:

> You know that those who are regarded as rulers of the Gentiles lord it over them, and their high officials exercise authority over them. Not so with you. Instead, whoever wants to become great among you must be your servant, and whoever wants to be first must be slave of all. For even the Son of Man did not come to be served, but to serve, and to give his life a ransom for many [Mark 10:35-45, NIV].

In Christ's kingdom, the king is the servant of all—*traditional ecclesiology has been turned upside-down!*

The author of Hebrews tells us that Christ, the new high priest, "offered himself"—not the sacrifices of others—for the sins of humankind (7:26-27). The ultimate symbol of the Christian message, the essence of the priestly communication of the gospel, is the sacrifice of one's self. Without diminishing Christ's redemptive work at Calvary, but in fact giving it its full content, the priestly ministry of Protestantism will have little effect unless it assumes the radically self-giving character of the mission of Jesus Christ (Phil. 2:5-8, 3:7-10). *In Christ Jesus traditional liturgy (worship) has been turned upside-down!*

Jesus also gave a new meaning to the prophetic ministry. When the ancient prophets spoke of God's command, at times dramatizing the message with actions, their identification with the people to whom they spoke was, at best, partial. But Christ, the divine word (*logos*) with God before creation, "became flesh and lived for a while among us" (John 1:1-3, 14). Being rich, he became poor; being God, he became man and died the death of an insurrectionist. The ultimate communication—the essence of Christian mission—is the incarnation. In Jesus Christ, the Son of God and Son of Man, *traditional mission has been turned upside-down!*

The Catholic CEBs challenge Protestant mission because they have stamped a radical question mark upon the doors of our churches. They question our Protestant structures, actions, and witness. And they are doing it "from below." Whether or not we agree with their doctrinal interpretations, and despite the fact that we can single out their theological deficiencies, we dare not turn our backs on their challenge to our ecclesial and missionary lifestyle. We are being called back to our roots, back to the poor who have always been the true strength of the church. We are, in fact, being summoned to the heart of the mission of God:

> Stop doing wrong, learn to do right! Seek justice, encourage the op-pressed. Defend the cause of the fatherless, plead the case of the widow. Come now, let us reason together, says the Lord. Though your sins are like scarlet, they shall be as white as snow; though they are red as crimson, they shall be like wool [Isa. 1:13-18, NIV].

## THE CHALLENGE OF THE CEBS TO ROMAN CATHOLICISM

The greatest challenge of the Catholic *comunidades de base*, is, of course, to their own church in Brazil, the rest of Latin America, and throughout the world. Ultimately, it is a challenge to the Roman See. They challenge it, as we have seen, at the levels of sociology, ecclesiology, theology, and mission. How will a church that is one of the wealthiest, most centralized, and traditionalist institutions on earth respond to this challenge from a church of the poor? The fact that the challenge comes not only from one of the most politically advanced but from the largest Catholic church in Latin America and the third largest in the world (after Italy and the United States; CRIE 1980: 2:6, 4:2), makes the challenge difficult to ignore.

## From Medellín to Puebla: Changing Attitudes toward the CEBs

There was a notable cooling in the attitude of CELAM toward the CEBs between Medellín and Puebla. What Medellín called "the first and fundamental ecclesial nucleus, . . . the initial cell of the ecclesial structures, and the focus of evangelization" (CELAM II 1973: 15:10), Puebla merely calls "a cell of the larger community" (CELAM III 1979: 489).

The intent at Medellín was to turn the *comunidades* loose—to develop and strengthen a variety of leadership roles, particularly among the laity, with a view to periodically revising and readjusting ecclesiastical structures, as part of a decentralized "combined pastoral plan" (CELAM II: 15:9, 11, 13). Puebla is more ambiguous. Approvingly, it quotes Paul VI's encomium of the *comunidades*—"the hope of the church" (EN: 58)—and defines the CEBs somewhat condescendingly as "an expression of the church's preferential love for the simple people" wherein their popular religiosity is purified and they are encouraged to take part in the transformation of the world (CELAM III: 477, 490–91).

In an earlier section, Puebla warns against the critical attitude of some *comunidades*. In an obvious allusion to the self-awareness of the grassroots church as "a church born from below," the authors of this section of the document point out that "the church is always born out of a first initiative 'from above,' from the Lord [who] summons [it]" (1980: 162). This has a nice orthodox ring to it. But the bishops had carefully laid the groundwork for this assertion by pointing out that "the church, as the people of God, recognizes only one authority: Christ"—and by further adding that this authority consists in a mysterious relationship in which "Peter and the Twelve where chosen by Jesus to participate . . . with the church" (CELAM III: 156–57). By implication, then, the divine summons to be the church is mediated through the hierarchy—not through the whole people of God, as is the conviction of the CEBs.

The ambiguity of the Puebla document must be understood in light of the power struggle within the Latin American Conference of Bishops (CELAM) in the decade between Medellín and Puebla—in some respects, a reflection of shifting perceptions and alliances, and a change of leadership in the Vatican.

*Concern in the Vatican*, even before the death of Paul VI, over what was perceived as an ecclesial transformation that had moved too far and too fast, prompted Paul to convene the third general assembly of the Synod of Bishops (1974) to discuss the topic of the evangelization of the modern world (final document, EMW). The bishops paid special attention to "the mutual relationship between evangelization ('proclamation' and 'church planting') and integral salvation or the complete liberation of man and of peoples." They "experienced profound unity in reaffirming the intimate connection between evangelization and liberation." While promoting "generous dedication to the service of all men—the poor especially and the oppressed" in order "to eliminate the social consequences of sin"—the synod warned against remaining "with the mere political and social [consequences], however important" (EMW; 12 in Gremillion: 597; 12).

## *Evangelii Nuntiandi (EN)*

One year later (1975) Paul VI's apostolic exhortation, EN, was more specific in its definitions of the nature of evangelization. In this stirring document, the pope established the christological foundation of evangelization, its meaning, content and means, the objects and subjects of the good news, and the "spirit of evangelization." The ringing call to conversion, its high view of Jesus Christ, the openness (though qualified) to renewal, with its recognition of the important role of the laity and awareness of culture and of the need for message contextualization, the first official mention of the CEBs, and a flat rejection of secularized ideologies that distort the Christian message—these are a few of the strong points of EN.

On the debit side, one can perceive strong hints of Vatican fears that it was beginning to lose control of events (EN: 66–69, 74–80). The pope's homage to Mary in the closing paragraphs is a symbol of the underlying conservatism and fundamentally institution-centered ideology of the Roman curia. With all its strengths, EN perpetuates a verticalist ecclesiology; it understands evangelization from the apex of the hierarchical pyramid, not from its base.

## Puebla

Preparations for the third general assembly of the Latin American Episcopal Conference (Puebla) began almost immediately after the Vatican announcement of the event on December 5, 1976. The consultation document, which was circulated the following year, stirred up a storm of protest. Literally hundreds of responses were prepared by groups of theologians, theological journals, and national episcopal conferences.[177] Critical reactions can be summarized as follows: (1) The historical vision is from the top downward. (2) The diagnosis of Latin American reality is descriptive and not sufficiently analytical. (3) The implicit goal of evangelization is not integral liberation but the creation of a new social Christendom. (4) The theoretical and theological framework of the document is faulted for its docetic christology, deficient understanding of the kingdom message, too traditional ecclesiology, and naive and paternalistic social doctrine. And (5) the document is criticized because the few pastoral recommendations are too clergy-centered. In brief, the "structuring principle" of the consultation document does not represent the cry of the oppressed and the trials of the grassroots church, but an institution-centered vision of a "new civilization" wherein the Catholic Church would be the guiding light. Not surprisingly, the *comunidades* are given short shrift (REB 149: 5–10, 20–23, 33–58; Boff, Dussel et al., 1978: 3–41, 86–101, 118, 120).

*The Socio-Political Dynamics of Puebla.* CELAM III was convened by Paul VI, ratified by John Paul I, and inaugurated several weeks behind schedule by John Paul II. As with Medellín, the political climate in Latin America at the time had much to do with its preparation. Before and during Medellín the socio-political climate had been relatively quiescent—although the causes of unrest were beginning to make their presence felt. Medellín was also motivated by the continuing optimism in the wake of the changes initiated by Vatican II. The Latin American bishops felt free to be innovative and to speak out clearly on social issues. Significantly, many of the future "liberation theologians" were present and active at Medellín.

Not so with Puebla. In the intervening decade, political polarization, terrorism, armed liberation movements, and institutionalized violence had become common. Violence was even directed against servants of the church. The curia and the CELAM III secretariat had become very jittery. They saw in Puebla a way of slowing down the radicalization of the Latin American church.

Faced with mounting criticism of the consultation document, a second working document was prepared; although still conservative, it spoke a little more specifically to the issues in Latin America. It recognized, though cautiously, the positive contributions of the CEBs and of the liberation theologians.

Meanwhile, the CELAM secretariat was maneuvering behind the scenes to assure that progressive bishops and liberation theologians would be kept away from the conference. As a result, about a fifth only among the almost two hundred Latin American prelates who were present were truly identified with the aspirations of the poor. There was also, in the words of a European bishop who was present, "an excess of Romans," and a dozen conservative Latin American bishops who had been named by the pope. The choice of Puebla, an archconservative city in a very conservative Catholic nation (Mexico), was symbolic and exerted pressure upon the participants to remain close to the old Catholicism. The assembled bishops fell into three categories: those who professed political neutrality, a relatively small group; progressives; and a large body of uncommitted bishops who, as one of them observed, were "learning about Medellín at Puebla" (*Páginas*: 23, 32–33).

Said Cardinal Arns:

> We all went to Puebla as condemned men. We knew for a certainty that we would not satisfy what was expected of us. Undoubtedly we would not fulfill the wishes of the economists, sociologists, theologians, pastoralists, and *comunidades de base* specialists [*Páginas*: 28].

But to everyone's surprise, Puebla turned out to be a minor victory for the progressive forces and a temporary setback for the conservatives. Though there was no outright endorsement of the "popular church," neither was there specific condemnation. The polarization generated a creative tension that served to force the uncommitted prelates to take positions they had hitherto avoided. The uninvited liberation theologians operated *extra muros* in a low-key advisory capacity, and the assembled bishops were able to shove aside the officious secretariat and replace it with a more sympathetic "connecting commission" (*Páginas*: 28, 35; Cox and Sand 1979).

The decisive factor was probably John Paul II. Despite his innate conservatism, his charismatic interaction with the people and face-to-face confrontation with some aspects of the subhuman reality of the poor in Mexico may have caused him to moderate his views. Or it may have been part of a "pastoral" Vatican strategy from the beginning. In any case, he gave just enough encouragement to the progressives—in the context of his cautious warnings against excesses—to allow them some room to maneuver (CNBB 1980: 5–14, 19–35, 43–70, 81).

*The Puebla Document*. Despite a conference structure that isolated working groups from one another and limited plenary debate, the document has a number of points to commend it. Though at times ambiguous and contradictory in its ideological commitment—a reflection of the lack of internal communication at Puebla—it is a great improvement over the consultation document. *Evangelii Nuntiandi* continues to be the magisterial reference point, but not as much so as in the earlier versions. Medellín and the CEBs, though somewhat emasculated, cannot be entirely overlooked. The sociological analysis is more precise and avoids falling into the functionalist trap. The theology, predictably, is fairly traditional, but often in ways that find an echo in the hearts of many Protestants.

The missiological content attempts to balance the Vatican II definition of evangelization with Medellín and post-Medellín concerns for human promotion. The stated goal of evangelization is to lead persons to a knowledge of Jesus Christ as Lord, the result of which is an outpouring of "the fruits of justice, forgiveness, respect, dignity, and peace." This includes "liberation from everything that oppresses mankind . . . above all, liberation from sin and from the evil one." Human promotion is "intimately related ('an integral part') to salvation" (CELAM III: 244ff.).

Earlier the document had defined evangelization as "the duty to announce the liberation of millions of human beings, among whom the church identifies many of its children; the duty of accelerating this liberation of giving witness, and of insuring that it is complete" (CELAM III: 15).

*Puebla and the CEBs*. At the same time, there is enough traditional content in the Puebla document to give support and comfort to those who would suppress the grassroots church and its concerns. Although the *comunidades* are neither overlooked nor condemned, fairly precise limits are placed upon their actions. This can be appreciated best by briefly analyzing the Puebla definitions of the CEBs.

*Community* is stated in terms of family and age units, and of their personal Christian commitment. Nothing is said about the cultural and economic variables that define community. *Ecclesial* is narrowly defined in terms of the liturgical symbols of the church, and ambiguously expressed in the context of "solidarity and commitment to the new commandment of the Lord." There is no mention of the radical nature of ecclesial commitment, or of its primary orientation—not to a commandment, but to persons: toward Jesus Christ and one's needy neighbor. *Base* takes on the one meaning of a small group, "a cell in the larger community," without defining its socio-economic and political content and context (CELAM III: 489).

In the Puebla document the CEBs have been scrubbed and sanitized. The sting was taken out of them, at least on paper. It was an attempt to render them harmless to the institutional church and to circumscribe them to a mere token resistance to oppressive social structures. But Puebla did not deter the evolution of the *comunidades* in Latin America.

## GRASSROOTS COMMUNITIES IN LATIN AMERICA TODAY

What is the status of the CEBs in Latin America since Puebla? As far as Brazil is concerned, part of the answer to this question can be found in the events surrounding the pope's visit there (July 1-12, 1980), in the press notices of the escalating tension between the church and state, and in the comments of the CNBB and *comunidade* representatives.

*John Paul II's visit to Brazil* was preceded by a great deal of interest and speculation. The political-military establishment in Brazil fully expected an anticommunist pope to rubber-stamp their ruthless fight against "Marxist subversion." Much was made of the pontiff's criticisms at Puebla of the theologies of liberation and of his generally conservative stance. At the same time, Brazilian labor and CEB leaders, along with progressives in the clergy and hierarchy, were pointedly expressing their hopes of support from their spiritual leader. As one priest observed:

If the pope is used as a kind of tool and idol to deceive the people and make them forget for a moment the hunger, misery, and oppression in which they live, then his visit will not serve any useful purpose, since, after his return to Rome, we will continue in the same situation in which we now find ourselves [CRIE 1980: 4].

Influential members of the hierarchy, including Cardinal Lorscheider, were publicly expressing their disappointment with the Vatican meddling in the pope's visit to the Eucharistic Congress in Fortaleza—the religious purpose of his visit to Brazil. And mere days before John Paul II touched down in Brasilia, the CNBB pointedly reaffirmed its commitment to defend the cause of the poor and denounce injustice, expressing the wish that the pope's words might be on the side of peace and justice.

One item of heated debate was whether the pontiff was coming as the Vatican head of state, with all this implied in protocol and relationships with the Brazilian state, or as the supreme shepherd of the Catholic flock. In the end he came as both but, to the gratification of many and the discomfiture of officialdom, John Paul II played down his secular role in favor of the religious (CRIE 1980: 1:4; 2:3–4).[178]

Interspersed with blaring headlines that announced the pope's condemnation of violence and of liberation theologies and his affirmation of traditional Christian values, the overwhelming mass of news coming out of Brazil emphasized John Paul II's outspoken defense of human rights and surprisingly direct criticism of the socio-economic policies of the Brazilian government, his rapport with the masses, and his pointed snubbing of officialdom (CRIE: 2:6, 9; 3:1, 5, 7. 9; 4:6; 7:6; 8:5–6; 9:8–10; 10:9).[179]

The pope wasted no time in getting to the point. In a speech at the Palacio do Planalto (presidential palace) during his brief protocol stop in Brasilia, he pointedly addressed the issue of the doctrine of national security. After emphasizing the concern of the church for human rights, John Paul observed:

> The church encourages those who are responsible for the common good to undertake, before it is too late . . . reforms with conviction and courage, with prudence and efficiency, on the basis of Christian principles and criteria, objective justice, and an authentic social ethic. . . . To promote these reforms in this way is also a way to keep others from promoting them based on the impulse of currents that would not hesitate to use violence. . . . Never will a transformation of socio-political and economic structures be consolidated if it is not accompanied by a sincere "conversion" of the human mind, the will, and the heart with all that this entails [CNBB 1980: 23–25:14–15, 18].

During his dramatic visit to the Vidigal *favela* in Rio, which had been sanitized and reportedly depopulated of a number of less desirable residents (CRIE 4:3–5), the pontiff told the *favelados* who remained that "the church, in Brazil, desires to be a *church of the poor*. . . . It wants the first Beatitude of the Sermon on the Mount to become a fact." Speaking about the "poor in spirit," the pope asked:

> Do the words of Jesus about the poor in spirit make us by any chance forget injustices? . . . The words of Jesus . . . are not aimed at suppressing these problems. On the contrary, they make them stand out, while emphasizing the most essential points, which is humankind, the human heart, which involves every person without exception [CNBB 1980: 51–52:9–10].

On July 3 the pontiff spoke to a football stadium full of workers—militants in the bloody encounters between church-supported labor unions and the police (CRIE 5:3–4). There he reiterated the support of the church for an equitable distribution of the products of workers' labors. Though rejecting class struggle, he condemned the injustice of employers and the self-serving of the various power and interest groups (CNBB 1980: 102–11:6–8).

Yet one cannot help but notice the relatively few references to the CEBs in the papal speeches, despite the tremendous significance of the *comunidades* for the Brazilian church and for human promotion. John Paul devoted a very brief section to them in his speech to the CELAM bishops at Fortaleza, and left behind a brief admonitory "Message to the CEBs." In both instances he cautiously followed the line of *Evangelii Nuntiandi* and chose to emphasize the ecclesiality of the communities with barely a mention of their grassroots nature (CNBB 1980: 69:55, 57–61).

The pope's visit to Brazil highlights the dilemma of the Vatican in the face of what is taking place in Latin America. The social doctrine of the Catholic Church, reemphasized and expanded since Vatican II, and John Paul's credentials as a fighter for justice in this native Poland, do not make it easy for the Vatican to retreat to an Ultramontane view of the church, as much as some members of the hierarchy and curia might like it to do so. The challenges of modernity and secularization, coupled with an awareness of the stultifying effects of overcentralization, have caused the Holy See to cautiously welcome the initiative of the CEBs. However, once the door for reform and lay participation has been opened, once the church has pronounced itself in favor of the poor and disadvantaged, there is no turning back.

So the pontiff attempted to strike a balance. A close scrutiny of his pronouncements in Brazil will show that he had not budged one inch from his position as expressed at Puebla. What gave the illusion of a greater openness was the atmosphere of frontal confrontation between church and state, coupled with a need for institutional solidarity. This was spiced with the pope's natural outspokenness in response to human issues that touch him deeply—as his visit to Brazil undoubtedly did. Also John Paul did not arrive in Brazil totally unprepared. At his request, he had received from his episcopal colleagues, well in advance, suggestions for the contents of his various speeches. The progressive Brazilian hierarchy was well rewarded for its efforts in "conscientizing" their supreme leader (CRIE: 1:5:7).

Though the pope did not get to the root of the problems that trouble Brazil, his major function, in the view of his fellow bishops, was to raise issues, to use his considerable charisma to make others aware of those issues, and to mobilize a vast popular movement unlike anything the rival political parties had ever been able to achieve. In brief, *the pope dramatized the popular strength and influence of the Brazilian Catholic Church as a critical point of confrontation with a very worried government* (CRIE: 11:4–7; 12:1–7). The delicate balance that existed until recently between the totalitarian state and the grassroots church in Brazil, and the eventual evolution to a political democracy, is probably due in great measure to the impact of the visit of John Paul II to Brazil—as well as to the continued upward pressure of thousands of CEBs.

Vatican concern over the CEBs has not ceased, however. A cause célèbre in Brazil midway in 1981 was an accusation of Marxist infiltration by Cardinal Agnelo Rossi, prefect of the Sacred Congregation for the Evangelization of the Peoples. Dom Agnelo, it will be remembered, in 1956 had set in motion one of the earliest CEB experiments in Barra do Pirai (Natal), in response to the challenge of the rapid spread of Protestantism (see chap. 4, above). Later, as cardinal archbishop of São Paulo, he had led the conservative forces that supported the military revolution in 1964, for which Paul VI moved him out of the way into a recent Vatican position (see chap. 5). In May 1981, returning to Brazil to celebrate his episcopal jubilee, the cardinal, soon to retire, dropped a bombshell in the lap of the CNBB.

He announced the existence in Europe of a series of cassette recordings, Marxist in content, that were intended for the CEBs (*Folha de São Paulo*, May 10, 1981). He further accused certain theologians of promoting the politicization of the CEBs (*Jornal do Brasil*, May 11, 1981). The CNBB denied the existence of the recordings, and the more conservative bishops made clear their opposition to this alleged infiltration. Cardinal Arns was quoted as saying diplomatically that "when you make an accusation, either you love the ones whom you are trying to protect very much, or you mistrust those who are involved in the CEBs. I imagine that Dom Agnelo is in the first category; he loves the CEBs and wants to protect them. In São Paulo we do not want exaggerated protection, nor do we accept anarchy."

An episcopal spokesman offered the opinion that the suspicions of Cardinal Rossi could be attributed to the fact that "he has been so long in the Roman curia that he is perhaps unaware of the reality of the CEBs in Brazil." He pointed out that in Europe such communities are in confrontation with the church, but in Brazil they remain in close community with it. The CNBB promptly launched an investigation of the matter, while Dom Agnelo continued to defend the veracity of his charges in strong terms, promising to report the matter to the pope. Dom Luciano Mendez, the CNBB secretary general, and several cardinals and bishops stoutly defended the integrity of the CEBs and called for an end to the debate.

Later, when the CELAM secretariat announced that the cassettes would not be allowed in Latin American CEBs, the CNBB was able to reveal that the material was not of recent vintage, nor was it intended for Brazil. "A Man Called Jesus" had been prepared in Spanish, in 1978, by a para-ecclesiastical radio literacy agency for use in Central America and the Caribbean. When the content of the tapes and accompanying booklet were finally revealed, they proved to be somewhat anticlimactic. "A Man Called Jesus," judging at least from the newspaper summary, is rather innocuous: quite biblical in content, popular in style, and only slightly to the left of the books of Micah, Amos, and St. James![180]

Whether this faux pas was the result of a Vatican foray against the CEBs or simply the crotchet of an aging conservative churchman may never be known. The fact, however, remains that the relationship between the Holy See and the CNBB leadership was somewhat strained over the latter's unconditional support of the *comunidades* and all that they imply. Despite the pope's show of support in 1980, the Vatican is evincing unmistakable signs of concern over the growing politicization of the Brazilian Catholic Church.

## The Role of the CEBs in the Current Political Milieu

All the way across the political spectrum of Brazil, the Catholic grassroots communities are both feared and wooed. This can be perceived by glancing through the newspapers since the *distenção* was announced in 1979. Here and there a politician will insist that he and his party have the support of the CEBs. Others initiated community action programs of their own to counteract the impact of the *comunidades*. Bishops and priests protested the ideological manipulation of the CEBs by the five legal political parties. Cardinals Arns and Lorscheider declared categorically that they did not want the political parties within the church, though Cardinal Arns acknowledged that the CEBs did indeed exert political pressure on the political parties. He sees them as schools for democracy.

### The Challenges of the CEBs to Marxism

A growing volume of press commentary points to the increasing politicization of the *comunidades*. In fact, Dom Pedro Casadáliga, the so-called red bishop of São Féliz do Araguaia, has defended the right of the CEBs to participate in the political process, pointing out that the left-of-center parties are the ones that have demonstrated the greatest degree of openness to the needs of the people. The press had noted the seeming predilection of many *comunidade* members for the *Partido dos Trabalhadores* (PT; Workers' Party), of a radical Social Democratic orientation, and had speculated over the possibility that the CEBs might be co-opted by Marxist groups, although this seemed to be less of a possibility in Brazil than elsewhere (*Jornal do Brasil*, Sept. 22, 1980).[181] In an oral report on the Brazilian CEBs (in San José, Costa Rica), Leonardo Boff commented, perhaps naively, that doctrinaire Marxists who have attended the *comunidades* "soon tire of all that Bible reading, chorus singing, and praying—and they move on!"

Tristão de Athayde (Alceu Amoroso Lima), the Brazilian man of letters who was a leader of the anticommunist Catholic Nationalist Movement in the 1940s and 50s, is today a supporter of the CEB movement. He insists that the expansion of communism in recent years is due to the earlier withdrawal of the church from the social sphere, particularly during a period of social and technological revolution:

If the church, at the right moment, had opted for the poor, as did Marx and his partisans and successors, the face of the earth would have been changed by the Holy Spirit and not by the spirit of pseudo science, of a historical determinism that has been sidetracked from its transcendental sources. What the spirit of the *comunidades ecclesiais de base* is attempting to reintroduce in history, in the light of the encyclicals and of the theology of liberation, is precisely the only authentically scientific process that can respond to the false science [*Folha*, April 12, 1979].

Frei Betto argues emphatically that the CEBs do not have a "Marxist scientific instrument of analysis." They are merely living the process of analysis or reality that Marxism had previously systematized. In a number of points this may coincide with Marxism, but it is not Marxist. It is "biblical and prophetic" (interview, Feb. 13, 1980).

In any case, a Christian critique of the social structures by the oppressed themselves is a response that doctrinaire Marxists had not met before. It can be considered a threat, as well as a challenge, to their deterministic and simplistic explanation of historical processes. For this reason, presumably, they would not hesitate to use the *comunidades* for their own purposes if they are permitted to do so. At the same time, the radical-sounding social rhetoric of the government party during the closing years of the military regime was clearly aimed at manipulating the *comunidades*. There is danger for the CEBs from both extremes.

For a time the CEBs in Brazil gave evidence of an *identity crisis* in a sociopolitical context that was, for a short time, not as repressive as it once was.[182] Cardinal Arns prophetically observed in early 1980 that the great challenge for the grassroots Brazilian church in the immediate future was to maintain its ecclesial identity in the face of competing ideologies (interview, Feb. 16, 1980).

Catholic sociologist Ribeiro de Oliveira is quoted as stating that in spite of the irreversible nature of the social commitment of the church, the CEBs "are at present passing through a difficult situation and are subject to some retreating." Nevertheless, he judges that the disappearance of the *comunidades* would be impossible because it would produce a schism in the church. If the current political process is allowed to evolve into a viable democracy, Oliveira foresees a "relative emptying of the *comunidades* in favor of new popular options such as labor unions and neighborhood associations." But "without democracy, the *comunidades* will become even stronger" (*Estado*, Dec. 15, 1981).

This poses a great dilemma for the Brazil hierarchy, only about 25 percent of which, according to Oliveira, are truly committed to the CEBs.[183] Unless they are able to deepen the grassroots community understanding of the Christian faith, and of the gospel of the kingdom, together with an adequate orientation in their rights and privileges as citizens,[184] the Brazilian Catholic Church is in danger of losing not only its imposing power base, but its raison d'être. That the bishops are not unaware of this danger is demonstrated by the importance that the CNBB continues to place upon the *comunidades* in its annual and quinquennial plans. In 1982 it created a special commission to evaluate the work of the CEBs.

The *comunidades'* role in the advance toward what some are now calling Brazil's "New Republic" will presumably ensure them a measure of acceptance after a brief resurgence of harassment by rural landholders and police. Nonetheless, they are viewed with increasing suspicion by an uneasy Vatican, as the pressures recently brought to bear upon CEB-related Leonardo Boff and Gustavo Gutiérrez by the Congregation for the Doctrine of the Faith testify.

If, as seems evident, the Vatican is so pressured by the demands of power politics and by the interests of institutional integrity that it has begun to crack down on the *comunidades* through their best-known spokesmen, what will be the reaction of the CNBB? Presumably it would eventually have to submit, in loyalty to the church. Outright rebellion, at least at the top, seems unlikely at this point.

If abandoned by its official leadership, what would be the reaction of the grassroots church, including committed priests and bishops? Officially, the possibility of a confrontation was stoutly denied, while, privately, some of the persons whom I interviewed conceded that it might happen, and if so, that significant numbers of the *comunidades* would go their own way. This possibility may have crossed the minds of curia personnel also—and may have something to do with the Vatican's cautious treatment of liberation theologians.

Whether autonomous CEBs evolved into a new popular church or became a powerful grassroots political movement, much depended upon the depth of their Christian faith and upon the quality of their political commitment, as well as upon the continuing interaction of both dimensions of their base community praxis. To be sure, the Brazilian CEBs are being watched very closely by the rest of Latin America, because of their sheer size and political impact. The way they go may decide the future of the CEB movement—and of the church— throughout Latin America.

The Catholic communities are at *a crucial point in their history*. In the same way as Protestant communities have leaned too far in the direction of the otherworldly dimension of the gospel and have thus alienated themselves from the reality of the poor, the Catholic CEBs in Brazil could either be swallowed up by the socio-political world or be forced into submission by a powerful curia. In either case, they would be alienating themselves from a full-orbed ecclesiality and vital Christianity. If this should happen, then, despite its minuscule size, Central America and its numerous clandestine CEBs may now become the place to watch. It seems increasingly possible that the crucial battle for the integrity of the Christian church and of the biblical message at every level is being fought in Latin America, and in particular in Central America, as well as Brazil. The foregoing study of the CEBs may, I certainly hope, provide some clues for mission action in the days ahead.

My prayer is that the *comunidades de base* in Latin America continue to be the "hope of the church" and "the expectation of the poor"—but from within, not as a separate ecclesiastical institution, as a partisan political movement, nor as a mere appendage to a traditional church. Ecclesiastical schism, degeneration into a mere political movement or institutionalization would spell the end of one of the most significant ecclesial movements and social forces in the twentieth century.

# Notes

1. In the Glossary I have defined the Portuguese and Spanish terms that I have chosen to maintain for the sake of authenticity. Technical definitions and necessary addenda or clarifications will appear in these notes that will also serve to provide additional information on matters that would interrupt the flow of the basic material. Only when such information is extraneous to the main subject matter—yet required in order to provide the necessary documentation for a particular point—will it appear in the notes.

2. Portuguese; in Spanish, *comunidades eclesiales de base.*

3. "Reality" is the literal translation of the Portuguese *realidade,* which is also rendered "actuality" or "fact" in *The New Michaelis: Illustrated Dictionary,* vol. 2 (Portuguese-English), São Paulo: Edições Melhoramentos, 1961. Roughly, it conveys the idea of "the situation as it *really* is." Sociologically, it is used to refer to empirical facts. The sociology of knowledge defines "reality" as "a quality appertaining to phenomena that we recognize as being independent of our own volition" (Berger and Luckmann 1967: 1). Following Berger, J. B. Libânio (1979b: 63, 65) elaborates: "It is not incorrect to say that man is a product of his environment. But, on the other hand, reality is socially constructed. . . . In other words, man is both the producer and the product of social reality." This subject will be discussed at length in chap. 6.

4. The creativity of the *comunidade* movement is so great that this writer has been kept on his toes during the two and a half years that it took him to do this research. It has meant repeatedly going back to incorporate new data. Since completion of the project, the productivity of the *comunidades de base* has not abated and bibliography on the subject continues to expand. Perhaps the most up-to-date Protestant library on the *comunidades* is at Princeton Theological Seminary.

5. Marvin Harris, *The Rise of Anthropological Theory,* New York: Crowell, 1968, p. 163.

6. For more on the Radical Evangelical perspective, see Hubbard 1979; Quebedeaux 1974; Wallis 1976 and 1981.

7. Increasingly, Latin American social scientists and Catholic theologians are turning to a modified Marxist dialectical analysis, if not always to classic Marxist solutions, as a tool for "unmasking" social reality and for understanding the root causes of poverty and social alienation. Although admitting that Marxist theory does not satisfactorily explain every dimension of social reality (IECT 1980: 94), they point out the difference between using it as an analytical tool, as a philosophy of history, and as a absolute political-economic system. Even if the philosophy and the system are open to question on the basis of both theory and practice, the social analysis, they believe, can be useful (Segundo 1976: 57–62; LADOC Keyhole 15: 53–60).

8. The Iberian word *base* is difficult to render adequately in English. Most often it is translated by the term "basic," as in "basic ecclesial communities." "Basic" (i.e.,

"fundamental") is of course one of the meanings of the English noun-adjective "base." It is derived from the Latin *basis* (pedestal) from which the Spanish-Portuguese word *base* also derives a meaning. This is, for example, what Medellín means when it calls the *comunidades* "the first and fundamental ecclesial nucleus . . . the initial cell of the ecclesiastical structures" (CELAM II: 15:10). This usage was echoed by Puebla, which stated that a community is *de base* because it is "a general cell in the community at large" (CELAM III: 389). But "basic" is only one facet of the complex meaning of the term as it is understood sociologically in Latin America. A more literal—and problematical— rendering of *base* would be "base," derived from the Latin *bassus,* meaning "fat" or "low." In English it conveys the idea of low social station, which implies that we are looking down on the communities, for example, a perspective which is in disharmony with an attitude which is informed by a view "from below" (see Bruneau 1980: 227–28). The International Ecumenical Congress of Theology (IECT, São Paulo, Feb. 9 to March 2, 1980) referred to *comunidades cristianas populares* (IECT 1980: 8–9), which has been translated into English as "peoples' ecclesial communities" (Torres and Eagleson 1981: 231; *Occasional Bulletin* 1980: 4/3: 127). But "popular" is also ambiguous in English. These communities are "popular" only in the sense that they are "of the people"—the poor, though they are far from popular in certain sectors of the church and in the eyes of the secular powers! A literal, though somewhat clumsy, rendering of *comunidades de base* would be "communities of the base." The closest English equivalent to this is "grassroots communities," a term that I will henceforth use interchangeably with *comunidades* or communities and with the commonly accepted abbreviation CEB (for *comunidades eclesiales de base*).

9. Functionality cannot be studied apart from the problem of power. What may be functional for the powerful may be highly dysfunctional for the powerless. This is of more than academic interest to the discipline of missiology, which purports to further the mission of God who entered into self-identification with the powerless to achieve human freedom and redemption.

10. Frei Betto attributes this figure to CERIS (SEDOC: 12/126, 450). Cardinal Arns would not give me any figures, admitting that he did not know where these estimates had come from. There are no official statistics on the movement.

11. Proto-Iberians, Celts, Phoenician and Greek traders, Roman legions, diaspora Jews, Germanic tribes, and Moorish followers of the prophet Muhammad.

12. In *O Brasileiro entre os Outros Hispanos* (1975), Freyre—a product of the Franz Boas "cultural trait" school of anthropology—brings together a number of essays in Portuguese, Spanish, and English. He postulates that the dominant Iberian traits are "poetic vision," "shrewd realism," and a different time valuation. The last-named is manifested in a unique gift for improvisation and in a characteristic attitude toward work, which, he argues, fits into neither the capitalist nor Marxist work ethics. If he is correct, the Marxist political system should have little appeal to the CEBs. See also his studies of the cultural environments of Brazil (Freyre 1964 and 1968) (e.g., Amerindian, African, and European), which, in the process, have lost many of their unique cultural patterns, while contributing elements to an evolving new culture. Brazil is the outstanding example of this configuration, and, to a lesser degree, Paraguay, Chile, Venezuela, Colombia, and the Greater Antilles (Ribeiro 1980: 53–59).

13. Darcy Ribeiro had developed his theory of human history in *The Civilization Process—Stages in Sociocultural Evolution,* Washington, Smithsonian Institution, and New York, Harper & Row, 1971. His application to the New World can be found in *The*

*Americas and Civilization,* New York: Dutton, 1971. Ribeiro's presuppositions are qualified Marxism. He makes the point that Marx focused in detail on only one world system—capitalism. A man of his time, Marx held a view of socio-economic history that was linear and evolutionary and in which slavery, feudalism, and capitalism had each followed the other in a logical and inevitable sequence. Consequently, the next stages— socialism and communism—were also inevitable. Ribeiro, however, is neither linearly evolutionary nor historically deterministic, though he maintains in his theory of world cultures the Marxian belief in the dynamic role of class struggle in any stratified society (1980: 28–30, 154–66).

14. "Cultural-historical configurations" are more concrete in character, says Ribeiro, than the great "civilization traditions" such as the Chinese, Greco-Roman, Islamic, English, Iberian, etc. On the other hand, these "configurations" do not have the same cohesive force as macro-ethnic groups—e.g., the Spanish American peoples— or their smaller ethnic components. Ribeiro isolates four cultural-historical configurations in recent human history, all of which are represented in the New World: (1) The *witness peoples,* such as the Chinese, Muslim, Aztec, Maya, and Inca cultures, which collectively bear witness to ancient cultural glories. (2) The *transplanted peoples:* nations of immigrants (e.g., Argentina, Uruguay, Canada, and the U.S.A.), mainly of European origin, who have managed to preserve much of their original cultural patterns with only superficial adaptations. (3) The *emerging peoples* are beginning to appear in Asia, Africa, and the Caribbean. (4) The *new peoples* have developed from a coming together and melding of disparate cultures (e.g., Amerindian, African, and European), which in the process, have lost many of their unique cultural patterns, while contributing elements to an evolving new culture. Brazil is the outstanding example of this configuration, and, to a lesser degree, Paraguay, Chile, Venezuela, Colombia, and the Greater Antilles (Ribeiro 1980: 53–59).

15. The complex interaction of temporal, social, and regional factors in Brazil has produced a highly heterogeneous society. At the *temporal* level, says Ribeiro, successive historical configurations (colonial, neocolonial, national) interacted during the "civilization process" with overlapping economic systems (agrarian-mercantile and urban). At the *social* level we must deal with the stratifications that developed in the interacting rural-urban and manorial-slave cultures. At the *regional* level we find "different ecological adaptations that structured themselves into different cultural areas." The homogenizing agents in this complex process were the socio-cultural institutions of Iberian Europe. To quote Ribeiro, "Throughout its almost five centuries of history, Brazilian culture shows the widest variations within these bounds. In fact, the only constant is, principally, its spurious character, caused by cultural displacement and the consequent vicissitudes of a culture that is both alienated by and alienates its own participants" (Ribeiro: 142).

16. The Latin American working class was never more than an "external proletariat" at the service of the industrial European societies. But the dominant class also lacked an autonomous culture. It existed only as a surrogate of the distant metropolis. The only aspiration of this class was to adopt the customs of their white alien role models—successively Portuguese or Spanish, English, French and, more recently, North American. Their lack of cultural creativity throughout the centuries is the consequence of this dependence upon alien cultures and of their lack of a truly autochthonous intelligentsia (Ribeiro: 142ff.)

17. Calculations based upon official census statistics as graphed in Read and Ineson

(1973: 8, 10). Government policy aimed at stemming the massive tide to the urban centers, and massive unemployment in the early 1980s, began to reverse the flow. This has served only to increase tensions in the newly lucrative Amazon region (*Newsweek,* Jan. 25, 1981: 4:6–9).

18. The Christendom model of the church was essentially a sacralist worldview, a carryover from the religion of imperial Rome. In sacralism—the opposite of secularism—the sacred and the secular, religion and everyday life, church and state are indistinguishable; they are two sides of the same coin. In this worldview all the citizens of a state belong to the state religion by reason of birth and not out of personal commitment. After Christianity became the imperial religion, pagan sacralism gradually gave ground to Christian sacralism.

19. After centuries of living side-by-side with Muslims on more or less amicable terms, the Christian princelings of the numerous Iberian kingdoms of the 14th and 15th centuries found in a Holy Crusade against Islam the religious justification for their strivings for political hegemony over the entire peninsula. In this way, the enemies of the homeland came to be considered enemies of the faith and vice versa.

20. Spanish, *patronato*; Portuguese, *padroado real.*

21. In addition, the Portuguese king and his successors were rewarded in 1522 by a grateful Pope Adrian VI (for this monarch's battles against the Moors) with the title of Grand Prior of the Order of Christ. This order was the successor in Portugal of the crusading Knights Templar who had been disbanded in 1310 by Pope Clement V. By pontifical bulls, all the colonies of Portugal were entrusted canonically to the Order of Christ, in much the same way in which a prelacy would be entrusted to a religious institution. By so doing, the papacy sacralized Portuguese colonial expansion and made the church virtually the religious department of the crown. This policy came to be known as *regalism.*

22. Missionary-colonialist expansion in Brazil took place in four overlapping cycles. The *first missionary movement,* during the second half of the 16th century along the Atlantic seaboard, was closely tied to the exploitation and ultimate destruction of the vast brazilwood forests, and later to the sugarcane plantation system in the Brazilian northeast. This was the period of the heroic Jesuit pioneers who preceded by only a few years the creative apostolates of Mateo Ricci and Roberto de Nobili in China and India. The *second missionary advance* was conditioned by the occupation of the vast Brazilian interior plain or *sertão.* During the second half of the century, monks of several nationalities and orders navigated the São Francisco river basin seeking to take the gospel to the natives under the aegis of the Portuguese crown. The *third missionary thrust* took place during this same period, and in the first half of the following century. Gifted Jesuits, traveling along the vast Amazonian waterways, moved into the north equatorial province of *Maranhão,* after it had been wrested from the French. The *fourth and final missionary thrust* of the colonial period was unclerical and unplanned. It was a lay movement in which the church had very little to do. During the 18th century, hermits, "miracle workers," and lay religious brotherhoods spread a grassroots version of Catholicism throughout the large "wild-west" mining territory of Minas Gerais. The brotherhoods were, in part, a response to the scarcity of priests. But they were also one answer to cultural alienation and racial discrimination in a changing social order. Historian Paul E. Pierson points out that "these groups were important, not only in expressing and enhancing the identity of their members, but also in changing the traditional relationship between clergy and laity" (Pierson 1974: 3). The brotherhoods

and the extended-family lay religiosity in the plantation culture highlight the fact that in large areas of Brazil Christianity was disseminated almost exclusively by grassroots movements. This has had a profound effect upon the lay religiosity and leadership development in the subordinated classes, a fact that is not without importance for the emergence of the CEBs.

23. This is why, says Hoornaert, the evangelization of the Amerindians was so crucial to the colonialist project. It facilitated their enslavement under the patronage system. It is therefore important to study the problem of land ownership in Latin America and its implications for the formation of the particular Latin American form of Christendom.

24. The jurisdictional controversies that erupted along the Portuguese-Spanish frontiers between missionaries (even among those of the same order!) serving the interests of their respective monarchs make evident the fact that the "reduction" of natives into protective *aldeamentos* by the missionaries was based, at least in part, upon land competition between the great colonial powers.

25. This is what happened when the Dutch were expelled from their 50-year rule over northeastern Brazil by guerrillas at the service of *fazendeiros*.

26. In the words of Hoornaert, "It is within the context of the slave trade as practiced by the religious orders or tolerated by them that the catechesis of Africans in Brazil must be studied. The Jesuits, at the same time that they sent slaves here, also sent priests to catechize them" (1979: 262).

27. Gilberto Freyre insists on the importance of the *engenho,* as over against the official church, in the religious formation of Brazil. The central religious figures in the sugar mill culture were the landlord and his loyal mestizo or mulatto chaplain. But they were not the only transmitters of rural Catholic religion. The lady of the house, the black wet nurse, the maids and servants, the black playmates of the heirs of the manor, as Freyre so vividly portrays, were all communicators of a typical and original genre of rural Catholicism. In this triangle—the *casa grande* (manor house), *senzala* (slave shed), and *capela* (chapel)—"the Big House overcame the church. . . . The lord of the manor was nearer to being the true lord than the viceroys and bishops . . . the Big House and the slave shed represent the entire social and political system," to which the Catholic Church was a willing servant. This subservience was symbolized by the location of the chapel in the shadow of the *casa grande.* The "uncle-priest" often was a close relative of the plantation master (Pierson 1974: 2). In this system of monoculture and slave labor it was inevitable that the plantation chaplaincy should become corrupted by the venality and moral laxness of the masters of the Big House, whose lives "revolved around the hammock: sleep, rest, eat, play, sex" (Freyre 1964: 7–13, 344, 347, 380–81; see also de Kadt 1970: 14).

28. The major cities of Brazil became rich from the slave trade. Rio de Janeiro, for example, began to prosper and grow after its merchants had raised enough money in 1648 to finance an expedition that recovered the African territories of Portugal from Holland in order to take over the lucrative trade of the Dutch. Salvador de Bahia, the first colonial capital, was the principal slave port of Brazil and possibly of the entire Atlantic-American seaboard. One-eighth of all the slaves who came to the New World were funneled through the quintessentially African colonial city. As a result, between 1650 and the demise of the slave trade in 1880, a majority of the inhabitants of Brazil were black (Hoornaert 1979: 267–70). This reality has profoundly influenced all of Brazilian Christendom—a fact that should become

even more clear when we look at Afro-Brazilian religiosity in chap. 3.

29. This squares with a Freyre quote from a slaveholding planter's manifesto, "The most productive feature of slave property is the generative belly" (1946: 278, 356 ff.).

30. Meanwhile, in Spanish America, though Amerindians have always been discriminated against, miscegenation and intermarriage *(mestizaje)* continue to be a door to social acceptance. Native Amerindians were also accepted once they had abandoned their traditions or, as in a very few cases, had managed to prosper on the white man's terms.

31. Because of this definition of ecclesial reality, the post-Tridentine church continued to place great stress upon the outward symbols of the faith: feasts, processions, holy days, pageantry, etc. (Galilea 1978: 43–44). This self-understanding was at the root of the crusading and inquisitorial spirit to which I have alluded earlier.

32. Not that there was an abundance of bishops in colonial Brazil! It was not until 1551 that Brazil had its first bishopric. More than a century later three additional sees were created. Three new ecclesiastical jurisdictions were set up during the early part of the 18th century. These seven sees and prelacies alone were responsible for a vast territory until independence in 1821 (Gregory 1965: 99–112; see also Perez, Gregory, and Lepargneur 1964: 31–52). This weak structure was in marked contrast with the Spanish ecclesiastical organization of the colonies, where numerous bishoprics were created in rapid succession beginning in the 16th century. To make the situation more acute, Brazilian sees were frequently vacant, or left unattended for long periods of time by absentee prelates, a fact that further contributed to the demoralization and venality of the lower clergy, and to the pastoral neglect of the masses.

33. Even the architecture, interior, and location of the colonial chapels, under the shadow of the Big House, reflected the reality of cultural, socio-economic, and sexual domination and discrimination of the times (Hoornaert 1979: 170–241; dos Santos: 48–49; Pierson 1964:2).

34. The theological training of the clergy, according to Hoornaert, was doctrinaire, theoretical, and domesticating. By and large there was no such thing as contextualized reflection in the seminaries, although some intriguing examples of attempts to grapple with contemporary issues can be found in sermons, missionary correspondence, and writings of the time. When priests indoctrinated slaves, they often played upon their superstitious fears, while seeking to take the place of the tribal shamans. Their catechesis was repetitive, demeaning, and domesticating. It was also hampered by the barriers of language and by the lack of a trained clergy. Because of the shortage of priests, much of the indoctrination was done by the slave masters themselves. In contrast with the native catechesis, which was haltingly taught by the religious orders in the native languages, all communication with blacks took place in Portuguese or Latin. The African languages were considered subversive and were used by the slaves only in secret. As a result, the real religious sentiments of the enslaved populace were expressed clandestinely (Hoornaert 1979: 322–26).

35. But the subordinated masses had a more complex, and seemingly contradictory, view of Christ. Though they developed the legend of the "beggar Christ" who traveled the world incognito in the company of St. Peter defending the poor and putting to the test the compassion of the rich (Hoornaert 1979: 344, 346), the Jesus of their devotions remained basically a dehumanized Christ. At one and the same time he was the helpless Christ of the cross, and the first of the *santos* (Leers 1977: 79–80) and a deity who was often indistinguishable from God the Father. Segundo Galilea puts forth the hypothesis

that the last-named strand of belief was the result of orthodox Catholic reaction to the early spread of animism in the Iberian peninsula. In the void left by a dehumanized Christ there arose the worship of Mary and the saints (Galilea 1978: 65, 67, Leers: 84, 88).

36. The distinctly Catholic devotion to Mary and the saints also meant different things to the colonial masters and to their slaves. The colonizers were intensely devoted to Mary, as manifested by the numerous churches that they founded in her honor. The role of Mary and of other female saints was closely related in the colonial mind with the domesticating role of the wife and mother of the plantation rulers. She was also pictured as a warrior who had fought side by side with the conquerors of the land. The various saints were also portrayed in the colonial hagiography as warriors and richly attired lords, or even as privileged black servants caring for white children. St. Anthony, John, Peter and the warrior St. George were the protectors of the privileged and of the rich. But the poor also identified Mary and the saints with their own spirits and deities, and looked to them "as protectors . . . since the powerful did not protect them." In Brazil, St. George's counterpart, the African God Ogun, was the champion of the slaves (Freyre 1936: 166, 302, 315). Whom did the saints heed? As Hoornaert observes, "The popular saints reveal the social truth about Brazil" (1979: 320–53).

37. In the 17th century, Gallicanism had tried to make the French church administratively independent of Rome. Even earlier, Jansenism, a radically Augustinian and relatively antipapal movement, was set in motion by Bishop C. O. Jansen of Ypres as an attempt to combat the Reformation and Counter-Reformation.

38. Ultramontanism, a 19th century movement to restore papal authority in the Catholic Church, derived its name from those clerics who looked beyond the alps *(ultramontanus)* to Rome for help against the still strong Gallican influence in powerful sectors of the European church. Ultramontanism was a highly centralized and verticalist movement that rejected all forms of liberalism and the involvement of the church in temporal activities. It came to a head in Pius IX's unilateral proclamation of the immaculate conception of Mary and in the Vatican I (1869–1879) proclamation of papal infallibility.

39. The Catholic Church in Spanish colonies was never as weak as in Brazil, despite regalism. But the local clergy maintained a measure of autonomy from a weakened Rome. Several prelates were active in the independence movements of their respective nations. After independence, the church continued to be influential, and became even more so following the Ultramontane revitalization. Rome began a forceful defense of its authority as a powerful supporter of conservative political movements, in belligerent opposition to liberal movements—which early on saw in Protestantism a potential ally.

40. The wave of democratic sentiment that accompanied the end of World War II forced Vargas, who had remained in power with military support long after the end of his term, to bow to pressures that came from all sides for a return to constitutionality. The officer class—the ultimate power brokers—having so recently fought in Europe "to save democracy," could scarcely afford to continue supporting a fascist dictatorship at home. After Vargas's overthrow, tensions surfaced that were exacerbated by the changes that he had set in motion. Political allegiances shifted as the various power interests—the new urban middle class and labor unions, large landholders, liberals, the military, and the Communist Party—vied for control. In all this, the marginalized masses were still excluded from the electoral process. After Vargas was reelected, as a populist-style politician, he was forced to deal with a more clearly defined class structure

and with a growing preoccupation with economic development. His economic policies became increasingly nationalistic. But opposition to his policies grew. Inflation-aggravated social tensions and the fears of leftist subversion, astutely played up by the right-wing opposition, eventually led to his final downfall. Faced with a military ultimatum to resign, and in failing health, Vargas aimed a bullet through his heart (Skidmore 1967:3–142).

41. Quadros, an idealistic "outsider," was swept into power on a conservative fiscal reform ticket and then resigned in frustration, or perhaps as a ploy to win public support. His resignation was accepted. "Jango" Goulart was inept and indecisive as well as corrupt. As the political spectrum coalesced into radical extremes—leaving the majority of Brazilians, and in particular the disenfranchised, without effective political representation—his policies became even more radical.

42. It is precisely this unique ecclesiastical fact that sets Brazil apart from the rest of Latin America. To my knowledge, only in Brazil does the base church figure as a prominent goal in the planning of the conference of bishops and have the active support of prominent cardinals. Decisive hierarchical support, which seems to be one prerequisite of CEB success, appears elsewhere in Latin America only in Chile and El Salvador. Elsewhere, the CEBs are fostered mainly at local diocesan levels, as was the case, for example, in Bishop Mendez-Arceo's Cuernavaca (Mexico) diocese, and continues under Bishop Leonidas Proaño in the Chimborazo province of Ecuador. Here and there, national sees will give the CEBs guarded support.

43. AI-5 was based upon the state-of-siege powers that are granted to the president by the revised constitution of 1967 for cases where the security of the state is threatened by dangerous foreign ideologies. It gave the chief executive of Brazil the power to "close congress and other legislative assemblies, remove citizens from office and divest them of their political rights, and eliminate the rights of habeas corpus" of anyone suspected of attempting to conspire against the security of the state. It in effect subverted the very constitution that had been dictated by the military (Bruneau 1974: 178; Antoine 1973: 205–6).

44. Brazil is constitutionally a federal republic with authority at all levels of government divided between the executive, legislative, and judicial branches, at both state and national levels. However, since the Vargas years, power has increasingly been concentrated in the federal government, particularly in the executive branch (Wagley 1963: 4, 254ff.). From the *Revolucão* until 1983, the president appointed all state governors and they, the mayors of the state capitals. The president is assisted by the National Security Council (CNS) and by the National Information (Intelligence) Service (SNI), which combine to form a kind of "power behind the throne." They are entrusted with major policy decisions on matters ranging from economics to repression of social unrest. The secretary general of the CNS, a shadowy figure, had many of the attributes of his counterpart in the party secretariat of a communist country (Antoine 1973: 115). Significantly, two of the five military presidents have been SNI directors. The military regime has attempted to maintain the semblance of a democratic government during most of this period, including an artificial two-party system. Indeed, the Constitution of 1945 (revised in 1967) begins with the full text of the Universal Declaration of Human Rights (*Constituição* 1970: 8–11). All of this notwithstanding, the favorite legislative instruments of the presidency during this period were the "institutional acts"—the series of presidential decrees appended to the constitution for indefinite periods.

45. Ironically, the self-effacing and soft-spoken Golbery—who was the *eminence grise* behind the two more recent presidents of Brazil—is a leader of the "moderate"

faction of the Brazilian War College. A realist, he has warned, "Beyond certain limits the sacrifice of freedom will be harmful to security. Slaves are never good fighters. This is a lesson which tyrants have learned throughout history" (*Pro Mundi Vita: Dossiers* 1977: 15). Because of his espousal of tactical concessions to the increasingly restive population, Golbery was labeled a "radical leftist" by military hard-liners (LADOC Keyhole 8:1–5; IDOC International 1978:30–42) who apparently forced his resignation in August of 1981 (*Folha* 1981c:8/23:5).

46. The national security doctrine uses religious symbols to legitimize its actions. In 1970 representatives of the Evangelical Church Lutheran Confession presented to President Medici a copy of the Declaration of Curitiba in which, among other things, they addressed themselves to the *educação moral e cívica* program that was being substituted for religious instruction in public schools. They criticized its "declared ideological base," which "confuses for many citizens the pertinent areas of the State and the Church" (Costas 1976:42).

47. At least Marxist-Leninism does not profess Christian values. But a geopolitical philosophy that, in its most extreme forms, has meant death to countless thousands and has, in any case, been responsible for the subhuman conditions in which millions in the world are living—in the defense of a supposed Christian heritage—has a lot to account for!

48. Invoking his power under AI-5, Geisel closed congress long enough to emit certain decrees that would ensure the continued political dominance of the regime in the face of the congressional gains of what was now becoming a bona fide opposition party. The opposition strength was shrewdly diluted with the creation of a five-party system, which covers the political spectrum from the relative radicalism of a workers' party to the extreme conservatism of the traditional oligarchy. Astutely, the government party self-defined itself as left of center!

49. The social consequences of acute economic crisis in Brazil manifested itself in a wave of looting in São Paulo in April 1983, and again in São Paulo and Rio in September. Hundreds of hungry and unemployed sacked stores and supermarkets, causing alarm among leaders of both church and state. Prominent leaders predict a social crisis of unprecedented dimensions if present inflation and unemployment levels continue. A senate commission recently reported that "if the government maintains its present economic policies, President Figueiredo's term will end with six million unemployed and seven million underemployed—27 percent of the economically active population" (*Latinoamerica Press* 15:40, Nov. 3/83). Although Rio and São Paulo states are governed, for the first time in almost two decades, by democratically elected opposition parties, they have neither the power nor the resources to significantly improve the situation. Nor have they been able to establish strong ties with the people. Meanwhile, church and state grassroots organizations—in which the CEBs play a significant role—are making efforts to alleviate the situation in order to head off an ultra-rightist coup. The air is full of alarming predictions of imminent social convulsions.

50. The word "religion" derives from the Latin words *religare*—to bind back—and *religio*—bond between man and the gods (Heritage Dictionary 1970).

51. This is my estimate, based upon figures given by the IBGE as quoted by Read and Ineson (1969: 23, 77–78). The IBGE does not have more recent statistics. Brazil is the third Protestant nation in Latin America, according to a study of Central American church growth (by what is now the PROCADES project of the Instituto Misionológico de las Américas [IMDELA]). Guatemala now has the highest Protestants-to-population

ratio in Latin America (Clifton L. Holland, ed., *World Christianity: Central America and the Caribbean,* Monrovia, Cal., MARC, 1981).

52. The Iberian noun *pastoral* is roughly equivalent to "ministry" in Protestant English parlance. It is the practical side of mission, involving evangelization and social involvement. It is everything that the church does on behalf of the world. In this sense, "pastoral" also includes the apostolic, prophetic, and evangelistic dimensions of mission.

53. The peasant leagues began in 1955 on a *fazenda* near Recife when lawyer Francisco Julião was asked to defend from closure and eviction the mutual-benefit association of a group of sharecroppers. His success led to the establishment of other *ligas,* which gradually began to demand more and more rights for the peasants, and to establish Julião as a political force to be reckoned with—as well as a threat to the *fazenda* system in the northeast (de Kadt: 25–30).

54. Associated Press, June 30, 1980. Betto (Carlos Alberto Libânio Christo), a one-time JUC national coordinator, was imprisoned for four years without due process and tortured despite the intervention of the Vatican on his behalf (Betto 1977a, 1980). See also the account of the Rosebaugh and Capuano affair in LADOC 1978:8/5:20–24.

55. The Catholic Charismatic Renewal, instead, has highlighted the role of Mary as a Spirit-filled example to the church. She was the one who joyfully received the seed of the Holy Spirit into her womb. But today, even ecumenically-minded Protestants are disturbed by the divisive emphasis placed by Pope John Paul II on devotion to Mary and its reappearance, even in the Charismatic Renewal. Progressive Catholics, as well as Protestants, in Latin America are further concerned over the way in which the figure of Mary is being used by the conservative hierarchy to reinforce oppressive social structures and convey right-wing ideological symbols.

56. Iberian esotericism is the result primarily of 500 years of Moorish domination of the peninsula. During much of this time there was considerable, and fairly peaceful, intercourse between Christians and Muslims. The mysterious practices of Jewish cabals seeped into Iberian Catholic religiosity during seven centuries of influential Jewish participation in Spanish and Portuguese life. Later, when Ferdinand and Isabel and their successors forced all Jews in the realm into conversion to Catholicism or expropriation and exile, a number of them (the Marranos) opted for nominal Christianity, while secretly continuing to practice Judaism and esotericism.

57. The Tupi-Guarani Amerindians of Brazil worshiped a pantheon of spirit-gods, which included the supreme god Guarani, the thunder god Tupan, the evil spirit Jurupari, and many other spirits. Their key religious figure was the *page* (shaman) who alone, when possessed, was able to communicate with the spirit world. However, the Portuguese exterminated the Tupi-Guarani far too quickly for them to have had much of an influence upon the Portuguese at that time. Traces of their beliefs infiltrated the cults of fugitive African slaves and through them became a part of present-day Brazilian spiritism (Johnson 1969: 86–87; dos Santos 1978; 61–62).

58. The infamous slave trade in which the European colonizing powers had a part resulted in one of the most massive relocations of peoples in known history. Entire tribes were forcibly resettled throughout the Atlantic seaboard in the New World. Africans brought much of their culture and religion with them. Although, according to Roger Bastide, who is the foremost student of this phenomenon, few African tribes escaped this fate, certain tribes and peoples predominated in each region in accordance with local economic demands. The hardy South Equatorial Bantu tribes of Congo and Angola were highly prized as field hands. Though they spread their folklore throughout

the Americas, few traces remain of their animistic world view. In Rio and São Paulo, their cult of the dead, totemism, and especially the Bantu belief in transmigration were assimilated by other African cults and eventually found a point of contact with the belief in reincarnation of "higher" spiritism to become what is known today as Umbanda. The haughty Muslim Hausas and Fulanis of northern Nigeria were highly prized as house slaves, because of their superior Islamic culture. However, they were eventually eliminated as a result of their involvement in a number of slave uprisings. But they left behind them a small legacy of fetishist Islamic practices, which have been assimilated into the dominant Afro-spiritist groups of Brazil. The "Sudanese" Yoruba and Fon tribes from Nigeria and Dahomey had a more complex type of diffuse monotheism intermingled with strong polytheistic and pantheistic elements. Their beliefs found an ideal breeding ground in the superficial Christianity that the Portuguese imposed upon their slaves. Baptized en masse, and without benefit of meaningful catechesis, the slaves never abandoned their ancestral beliefs. They merely "christianized" their African gods, and later the Indian spirits which they would assimilate.

59. "Higher" spiritism or Kardecism takes its name from Alan Kardec, the founder of this cult. His writings found a ready audience among the Francophile Brazilian elite at the beginning of the Brazilian Empire. Because Kardecism did not consider itself a religion but a philosophy with heavy positivist overtones, it attracted eminent members of the medical and legal professions. One of its principal tenets is the transmigration and reincarnation of the soul. Maintaining a supercilious distance from African spiritism, it appeals to the wealthy and dilettantish upper classes (Brandão 1980:104–8). By the mid-20th century it had achieved an astonishing growth.

60. The multiplicity of spiritist cults could not escape the effects of the increasing geographical and social mobility that characterizes the 20th century. There came a time when a Kardecist medium was visited, not by a long-dead French or Brazilian intellectual as had previously been the case, but by an Amerindian *cabôclo* and by a *Prêto velho*. They represented the ancestors of the enslaved and marginalized masses of Brazil. When Amerindian animism and Bantu ancestor worship reached out to upper-class "scientific" Kardecism through their common communion with the departed spirits, a "planned new religion," Umbanda, made its appearance. Umbanda then baptized its modified pantheon with Catholic names (McGregor 1967:165–69). Most Umbanda practitioners are nominal Catholics from the upper-lower to middle class of Brazilian society who for all practical purposes have been lost to the church. While the church was grasping for power and influence, it lost its people to religious systems that seemed to provide solutions to the profound existential needs that Brazilians at every social and economic level experience (CNBB-LESTE 1976: passim). See Bastide 1971, Herkovits 1958, Johnson 1969, and McGregor 1967 for in-depth studies of Afro-Latin American spiritism from different perspectives.

61. Protestantism will be analyzed in some detail in chap. 10.

62. Santa Ana writes in his study of popular culture: "Although one may say that the growth and perpetuation of property are mainly due to the way in which economic relationships are organized, there are other forces at work, such as cultural and ideological mechanisms which exert influence on the people or try to dominate them. It is important to keep this in mind when discussing popular culture and religiosity." On the other hand, the study adds: "The religion of the people . . . cannot evade the social and economic structures which characterize the existence of poverty" (Santa Ana 1981:48–49).

63. To quote Brandão: "Religious involvement of whatever kind, though apparently

a free option, in fact obeys the guidelines and limits of social class (as both religiously and secularly expressed), which prescribe codes of conduct, choose its agents, and distribute the various peoples among the several faiths" (1980a: 64).

64. In fact, Brandão points out, religion is precisely the ideological sphere where the poor and the disadvantaged manage to be most creative. He points to their "growing vocation for resistance; their capacity for reclaiming traditional modes of belief and practice, or for creating new religious forms. Few are the sectors of religious society where the power of the weak manages to be so consistently creative" (1980a: 31; see also Santa Ana 1981: 48).

65. By this Brandão means that social relationships are marked by vertical class divisions, whereas interconfessional relationships tend to be within the same class.

66. The same criteria would seemingly apply, from indirect references that Brandão makes, to a number of the *comunidades* that he encountered in his field research.

67. The lay pastor of a grassroots Pentecostal sect aptly summed up the general attitude of his peers toward religious differentiation: "I pick up everything on the radio that comes my way: Mass, spiritist service, everything." This eclectic attitude is not so much syncretism as a characteristic folk attitude toward the supernatural—a willingness to resort to any being or force that might have the power to resolve what they themselves are powerless to attain. In the words of one folk practitioner: "As long as it is religious and it is for our good, it is all the same thing" (Brandão 1980a:127).

68. One example of how this happens can be found in the way in which the characteristically grassroots total body involvement—frenzied dancing, hand-clapping, and spasms of possession—becomes more subdued when it appears in the upwardly mobile Afro-spiritist cults and Pentecostal denominations. It altogether disappears in the traditional confessions as these unfettered religious expressions give way to formalism under pressure from upper-class religiosity (Brandão 1980a:124).

69. In contrast to the attitude of established Catholics and Protestants, who see the miraculous as extraordinary breaks in the natural order, serving the purpose of demonstrating the absoluteness of divine power, the devotees of popular religion in the lower *bairros* take miracles for granted as everyday occurrences with or without the help of a church or of human and supernatural mediators. Far from being a break in the natural order, miracles are perceived by peasants and the urban poor as necessary for the maintenance of the divine-social equilibrium (Brandão 1980:131). However, all but imperceptible changes in the way miracles are perceived also signal changes in the approach to the social order. Says Brandão, "In the churches and faith groups of the "lower *bairros*," miracles are, therefore, necessary, readily available, and routine happenings. . . . [But] attempts to control them [even] with the help of gods and demons . . . are one of the first evidences of the institutional origins of a religious group, or of its later institutionalization" (1980a:132).

70. "I am defending here [the thesis] that the reconquest of 'space' for popular religion, when it is accomplished by subordinated peoples, and reacted against by those in dominant positions, is a political act by a [dominated] class, whether the end result be . . . popular Catholicism, autonomous agencies dealing with spirit possession, or the small outcast sects of Pentecostalism" (Brandão 1980a:138).

71. Brandão emphasizes that, "What gives consistency to peasant Catholicism is the presence of a complex network of positions, of practices, and of types of agents and practitioners which is accompanied by a code of service exchanges which has been established with a rigor that is very close to that of any church" (1980a:53–54). However, this code is not that of a true ecclesiastical order "but a communitarian sector

which has been constituted as a religious system" (ibid., 155).

72. Brandão shows that the closer a popular leader is to the grass roots, the more likely he is to belong to the community that he serves and to have been initiated in the "mysteries" of his religion in the same locality and among his own kind of people. Although most grassroots leaders either originated or picked up their expertise locally, the "intermediate" leaders usually came from the corresponding social class in other regions of Brazil and had acquired practical experience in their religion in the big cities. Invariably the priests, mediums, and pastors of the "upper-class" religions were outsiders in every sense of the word (Brandão 1980a:35–48). The process of religious institutionalization and the upward social mobility can be charted. Once they had submitted to the priests, the once-autonomous "pray-ers" and lay "chaplains" eventually found a place within traditional Catholicism. This did not happen, however, to the "healers," because their trade fitted into neither official Catholicism nor scientific medicine. Among the practitioners of popular Catholicism, the autonomous "blessers" are the closest to the cultural norms and values of their people. They manage to keep their distance from parish life, while professing allegiance to official Catholicism. Exorcists comport themselves in a similar manner vis-à-vis Kardecist spiritism. Some, however, prefer to identify with Umbanda, whether as autonomous agents or as the founder-leaders of local *terreiros*.

73. Brandão points out that one of the local parishes that he researched attempted, with only limited success, to enlist the members of the subordinated classes and the agents of popular Catholicism in the *comunidades* (1980a:101; cf. 76, 122). Whether or not it is possible to generalize from so small a "universe," he sees this as a demonstration of the validity of his hypothesis.

74. José Míguez Bonino addresses himself to the growing awareness among Catholic pastoralists of the potential for social change in popular piety, "in terms of the authentic transforming power of the Christian faith." But he points out that popular religiosity cannot be a factor for change until it has undergone a crisis of faith. "At heart, a new faith has to emerge, not a mere growth." It "has to die to give birth to an adult and responsible faith." Because this kind of change will not be a mass phenomenon, it requires "the creation of conscientious and committed Christian minorities which, in the end, are the only kinds of communities that correspond to the demanding character of the gospel." Ultimately this will demand, Catholic pastoral guides believe, the "conversion and dealienation" of popular piety, radically altering the content of its religious understanding, through the dialectical interaction of action and reflection in solidarity with the oppressed (IDOC:81–84; LADOC 1977/27:37–41).

75. *Rerum Novarum* was, in fact, the distillation of a half century of Catholic search for a new social posture in a changing world order. The philosophical frame of reference for the RN definition of the rule of law in human intercourse is neo-Thomism (see LADOC Keyhole 13:34–45 for a critique of RN from a Marxist perspective).

76. *Mater et Magistra* (1961), *Pacem in Terris* (1963), *Gaudium et Spes* (1965), *Populorum Progressio* (1967), and *Octogesima Adveniens* (1971) (Gremillion 1976: 139–40; Latorre Cabal 1978: 11–24). In 1975 Paul VI dedicated a long section to the CEBs in *Evangelii Nuntiandi*.

77. Methodist colporteur D. P. Kidder, in the 19th century, told of attending evening prayers in a São Paulo plantation—prayers led by an old black slave: "I had observed a great number of slaves entering, who in succession addressed us with crossed hands and the pious salutation, 'Praised be our Lord Jesus Christ.' Presently there commenced a chant in the adjoining room. . . . I was told that [the priest] attends these exercises

merely as any other member of the family, the singing and prayers being taught and conducted by an aged black man. . . . This assembling of the slaves, generally at evening, and sometimes both morning and evening, is said to be common on plantations in the country, and is not infrequent among domestics in the city. On those occasions, masters and servants are all equal" (Pierson 1974:6; see also Léonard 1963:34).

78. One of the most significant of these movements, the Canudos Rebellion, has been immortalized by Euclides da Cunha in *Rebellion in the Backlands* (University of Chicago Press, 1894). The strange ascetic Antonio Conselheiro began to gather a following in the backlands of the parched northeast around 1874. In 1896–97 his movement was totally wiped out because it was deemed subversive to the new liberal Republican order. Canudos is an example of an unofficial folk Christianity pitted against both church and state, though the two were no longer officially one. In the early 1900s, a succession of "monks" led a "holy war" against the Republic in the southern Contestado region. During the same period Fr. Cícero Romão Batista led the backwater small northeastern hamlet of Joazeiro to prosperity and, in the process, acquired the reputation of a thaumaturge—and ran afoul of canon law (Willems 1967: 32–33; Foreman 1975:227–35). Other, lesser known messianic movements were "the City of Heaven on Earth" (1817–20) and the "Enchanted Kingdom" (1836–38), both in Pernambuco, and the "Muckers" (1872–98).

79. Dom Agnelo would become the archconservative primate of São Paulo, before his "promotion" to the Prefecture of the Sacred Congregation for the Evangelization of the Peoples. He later charged the Brazilian CEBs with Marxist infiltration.

80. The term *conscientização* was coined around 1964 by a team of professors at the Instituto Superior de Estudos do Brasil (ISEB), was picked up by Paulo Freire, and was brought into English by Dom Hélder Câmara (Freire 1973a:29). Paulo Freire contrasts *conscientização*, which he equates with true communication, with *extensão* (extension), which denotes a vertical, paternalistic transmission of information. It implies "messianism" on the part of the communicator, the superiority of the source over the receiver, a mechanistic approach to education—in sum, a "cultural invasion" (1970:39–55). According to Freire, who was the first to make extensive use of the term, *conscientização* means "an awakening of conscience." It is a mentality that requires that persons be able to understand "realistically and correctly" their place in nature and society. It is the human "capacity to critically analyze the causes and consequences of human reality and to establish comparisons with other situations and possibilities." In the process of *conscientização* persons are led to discover, through interpersonal dialogue, the meaning of their own humanity and worth. Inasmuch as consciousness of reality, of whatever kind, always leads to some form of action, one of the virtually inescapable consequences of *conscientização* is "political involvement and the formation of interest and pressure groups" (Freire 1969:17–18). Freire contrasts "critical consciousness," which is the goal of *conscientização*, with the "magical consciousness" that he associated with a passive and fatalistic acceptance of reality. The role of education is to help persons—and in particular those who are illiterate and socio-economically dominated—to overcome this "magical consciousness" (1969:124–125). The way to do this, he has successfully demonstrated, is through an active, participant, and dialogical methodology. The "Freire method" consists of five steps: first discovering the vocabulary of the target group, then vocabulary selection, and then the creation of existential situations that are typical of the target group. Steps 4 and 5 have to do with the conceptual elaboration of suitable training tools (Freire 1969:133–38). Freire's methodology has been adapted to the context of the CEBs by Freire himself and by the coordinators of the CEBs (Freire 1974: passim; other examples in SEDOC 1975: 73–74, 80).

81. "Natural communities" are groups of persons who share common subcultures of poverty and alienation, which are the result of socio-economic exploitation. Ties of race, family, and place, though important, do not inform "natural communities" in isolation from their socio-economic context (Alicino 1977:55–59, 63–70).

82. The ideological evolution of the MEB leaders must be understood in order to grasp the ideology of the *comunidade* pastoral guides who would later build upon the MEB infrastructure. (a) Early in their involvement in the change process, the ideology of the young Catholic militants in Brazil was based upon a modified version of Maritain's neo-Thomism. It was a sort of ideal construct of social reality, a theoretical idea of what social reality should be like "not as a finished thing, but as a thing in process" (de Kadt:63–64). (b) But the "central line in the more radical philosophy of history of the quasi-political AP in which a number of the young activists became involved was *the process of socialization*—i.e., "the increasing density and ambiguity of social [as opposed to individualistic] arrangements of human intercourse" (1970:85). Before *Mater et Magistra* introduced what had previously been a pejorative term into the mainstream of Catholic thought, "socialization" was a key concept in the thinking of Teilhard de Chardin. This had a strong influence upon the thought of the young radical intellectuals in the Brazilian AC who were later to lead both the AP and MEB movements. Teilhard's evolutionary view of science, history, and philosophy has at least two points of contact with the Marxism that would later influence these intellectuals to some degree: first, his emphasis upon an inevitable forward dynamic—the "pull" or "supernatural salvation" exerted by "the Omega point in history," which Teilhard identified with Christ, the Man-God; and second, his appeal to science for explanations of past history and of the future of humankind (Libânio 1976:172–73). (c) The *philosophy of history* of the young Catholic radicals was further modified by Hegelian dialecticism, with the additional input of Karl Marx's concept of class struggle. The "historical ideal" that was at the heart of the neo-Thomism that had fascinated these intellectuals was transmuted into a more concrete and more *critical "historical consciousness."* The transformation ("hominization" or humanization) of the world, according to their reinterpretation of Marx, is based upon "an understanding of the real conditions found in the here and now (and their historical roots)" (de Kadt:88). For the young Catholic intellectuals, this "Omega point," this "hope beyond history, became transformed into a belief in the actual possibility of Utopia." It became something like "an article of faith without a theological anchoring, rather like the Marxist credo of the classless society" (de Kadt:81–90). This evolutionary philosophy of history, which was later elaborated more systematically by Karl Rahner in another context, can be seen in several of the writings of the theologians who have had the most influence upon the thinking of the Brazilian *comunidade* leaders (Rahner 1978: passim; L. Boff 1978a, 1978b; C. Boff 1978b). (d) A further philosophical element was injected into this evolving ideology by the *"personalist Christian existentialism"* of Emmanuel Mounier who emphasized the supreme importance of person-to-person relationships and the need of every human being to be open to "the other." But Mounier lacked a sociological theory to serve as a framework for his psychological theory. This, according to de Kadt, is one reason for the fuzziness of Mounier's view of the future. In the absence of such a sociological framework, Mounier's emphasis upon living a life of "authenticity" in the face of the daily options of human existence was integrated into a concept of "historical consciousness." According to this view, we make authentic choices on the basis of our critical understanding of both past history and the direction in which history is moving. Authenticity also requires that the freedom of choice of "the other" be respected. This means that in order for the organization of the masses to achieve social change, it must

not take place until persons have been made aware of the nature of their problems (through the conscientization process) and have freely opted for change. Because of this deep conviction, Catholic radicals were as strongly opposed to the efforts at "massification" of the government as they were to the collectivization by Marxist cadres (de Kadt:90–94). (e) At the heart of the young Catholic radicals' analysis of Brazilian social reality was the conceptual dyad: the "dominant pole" (those who control production, distribution, and the formation of public opinions) and its opposite, the "dominated pole." This interpretation of reality owed much to Marxist dialectical analysis. Their use of Marxist analytical tools does not mean that Catholic radicals were prepared to make common cause with card-carrying Marxists in the Brazilian Communist Party. They excoriated international communism both for this creation of a "new pole of domination"—a state bureaucracy—and for its willingness to collaborate opportunistically "with all nationalists and democrats . . . irrespective of their class position and party affiliation" (1970:98, 101). This complex ideology of the AC and MEB movements is the key to understanding the ideology that informs the theology of the *comunidade* coordinators in Brazil. Although by no means identically, the "young radicals" who are now the prominent pastoral or liberation theologians in the rest of Latin America have absorbed inputs from a number of sources, so that it is inaccurate and unfair to label them "Marxists."

83. See note 10, above.

84. The self-understanding of the grassroots communities is expressed at two interrelated levels: directly, through the recorded comments of *comunidade* members at regular meetings and *encontros* or regional convocations; and indirectly, through the interpretation of the CEB praxis by its coordinators and pastoral guides. I have compared both with my personal observations and research with the *comunidades*.

85. The 1976 *encontro*, also in Vitória, met around the theme of "The Church, a People on the Move." The 1978 convocation in João Pessoa used the theme, "The CEB Church: The People Liberating Itself." The theme of the 1981 *encontro* (Itaici) was "The Church: An Oppressed People Organizing Itself for Liberation." The fifth convocation, in 1983, in Canindé was called to reflect upon "The CEBs, A United People, Seed of a New Society" (Betto 1983).

86. Vatican II emphasizes this dimension, pointing out that the church is both a *historical* and a *messianic* community (LG:9–10; GS:1). The church has been called within human history to be the people of God, by virtue of its faith and submission to Christ, in the power of the Holy Spirit. It makes itself visible in concrete historical situations and "in accordance with diverse powers and services," and is "a church that is born and becomes constituted at the *base* with the life and culture of diverse nations and human communities . . . a church that is incarnate in reality." The messianic character of the church relates to its mission to "proclaim to all the world the power of God who has called us out of darkness into his wonderful light." In this role the church is salt and light, "a source of unity, a hope of salvation, and . . . an instrument of universal redemption . . . the sacrament of salvation" (Alicino:28–36; see LG:9).

87. David Prior, citing my research at some length, picks up on this theme in his insightful book, *The Church in the Home* (London: Marshall, Morgan & Scott, 1983). However, he fails to see that the CEBs do not fit neatly into the "home church" category around which he builds his argument. Aside from the fact that they do not always meet in homes, what sets the CEBs apart is the radicality of their approach to social evil.

88. This remark gets to the heart of a fundamental difference between an establishment Protestant approach to the basic community and the base community experience

of the poor in the Catholic Church. Grassroots community already exists as a socio-cultural fact. It remains only to transform it into an ecclesial community—i.e., an authentic expression in every way, albeit in microcosm, of the universal church. In a helpful analysis, Delespesse observes that "a community is essentially heterogeneous." Homogeneity is manifested in the organizations of special interest groups and not (only of a real sense of community). But a true community is composed of all age groups and social levels. *Heterogeneity is not the opposite of community*, because the Spirit of Christ transforms human variety into true community. Although the homogeneity of a given community may be the product of a commonality of problems, traditions, and customs, community heterogeneity "is an indispensable guarantee of equilibrium and realism in the communal development of the church. A group that attempts to be a community while remaining homogeneous will almost inevitably be condemned to vegetate" (Delespesse: 52; Alicino:59).

89. Pablo Richard is a Chilean-born former priest who works with CEBs in Central America. An extremely competent scholar with doctorates in biblical studies and the social sciences, he is on the staff of the Departamento Ecuménico de Investigación (DEI) in San José, Costa Rica.

90. A report given at the Itaici *encontro intereclesial*, in 1981, mentioned the fact that some 240 *comunidades* in Espíritu Santo state had originated in the strongly parish-oriented *cursillo* movement (REB 41:287)—an indication, perhaps, of growing strength for this wing of the CEBs.

91. This typology, I submit, is borne out by the statistics of IBRADES that C. Boff quotes. The relationship of the *comunidades* with their parishes breaks down statisti-cally as follows: "renewal" (40.8%), "coordination" (8.9%), "juxtaposition" (21.8%), "independence" (6.9%), and "no CEBs in the parish" (21.8%). The first three catego-ries would seem to correspond, respectively, to the three—(1) *comunidade*, (2) *eclesial*, (3) *de base*—types (see C. Boff 1978a:58).

92. O. Massing, writing from the perspective of basic Christian communities in Europe, comments that according to "organization theory," the church as institution "will give first place to those functions that guarantee its stability and will seek to reject any aspiration that is cloaked in criticism of the system." A corollary of this is that "all grass roots activity [critical in its posture toward the church] represents a threatening challenge to the existence of the ecclesiastico-administrative system and to its represent-atives" (Concilium 1975:52, 59).

93. Paul VI seems to support these attempts in his encyclical *The Cult of the Virgin Mary*, when he states that, on the basis of Scripture, modern science, and new realities, and under the Holy Spirit's guidance, "Mary can very well be taken as a model for that which mankind yearns for in our day" (see L. Boff 1978a:119).

94. A *connotative meaning* is "the totality of the attitudes constituting the meaning of a term." A *denotative meaning* is designative or explicit *(Heritage Dictionary)*. It is a formal, generic, or operational definition.

95. The most perceptive statement that I've read on Marxism is by historian Robert Goldston: "Like all systems of ideas, Marxism was a long time developing. It did not spring entirely from the mind of the man whose name it bears, nor was it a scheme devised to be forced upon an unwilling world by a small band of conspirators. It was and remains a flawed but very useful view of the world and man's place in it. Like any system of thought that pretends to be universal, it has many inconsistencies; many of its prophecies have never come to pass, many of its analyses are demonstrably false. Marxism has been used and abused as a sort of intellectual bludgeon by radicals, while

to conservatives it has become somewhat of a bogey. Nevertheless, many of its views of history, many of its principles, are a permanent part of the intellectual heritage of all men. It is primarily a system of analysis—a key among others for the unlocking of some of the mysteries of man's behavior. If the key fails to fit many locks, it remains nonetheless useful when properly employed. There are today no serious statesmen, economists, or historians anywhere in the world, no matter how conservative, who do not make use of it one way or another" *(The Russian Revolution,* Greenwich, Ct.: Fawcett Publ., 1966, pp. 27–28).

96. The sociology of knowledge is concerned with "the relationship between human thought and the social context within which it arises" (Berger and Luckmann 1966: 4–5; Berger 1967: 15, 17). Despite "the fact that much of the sociology of knowledge was explicitly formulated in opposition to Marxism," the "immediate intellectual antecedent" of this branch of sociology is, in fact, 19th-century Marxism. It derives its root propositions from Marx (Berger et al. 1966:5–6). Karl Mannheim is the best known formulator of the sociology of knowledge. His principal concern was with the problem of ideology *(Ideology and Utopia,* New York: Harcourt, Brace and World, 1936), not only in one's own thinking but also in the thought of one's opponent.

97. I have taken the liberty of restructuring Libânio's argument, which was written primarily with monastic communities in mind, by combining it with parallel statements concerning the CEBs in IRM (1979: 68, 243–65, 272).

98. The very existence of the *comunidades* is a factor for legitimization. In the words of one community member, "One begins to feel like a person." A very important aspect of this new identity is the CEB awareness of being the church ("We are the church"). The presence of the pastoral guides who work at the grass roots is still another legitimizing factor. Numerous "therapies contribute to the cohesion of the *comunidades*: frequent intra-group contact . . . traditional gatherings of the people . . . the increase in level of companionship . . . meetings for Bible reading . . . the reexamination of life which characterizes certain groups . . . and popular festivals." After the newness of belonging to a *comunidade* wears off, the group will find that it needs various forms of social control, but not to keep members in line, or in order to "guarantee canonical purity," but to ensure the involvement of every member in the community. Ultimately, says Libânio, the meetings themselves are the best form of social control, because when someone fails to attend, fellow CEB members will certainly notice the fact (IRM 271: 257–62).

99. When persons are confronted by realities or facts that contradict their own ideological presuppositions, their attitudes, as a rule, will remain unchanged, or will be reinforced by defense mechanisms. A few may seek to resolve the contradictions by rationalizations or perhaps through ways that do not substantially threaten their comfortable assumptions. Only a very few will be willing to make the qualitative leap into a new perception of reality—an experience that has been likened to a kind of conversion. Without a theoretical framework into which one can fit a new perception of reality, attitudes will usually remain unchanged, or at best, change only superficially. This is why a coherent social theory is so important. But theory, as Libânio shows, no matter how plausible, nor how ideologically potent, will lack the power to bring about significant change if it is unrelated to the everyday lives of the persons involved. This is why praxis is so important. Social theory, for the Christian, will be informed, in varying degrees, by a biblical worldview, and vice versa. It should honestly face up to social contradictions and seek to deal with them within the context of a genuinely Christian worldview. Only then can it adequately participate in bringing about change. The problem in Latin America is that the majority of Christians, Catholic and Protestant,

have a proof-text knowledge, at best, of the Scriptures, and are virtually ignorant of their own secular and sacred histories. In consequence, they are unable to articulate a coherent Christian understanding of social reality. They are then easily manipulated by ideological extremes and tendentious theologies (plausibility theories), which serve to justify vested interests and blind persons to the cold facts of their own or their neighbors' realities.

100. A Protestant would want to add a fourth category: *kerygma* (calling persons to repentance and faith in Christ). But we should ask of it the same critical questions that Libânio suggests at each level and step of the process if we are to be faithful to the "Protestant principle" of prophetic criticism.

101. In fact, as I was informed by Frances O'Gorman of FASE Programa Nuclar in Rio, the term *comunidades ecclesias de base* is a generic term that many CEBs do not use. They give themselves a variety of names.

102. See the annotated bibliography at the end of Eduardo Bonin (ed.), *Espiritualidad y liberación en América Latina* (San José 1982, DEI) pp. 183–200. The book is a collection of monographs by twelve Latin American theologians, the majority of whom have some relation to CEBs. Five works on a spirituality of liberation have been published by Orbis Books: Hélder Câmara, *The Desert is Fertile* (1976), Segundo Galilea, *The Beautitudes: To Evangelize as Jesus Did* (1984), Maryknoll, N.Y.: Orbis and Dublin: Gill and Macmillan, J. B. Libânio, *Spiritual Discernment and Politics: Guidelines for Religious Communities* (1982), Leonardo Boff, *The Lord's Prayer: The Prayer of Integral Liberation* (1983), and Gustavo Gutiérrez, *We Drink from Our Own Wells: The Spiritual Journey of a People* (1984). See also my article on the subject in *Missiology* 12:2 (April 1984) 224–32.

103. Clodovis Boff has a helpful analysis of the dialectical "levels of operation" of the "hermeneutic circle": (1) Word of God and Scripture, (2) meaning encoding and meaning decoding, (3) form and meaning, (4) present and past, (5) technique and exegesis (C. Boff 1978b: 238–50).

104. It is important to understand the dialectical relationship that exists between the CEBs and the pastoral theologians of the Catholic Church. The theologians are reflecting out of their involvement in the action of grassroots communities, and they return to the *comunidades* with theoretical framework for ongoing mission action in the communities (Libânio 1979b: 31–42). Antonio Gramsci, the Italian Marxist theorist, coined the phrase "organic intellectual" to describe those intellectuals who, having been born for the most part among the affluent classes, came to understand historical processes in such a way that they identified organically with the aspirations of the oppressed classes. This is something new in history, says Gramsci, because heretofore, though "traditional intellectuals" could often trace their roots to the poor, they consciously turned their backs upon their class in order to serve the ruling classes. See James Joll, *Gramsci,* Glasgow: Fontana Books, 1977, pp. 90–94. See also Antonio Gramsci, *La formación de los intelectuales,* Mexico City: Grijalbo, 1967, pp. 26ff., and Hughes Portelli, *Gramsci y el bloque histórico,* Mexico City: Siglo XXI, 1973, pp. 101–3.

105. I once asked Frei Betto whether he thought Protestant evangelicals had a role to play in the current religious and political process in Latin America. By way of illustrating his negative reply, he said: "Evangelicals remind me of persons who are walking along a dark path with a flashlight. They are so fascinated by the light that instead of shining it down and ahead on the path, they point it at themselves . . . staring at it . . . when they are not aiming it up to heaven! According to the Psalmist, God's Word is a lamp unto our *feet,* and a light unto our *pathway.* You Evangelicals are pointing the Bible in the wrong direction!" (1980 interview).

106. My criticism in no way diminishes my profound admiration for Leonardo Boff, for his deep spirituality and commitment to the poor. I have been immensely helped by his profound insights and have appreciated the opportunities that I have had of interacting with him. Yet it seems to me that Boff's appropriation of Bultmannian categories, in his approach to a historically-rooted christology, not only weakens the authority of Scripture, but does little or nothing to serve the cause of the poor.

107. The "epistemological privilege of the poor," an expression perhaps first used by Hugo Assmann (Sergio Torres [ed.], *Theology in the Americas,* Maryknoll, N.Y.: Orbis, 1976, p. 300), does not mean that only the poor can understand scriptural truth. It does signify that they are privileged receptors of truth, in line with the Lucan statement of Jesus, "Blessed are you who are poor, for yours is the kingdom of God" (6:20). This is first because God defends the cause of the poor and announces judgment upon their oppressors. But it is also related to the very content of Scripture, the major portion of which was written by and for persons of a peasant culture. Because of this, the poor everywhere, even today, can identify more readily with the language and imagery of the Bible than can we who belong to the ranks of the affluent. We are forced to resort to exegetical tools in order to understand the Word of God—when we are not trying to obfuscate its meaning with ingenuous allegories or archaic translations. The Matthean version of the statement of Jesus (5:3, "Blessed are the poor in spirit . . . ") could well be meant as a reminder to us that only as we begin to look at God's Word from the perspective of the poor, will we begin to understand the significance of the kingdom of God. The recent interest in Scripture exegesis from the perspective of the poor should be taken not as something negative, but as a gift from the Spirit of God to guide us on our way. For those who may be interested in pursuing this subject further, from several perspectives, may I suggest the following: José Miranda 1974; Elsa Tamez, *Bible of the Oppressed,* Maryknoll, N.Y.: Orbis, 1982; Kenneth E. Bailey, *Poet and Peasant,* Grand Rapids: Eerdmans, 1976; idem, *Through Peasant Eyes,* 1980, republished by Eerdmans in one volume, subtitled *A Literary-Cultural Approach to the Parables in Luke,* 1983; Norman K. Gottwald's formidable *The Tribes of Yahweh: A Sociology of the Religion of Liberated Israel, 1250–1050 B.C.E.,* Maryknoll, N.Y.: Orbis, 1981; idem (ed.), *The Bible and Liberation: Political and Social Hermeneutics,* Maryknoll, N.Y.: Orbis, 1983; Willy Schotroff and Wolfgang Stegemann (eds.), *The God of the Lowly: Socio-Historical Interpretations of the Bible,* Maryknoll, N.Y.: Orbis, 1984.

108. By this Boff presumably means that the preexistent Christ permeates the pages of the Old Testament and was at work in human history even from before creation. This is the "christic structure" that permeates the entire Bible. I am, however, disturbed by the pantheistic and universalistic overtones of this statement, which I find difficult to square with Scripture.

109. Mesters follows the same methodology in his two-volume *Palavra de Deus na Historia dos Homens* ["the Word of God in human history"], where he relates the lives of the men and women of the Bible to the present reality of the Brazilian people (1973 and 1977: passim). He makes his reflection material even more practical for *círculos* participants in a series of sixteen booklets. Each contains four topics, and each topic consists of a simple liturgy, a contextual homily, a Scripture text in popular language, and questions for reflection applied to real-life situations. The lessons cover five main themes: the wisdom of the people (the wisdom literature), the parables, the Sermon on the Mount, the person of Christ, and a new heaven and a new earth. *Círculos* leaders can find help in the General Introduction and Guide, and in supplemental booklets for each of the five themes (Mesters 1972–1978: passim).

110. Other examples of Mesters' reflections are: On the Sermon on the Mount ("A

new and strange happiness!"): "Do the words of Jesus help you to understand that strange happiness [blessedness] of Alfredo, of Carlos Alberto, of that grey-haired mother, of the apostles?" On the mother of Jesus, Mesters comments: "The devotion to Our Lady runs very deep." He then asks, "Does the way in which we relate to Our Lady always accord with the place she wants to have in our lives?" (1977:29:5, 10:23:32). On hell (in this life and in the hereafter): "Instead of always looking toward hell in order to scare the life out of people, it is better to look toward the wonderful future that God offers to those who hear his Word, and put it into practice now." On the hope of the resurrection: "Is it enough to wait for heaven or shouldn't we work to change things down here? Why?" (1973:38:16,21). Mesters is not the only Brazilian pastoral leader who is developing materials for grass roots reflection. Gilberto Gorgulho, Ana Flora Anderson, José Luiz Gonzaga do Prado, and others have prepared studies and paraphrases of books of the Bible.

111. In *Puebla para o Povo* ["Puebla for the people"], Frei Betto contextualizes the Puebla document with grassroots dialogue, brief commentary, and provocative cartoons.

112. See Teófilo Cabestrero, *Mystic of Liberation: A Portrait of Bishop Pedro Casaldáliga of Brazil,* Maryknoll, N.Y.: Orbis, 1981.

113. Subsequent lessons in this booklet begin with such provocative titles as "Don't Make Fun of God!," "Don't Throw Baptism into the Trash Can!" ("Everybody says he's a Christian because he was baptized—but they're baptized people who ain't Christian: money-grabbers, oppressors, etc."), "Baptism Ain't for Softies!," "A True Christian Must Have Faith in Jesus Christ." Each lesson ends with some study questions and additional Scripture passages for *comunidade* reflection (Casaldáliga 1980b).

114. The Eucharist is "AN AGREEMENT THAT HAS BEEN SEALED WITH BLOOD: the blood of Jesus." God has made this agreement with us; "God's never gonna abandon his people unto the end of the ages." Each time that we eat the bread and drink the wine we renew the agreement that binds us to fulfill our commitment to Christ and to his kingdom of justice and love. Just as the Eucharist was born during the "fiesta" that celebrated the liberation of the people of Israel, "every Mass is a celebration feast because it commemorates and helps us relive the resurrection of Jesus." The resurrection is "the great liberation that assures us of the liberation of the people." This feast is also the firstfruits of "a new world, of a new society wherein all the fruits of human labor and all the blessings of nature will serve everyone equally and will be distributed equally among all." This new world "begins here and now and will be completed in the new heaven and new earth when Jesus will return to wipe away all tears and to do away with all pain and suffering." Then the joy will be completed and the "fiesta" will never end (Casaldáliga 1980a: 7–20).

115. Popular discontent from every corner of Brazil and pressure from the CEB-supported Catholic hierarchy forced the government to back down. Shortly after the above incident of which I was an observer, it was announced that the new taxes would come out of the pockets of employers.

116. This is the expression that Methodist Bishop Mortimer Arias uses in "Contextual Evangelization in Latin America: Between Accommodation and Confrontation," in *Occasional Bulletin* 1978: 2:9–25. He had developed the theme earlier at Nairobi (IRM 257: 18–19; Anderson and Stransky 1976: 92–93).

117. Indeed, as is well known, many of the terms that have become sacred to us were originally of everyday sacred and political usage—e.g., *euangelion, ekklesia, leiturgia,* and *episkopos.*

118. Recent textual research hints at the fact that even the Apostle Paul may have had

a clearer understanding of the social significance of justice as it relates to justification than our traditional exegesis has allowed us to believe. See Thomas Hanks, *God So Loved the Third World,* Maryknoll, N.Y., Orbis, 1983, and Jacques Pons, *L'oppression dans l'Ancien Testament,* Paris Letouzey et Ané, 1981. The Hanks book also contains a listing of Orbis publications related to biblical exegesis.

119. Nevertheless, we usually manage to abstract biblical truth by the simple expedient of applying it to "safe" historical events of the past, then transmogrifying it into "spiritual" applications in the present or, at best, keeping it within the bounds of individual human actions.

120. The Rio-based *Federação de Orgãos para Assistência Social e Educacional* (FASE) is a unique Catholic para-ecclesiastical institution. It was founded by Edmund Leising, an American priest. His associate is Dr. Frances Elsie O'Gorman, a Brazilian ex-nun who is an expert in popular communication. FASE was dedicated exclusively to social development and popular education programs. Now, through its *Programa Nuclar,* it works closely with urban *comunidades,* helping them to integrate Catholic spirituality with their socio-economic aspirations.

121. These are the thoughts of a Catholic researcher, James Pitt. As an evangelical missiologist, I should prefer to put justice (denunciation) on one side of the coin and the announcement of the good news of total redemption and liberation on the other.

122. Cardinal Arns has chosen as his own permanent "integrated" pastoral objective "to promote the continuity, organic development, and integration of the permanent pastoral ministry of the communities of the church in the city of São Paulo." One indication of how the São Paulo primate's goal is being carried out may be observed during almost any lunch-hour period in the nave of his vast cathedral: small groups are gathered here and there around flannelgraph boards to participate in a Bible lesson being taught by a lay *animador* (see also SEDOC 12/126:454,483).

123. The concern for a broader understanding of church planting and growth is, of course, not entirely new to Christian mission. Von Zinzendorf (1700-60), the founder of the passionately missionary Moravians, arrived at this conviction out of his interaction with Catholics and followers of other religions (Schattschneider 1975:78, 89–98).

124. The question that Evangelicals, no matter how radical their social position, would have to ask at this point is, How much of the real core is allowed to come through in the post-Medellín understanding of mission in the Catholic Church? Even if the announcement of redemption is taken for granted by those who know it and have received it (and we dare not take it for granted), what are we to do about those who have never heard it, except, perhaps, in some garbled form? See my treatment of this subject in chap 9.

125. *Lumen Gentium* uses such institution-centered descriptions of the church as "sheepfold," "that Jerusalem which is above," "our Mother," "the spotless Lamb," etc. (LG:6 in Abbott:18–19).

126. This new attitude was eloquently expressed a little more than a year after the start of the council (in Dec. 1965) in *Gaudium et Spes*: "The Council focuses its attention on the world of men, the whole human family along with the sum of those realities in the midst of which that family lives. It gazes upon that world which is the theater of man's history, and carries the marks of his energies, his tragedies, and his triumphs; that world which the Christian sees as created and sustained by its maker's love, fallen indeed into the bondage of sin, yet emancipated now by Christ. He was crucified and rose again to break the stranglehold of personified Evil, so that this world might be fashioned anew according to God's design and reach its fulfillment" (GS:2 in Gremillion 245 or Abbott 200).

127. The same four emphases can, of course, be found among Evangelicals in Latin America, for example, a conservative theology, which always had a substratum of conservative ideology, has been welded by fear into a hermetic "spiritualizing" and reactionary ideology. But this is, in part, a reaction against the early extremes of a small but doctrinaire group of radical "young Turks" who bought the entire liberation theology package without having passed it through the grid of a grassroots Protestant ecclesial experience. They were also reacting against a decontextualized theological fundamentalism. But between these extremes there is a growing minority of Evangelicals who are endeavoring to integrate evangelization and social concern. Although the majority of these Christians give the priority to evangelism, others—including a number of the above-mentioned "young Turks"—prefer to maintain a dialectical tension between both dimensions, believing and practicing the importance of both sides of the same gospel. It is fair to say that much the same kind of situation obtains throughout Latin America with local nuances. In Brazil, my impression is that the apex of ultraconservative Protestant reaction was reached about midway through the 1964–74 decade, when every other position either went underground or kept its mouth shut. The time has come, however, when a growing number of thinking conservative Evangelicals are beginning to address themselves to social issues, while maintaining the primacy of evangelism. They are, on occasion, even willing to make common cause with more radical Evangelicals who share their concern for evangelism, while insisting that, in the social context of Brazil, evangelism is meaningless if it does not also address social sin.

128. This dimension was clearly enunciated in São Paulo by a group of Third World theologians: "The power of the Spirit leads to conversion, to a radical change of life; thus an apostolic community is constituted, the seed and the model of the first ecclesial *communities"* (IECT in *Occasional Bulletin* 1980b:4:3:130; Torres and Eagleson: 239/ 46).

129. Missing here is an explicit statement of the divine action in this process. St. Paul deals with the subject of freedom from fear of "elemental forces" *(stoicheia)* in Gal. 4:3–9 and Col. 2:8, 20 (cf. Rom. 8:38, etc.). Libânio's "first step," in fact, comes about by a deliberate transfer of authority through personal confession of Christ's lordship (Rom. 10:9–10). "I-awareness" is inseparable from the awareness of our divine sonship through Christ, which enables us to become the subjects of our own history (Gal. 4:6–7). Conversely, "social awareness" will happen only when we are confronted with the specific needs of a specific people out of a specific and historically-rooted theology and respond to these needs with specifications (Neh. 1).

130. Unfortunately, in the polarized times in which we live, it has become very difficult to dialogue in an atmosphere of mutual respect on the basis of our common faith in Jesus Christ. Over the years, I have come to see that persons who cannot dialogue are psychologically insecure and, at heart, unsure of the beliefs that they so ardently defend.

131. For Boff human history is not limited by death. He locates eschatology within the compass of earthly history and explains heaven, purgatory, and hell in historical terms. He seems to identify death as the point where persons will be given their final opportunity for commitment to Christ. This enables him to conceive of purgatory as "the gracious possibility granted by God to human beings, as an opportunity and as a duty, to become radically mature" (1978c: 26–32, 55–61).

132. I have often been asked about the CEB attitude toward upward mobility. Will not the *comunidades* lose their driving force once they have achieved even a minimum of their just material needs, and begin, inexorably, to move up in the social scale? It may well happen. Yet this is less likely to take place, and to have the negative effects that it has

shown in our Protestant congregations because of a unique difference between the CEB ethic and the Protestant ethic. Whereas we Protestants, as a rule, have prospered individually (whether as persons or local congregations), forgetting our roots, the base community ethic involves everyone in the struggle to better the lot of an entire community—ecclesial and socio-cultural.

133. One often hears the objection that liberation theologians might be more credible if they also directed their critique at totalitarian communism. This criticism fails to take into account the fact that the totalitarianism that most Latin Americans suffer under comes from another source! This criticism should not, however, be dismissed out of hand. It has a point. Increasingly one finds among liberation theologians a disposition to aim their social critique at the Soviet Union. This is the case with J. B. Libânio, Julio de Santa Ana, José Míguez Bonino, and others in some of their public and private discussions.

134. José Porfirio Miranda, *Marx against the Marxists,* Maryknoll, N.Y.: Orbis, 1980.

135. Unfortunately, this has become accepted practice in conservative Evangelical circles in North America, Europe, and Latin America. Reputations are being ruined and innocent lives have been sacrificed by so-called Christian brothers who presume they have a corner on biblical truth.

136. A remark attributed to Mennonite anthropologist Jacob Loewen.

137. Both Protestant and Catholic theology suffer from a systematization syndrome. No matter what the starting point—whether "from above" or "from below"—we are tempted to formulate our theories on the basis of presuppositions that may, in fact, be alien to our point of departure.

138. Brooks Foss Wescott, ed., *The Gospel According to Saint John,* Grand Rapids: Eerdmans, 1954, pp. 224–25.

139. This does not, in my view, negate the existence of propositional truth. What it does is emphasize the historical rootedness of these truths, the historical conditioning of their interpretation, and the historical pertinency of their application.

140. With this Emilio Castro agrees: "Conversion means that we become conscious of a relationship to Jesus Christ, and this will eventually mean a relationship with our neighbor. It means to become a part of the discipleship of those that serve him. These two elements—relationship with Jesus Christ and relationship with my neighbor—can be distinguished but not separated. There is no such thing as a relationship with Jesus Christ that is not a relationship with our neighbor. . . . The lack of a correct relationship with our neighbor is authentic proof of a lack of a correct relationship with God" (Castro 1970:167).

141. The WCC "Ecumenical Affirmation on Mission and Evangelism" states it very well: "Conversion as a dynamic and ongoing process 'involves a turning *from* and a turning *to.* It always demands reconciliation, a new relationship, both with God and with others. It involves leaving our old security behind (Matt. 16:24) and putting ourselves at risk in a life of faith. . . . While the basic experience of conversion is the same, the awareness of an encounter with God revealed in Christ, the concrete occasion of this experience, and the actual shape of the same differs in terms of our personal situation. The calling is to specific changes, to renounce evidences of the domination of sin in our lives and to accept responsibilities in terms of God's love for our neighbor' " (EAME: 11–12). The specific manifestation of conversion could be religious, taking place in a religious environment, or it could be a very secular happening, in the midst of struggles for social justice, "but it should always have a concrete religious reference to

Jesus Christ, his life, ministry, death, and resurrection," and have a concrete historical content (IRM 72: 287, 310–11; cf. EAME:11).

142. An excellent beginning to a much-needed Evangelical reassessment of our traditional view of conversion can be found in Jim Wallis, *The Call to Conversion,* San Francisco: Harper & Row, 1981.

143. Most Latin American Protestants seem to assume a void of 1,800 years between New Testament Christianity and their present experience, which they often perceive as being the only true and authentic Christian expression at that point in time. We Protestants take for granted that true Christianity, after the New Testament period, began with the Reformers, faded from view as the Magisterial Reformation became more clericalized and sacramental, and reappeared in purified form with the arrival of the first missionaries in Latin America. Although admittedly, this is a broad generalization, it accurately reflects our Protestant popular religiosity. I suspect that it has a great deal to do with our present crisis of identity and theological stagnation in Latin America. We urgently need to recapture a sense of history in order to understand our place in the stream of salvation history, and to identify with what God is doing today in the world.

144. Not every religious grassroots community would qualify as a "base" movement, in the exact sense in which I have used the term in previous chapters. But each case needs to be evaluated in historical perspective. Despite the "middle class" origins of some of the movements that we shall consider, I would insist upon the "base" relatedness of most of them. They were often marginalized and oppressed, whatever their socioeconomic status, or consciously threw in their lot with the oppressed poor, at least in their initial stages.

145. An expression used by Gustavo Gutiérrez in *La fuerza histórica de los pobres,* Lima: CEP, 1979; English trans., *The Power of the Poor in History,* Maryknoll, N.Y.: Orbis: 1983. As historian Christopher Hill observes, "Upside down is . . . a relative concept. The assumption that it means the wrong way up is itself an expression of the view from the top" (1972: 386–87).

146. According to this theory, every social movement follows a three-step process: "charismatic," "institutionalizing," and "institutionalized" (Nottingham 1964: 141–45).

147. A great deal has been written about the sociology of the New Testament church, from various perspectives. See Robert M. Grant, *Early Christianity and Society: Seven Studies,* San Francisco: Harper & Row, 1977; Abraham J. Mahlerby, *Social Aspects of Early Christianity,* Philadelphia: Fortress, 1982. See also the articles by Robin Scroggs, George Pixley, John G. Gager, and Robert H. Smith in Norman K. Gottwald (ed.), *The Bible and Liberation: Political and Social Hermeneutics,* Maryknoll, N.Y., Orbis, 1983. An excellent study written from an Evangelical perspective is that of Robert Banks, *Paul's Idea of Community : The Early House Churches in Their Historical Setting,* Grand Rapids, Eerdmans, 1980.

148. French sociologist G. Gurvitch's "three levels of sociability" model is based on the interaction of the "I-We" poles of human intercourse. At the "I" pole is the individualism and impersonality of "mass-sociability," whereas "communion-sociability" is characterized by a closed and tightly knit "we-consciousness." Between them one rarely finds cases of "community sociability" in which both extremes are kept in creative balance. "Community sociability" accepts the centripetal cohesion that is offered by group homogeneity while availing itself of the centrifugal diversity inherent in mass homogeneity (Ribeiro Guimarães 1978:78–79).

149. Garsoïan theorizes that their heterodox beliefs came to them from the Adoptionist-leaning Syrian church, which first evangelized Armenia in the late second or early third century. Reacting against the materialism and idolatry of the state churches, the faith of the most visible Paulician sect became increasingly dualistic, earning for itself the label "Manichean." Whether deserved or not, this pejorative had the same effect in their day as it is to be a "Marxist" in our time. Manicheism was the only heresy to be outlawed by imperial decree and made punishable by death.

150. Once again I have singled out Brazil as a case study, in part because it was important to be able to compare Protestant and Catholic ecclesial realities in the same general locale. But there are more compelling reasons for focusing on Brazil. It is the Latin American country with the largest number of historical churches (and with the largest memberships in these churches). In the majority of Hispanic American countries, independent and "faith mission" churches outnumber historical churches. And the largest grassroots Protestant movement in Latin America, autochthonous Pentecostalism, is also in Brazil. Although the conclusions that I hope to reach on the basis of a Brazilian case study may not always be precisely applicable to every situation in Spanish America, it is my observation that the crisis in Hispanic American Protestantism is, if anything, more acute. This may be due to the absence of even the minimum of historical continuity that the historical churches have been able to contribute in the case of Brazil. It is probably also a function of the overdependence of the large "faith mission" churches upon their North American metropolis, a situation from which Brazil has, to a certain degree, been spared.

151. Luther even went so far as to set down his enlightened ideas concerning a "truly evangelical order," but because he was unable to find those "who want to be Christians in earnest and who profess the Gospel with hand and mouth," he eventually threw in his lot with the territorial church and denounced the Anabaptist sectarians as "false prophets" (Durnbaugh 1968:3; Littell: 9–15).

152. Baptists John Bunyan *(Pilgrim's Progress)* and William Carey, founder of the modern Protestant missionary movement, belonged to the lower strata of society, as did Baptist churches in the U.S.A. for many years.

153. Pietists addressed themselves to the ills of the territorial churches of northern Europe. Where church and state are united, the evils of one become the ills of the other.

154. In a significant parallel, Ralph Della Cava suggests that the strong support the Catholic CEBs are receiving from the hierarchy and "a clergy descending from the pronouncedly European, rural immigrant milieu elaborated for more than a century in the states of southern Brazil" may have something to do with the fact that the immigrant experience until this present generation "was rooted in virtually clergyless church services sustained by lay preachers, home catechesis, and the communitarian fraternity typical of agrarian small-holders." He asks, "Are the current church fathers discerning in their own past a model for Brazil and Catholicism's future?" (IDOC 1978:48). When I asked Cardinal Arns the same question, he was intrigued by it, granting that this was a possibility he had not thought of.

155. Conversation with Reformed pastor Peter Gilhuis, São Paulo, July 1980, who received his information from a Lutheran colleague.

156. A remark attributed to Hugo Assmann, currently a professor at the Methodist University in Piracicaba, São Paulo, during a talk in 1981 at the Faculty of Theology of the Instituto Metodista de Ensino Superior, São Paulo.

157. A Methodist pastor in Brazil asked me to disband the small cell groups I was coordinating in his local congregation because his bishop, since deceased, was of the

opinion that small house groups are dangerous. "They spawn too many strange ideas!" This attitude, though probably not that of every Methodist, I suspect is fairly represent-ative of the majority of the clergy.

158. Kalley wrote home about these early house churches, small basic communities, telling how "on the Lord's Day" they "sat around the dining room table, reading verses from some Scripture passage. . . . We always discuss them as familiarly and freely as we would at any other kind of social gathering. We pray and sing some stanzas without any particular order of service" (Reily Documents:18).

159. Donald W. Dayton documents a number of such instances in which references to human rights issues have been edited out of Finney's writings and sermons. He shows that Finney, as president of Oberlin College, "a hotbed of radicalism," made major contributions to feminism, the peace movement, the doctrine of civil disobedience, temperance, and other reforms of the era (1976:35).

160. Catholic sociologist Carlos Brandão observes that in a small São Paulo town traditional Protestants abandoned the field of evangelism to Pentecostals once they had achieved a congregation capable of supporting a pastor. "The Presbyterians in the town have now become a 'Protestant parish' where religion has reached the optimum balance between regular routine and respectability" (1980a:108).

161. These contrasting approaches to church planting are rooted in two distinct views of the church. Baptist ecclesiology focuses almost exclusively upon the local church. By the time of the New Hampshire Confession (1833), which would become normative for most North American Baptists, earlier references to the universal church were omitted. The "visible church of Christ" is the local congregation of baptized believers who perceive themselves, in fact, as a basic Christian community, with all the privileges and responsibilities this implies (Costas 1980: 3,9). On the other hand, Presbyterians stress the connectional nature of the church—i.e., the intrinsic relationship of the local congregation to the institutional church through its various judicatories, and ultimately to the universal church.

162. More recent information confirms the downward trend in Brazilian Baptist numerical growth. In 1970, Baptist membership stood at 330,500, for an average annual growth rate (AAGR) of 5.9% (see Table 9). In 1979, the latest figures available to me, total membership was estimated at 503,490, an AAGR of 4.8%. That 1979 estimate was arrived at (in the official Baptist journal) by projecting an unrealistic 7% over the previous year's figures, to account for nonreports from almost one-third of the state Baptist conventions. It is possible that the real AAGR is even smaller than 4.8%, especially if this practice has been going on for a long time. Baptist projections of a 9% and 11% growth by 1980 and 1981, respectively, therefore, seem over optimistic *(Jornal Batista* 1981: 16/8:3). A comparison between their 76.8% growth in the 1960–70 decade and 60% during the 1970–80 period, which can be calculated on the basis of available information, also demonstrates a slowing down of Baptist growth.

163. At the time of my research, Baptists had no mechanism for tracking migrations within the *Convenção*; hence it was impossible to discover the true causes of this uneven growth. Some facts can be inferred, however. The slow growth in #4 (Table 10) is as much a reflection of the low number of rural (i.e., grassroots) Baptist churches as it is of the migration trends to the cities. The large number of transfers from churches in the interior of the state leaves open the question as to *why* and *where* they transferred. My hunch is, admittedly, a hypothesis, which demands proof, as is the hypothesis that the growth factors are due primarily to internal migrations. I hope that someone will take up the task of researching this.

164. The equivalent of almost one-fourth of the number of persons received in the churches we surveyed were put under discipline, but only 30% of those disciplined were reinstated—according to the research that I did for the Brazilian Baptist Board of Evangelism in 1976.

165. Article 1 of the New Hampshire Confession of Faith of 1833 reads: "[We believe] that civil government is of divine appointment, for the interests and good order of human society; and that magistrates are to be prayed for, conscientiously honored, and obeyed, except [only] in things opposed to the will of our Lord Jesus Christ, who is the only Lord of the conscience, and the Prince of the kings of the earth" (*Baptist Confessions of Faith,* William L. Lumpkin (ed.), Philadelphia: Judson, 1959, p. 366).

166. Hollenweger is relying largely upon the research of Key Yuasa, a Japanese-Brazilian Holiness pastor who is doing his doctoral research on the heritage of Luigi Francescon.

167. I found support for this hypothesis in my field research in the Canhema *favela,* in the greater São Paulo suburb of Diadema, to which I have alluded earlier. Rivail Pereira de Souza belongs to the *Congregação Crista.* He also participates in the food and brick-making cooperative that is administered by the local CEB. A member of the São Paulo growing class of "new poor," Rivail was a control-panel supervisor at a large industrial plant, but was unable to support himself and his family of five because of the skyrocketing rent and cost of basic services. So he moved his family to a drafty one-room squatter's shanty hard by the Catholic chapel. From what he saved on rent, he was making payments on a small plot of land in a distant suburb to which he hoped someday to move.

168. In another article, Rolim describes the grassroots ecclesial structure of a local *Assembleia de Deus* in a way that not only seems to confirm their CEB nature, but also illustrates how different ideologies inform the same church at different social levels. The mother churches are presbyterially organized and the faithful have very little say in the choice of their leaders. But the "preaching points," which he calls *unidades de base* (grassroots units) enjoy a fairly high level of local autonomy. The mother church presbytery makes the decision as to when a "preaching point" becomes a *congregação* with a more centralized structure, but the lay membership of the "grassroots units" must also be in agreement (Rolim 1977: 45–47).

169. The awakening of a political consciousness among the Protestant poor is a relatively recent phenomenon, which no amount of political and ecclesiastical harassment (the term is too mild) will be able to suppress—if church history is any guide to future events. It is the result of the interaction of two historical processes in which the Holy Spirit is at work. On the one hand, the very success of the Evangelical witness is producing unprecedented numerical growth at the grass roots. Poor *evangélicos,* who far outnumber their relatively affluent leadership, are precisely the factor that is thrusting the once minority Protestants into the limelight. Entire Amerindian populations in the Andean region of South America and in Middle America have opted for the Protestant faith, much to the concern of the Catholic hierarchy. These "people movements," inevitably, are swelling the ranks of marginal urban dwellers. Coupled with this is the widespread distribution of Scripture, in which Protestants and Catholics now participate. The Bible has become a ferment at the very base of the socio-economic pyramid in all of Latin America, no matter what the religious affiliation. The power of the Word is enabling the Mayans of Central America to stand up against unscrupulous landlords or greedy multinational interests, even when this has meant torture and death. Scripture is overcoming the fatalism of underemployed Pentecostals in Lima, and

giving courage and hope to Evangelical community leaders in Nicaragua who have been singled out for extermination by U.S.-supported *"contras"*. No less significant is a sociological fact that has generally been overlooked by students of church growth. The traditional Protestant work ethic is being effectively neutralized by the very magnitude of the socio-economic crisis that is gripping Latin America today. One can no longer accept as a given that the new dynamism unleashed in such force by Protestant Christianity will gradually move those Protestants upward in the social scale, into the comfortable middle class. The Latin American middle class is shrinking at an alarming rate. The social pyramid, though narrow at the apex, is so top-heavy with the vested interests of the powerful rich that it is squeezing out the narrow middle-class fringe, while it bears down upon the millions of poor—whatever their faith—with crushing force. Scripture, read in small rural and Amerindian congregations, is slowly becoming a very dangerous political instrument for those who would like to "keep these people in their place." To attribute this to Marxist influence is to delude ourselves. It also underestimates the power of the Holy Spirit at work in the church through the leaven of the Word. Those who refuse to learn from history are condemned to repeat it.

170. A spokesperson for the Protestant-run *Centro Ecuménico de Documentaçâo e Informaçâo* (CEDI) told me in August 1981 that they had recently conducted a workshop for CEB pastoral ministers. The topic: idiosyncrasies of the Pentecostals!

171. "We are coming from where you are going," Fr. José Marins is reputed to have observed to a Pentecostal pastor who was proudly showing off the large church structure he was completing.

172. *Proyecto histórico,* a particularly dense term often used in Latin American liberation writings: a consciously chosen, goal-oriented self-projection into the future, in pursuit of concrete betterment.

173. My conviction is based not upon Marxist "historical inevitability" but upon my reading of prophetic Scripture, of history, and of the "signs of the times". A balanced biblical understanding of the kingdom of God should motivate us to act as salt and leaven in society, infusing kingdom values into new social structures, even though we recognize their tendency to sinfulness and abuse.

174. John Stam in *Hacia una teología de la evangelización,* Orlando E. Costas, ed., Buenos Aires: Aurora, 1973, pp.87ff.

175. St. Paul's Jewish listeners in Thessalonica very quickly perceived the "subversive" implications of his announcement that "Jesus is the Christ," though they were obviously twisting this to their own ends when they translated Christ's lordship into a direct "political" confrontation with Caesar. Nonetheless, Christ's lordship is indeed a glove flung in the face of all the absolutist powers of this world.

176. The author of Hebrews uses the words *hypodigma* ("example, model, pattern, copy, imitation, image"), *skia* ("foreshadowing of a future reality"), and *tupos,* which means "visible impression, copy, image, archetype, pattern , or model" (Kittel and Friedrich 1964:2:32–33; 7:394ff.; 8:246ff.; see also Arndt and Gingrich, *Greek-English Lexicon* 1957:763, 837, 851). All these can be summarized by the terms "image," "sign," and "symbol" used in modern communication theory.

177. José Marins and his team have done a thorough job of documenting and excerpting the 115 most important national episcopal conferences and 342 lesser events between 1968 and 1978, and of cataloguing them into periods from Vatican II until after Puebla (Marins 1979a). The archdiocese of San Salvador (C.A.) carried out an inquiry of popular attitudes toward the issues to be discussed at Puebla. The results have been quantified and presented in "Radiography . . . " (CELAM III Documents).

178. John Paul II covered more than 30 thousand kilometers in Brazil during which he addressed some 17 million persons in 13 major religious services and made 44 speeches in 13 cities, not counting side trips to a hospital and a leprosarium (CRIE:1:5).

179. My primary source for news information is the clipping and news analysis provided by the documentation service of the *Centro Regional de Informaciónes Ecuménicas* (CRIE), located in Mexico City.

180. The entire documentation for this case is listed in the Bibliographic References: *Estado do São Paulo,* May 20, 21, 23, 26; *Folha de São Paulo,* May 12, 13, 21, 23, 27, 28, 30; *Jornal do Brasil,* May 11, 14, 15; and *O Globo,* May 30. My source, CEDI of Rio and São Paulo, has the most complete clipping service of the CEBs of any place in Brazil and probably the world. Much of this material may also be secured from Princeton Seminary Library.

181. Indeed, the PT made a very poor showing in the 1982 elections. Indications are that in the south and southeast the CEBs threw their weight behind parties of a Christian Democratic and moderate Social Democratic orientation, whereas in the impoverished north and northeast, they voted massively for the government party.

182. There are, however, indications that repression is again on the increase in Brazil, not only against striking workers of São Paulo, but on the *fazendas* in the vast interior (private conversation with L. Boff, Nov. 24, 1981).

183. Despite recent onslaughts from "reactionary" bishops, the small group of "progressive" CNBB prelates continues to enjoy the support of the large "moderate" middle. But for how long? Dom Hélder Câmara, pioneer of the social activism of the Brazilian church, will one day have a successor. Observers in Brazil are attaching great importance to the identity of his successor. It will be taken as an early indicator of the Vatican position regarding the orientation it desires for the Brazilian church *(Jornal do Brasil,* Aug. 16, 1981).

184. In preparation for the 1982 elections, the São Paulo archdiocese prepared a workbook and slide show reviewing the past and present political history of Brazil, and orienting CEB members on the basics of the democratic process *(Jornal,* Aug. 2, 1981).

# Bibliographic References

ABBOTT, Walter M. (ed.)
1966     *The Documents of Vatican II,* New York, America Press.
ALICINO, Rogério
1977     *Comunidade, Lider, Parróquia,* São Paulo, Paulinas.
ALTMANN, Walter
1980     "Algunas Experiências de Base na Igreja Evangélica de Confissão Lu-
         terana no Brasil," report at the International Ecumenical Congress of
         Theology, São Paulo, 1980.
ALVES, Rubem
1982     *Dogmatismo e Tolerancia,* São Paulo, Ediçoes Paulinas.
ANDERSON, Gerald H., and Stransky, Thomas F.
1976     *Mission Trends No. 3: Third World Theologies,* New York, Paulist Press
         and Grand Rapids, Eerdmans.
ANTOINE, Charles
1973     *Church and Power in Brazil,* Maryknoll, N.Y., Orbis.
AQUINAS, Thomas
1967     *Summa Theologica,* Chicago, Henry Regnery.
ARIAS, Esther and Mortimer
1980     *The Cry of My People: Out of Captivity in Latin America,* New York,
         Friendship Press.
ARNS, Cardinal Paulo Evaristo
1974     *Cristãos em Plena Vida,* São Paulo, Loyola.
1980     Interview in São Paulo, Feb. 16.
AYER, Joseph Cullen
1952     *A Source Book for Ancient Church History from the Apostolic Age to
         the Close of the Conciliar Period,* New York, Scribner's.
AZEVEDO, Fernando de
1950     *Brazilian Culture: An Introduction to the Study of Culture in Brazil,*
         New York: Macmillan.
AZEVEDO, Irland Pereira (ed.)
1980     "A Cidade de São Paulo, Brasil." Unpublished study of Protestant
         churches in São Paulo.
AZEVEDO, Thales de
1963     *Social Change in Brazil,* Gainesville, University of Florida Press.
1981     A Religião Civil Brasileira: Um Instrumento Político, Petrópolis, Vozes.
AZZI, Riolando
1978     "Formação Histórica do Catholicismo Popular Brasileiro." *A Religião
         do Provo,* B. Beni dos Santos (et. al.), São Paulo, Edições Paulinas.
1984     "Moral Católica e Sociedade Colonial." Unpublished paper.

BAINTON, Roland H.
1968       *Early Christianity,* Princeton, N.J., Van Nostrand.
BANKS, Robert
1980a      *Paul's Idea of Community: The Early House Churches in Their Historical Setting.* Grand Rapids, Eerdmans.
1980b      *Going to Church in the First Century,* Greenacre, Australia, Hexagon Press.
BARAGLIA, Mariano
1974       *Evolução das Comunidades Eclesiais de Base: Experiências Comunitarias na Cidade de São Paulo,* Petropolis, Vozes.
BARKLEY, John M.
1959       *A Short History of the Presbyterian Church in Ireland,* Belfast, Church Publications Board.
BARRA DE TIJUCA (Rio de Janeiro)
1981       Participation in a construction workers' and live-in maids' *comunidade,* accompanied by Fr. Edmund Leising and Dr. Frances E. O'Gorman of FASE, Aug. 9.
BARREIRO, Alvaro
1982       *Basic Ecclesial Communities: The Evangelization of the Poor,* Maryknoll, N.Y., Orbis.
BASTIDE, Roger
1971       *African Civilizations in the New World,* New York, Harper and Row.
BAX, E. Bedford
1968       *The Peasants' War in Germany,* 1525-1526, New York, Russell &Russell. Originally published in 1899.
BEOZZO, José Oscar (ed.)
1980       *História da Igreja no Brasil,* vol. II/2, CEHILA Project, Petrópolis, Vozes.
BERGER, Peter L.
1967       *Introducción a la sociología.* México City, Edit. Limusa Wiley. Original edition, *Invitation to Sociology: A Humanistic Perspective,* Garden City, N.Y., Doubleday, 1963.
1969       *The Sacred Canopy: Elements in a Sociological Theory of Religion,* New York, Doubleday.
BERGER, Peter L., and Luckmann, Thomas
1967       *The Social Construction of Reality,* Garden City, N.Y., Doubleday Anchor.
BERKHOF, Hendrik
1977       *Christ and the Powers,* trans. John H. Yoder, Scottsdale, Pa., Mennonite Publ.
BERRYMAN, Phillip
1984       *The Religious Roots of Rebellion: Christians in Central American Revolutions,* Maryknoll, N.Y., Orbis.
BETTENSON, Henry (ed.)
1976       *Documents of the Christian Church,* London, Oxford University Press. Originally published in 1943.
BETTO, Frei (Carlos Alberto Libânio Christo)
1971       *Against Principalities and Powers: Letters from A Brazilian Jail,* Maryknoll, N.Y., Orbis.

1976    "Evangelización Popular, Ideología y Liberación." *Mensaje Iberoamericano,* no. 129–30 (July-Aug.).

1977    *O Canto do Galo* (Relatorio Pastoral de uma visita à Prelazia do Acre e Purus). Separatas of the *Revista Eclesiástica Brasileira,* Petrópolis, Vozes.

1979a   *A Semente e o Fruto: Igreja-Comunidade,* Petrópolis, Vozes.

1979b   *Prática Pastoral e Prática Política,* Petrópolis, Vozes.

1980a   "Por la liberación del pueblo." *Cuadernos de Marcha,* 2:8:61–66, Mexico City.

1980b   *Puebla para o Poro,* Petrópolis, Vozes.

1980c   Interview on his early work in CEBs and present service in workers' pastoral ministry in ABC suburbs of São Paulo, Feb. 13.

1981    *O qué Sao as CEB?* São Paulo, Editora Brasilense (Coleção Primeiros Passos).

1982    "Church Born of the People." LADOC, 12:3 (Jan.-Feb.) 1–19.

1983    *CEBs: Rumo à Nova Sociedade,* São Paulo, Paulinas.

BETTO, Frei et al

1978    *O Canto na Fogueira,* Petrópolis, Vozes.

BOFF, Clodovis

1978a   *Teologia e Prática: Teologia do Político e suas Mediações,* Petrópolis, Vozes.

1978b   "Comunidades Cristãs e Política Partidiaria." *Revista Eclesiástica Brasileira* 38:151 (Sept.) 386–401.

1978c   *Comunidade Eclesial: Comunidade Política,* Petrópolis, Vozes.

1979    *Sinais dos Tempos: Princípios de Leitura* Sao Paulo, Ediçoes Loyola.

1981    *Comunidades Eclesiais de Base e Políticas de Libertação,* Petrópolis, Vozes.

1984    *Teologia Pé no Chão* (Feet-on-the-Ground Theology), Petrópolis, Vozes.

BOFF, Leonardo

1976a   *A Ressurreição de Cristo—A Nossa Ressurreição na Morte,* Petrópolis, Vozes.

1976b   "Eclesiogénesis: Las comunidades eclesiales de base reinventan la iglesia." *Servir* 12:65/66:401–46.

1977    *Eclesiogênese: As Comunidades Eclesiais de Base Reinventam a Igreja,* Petrópolis, Vozes.

1978a   *A Fe na Periferia do Mundo.* Petrópolis, Vozes.

1978b   *Jesus Christ, Liberator,* Maryknoll, N.Y., Orbis.

1978c   *Paixão de Cristo, Paixão do Mundo,* Petrópolis, Vozes.

1978d   *Vida para Alem da Morte,* Petrópolis, Vozes.

1979    "Os Ganhos de Puebla." *Revista da Arquidiocese* 3 (March) 167–70.

1980    *Way of the Cross—Way of Justice,* Maryknoll, N.Y., Orbis.

1981    Series of lectures on liberation theology and CEBs sponsored by CONCORD (National Conference of Religious Orders) in San José, Costa Rica, Nov. 23–27.

1983    *The Lord's Prayer: The Prayer of Integral Liberation,* Maryknoll, N.Y., Orbis.

BONIN, Eduardo (ed.)

1982    *Espiritualidad y liberación en América Latina,* San José, Costa Rica, DEI.

BOSCH, David L.
1980 *Witness to the World: The Christian Mission in Theological Perspective,* Atlanta, John Knox.
BRANDÃO, Carlos Rodrígues
1980a *Os Deuses do Povo,* Rio de Janeiro, Editora Brasilense. Summary in *Missiology: An International Review* 10 (April 1982) 2:245–56.
1980b *Memória do Sagrado: Religiões de Uma Cidade do Interior,* Cadernos de ISER, Rio de Janeiro, Tempo e Presença.
1980c Notes on a lecture at WCC Preconsultation on Evangelization, Rio de Janeiro, Focolares Retreat Center, Feb. 26.
BRAVO, Antonio
1979 Interview with administrator of the diocese of Rio Bamba, Ecuador, on operations of Quechau CEBs, and popular religiosity, Sept. 15.
BROCK, Peter
1957 *The Political and Social Doctrines of the Unity of Czech Bretheren in the Fifteenth and Early Sixteenth Centuries,* London, Mouton.
BROCKMAN, James R.
1982 *The World Remains: A Life of Oscar Romero,* Maryknoll, N.Y., Orbis.
BRUNEAU, Thomas C.
1974 *The Political Transformation of the Brazilian Catholic Church,* London, Cambridge University Press.
1980 "Basic Christian Communities in Latin America: Their Nature and Significance (especially in Brazil)," in *Churches and Politics in Latin America,* Daniel H. Levine (ed.), Sage Focus Editions 14, Beverly Hills, Ca., Sage, pp. 226–37.
BULLOCK, James
1963 *The Life of the Celtic Church,* Edinburgh, St. Andrews Press.
CÂMARA, Hélder
1971 *Revolution Through Peace,* New York, Harper & Row.
1974a "The Gospel of Liberation," LADOC 6 (Sept.-Oct.) 3a:30–34.
1974b "What Would Thomas Aquinas do about Karl Marx?" LADOC 6 (Sept.-Oct.) 3a:35–36.
1976a *The Desert Is Fertile,* Maryknoll, N.Y., Orbis.
1976b "The Force of Right or the Right of Force?" *Mission Trends,* no. 3, Gerald H. Anderson and Thomas F. Stransky. eds, New York, Paulist; Grand Rapids, Eerdmans.
1980 I accompanied him on a pastoral visit to an "Assembly of the People" in Cruz de Rebouças, PE later joined Fr. Luigi Rocco and CEBs in communal meal, July 26.
CAMERON, Richard M.
1961 *Methodism and Society in Historical Perspective, vol. 1, Methodist and Society,* New York, Abingdon.
CANHEMA FAVELA (DIADEMA, S.P.)
1981 Participation in work project and liturgical celebration with pastoral team led by Fr. Rubens Chasseraux, coordinator of CEBs for the ABC industrial suburbs of São Paulo, Aug. 16.
CARRICK, J.C.
1980 *Wycliff and the Lollards,* Edinburgh, Clark.
CASALDÁLIGA, Pedro
1979 *I Believe in Justice and Hope,* Notre Dame, Ind., Fides-Claretian.

CASALDÁLIGA, Pedro and pastoral team
1980a    *Missa, O qué é?* Petrópolis, Vozes.
1980b    *O Batismo, o qué é?* Petrópolis, Vozes.
CASTRO, Emilio
1970     "Conversión y transformación social." *Hacia una revolución responsable: Ensayos sobre socio-ética cristiana,* Richard Shaul, et al., Buenos Aires, Aurora.
1975     *Amidst Revolution,* Belfast, Belfast Christian Journals, Ltd.
CELAM
1975     Special bulletin on Base Ecclesial Communities (Nov.-Dec.).
CELAM II (Medellín)
1973     *The Church in the Present-day Transformation of Latin America in the Light of the Council,* Washington, D.C., United States Catholic Conference.
1976     *Iglesia y Religiosidad Popular en América Latina,* Bogotá, CELAM. Study paper (August).
1978b    "Tercera conferencia del Episcopado Latinoamericano: Puebla 1978: Síntesis del Documento Preparatorio," Bogotá, CELAM.
CELAM III (Puebla)
1977     *Documentation: Radiography of a Local Church in View of Puebla,* Rome, IDOC.
1978     "La evangelización en el presente y el futuro de América Latina: Documento de consulta a las conferencias episcopales: Puebla 1978." *Mensaje,* no. 267 (April), Santiago, pp. 167–74.
CHASSERAUX, Rubens
1981     Interview in parish house in working-class suburb of Rudge Ramos, São Bernardo do Campo, S.P., Aug. 7.
CIET
1980     *La irrupción de los pobres en la iglesia,* San José, Costa Rica, DEI. English version in *Occasional Bulletin of Missionary Research,* 4 (July) 3: 127–42, and in Torres and Eagleson 1981: 231–46.
CLARK, David
1977     *Basic Communities: Towards an Alternative Society,* London, SPCK.
CNBB
1975a    *Diretrizes Gerais da Ação Pastoral da Igreja no Brasil (no. 4), 1977–78,* São Paulo, Paulinas.
1975b    *Comunidades: Igreja na Base: Estudos da CNBB,* São Paulo, Paulinas.
1976     *Manual sobre as Comunidades Eclesiais de Base,* Secretariado Regional Sul II, Equipe de Coordenação da Pastoral Rural.
1977a    *Quarto Plano Bienal dos Organismos Nacionais: 1977–78,* São Paulo, Paulinas.
1977b    "The Christian Requirements of a Political Order," LADOC 8 (Jan.-Feb.) 3:1–14.
1979     "A Marca do Povo de Deus na América Latina." Assembleia Regional Nordeste II, *Estudios da CNBB,* no. 23. Published in Spanish by MIEC-JECI, Servicio de Documentación, no. 22, Lima, Peru.
1980     *Todos os Pronunciamentos do Papa no Brasil,* São Paulo, Loyola.
1981a    "Indicações Pastorais frente ao Compromisso Político Partidário." Confidential document, April 27.

1981b    "Seminário sobre Religiosidade Popular e Comunidades Eclesiais de Base." Confidential document.

1981c    "Seminário sobre Religiosidade Popular e Comunidades Eclesiais de Base." Confidential paper.

COMBLIN, José

1974    "Comunidades y Servicios." *Selecciones de Teología,* 52:294–300.

1977    *The Meaning of Mission: Jesus, Christians and the Wayfaring Church,* Maryknoll, N.Y., Orbis.

1978    *A Ideologia da Segurança Nacional: O Poder Militar na América Latina,* Rio de Janeiro, Civilização Brasileira.

COMBLIN, José et al.

1972    *Comunidad de base y prospectiva pastoral en América Latina,* Quito, IPLA.

*EL COMERCIO* (Quito, Ecuador)

1979    "Nuevo giro en el Brasil." Sept. 7.

CONCILIUM

1975    Edition dedicated to Base Ecclesial Communities; Spanish no. 104. Articles by Comblin, Marins, Libânio, and others.

CONSTITUÃÇO DO BRASIL

1970    *Novissimo Vade-Mecum Forense,* vols. 1 and 5, 7th edition, Rio de Janeiro, José Konfino Press.

CONYBEARE, F. C.

1898    *The Key of Truth: A Manual of the Paulician Church of Armenia; Armenian text edited and translated with Illustrative Documents and Introduction,* Oxford, Clarendon Press.

COOK, William (Guillermo)

1978a    "Basic Christian Communities in the Catholic Church: A Protestant Perspective." Unpublished paper presented for credit at the Maryknoll Mission Institute, Ossining, N.Y. (July).

1978b    "Baptist Growth in the State of São Paulo." Unpublished paper submitted to Advanced Church Growth course at the School of World Mission, Fuller Theological Seminary.

1980    "From a Hand-carved Dove, A Call to Repentance." *The Other Side* (April 1980) 14–16.

1980    "Base Ecclesial Communities: A Study of Reevangelization and Growth in the Brazilian Catholic Church." *Occasional Bulletin of Missionary Research,* 4:3 (July) 113–17.

1981    "Base Ecclesial Communities in the Brazilian Catholic Church: A Study of Re-evangelization and Growth." *Evangelical Review of Theology* 5:7 (April) World Evangelical Fellowship Theological Commission.

1983    "An Evangelical-Protestant Analysis of the Base Ecclesial Communities." Paper presented before the Ventnor[N.J.] Study Group (Dec. 2–3). Not for circulation.

1984a    "Base Ecclesial Communities in Central America." *The Mennonite Quarterly, Review* 410–423, and *Occasional Essays,* 11:2:78–113.

1984b    "The Protestant Predicament: From Base Ecclesial Community to Establishment Church—A Brazilian Case Study." *International Bulletin of Missionary Research* 8:3 (July 1984) 98–102.

COOK, William (ed.)

1984    "Spirituality in the Struggles for Social Justice: A Brief Latin American Anthology." *Missiology: An International Review,* 12:2 (April) 224-32.

COSTAS, Orlando E.

1976    *Theology of the Crossroads in Contemporary Latin America: Missiology in Mainline Protestantism, 1969-74,* Amsterdam, Rodopi.

1978a   "Grupos de base: Uma Resposta ao Desafio do Discipulado." Notes from a lecture at the Seminário Batista do Nordeste, Recife, Brazil.

1978b   "Conversion as a Complex Experience—A Hispanic Case Study." *Occasional Essays* 5 (June):1:21–40. San José, Costa Rica, CELEP.

1979    *The Integrity of Mission: The Inner Life and Outreach of the Church,* New York, Harper & Row.

1980    "The Nature and Mission of the Church. A Commentary on the Ecclesio-Missiology of EBT's Doctrinal Basis." Theological colloquium at Eastern Baptist Theological Seminary, Dec. 5.

1982    *Christ Outside the Gate: Mission Beyond Christendom,* Maryknoll, N.Y., Orbis.

COUTO E SILVA, Gen. Golbery

1981    *Cojuntura Política Nacional, O Poder Executivo e Geopolítica do Brasil,* Rio de Janeiro, José Olympio Editora.

COWEN, Ian B.

1976    *The Scottish Covenanters: 1560-1688,* London, Gollancz.

COX, Harvey, and SAND, Faith A.

1979    "What Happened at Puebla?" *Christianity in Crisis* 39:4 (March 19).

CRABTREE, A.R.

1953    *Baptists in Brazil,* Rio de Janeiro, Baptist Publishing House.

CRIE (Centro Regional de Informaciónes Ecuménicas)

1980    *Vista del Papa al Brasil,* nos. 1–12 (July), Mexico City.

CROSSLEY, Robert N.

1974    *Luther and the Peasants' War: Luther's Actions and Reactions,* New York, Exposition Press.

d'ABLEIGES, Xavier G. de M.

1979    *Curso Bíblico para as Comunidades Eclesiais de Base,* São Paulo, Paulinas.

DALE, R. W.

1907    *History of English Congregationalism,* London, Hodder & Stoughton.

DAVIES, Horton

1948    *The Worship of English Puritans,* Glasgow University Press.

DAVIES, Rupert E.

1963    *Methodism,* London, Penguin.

DAYTON, Donald W.

1976    *Discovering an Evangelical Heritage,* New York, Harper & Row.

de JESUS, Maria Carolina

1962    *Child of the Dark,* New York, New American Library.

de KADT, Emmanuel

1970    *Catholic Radicals in Brazil,* London, Oxford University Press.

DELESPESSE, Max

1973    *Revolução Evangélica,* São Paulo, Loyola.

DELGADO, Isaac
1979      Interview with a lay *responsable* of a *comunidad neocatecumenal* in Quito, Ecuador, Sept. 11.

D'EPINAY, Christian Lalive
1968      *El refugio de las masas: Estudio sociológico del protestantismo chileno,* Santiago, Editora del Pacífico.

*DIÁLOGO ECUMÉNICO*
1977      Special issue on Base Ecclesial Communities, no. 43.

DIAS, Zwinglio Mota
1982      "Reflexões em Torno a Questão Pastoral Protestante e a Experiencia Acumulada pelo CEDI até Aquí." *Tempo e Presença: Protestantismo e Política* 29 (Aug.) 7–17, Rio de Janeiro, CEDI.

DILLENBERGER, John, and WELCH, Claude
1954      *Protestant Christianity—Interpreted through Its Development,* New York, Scribner's.

DIOCESE OF SANTO ANDRÉ, S.P.
1981      "Animador: Vocação de Cristo." *ABC Litúrgico* 2 (Aug. 23) 98.

DORR, Donal
1983      *Option for the Poor: A Hundred Years of Vatican Social Teaching,* Maryknoll, N.Y., Orbis.

dos SANTOS, B. Beni et al.
1978      *A Religião de Povo,* São Paulo, Paulinas.

DURNBAUGH, Donald F.
1968      *The Believers' Church: The History and Character of Radical Protestantism,* New York, Macmillan.

DUSSELL, Enrique
1976      *History and the Theology of Liberation,* Maryknoll, N.Y., Orbis.

ENSIGN, Chauncey David
1965      "Radical German Pietism (c1675-c1765)." Dissertation submitted in partial fulfillment of the requirements for the degree of Doctor of Philosophy, Boston University Graduate School.

ESCOTT, Harry
1960      *A History of Scottish Congregationalism,* Glasgow, Congregational Union of Scotland.

*O ESTADO DE SÃO PAULO*
1973      "O Catolicismo Brasileiro em Crise." Jan.

ESTEP, William R.
1973      *The Anabaptist Story,* Grand Rapids, Eerdmans, revised and updated.

*EXCHANGE*
1979      "Church Basic Communities in Latin America." Geneva, WCC (May 2).

FACKRE, Gabriel
1975      *Word in Deed: Theological Themes in Evangelism,* Grand Rapids, Eerdmans.

FASE (Federação de orgãos para a Assistência Social e Educacional)
1981a      "Movimento de Criatividade Comunitária." Programa NUCLAR.
1981b      "FASE-Programa NUCLAR: Proposta Referencial."

*FOLHA DE SÃO PAULO*
1979      "Comunismo e Comunidades de Base." April 17.

1980        "Igreja Condena Regime Vigente." Feb. 15.
1981a       "Comida, a Maior atração de Festa dos Favelados." Aug. 17.
1981b       "Seminário sobre Favelas Apresenta sua conclussão." Aug. 17.
1981c       "Generais Aumentam Espaço Político com a Queda de Golberi." Aug.
            23, pp. 1/5.
1981d       "Coordenador não quer favelados 'iludidos'." Aug. 26, p. 15.
FOREMAN, Shepard
1975        *The Brazilian Peasantry*, Columbia University Press.
FREIRE, Paulo
1964, 1969  *La educación como práctica de la libertad*, Montevideo, Tierra Nueva.
1970, 1975  *Extensão ou Comunicação?* Rio de Janeiro, Paz e Terra.
1973a       *Conscientización*, Bogotá, Asociación de Publicaciones Educativas.
1973b       "A Key Idea of Paulo Freire: Oppression . . . Dependence . . . Mar-
            ginalization." Summarized in LADOC, 6 (Sept.-Oct.) 3a:15-25.
1974        *Las iglesias, la educación y el proceso de liberación humana en la
            historia*, Buenos Aires, Aurora.
1982        *Education for Critical Consciousness*, New York, Continuum Publishing
            Corp.
1983        *Pedagogy of the Oppressed*, New York, Continuum Publishing Corp.
FREYRE, Gilberto
1964        *The Masters and the Slaves*, New York, Knopf. Original edition, *Casa
            Grande e Senzala*, Rio de Janeiro, José Olympio, 1946.
1968        *The Mansions and the Shanties*, New York, Knopf. Original edition,
            *Sobrados e Mucambos*, Rio de Janeiro, José Olympio, 1936.
1975        *O Brasileiro entre os Outros Hispanos*, Rio de Janeiro, Ministerio de
            Educaçãoe Cultura.
FUNG, Raymond
1982        *Households of God on China's Soil*, Geneva, WCC.
GAIRDNERS, James
1908        *Lollardy and the Reformation in England: An Historical Survey*, vol. 1,
            New York, Burt Franklin.
GALILEA, Segundo
1978        *Religiosidade Popular e Pastoral*, São Paulo, Paulinas.
GALLETT, Paul
1970        *Freedom to Starve*, Baltimore, Penguin.
GARSOÏAN, Nina
1967        *The Paulician Heresy: A Study of the Origin and Development of
            Paulicianism in Armenia and in the Eastern Provinces of the Byzantine
            Empire*, The Hague, Mouton.
GISH, Arthur G.
1970        *The New Left and Christian Radicalism*, Grand Rapids, Eerdmans.
GLASSER, Arthur F.
1981        "A Paradigm Shift? Evangelicals and Interreligious Dialogue." *Mis-
            siology: An International Review* 9:4 (Oct.) 393-408.
GONZALEZ, Justo L.
1980        *La era de los reformadores*, vol. 6: . . . Y hasta lo último de la tierra:
            Una historia ilustrada del cristianismo, Miami, Editorial Caribe/Latin
            America Mission Publications.

Bibliographic References

GORGULHO, Frei Gilberto, and ANDERSON, Sr. Ana Flora
1975 O Evangelho e a Vida: São Marcos—Círculos Bíblicos, São Paulo, Paulinas.
GRAHAM, Fred W.
1971 The Constructive Revolutionary: John Calvin and His Socio- Economic Impact, Richmond, John Knox.
GRANT, Robert M.
1970 Augustus to Constantine: The Thrust of the Christian Movement in the Roman World, New York, Harper & Row.
GREGORY, Alfonso
1965 A Igreja no Brasil, Rio de Janeiro, CERIS.
GREGORY, Alfonso et al.
1973 Comunidades Eclesiais de Base: Utopia ou Realidade? Petrópolis, Vozes.
GRELLERT, Manfred
1981 "Evangelização e Educação Teológica no Brasil." Paper delivered before ASTE.
GREMILLION, Joseph
1976 The Gospel of Peace and Justice, Maryknoll, N.Y., Orbis.
GROUNDS, Vernon C.
1969 Evangelicalism and Social Responsibility, Scottdale, Pa., Herald Press.
GUIMARÃES, Mother Terezinha Stella
1977 "On the Road to Joazeiro: A Pilgrimage to North East Brazil." Lumen Vitae, 32:1.
GUTIÉRREZ, Gustavo
1973 A Theology of Liberation, Maryknoll, N.Y., Orbis.
1979 Brief dialogue and interview at Seminário Bíblico Latinoamericano, San José, Costa Rica, Nov. 13.
1983 The Power of the Poor in History, Maryknoll, N.Y., Orbis.
1984 We Drink from Our Own Wells: The Spiritual Journey of a People. Maryknoll, N.Y., Orbis.
HAHN, Carl Joseph
1970 "Evangelical Worship in Brazil: Its Origins and Development." Thesis submitted for the degree of Doctor of Philosophy at the University of Edinburgh, Faculty of Divinity.
HALEVY, Elie
1971 The Birth of Methodism in England, University of Chicago Press.
HANKS, Thomas D.
1983 God So Loved the Third World: The Bible, the Reformation, and Liberation Theologies, Maryknoll, N.Y., Orbis.
HARNACK, Adolf von
1961 Mission and Expansion of Christianity, New York, Harper Brothers.
HARRISON, Archibald W.
1942 The Evangelical Revival and Christian Reunion, London, Epworth.
HASTINGS, Adrian
1972 "Should Church Reform Start from the Top, or from the Ground Level?" Ongoing Reform in the Church, Aloise Mueller and Norbert Grenachen (eds.), The New Concilium: Religion in the Seventies, New York, Herder and Herder, 73:89–96.

HAUCH, João Fagundes, FRAGOSO, Hugo, BEOZZO, José (et.al.)
1980    *História da Igreja no Brasil—Segunda Epoca: A Igreja no Brasil no Século XIX,* Petropolis, Vozes.
HERKOVITS, Melville J.,
1958    "African Gods and Catholic Saints in New World Religious Belief." *Reader in Comparative Religion: An Anthropological Approach* (1s ed.), William A. Lessa and Ever C. Vogt (eds.), Evanston, Row, Peterson and Co.
HIEBERT, Paul G.
1980    "Conversion, Culture, and Cognitive Categories." Unpublished pamphlet, Pasadena, Fuller Theological Seminary, School of World Mission.
HILL, Christopher
1972    *The World Turned Upside Down: Radical Ideas During the English Revolution,* New York, Penguin.
1979    *The English Revolution: 1640,* London, Lawrence and Wishart. First published in 1940.
*HISTORIA DAS ASSEMBLEIAS DE DEUS NO BRASIL*
1960    Rio de Janeiro, Assemblies of God Publ.
HOLLENWEGER, Walter
1972    *The Pentecostals: The Charismatic Movement in the Churches,* Minneapolis, Augsburg.
HOORNAERT, Eduardo
1978    "Comunidades de Base—Dez Anos de Experiência." *Revista Eclesiástica Brasileira* 38:151 (Sept.) 474–511.
HOORNAERT, Eduardo and associate
1980    Lengthy interview in colonial seminary of the archbishopric of Olinda-Recife, and visit to Câmara's austere dwelling in a working-class "suburb" of Recife, Feb. 27.
HOORNAERT, Eduardo et al.
1979    *História da Igreja no Brasil,* vol. 2, CEHILA Project, Petrópolis, Vozes.
HUBBARD, David Allan
1979    *What We Evangelicals Believe,* Pasadena, Fuller Theological Seminary.
HYMA, Albert
1950    *The Brethren of the Common Life,* Grand Rapids, Eerdmans.
1951    *Rennaissance to Reformation,* Grand Rapids, Eerdmans.
IDOC
1978    *The Church at the Crossroads: From Medellín to Puebla (1968-78),* Rome. Articles by Ralph Della Cava and Pablo Richard.
IECL
1980    *A Enchada,* Vitória (E.S.), mimeographed periodical.
*INTERNATIONAL REVIEW OF MISSIONS*
1979    "Mission Without Missions, " 68 (July) 271.
JOHNSON, Harmon
1969    "Authority over the Spirits: Brazilian Spiritism and Evangelical Church Growth," M.A. Thesis, Fuller Theological Seminary.
JONES, R. Tudor
1962    *Congregationalism in England: 1662-1962,* London, Independent Press.

JONES, Susanne, and TABIS, David
1974     *Guatemala,* New York, NACLA (North American Congress on Latin America).
*JORNAL DA BAHIA*
1980     "Classes Populares São um Desafio Para as Igrejas." Oct. 7.
*JORNAL DO BRASIL*
1980a     "Boff Teme que Comunidades de Base Virem Células Marxistas." Sept. 22, p. 13.
1980b     "Pais Atacam Teologia da Libertação." Sept. 22, p. 13.
1980c     "Comunidades em Risco." Sept. 27.
1980d     "Professor Acha que o Desafio da Igreja é Consciencia Popular," in reference to an observation by Dr. Jether Ramalho of CEDIS, Oct. 1.
1980e     "Penumbra Teológica." nd.
1981a     "O Medo das Comunidades." Tristão de Atayde. June 25.
1981b     "Os CEBs Já Não Estão Sós." July 7.
1981c     "CEBs de São Paulo Ensinam o Povo Como se Deve Votar." Aug. 2, p. 8.
1981d     "A Tres Anos de Aposentaduria: A Difícil Sucessão de Dom Hélder Câmara." Aug. 16, p. 6.
1981e     "Dom Waldir quer a Igreja no Política." Aug. 16, p. 8.
KAMINSKY, Howard
1967     *A History of the Hussite Revolution,* University of California Press.
KAUTSKY, Karl
1966     *Communism in Central Europe in the Time of the Reformation,* New York, Augustus M. Kelley. Originally published in 1897.
KERHONAN, J.W.
1923     *Rosemary Street Presbyterian Church, Belfast: A Record of the Past 200 Years,* Belfast, Belfast Witness.
KINSLER, F. Ross
1983     *Ministry by the People: Theological Education by Extension,* Maryknoll, N.Y., Orbis.
KIRK, J. Andrew
1979     *Liberation Theology: An Evangelical View from the Third World,* Atlanta, John Knox.
KITTEL, Gerhard
1978     *Theological Dictionary of the New Testament,* 10 vols., Grand Rapids, Eerdmans.
KLAASEN, John J.
1977     "Two Methods of Evangelism and Church Planting: A Case Study of the Brazilian Mennonite Brethren Convention." Dissertation presented to the Faculty of the School of World Mission, Fuller Theological Seminary, in partial fulfillment for the degree of D. Miss.
KLEIST, James A. (ed.)
1948     *Ancient Christian Writers,* Westminster, Md., Newman.
KOSINSKI DE CAVALCANTI, José, and DEELEN, Godofredo
1970     *Brasil: Igreja em Transição,* Cuernavaca, CIDOC.
KRAFT, Charles H.
1979     *Christianity in Culture: A Study in Dynamic Biblical Theologizing in Cross-cultural Perspective,* Maryknoll, N.Y., Orbis.

KUHN, Thomas S.
1970    *The Structure of Scientific Revolutions,* University of Chicago Press.
LADOC
1970-81   Bimonthly publication, vols. 1-10, Washington, D.C., United States
          Catholic Conference, vols. 11 and 12 by Latinamerica Press, Lima.
          Numerous articles on Brazil and CEBs.
1975    "Are Basic Communities Marxist?" 5 (Nov.-Dec.) 16-18.
1979    "Third Ecclesial Encounter of Basic Christian Communities—João Pes-
        soa." 9:3 (Jan.) 7-9.
1980    "Basic Communities of Brazilian Church in Action." 10:5 (May-June)
        11-32.
1981    "Base Ecclesial Communities in Brazil," by J.B. Libânio. 12:2 (Nov.-
        Dec.) 1-20.
1982    "Church Born of the People," by Frei Betto Libânio Christo. 12:3 (Jan.-
        Feb.) 1-15.
LADOC KEYHOLE SERIES
1982    *Brazil,* no. 8.
1975    *Latin Americans Discuss Marxism-Socialism,* no. 13.
1976    *Basic Christian Communities,* no. 14.
1978    *Repression Against the Church in Brazil (1968-78),* no. 18.
LAMBERT, Malcolm D.
1977    *Medieval Heresy: Popular Movements from Bogomil to Hus,* London,
        Edward Arnold Publ.
LAPSANSKI, Duane V.
1976    *The First Franciscans and the Gospel,* Chicago, Franciscan Herald
        Press.
*LATIN AMERICA PRESS* (Lima, Peru)
1979a   "Grass-roots Christian Communities Spearhead Social Change in Latin
        America." 2 (Sept. 6) 32.
1979b   "Communal Emphasis Promises New Dimension in Latin American
        Church." 2 (Sept. 13) 33.
1979c   "Christian Communities (III): Living the Faith and Changing the Struc-
        tures." 2 (Sept. 20) 34.
LATORRE CABAL, Hugo
1978    *The Revolution of the Latin American Church,* University of Oklahoma
        Press.
LATOURETTE, Kenneth Scott
1938    *The Thousand Years of Uncertainty,* vol. 2: *A History of the Expansion
        of Christianity,* New York, Harper and Brothers.
1975    *A History of Christianity,* vols. 1 and 2, New York, Harper & Row.
        Originally published in 1953 in one volume.
LEE, Jody, STEERS, Tom and STARK, Mike
1977    "The Relevance of Small Group and Base Community Movements for
        North American Protestantism." Term paper, Pasadena, School of
        World Mission, Fuller Theological Seminary.
LEERS, Bernardino
1977    *Catolicismo Popular e Mundo Rural: Um Ensaio Pastoral,* Petrópolis,
        Vozes.

LEFF, Gordon
1967    *Heresy in the Later Middle Ages: The Relation of Heterodoxy to Dissent, c1250-1450,* 2 vols., Manchester University Press.

LEISING, Edmund
1981    Visit to Barra de Tijuca *comunidade* and interview of FASE offices, Aug. 10. (Leising is founder and first director of FASE, coordinates the *Programa Nuclar* and is an advisor to the CNBB.)

LEITE, Bishop Nelson Campos
1981    "Mensagem da Igreja Metodista a Propósito dos Recentes Acontecimentos na Região de ABC, Grande Sâo Paulo" (April), mimeographed statement.

LENZ, M. M. et al
1976    *Evangelização no Brazil Hoje: Conteudo e Linguagem,* São Paulo, Loyola.

LEON, Edmundo
1978    *María y la iglesia profética,* Lima, CEP.

LÉONARD, Emile G.
1963    *O Protestantismo Brasileiro,* São Paulo, ASTE.

LEPAGE, Laurette
1974    *Comunidades: Seitas ou Fermento,* São Paulo, Loyola.

LERNAUX, Penny
1980    *Cry of the People: United States Involvement in the Rise of Fascism, Torture, and Murder, and the Persecution of the Catholic Church in Latin America,* New York, Doubleday.

LERNER, E. Robert
1972    *The Heresy of the Free Spirit in the Later Middle Ages,* University of California Press.

LIBÃNIO, João Batista
1976    *Evangelização e Libertação,* Petrópolis, Vozes.
1976b   "Uma Comunidade que se Redefine." SEDOC, 95 (Oct.) 295-325.
1978    "Igreja, Povo que se Liberta: III Encontro Intereclesial de Comunidades de Base." *SINTESE,* no. 14. Also published by SEDOC 11 (Oct.) 115 and 11 (Jan.-Feb.) 118, Petrópolis, Vozes.
1979-80 *Formação da Consciência Crítica,* vols., 1-3, Petrópolis, Vozes.
1979a   "Comunidade Eclesial de Base: Pletora de Discurso." SEDOC, no. 118 (Jan.-Feb.).
1979b   "A Community with a New Image." *International Review of Mission,* 68 (July):272:243-265. Also in *Concilium,* no. 104 (Sp.).
1980    "Experiences with the Base Ecclesial Communities in Brazil." *Missiology: An International Review* 8 (July) 3:319-38. A translation of "Experiência das Comunidades Eclesiais de Base no Brazil." Paper read at Pre-Melbourne Consultation, Huampaní, Peru (Nov. 1979).
1981a   "Base Ecclesial Communities in Brazil." LADOC 12 (Nov.-Dec.) 2:1-20.
1981b   "Povo Oprimido que se Organiza para a Libertacão." *Revista Eclesiástica Brasileira* 41 (June) 162:279-311.
1981c   Lengthy interview at João XXIII Institute on future perspectives of CEBs, Aug. 8.
1982    *Spiritual Discernment and Politics: Guidelines for Religious Communities,* Maryknoll, N.Y., Orbis.

LIETZMANN, Hans
1938–52   *A History of the Early Church,* 4 vols., New York, Scribner's.
LINDSAY, T. M.
1907      *The Church and the Ministry in the Early Centuries,* London, Hodder &
          Stoughton.
LITTELL, Franklin H.
1964      *The Origins of Sectarian Protestantism,* New York, Macmillan.
LOFFLER, Paul
1965      "The Biblical Concept of Conversion." *Study Encounter,* Geneva, WCC,
          Division of Studies.
LÓPEZ TRUJILLO, Cardinal Alfonso
1978      "Basic Ecclesial Communities and Evangelization in Latin America."
          *Worldmission,* 29:3 (fall).
LORSCHEIDER, Cardinal Alfonso
1977      "Basic Ecclesial Communities in Latin America." AFER, pp. 142–48.
MADURO, Otto
1982      *Religion and Social Conflicts,* Maryknoll, N.Y., Orbis.
MAINWARING, Scott
1982      "Igreja Católica, Educação do Povo e Política." Unpublished paper.
MARINS, José
1969      *La comunidad eclesial de base,* Buenos Aires, Bonum.
1970a     *Diaconado y comunidad de base,* Buenos Aires, Bonum.
1970b     *La década del '70: Signos de los tiempos. Nuevas dimensiones del
          encuentro de los hombres,* Buenos Aires, Bonum.
1971a     *Comunidad eclesial de base: Iglesia-Comunión,* Buenos Aires, Bonum.
1971b     *Entrenamiento intensivo sobre comunidades de base,* Buenos Aires,
          Bonum.
1971c     *Iglesia local: Comunidad de Base,* Buenos Aires: Bonum.
1971d     *Las religiosas en acción,* Buenos Aires, Bonum.
1972a     *Comunidad de base y civilización técnica,* Buenos Aires, Bonum.
1972b     *Operación Bumerang,* Buenos Aires, Bonum.
MARINS, José and team
1976a     *Comunidade eclesial de Base: Prioridade Pastoral,* São Paulo, Paulinas.
1976b     *Igreja e Conflictividade Social no América Latina,* São Paulo, Paulinas.
1977a     *Comunidade Eclesial: Instituição e Carisma,* São Paulo, Paulinas.
1977b     *Comunidade Eclesial de Base na América Latina,* São Paulo, Paulinas.
1977c     *Missão Evangelizadora da Comunidade Eclesial,* São Paulo, Paulinas.
1977d     *Modelos de Igreja: Comunidade Eclesial no América Latina,* São Paulo,
          Paulinas.
1977e     *Readidade e Praxis na Pastoral Latinoamericana,* São Paulo, Paulinas.
1978a     *Praxis Profética: Profetas—Cristo—Comunidade Eclesial Primitiva,*
          São Paulo, Paulinas.
1978b     "The Techniques of Ministries in Basic Christian Communities—
          Workshop Papers," Maryknoll, N.Y., Mission Institute, July.
1978c     Circular letter to Workshop Participants (Oct. 18).
1979a     *De Medellín a Puebla: A Praxis dos Padres da América Latina,* São
          Paulo, Paulinas.
1979b     "Basic Ecclesial Communities in Latin America," *International Review
          of Mission,* 68 (July) 271:235–42.

1980    *A Praxis do Martírio: Ontem e Hoje,* São Paulo, Paulinas. Original edition, *Praxis del Martirio—Ayer y Hoy,* Bogotá, CEPLA, 1977.

MARINS, José, TREVISAN, Teolide Maria, and CHANONA, Carolee
1978    Participation in an intensive workshop for CEB pastoral leaders at Maryknoll Mission Institute, July 23–28.

McGREGOR, Pedro
1967    *Jesus of the Spirits,* New York, Stein and Day.

McGAVRAN, Donald Anderson
1970    *Understanding Church Growth,* Grand Rapids, Eerdmans.

McNEILL, John T.
1974    *The Celtic Churches: A History—AD 200 to 1200,* University of Chicago Press.

MELIA, Pius
1870    *The Origins, Persecutions and Doctrines of the Waldensians,* London, James Tooney.

MELLIS, Charles J.
1976    *Committed Communities: Fresh Streams for World Missions,* S. Pasadena, Cal., William Carey Library.

MENDONÇA, Antonio Gouvêa
1983    "Uma Inversão Radical: Uma visão protestante das Comunidades Ecclesiais de Base no Brasil." Unpublished paper by a Presbyterian scholar who teaches theology at the Instituto Metodista de Ensino Superior in São Paulo.

1984    *O Celeste Porvir: A inserção do Protestantismo no Brasil,* São Paulo, Etudões Paulinas (*The Heavenly Future: Protestant Involvement in Brazil).*

MESTERS, Carlos
1971    *Deus, Onde Estás? Curso de Bíblia,* Belo Horizonte, Vega.

1972–78    *Círculos Bíblicos,* Petrópolis, Vozes. (Sixteen booklets for use in Scripture reflection of the CEBs, including introductory and teachers' manuals.)

1973    *Palavra de Deus na História dos Homens,* 2 vols., Petrópolis, Vozes. (CEB reflection material.)

1974    *Por Trâs das Palavras,* Petrópolis, Vozes. (CEB reflection material.)

1976a    "La Biblia en manos del pueblo." *Servir,* 12:65/66:483–506.

1976b    "Una iglesia que nace del pueblo." MIEC-JECI Servicio de Documentación, no. 17–18.

1979    "A Brisa Leve: Uma Nova Leitura da Bíblia." SEDOC, no. 118 (Jan.-Feb.) 733–64.

1981    *A Missão do Povo que Sofre,* Petrópolis, Vozes.

1983    "The Use of the Bible in Christian Communities of the Common People," in *The Bible and Liberation,* Norman K. Gottwald (ed.), Maryknoll N.Y., Orbis, pp. 119–33.

MÍGUEZ BONINO, José
1975    *Doing Theology in a Revolutionary Situation,* Philadelphia, Fortress.

1976    *Christians and Marxists: The Mutual Challenge to Revolution,* Grand Rapids, Eerdmans.

MÍGUEZ BONINO, José (ed.)
1984     *Faces of Jesus: Latin American Christologies,* Maryknoll, N.Y., Orbis.
MILLET, Richard
1977     *Guardians of the Dynasty,* Maryknoll, N.Y., Orbis.
MIRANDA, José P.
1974     *Marx and the Bible: A Critique of the Philosophy of Oppression,* Maryknoll, N.Y., Orbis.
1980     *Marx Against the Marxists,* Maryknoll, N.Y., Orbis.
*MISSIOLOGY: AN INTERNATIONAL REVIEW*
1980     "Experiences with the Base Ecclesial Communities in Brazil," by J. B. Libânio. 8 (July) 3:319–38.
1983a     "Let the Basic Christian Communities Speak—Some Pastoral Theological Reflections on Portezuelo and Beyond," by Joseph G. Healey. 11 (Jan.) 1:15–30.
1983b     "The Church of the Poor: Church of Life," by Jane Casy Peck. 11 (Jan.) 1:31–46.
1983c     "Evangelical Reflections on the Church of the Poor," by William Cook. 11 (Jan.) 1:46–53.
1984     "Spirituality in the Struggles for Social Justice: A Brief Latin American Anthology" 12 (April) 2: 223–232.
MONTENEGRO, João Alfredo
1972     *Evolução do Catolicismo no Brasil,* Petrópolis, Vozes.
MONTGOMERY, Tommie Sue
1982     *Revolution in El Salvador: Origins and Evolution,* Boulder, Col., Westview Press.
MOODY, T. W.
1974     *The Ulster Question: 1603–1973,* Dublin, Mercier.
MOORE, John
1946     *Methodism in Belief and Action,* Nashville, Abingdon/Cokesbury.
MOORMAN, John Richard Humpidge
1968     *A History of the Franciscan Order from Its Origins to the Year 1517,* Oxford, Clarendon Press.
MORRIS, Fred
1980     Report on his experiences in northeast Brazil working with Dom Hélder Câmara; torture and expulsion from Brazil. San José, Costa Rica, Union Church.
MORTON, A. L.
1979     *The World of the Ranters: Religious Radicalism in the English Revolution,* London, Lawrence and Wishart.
MOURÃO FILHO, Gral. Olympio
1978     *Memórias: A Verdade de um Revolucionário,* Rio Grande do Sul, L & PM.
MOUREIRA ALVEZ, Márcio
1968     *O Cristo do Povo,* Rio de Janeiro, Sabiá.
MUELLER, William A.
1954     *Church and State in Luther and Calvin,* Nashville, Broadman Press.
MUGICA, Guillermo
1978     *Los Pobres en los padres de la iglesia.* Lima, CEP.

NAVAS, Luis
1979    Interview at Ingahurco parish house and participation in a *comunidad cristiana,* Ambato, Ecuador, Sept. 20.
*NEWSWEEK MAGAZINE*
1979    "Brazil's Fading Miracle." Nov. 12, pp. 32–35.
1981    "The Struggle for the Amazon." Jan. 25, pp. 6–9.
NIDCC
1979    *The New International Dictionary of the Christian Church,* J.D. Douglas (ed.), Grand Rapids, Zondervan.
NIEBHUR, H. Richard
1957    *The Social Sources of Denominationalism,* New York, Meridian.
NOTTINGHAM, Elisabeth K.
1954    *Sociología de la religión,* Buenos Aires, Paidós. Original edition, *Religion and Society,* Garden City, New York, Doubleday.
NOUWEN, Henri
1983    *Gracias! A Latin American Journal,* New York, Harper and Row.
OBOLENSKY, Dmitri
1948    *Bogomils: A Study in Balkan Neo-Manichaeism,* New York, AMS Press and Cambridge University Press.
*OCCASIONAL BULLETIN OF MISSIONARY RESEARCH*
*(INTERNATIONAL BULLETIN OF MISSIONARY RESEARCH)*
1980a    "Base Ecclesial Communities: A Study of Reevangelization and Growth in the Brazilian Catholic Church." 4 (July) 3:113–17.
1980b    "Final Document, International Ecumenical Congress of Theology, Feb. 20 - Mar. 2, 1980, São Paulo, Brazil." 4 (July) 3:127–33.
O'GORMAN, Frances Elsie
1981    Interview on work in Barra de Tijuca (Rio de Janeiro) *comunidade* and activities of *FASE-Programa NUCLAR.*
1983    *Base Communities in Brazil: Dynamics of a Journey,* Rio de Janeiro, FASE-NUCLAR.
O'HALLORAN, James
1984    *Living Cells: Developing Small Christian Community,* Dublin, Dominican Publ.; Maryknoll, N.Y., Orbis.
OLSEN, Charles M.
1973    *The Base Church: Creating Community through Multiple Forms,* Atlanta, Forum House.
ORR, J. Edwin
1978    *Evangelical Awakenings in Latin America,* Minneapolis, Bethany Fellowship.
*PÁGINAS: EN TORNO A PUEBLA*
1979    Lima, CEP, 4:23.
PAUL VI
1975    *Evangelii Nuntiandi: Apostolic Exhortation on Evangelization in the Modern World.*
PEREZ, Gustavo, GREGORY, Alfonso, and LEPARGNEUR, François
1964    *O Problema Sacerdotal no Brasil,* Rio de Janeiro, CERIS.
PESSOA DE MORAIS
1965    *Sociologia de Revolução Brasileira: Analise e Interpretação do Brasil de Hoje.* Rio de Janeiro, Leitura.

PETRIE, Ray C.
1964    *Francis of Assisi: Apostle of Poverty,* New York, AMS Press.

PIERSON, Donald
1951    *Cruz das Almas: A Brazilian Village,* Westport, Ct., Greenwood Press.

PIERSON, Paul Everett
1974    *A Younger Church in Search of Maturity: Presbyterianism in Brazil from 1910 to 1959,* San Antonio, Trinity University Press.

PIERSON, Stanley
1973    *Marxism and the Origins of British Socialism,* Cornell University Press.

PIN, Emile
1963    *Elementos para una sociología del catolicismo latinoamericano,* Fribourg, Switzerland, Oficina Internacional de Investigaciónes Sociales.

POPPINO, Rollie E.
1968    *Brazil, the Land and the People,* New York, Oxford University Press.

PRADO, Caio, Jr.
1947a    *Evolução Política do Brasil,* São Paulo, Edit. Brasilense.
1947b    *Formação do Brasil Contemporâneo: Colônia,* São Paulo, Edit. Brasilense.

PRADO, Gonzaga
1978    *O Clamor do Pobre pela Justiça,* São Paulo, Paulinas.

PRIOR, David
1983    *The Church in the Home,* London, Marshall, Morgan and Scott.

*PRO MUNDI VITA BULLETIN* (Brussels)
1976    "Let the People Be: 'Popular Religion' and the Religion of the People," (July).

PRO MUNDI VITA: DOSSIERS
1977    *The Brazilian Church and Human Rights* (Sept.-Oct.), no. 2.

PROAÑO, Bishop Leonidas
1979    Interview in his Rio Bamba office and later visit to the Retiro Santa Cruz training center for Quechua Amerindian *agentes de pastoral,* Sept. 15.

PURVES, George T.
1931    *Christianity in the Apostolic Age,* New York, Scribner's.

QUEBEDEAUX, Richard
1974    *The Young Evangelicals,* New York, Harper & Row.

RAHNER, Karl
1978    *Foundations of the Christian Faith,* New York, Seabury Press.

READ, William R.
1965    *New Patterns of Church Growth in Brazil,* Grand Rapids, Eerdmans.

READ, William, MONTERROSO, Victor, and JOHNSON, Harmon
1969    *Latin American Church Growth,* Grand Rapids, Eerdmans.

READ, William, and INESON, Frank A.
1973    *Brazil 1980: The Protestant Handbook,* Monrovia, Cal., MARC.

*REALIDADE* (São Paulo)
1972    "Nossas Cidades." (May).

*REB*
1976    "Trabalho Pastoral de Campo.," Martiene Groetelaars. 36:114:903–20.
1977    *Manual Sobre as Comunidades Eclesiais de Base,* Petrópolis, Vozes.
1978a    "Comunidades de Base: Busca de Equilíbrio entre Ministério e Comunidade Cristã." (Subsídios para Puebla). 38 (March) 149:80ff.
1978b    *Subsídios para Puebla/78.* 40 (March) 149.

1980　　"Teologia e Povo." 40 (March) 157.
1981　　*CEBs: Povo de Deus que se Organiza.* 41 (June) 162.
REILY, Duncan
1980　　"Os Metodistas no Brasil (1889–1930)." *Estudos Teológicos,* 20:2: 100–122, São Leopoldo, IECL.
1981a　　"Perspectivas Históricas do Protestantismo no Brasil." Unpublished paper presented at National Consultation on Evangelism, sponsored by WCC (Sept.), Itaici, S.P.
1981b　　*Metodismo Brasileiro e Wesleyano,* São Paulo, Imprensa Metodista.
1982　　"História Documentada do Protestantismo no Brasil." Manuscript of forthcoming publication by ASTE.
RIBEIRO, Darcy
1980　　*Os Brasileiros: 1. Teoria do Brasil,* Petrópolis, Vozes.
RIBEIRO GUIMARÃES, Almir
1978　　*Comunidades de Base no Brasil: Uma Nova Maneira de Ser em Igreja,* Petrópolis, Vozes.
ROLIM, Francisco Cartaxo
1970　　"Catolicismo no Brasil." *Limiar* (April).
1977　　*Protestantismo e Pentecostalismo,* Rio de Janeiro, CERIS.
1978　　"Abordagem Sociológica da Religiosidade Popular," *A Religião do Povo,* B. Beni dos Santos (et. al.) Sao Páulo. Edicões Paulinas, pp. 81–91.
　　　　"Pentecostalismo de Forma Protestante," in *A Religião do Povo,* B. Beni dos Santos (et. al.), Sao Paulo, Edicões Paulinas.
RUSSELL, Elbert
1942　　*The History of Quakerism,* New York, Macmillan.
SAMPAIO DE SOUZA, Geraldo and Geraldo José
1968　　*Geografia do Brasil,* vols. 1 and 2, São Paulo, Edit Brasiliense.
SAN JUAN CHALUC (name changed for security reasons)
1980　　Clandestine visit to an ecumenical *comunidade* and participation in celebration led by a Presbyterian pastor and an ex-priest, June 18.
SANTA ANA, Julio de
1977　　*Good News to the Poor,* Geneva, WCC; Maryknoll, N.Y., Orbis, 1979.
1980　　Report and dialogue on *comunidades* in Brazil. San José, Costa Rica, Seminário Bíblico Latinoamericano, June 12.
SANTA ANA, Julio de (ed.)
1980　　*Separation Without Hope: The Church and the Poor during the Industrial Revolution and Colonial Expansion,* Maryknoll, N.Y., Orbis.
1981　　*Toward a Church of the Poor,* Maryknoll, N.Y., Orbis. Originally published in 1979 by WCC.
SÃO PAULO JUSTICE AND PEACE COMMISSION
1978　　*São Paulo: Growth and Poverty,* London, Bowerdean Press and the Catholic Institute for International Relations. Original edition, *São Paulo, 1975: Crescimento e Pobreza.*
SCHAFF, Philip
1950　　*History of the Christian Church,* vol. 6, Grand Rapids, Eerdmans.
SCHATTSCHNEIDER, David Allen
1975　　" 'Souls for the Lamb': A Theology for the Christian Mission According

to Count Nicolaus Ludwig von Zinzendorf and Bishop Augustus Gottlieb Spangenberg." Dissertation submitted to the Faculty of the Divinity School of the University of Chicago in partial fulfillment of the degree of Doctor of Philosophy.

SCHISLER, William Filho
1977    "Teria Sido Cristo Expulso de Recife?" *Expositor Cristão* 92 (Oct.) 20:1-2.

SCOTT, Waldron
1980    *Bring Forth Justice,* Grand Rapids, Eerdmans.

SEDOC
1975    " 'A Igreja que Nasce do Povo'—Relatórios e Conclussões do Primeiro Encontro de Vitória, E.S." 7 (May) 81:1057-1216. Later published as *Uma Igreja que Nasce do Povo: Comunidades Eclesiais de Base-Encontro de Vitória, E.S.*

1976    " 'Uma Igreja que Nasce do Povo pelo Espírito de Deus'—Relatório e Conclusões do Segundo Encontro de Vitória." 9 (Oct.-Nov.) 95/96.

1978-79    " 'Igreja, Povo que se Libertao'—Relatório, Crónica, Conclusões e Estudos dos Peritos de Encontro de Joao Pessõa." 11 (Oct.) 115 and 11 (Jan.-Feb.) 118.

1979a    12 (Oct.) 125ff. Articles on church defense of peasants against injustices. Extensive documentation of injustice.

1979b    12 (Nov.) 126. Demands of rural laborers, Catholic indigenist policy, etc.

SEGUNDO, Juan Luis
1973    *The Community Called Church,* vol. 1, Theology for Artisans of a New Humanity, Maryknoll, N.Y., Orbis.

1974    *The Sacraments Today,* vol. 4, Theology for Artisans of a New Humanity, Maryknoll, N.Y., Orbis.

1976    *The Liberation of Theology,* Maryknoll, N.Y., Orbis.

SEMANA DE TEOLOGÍA
1980    Evening meetings for CEB *agentes de pastoral* during the International Ecumenical Congress of Theology, São Paulo, Pontificia Universidade Católica. Reports by Cardinal Arns, Gustavo Gutiérrez, Bishop Samuel Ruiz (Mexico), the Libânios, and others. Feb. 20-Mar. 2.

SEMMEL, Bernard
1973    *The Methodist Revolution,* New York, Basic Books.

*SERVIR: TEOLOGIA Y PASTORAL* (Mexico City)
1979    "El Reino de Dios y los pobres: Hacia una iglesia solidaria con los pobres." 15:83-84.

SHARPE, Eric J.
1969    "The Problem of Conversion in Recent Missionary Thought." *Evangelical Quarterly,* 41:4.

SHAW, Duncan (ed.)
1967    *Reformation and Revolution,* Edinburgh, St. Andrews Press.

SHEPPARD, David
1983    *Bias to the Poor,* London, Hodder & Stoughton.

SIDER, Ronald J.
1978    *Karlstadt's Battle with Luther: Documents in a Liberal-Radical Debate,* Philadelphia, Fortress.

SIDER, Ronald J. (ed.)
1980    *Cry Justice: The Bible Speaks on Hunger and Poverty,* Downers Grove, Ill., IVCF Press.
SIEPIERSKI, Paulo
1980    *Evangelização no Grande São Paulo,* São Paulo, CRESÇA.
SIMON, John S.
1937    *John Wesley and the Methodist Societies,* London, Epworth.
*SISTEMA PINICO—PROCESSO DE ENRIQUECIMENTO DE ÁGUA COM ESGOTOS PELA SABESP*
1981    Protest against dumping sewage in the lake that supplies water to São Paulo.
SKIDMORE, Thomas E.
1967    *Politics in Brazil: 1930-64,* London, Oxford University Press.
SMELLIE, Alexander
1975    *Men of the Covenant: The Study of the Scottish Church in the Years of the Persecution,* Edinburgh, Banner of Truth Trust. Originally published in London, Andrew Melrose, 1903.
SMITH, Lynn T.
1972    *Brazil, People and Institutions,* Louisiana State University Press.
SMITH, Timothy L.
1957    *Revivalism and Social Reform: American Protestantism on the Eve of the Civil War,* Nashville, Abingdon.
1977    *"Freedom through the Sanctifying Spirit: A Forgotten Chapter in America's Theological History."* Draft of a forthcoming book.
SNYDER, Howard A.
1980    *The Radical Wesley and Patterns for Church Renewal,* Downers Grove, Ill., InterVarsity Press.
SOYRES, John de
1965    *Montanism and the Primitive Church: A Study in the Ecclesiastical History of the Second Century,* Lexington, American Theological Library Association. Originally published by Deighton, Bell and Co., 1878, Cambridge.
SPENER, Philip Jacob
1964    *Pia Desideria,* Theodore G. Tapper (ed.), Philadelphia, Fortress.
STEVENSON, J. (ed.)
1957    *A New Eusebius: Documents Illustrative of the History of the Church to AD 337,* London, SPCK.
STEWART, A.T.Q.
1977    *The Narrow Ground: Aspects of Ulster 1609-1969,* London, Faber & Faber.
STOEFFLER, F. Ernest
1965    *The Rise of Evangelical Pietism,* Leiden, Brill.
1973    *German Pietism During the Eighteenth Century,* Leiden, Brill.
1976    *Continental Pietism and Early American Christianity,* Grand Rapids, Eerdmans.
TANNIS, James R.
1967    *Dutch Calvinist Pietism in the Middle Colonies: A Study in the Life and Theology of Theodorus Jacobus Frelinghuysen,* The Hague, Martinus Nyhoff.

TAYLOR, E. R.
1935     *Methodism in Politics,* Cambridge University Press.
*TEMPO E PRESENÇA* (Rio de Janeiro)
1981     "Operário em Construção," no. 168 (May-June), CEDI.
THOMPSON, John A. F.
1965     *The Later Lollards: 1414–1520.* Oxford University Press.
*TIME MAGAZINE*
1979a    "John Paul vs. Liberation Theology." Feb. 5, pp. 118–19.
1979b    "High Stakes in Latin America." Feb. 12, pp. 68–69.
1979c    "The Church of the Poor: Latin America's *comunidades de base* keep growing." May 7, p. 8.
TOEWS, John A.
1975     *A History of the Mennonite Brethren Church: Pilgrims and Pioneers,* Fresno, Cal., Board of Christian Literature/General Conference of Mennonite Brethren Churches.
TORRES, Sergio, and EAGLESON, John (eds.)
1981     *The Challenge of Basic Christian Communities,* Maryknoll, N.Y., Orbis.
TOURN, Giorgio
1980     *The Waldensians: The First 800 Years,* New York, Friendship Press.
TOWLSON, Clifford W.
1957     *Moravian and Methodist Relationships and Influences in the Eighteenth Century,* London, Epworth.
*AOS TRABALHADORES DE CONSTRUÇÃO CIVIL*
1981     Pamphlet prepared by construction workers' union and distributed at Barra de Eijuca *comunidade,* calling them to protest proposed social security payment increases.
TROELTSCH, Ernest
1960     *The Social Teaching of the Christian Churches,* vol. 2, New York, Harper & Row.
VALLIER, Ivan
1970     *Catholicism, Social Control and Modernization in Latin America,* Englewood Cliffs, N.J., Prentice-Hall.
van der GRIJP, Klaus
1976     "História do Protestantismo Brasileiro," text prepared for the third volume of the CEHILA project, São Leopoldo, Theological Faculty of the IECL.
VANN, Richard T.
1969     *The Social Development of English Quakerism: 1655–1766,* Harvard University Press.
*VEHA*
1980     "Os Bispos Divididos," no. 597, Feb. 13. Article on internal tensions in CNBB over the document entitled "The Church and Problems of the Land."
VELA, Jesús Andrés
1969     *Las comunidades de base y una iglesia nueva,* Buenos Aires.
1973     *Comunidades de Base: Conversión a Qué?* Bogotá: Indo-American Press/Paulinas.
VERDUIN, Leonard
1964     *The Reformers and Their Stepchildren,* Grand Rapids, Baker Book House.

*VIDA PASTORAL* (São Paulo)
1979    *Revista para sacerdotes y agentes de pastoral* 10 (Mar.-April) 85.
VINIEGRA, Francisco José Fernandes
1981    Interview with sociologist on staff of FASE who is an advisor to the CNBB on social issues, Aug. 10.
WAGLEY, Charles
1963    *An Introduction to Brazil,* Columbia University Press.
WALLIS, Jim
1976    *Agenda for Biblical People: A New Focus for Developing a Life-style of Discipleship,* New York and London, Harper & Row.
1981    *The Call to Conversion: Recovering the Gospel for These Times,* New York and London, Harper & Row.
WALZER, Michael
1976    *The Revolution of the Saints: A Study in the Origins of Radical Politics,* New York, Atheneum.
WARNER, H. J.
1967    *The Albigensian Heresy,* New York, Russell & Russell.
WEARMOUTH, R. W.
1948    *Methodism and the Common People in the Eighteenth Century,* London, Epworth.
WELLS, David W., and WOODBRIDGE, John D.
1975    *The Evangelicals,* Nashville, Abingdon.
WHITING, C. E.
1931    *Studies in English Puritanism: 1660–1688,* London, SPCK.
WILLEMS, Emilio
1967    *Followers of the New Faith: Social Change and the Rise of Protestantism in Brazil and Chile,* Vanderbilt University Press.
WILLIAMS, George Hunston
1962    *The Radical Reformation,* Philadelphia, Westminster.
WORKMAN, Herbert B.
1960    *Persecution in the Early Church,* London, Epworth.
1966    *John Wycliff: A Study of the English Medieval Church,* Hamden, Ct., Anchor Books.
*WORLD ALMANAC*
1983    New York, Newspaper Enterprise Association.

# Glossary of Portuguese/Spanish Terms

*Agentes de pastoral*—pastoral ministers/guides of CEBs.

*Aldeamento*—a village within the "reductions" *(reducciones/reduções)* into which Amerindians were forcefully gathered by colonial Catholic missioners, to protect them against the rapacity of the colonizers, and to facilitate evangelization.

*Animadores*—animators or lay catalyzers of CEBs.

*Bairro/barrio*—literally, neighborhood; here applied to those on the marginalized periphery of society.

*Base*—base; a term that has socio-political implications and is applied here to the marginalized sector of society.

*Beato/a*—an unusually pious or devout lay person.

*Canteiros*—"seedbed"; free schools for children and CEB–related activities in a rural section of northeastern Brazil.

*Casa grande*—"big house," the plantation manor.

*Círculos bíblicos*—CEBs oriented to Bible study, related to the method used by Carlos Mesters and his associates.

*Comunidad/comunidade*—"community."

*Conscientização/conscientización*—conscientization; the process of awakening and elevating socio-political awareness.

*Convivência/convivencia*—intimate sociability; from *con* (with) and *vivir/viver* (to live). Does not have a precise English equivalent.

*Delegados de la Palabra*—delegates/ministers of the Word; *animadores*.

*Distensão/distensión*—distension, expansion; used in Latin American political parlance to signify a relative opening up of the political process in situations where absolutism or authoritarianism had been the norm.

*Encuentro/encontro*—an encounter, a meeting, a gathering of persons; in this context, of CEB leaders.

*Equipo/equipe*—a team or task force.

*Favela*—a shantytown on the periphery and on vacant land of the large cities of Brazil.

*Favelados*—Persons who dwell in a favela.

*Fazenda*—(Portuguese) plantation.

*Fazendeiro*—plantation owner.

*Festas/fiestas*—religious feasts or holy days.

*Grupos de evangelização*—small witnessing teams, divisions of CEBs in the Amazonian prelacy of Acre-Purus; also, a name that the CEBs use in Dom Hélder Câmara's diocese of Olinda-Recife.

307

*Hacendado*—(Spanish) plantation owner.

*Hacienda*—Plantation.

*Iglesia popular*—the generic name for CEBs in Nicaragua.

*Mameluco*—in colonial Brazil, the child of a white father and an Amerindian mother.

*Monitores*—local leaders of the MEB study groups *(sistemas);* the name is sometimes used for CEB leaders *(animadores).*

*Padre*—(Spanish) father; in Brazil, a title given only to priests; in Portuguese, the term for a parental father is *pãe.*

*Praxis*—a Greek word signifying plan of action, way of acting, etc.; as used by liberation theologians and CEB pastoral leaders, it is "a course of action that demands reflection and reflects back upon action."

*Presbítero*—the term used in Brazil for the lay leaders of grassroots Pentecostalism.

*Realidade/realidad*—reality; in this study, it refers particularly to the socioeconomic, cultural, and religious situation of the Latin American poor.

*Reduções/reducciones*—"reductions"; concentrations of Amerindians into large self-sufficient societies under the supervision of Catholic missionaries; practiced by the Jesuits in a large area that now encompasses southeastern Brazil, Paraguay, and northeastern Argentina.

*Santos*—"saints"; images of saints venerated by the faithful and worshiped in popular Catholicism.

*Senzala*—slave house or quarter.

*Sertão*—hinterland, back-country, wilderness; more particularly, the semi-arid region in the interior of the Brazilian northeast.

*Sistemas*—the core groups in the MEB radio-transmitted literacy program that went underground and later emerged as nuclei for the CEBs.

# Index of Scripture Texts

# General Index

311